PERFECT COMMUNITIES

PERFECT COMMUNITIES

LEVITT, LEVITTOWN, AND THE DREAM OF

WHITE SUBURBIA

EDWARD BERENSON

Yale UNIVERSITY PRESS

New Haven and London

Yale University Press books may be purchased in quantity for educational, business, or promotional use. For information, please e-mail sales.press@yale.edu (U.S. office) or sales@yaleup.co.uk (U.K. office).

Set in Sabon and Berthold City type by IDS Infotech, Ltd.
Printed in the United States of America.

Library of Congress Control Number: 2024945266
ISBN 978-0-300-25954-4 (hardcover : alk. paper)

A catalogue record for this book is available from the British Library.

This paper meets the requirements of ANSI/NISO z39.48-1992 (Permanence of Paper).

10 9 8 7 6 5 4 3 2 1

For Chris and Melanie

Contents

Acknowledgments

Writing this book took me to many places, and in each one, several people generously gave me their time. Without their help I wouldn't have been able to do this project, especially since I did all of my research in the wake of the Covid pandemic. In Levittown, New York, Paul Manton and Bob Koenig took me to their wonderful Levittown Museum and showed me around the development, while answering a zillion questions. In Levittown, Pennsylvania, Dave Marable kindly allowed me to tour his house in Snowball Gate, which he has turned into a museum of Levittown history. In Willingboro, New Jersey, Linda Cope gave me access to the entire local history collection, and in Bowie, Maryland, Mike Bargeron shared his considerable knowledge of the community, showed me around, and gave me a pile of documents. Peyton Bramble found precious material for me in the archives of the Belair Mansion.

In France's Levitt developments, I'm grateful to Dorine Viltrouvé, Sophie Rodrigues Viera, Guillaume Vesnat, and Jean-Sébastien Detrait, who introduced me to their respective communities and spent many hours with me. Special thanks go to Elodie Bitsindou, an architectural historian and student of Levittown, who drove me from Paris to Le Mesnil-Saint-Denis, Lésigny, and Mennecy and gave me the benefit of her deep knowledge. The *mairie* of Le Mesnil-Saint-Denis generously scanned the commune's entire archive of Levitt documents for me.

In San Juan and Levittown, Puerto Rico, I couldn't have begun to do my work without the extraordinary help of José Eduardo Gerena and Ana Ortiz, who spent many days with me and drove me across their beautiful island to the gorgeous city of Ponce, which is still recovering from Hurricane María. My thanks go as well to the Toa Baja officials James Ramos Santiago and Rubén Pomales Rodriguez, who spent several hours with me. Jorge Lizardi Pollock of the University of San Juan's Escuela de Arquitectura also gave me crucial help and put me in touch with his student, Mónica Cruz Declet, who generously shared her work.

I've learned a huge amount from the work of Isabelle Gournay, who spoke with me at length about Levitt's French developments, and the work of Richard Longstreth, who talked with me about Belair at Bowie. I'm grateful to Paige Glotzer for discussing her work in progress on Levittown, Puerto Rico, and for sharing some sources with me. Thanks as well to my colleague Tom Sugrue for conversations over the years, and for his seminal work on civil rights, U.S. urban and suburban history, and especially his superb article on Levittown, Pennsylvania, and the Myers family. I've learned a lot about urban and suburban history from another colleague, Andrew Needham, with whom I regularly teach a course on the history of New York and Paris. Special gratitude goes to yet another colleague, Steve Hahn, for reading the entire manuscript and giving me enormously helpful comments.

Extremely helpful as well were archivists and librarians at the following institutions: the Centre nationale de recherche scientifique (Paris), the Fundación Luis Muñoz Marín (San Juan), the Archivo General de Puerto Rico, the U.S. National Archives, the Columbia University Special Collections Library, the Hofstra University Special Collections Library, Temple University's Special Collections Research Center, the Mercer Museum Library of the Bucks County Historical Society, the Friends Historical Library at Swarthmore College, the Belair Mansion in Bowie, Maryland, the Willingboro Public Library, and the Levittown Public Library.

I've presented aspects of the book at Princeton University, New York University, the Society for French Historical Studies, and the Kendal Lecture Series. My thanks to all those who participated and commented on my work. My thanks as well to the following current and former residents of Levittown, Pennsylvania, who did long interviews with me in person and on Zoom: Andrea Eisenberg, George Strachan, Anita Getz, Brian Higgins, Barbara Masson, Craig Zeke,

Michael Busler, Robert King, Joe Artley, Wayne Bossert, Bob Keiger, and Ed Gudusky. I'm especially grateful to Melanie Warhol Curtin for putting me in touch with many of these Levittowners. Thanks also to Peter Charapko for his architectural expertise and his memories of Levittown and Fairless Hills.

As always, my amazing agent, Sandy Dijkstra, and her colleagues read many drafts of my proposal, gave me precious advice, and found the perfect editor. Bill Frucht, a gifted editor, lent his deep wisdom and intelligence to this project and polished my prose. It's been a privilege to work with him. It's a privilege, too, to publish again with Yale University Press, and I thank Laura Hensley for her meticulous copy editing and Amanda Gerstenfeld and Jeffrey Schier for shepherding the book through the publication process.

For more than four decades, my wife, Catherine Johnson, has inspired me and given me the example of her sparkling prose. Our son, Chris, and his wife, Melanie, both public school teachers, have made Long Island their home and live just a stone's throw from the original Levittown. This book is dedicated to them.

PERFECT COMMUNITIES

Prologue
The Lure of Levittown

ON JANUARY 19, 1949, the Long Island newspaper *Newsday* carried the breathless headline "BUYERS STORM LEVITT FOR 2,500 NEW HOMES." After waiting "like matinee worshippers at a stage door," the paper informed readers, "young couples have been pouring into a Levitt & Sons model home . . . eager to own a Levittown House of 1949." *Newsday*'s story reflected an essential fact of postwar America: housing, especially the coveted single-family home, was in woefully short supply. The mass-produced, affordable houses marketed by Levitt & Sons became magnets for thousands of young families in search of a place to live. Four months later, when another tract of Levittown houses went up for sale, *Newsday* described the "HOME-RUSH" as "a scene reminiscent of the storming of the gates of Versailles and the Yukon gold rush." This was surely hyperbolic, but there was no mistaking the phenomenon: Bill Levitt had turned the staid, responsible process of home-buying into a craze.[1]

Levitt and a few other homebuilders and government officials had known for some time that too few private dwellings had been built during the Depression and World War II. With the birthrate already climbing in 1943—thanks to "goodbye babies" conceived just before servicemen shipped out—there would be an unprecedented housing shortage when the veterans returned home at the war's end. That, of course, is when the baby boom took off. By 1947, six million people had squeezed in with relatives and friends, taking up residence in basements, garages, attics, and barns. Another half million lived in Quonset huts and other temporary quarters. In Chicago, trolley cars were sold as homes, and an Omaha newspaper ad read, "Big Ice Box, 7–17 feet, could be fixed up to live in." One New York City couple installed themselves in a department store window to publicize their plight.[2]

A 1947 Senate committee report on the housing problem noted that returning veterans were forced to live in "garages, coal sheds, chicken coops, barns, tool sheds, granaries, and smokehouses." Such "hovels," the report added, "are merely gestures of contempt toward those who are desperate enough to take anything which is offered. . . . Structures with no water available, heating facilities so bad that bottled drinks will freeze in the same room with a large stove, no sanitary toilet facilities, primitive food storage, no sinks, cardboard windowpanes, and paper walls."[3] The authors mostly had white Americans in mind; for African Americans, the housing situation had long been dire. In the northern cities where they had flocked since the 1920s, Black families faced restrictive covenants, racist real estate practices, and everyday prejudice that for decades had confined large numbers of them to substandard dwellings in tight urban ghettoes.[4] Now white Americans faced a situation their Black counterparts knew all too well.

Few builders were doing anything about it. Of those who were, Levitt & Sons quickly became the most prominent, and the media-savvy William J. Levitt, the face of the firm, achieved a celebrity then rare for a businessman. "Each week," *Fortune* reported, he "gets a basketful of admiring mail," and letters to the editors of New York–area newspapers praised him as their savior. "Too bad there aren't more men like Levitt," wrote the wife of an air force veteran. "I hope they make a whopper of a profit."[5] Navy veteran William Snyder wrote, "I don't know what any of us would have done without Mr. Levitt."[6] Stories circulated of children who concluded their bedtime prayers with "God bless Mommy, God bless Daddy, and God bless Mr. Levitt."[7]

Worship of Bill Levitt became a central feature of Levittown lore, recounted in many personal memoirs and fictional accounts of the community. In W.D. Wetherell's story "The Man Who Loved Levittown," the narrator, Tommy DiMaria, lovingly describes his encounter with Levitt when he traveled out to Long Island to look at the houses under construction. "How much does one of these babies cost?" Tommy asks the homebuilder.

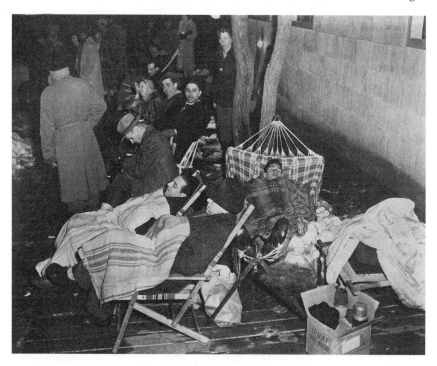

People camped out overnight to secure a Levittown house. (Levittown Public Library)

> "Seven thousand," he says, looking right at me. "One hundred dollars down . . ." "I only have eighty-three." He looks me over, "You a veteran?" "You bet . . ." He calls over to a man helping with the sinks. "Hey, Johnson!" he yells. "Take this guy's money and let him pick out whichever one he wants."

Tommy can't believe his good fortune: "Thanks to Big Bill Levitt we all had a chance. You talk about dreams!"[8]

So desperate were veterans for Levittown homes that many waited in line for two days and two nights for the chance to plunk down their deposit. Now-iconic photographs show hordes of people camped outside Levitt headquarters in hammocks and lawn chairs, swathed in blankets and sleeping bags to brace themselves against the cold nights.[9]

Other pictures show long lines of people in hats and winter coats outside the front doors of Levitt model homes. *Architectural Forum*

Dozens of people sign contracts to buy a Levittown house sight unseen, while dozen more wait to join them. (Levittown Construction Photograph Collection, Special Collections Department, Hofstra University)

reported that in one three-day period, "some 3,000 veterans lined up outside a model bungalow . . . to compete with each other for the privilege of putting a down payment on a house which did not yet exist."[10] "The crowd got so big," noted *Time,* "that police had to keep them in line." People arrived in fleets of cars and taxis, clogging the streets for miles. "Gotta get a house," yelled a motorist to a police officer vainly trying to keep the traffic under control.[11]

After trooping quickly through a sample bungalow, hundreds of people crowded into Levitt's makeshift sales center at the Village Bath Club in Manhasset, New York, eager to select their new home sight unseen: after all, the houses, now called ranches, were nearly identical.

"Facing the five lines of home purchasers," *Newsday* reported, "were three tables; the first manned by five Levitt salesmen, the second by five typist-clerks and the third by an assortment of bank, Federal Housing Association [he meant the Federal Housing Administration] and Veterans Administration representatives." It took couples an average of five minutes to select a homesite and not much longer to complete their paperwork and secure their loans. On August 15, 1949, Levitt & Sons sold 650 homes in five hours.[12] When the 1950 ranch was announced a few months later—like a carmaker, Levitt modified its product from one year to the next—forty thousand came to inspect the model house on its opening weekend. More than one thousand bought the 1950 ranch without even seeing the model.[13]

The fictional Tommy DiMaria's story is not very different from that of Robert Abrams, a real-life Levittown pioneer who told *Newsday,* "In my book Levitt will go down as a great guy. He responded to a need when my wife and I needed a house. He provided us with more than a decent life. He gave us a start in life."[14] Abrams, an overseas correspondent during the war, returned home to find himself and his four-member family crammed into his in-laws' small Brooklyn apartment. While riding the subway to his job in Manhattan, he read a story in the *Herald-Tribune* about a new rental development on Long Island. Shortly afterward, he signed a lease for a "Cape Cod" sight unseen. The first time he and his wife saw their house was when they parked in front of it on October 1, 1947—move-in day for the first three hundred residents of what was not yet called Levittown.

Two years later, Edgar Daniels, a veteran of the Pacific theater, moved to Levittown with his Omaha-born wife, Pat, as soon as new homes became available for sale and not just for rent. In Queens, the Danielses had been paying seventy dollars a month for a "hardly furnished" place with a minuscule bathroom and kitchen. "The door down to the basement," Edgar recalled, "got water rats. They were banging on the door." To escape Queens, Edgar lined up a day before the Levitt sales office was set to open. He and dozens of others waited through a freezing early-spring night, warming themselves around trash-barrel fires. Pat had set her sights on one of Levitt's six models, each different from the others only in a few details, but by the time the couple reached the head of the line, Pat's model was sold out. She didn't care: "I was so happy to get out of Flushing I would have taken anything that was clean and neat. And I mean it was; it was like a little doll house."

Mildred and David Glaser were equally desperate to flee the outer boroughs and their tiny, run-down apartment. But the first time they saw their new Levittown home, they had to use their imaginations.

Their newly installed street was covered in mud, and their home was nothing but a rectangular concrete slab. "We walk up," David said, "and there's this slab in the ground, and believe it or not, we're looking at it, and I said, 'Well let's see: the bathroom's over here; there's where the bedroom is. And I laid down right on it. The wet slab. [Mildred] said, 'Get up, you fool.' I said, 'Nah, look how wonderful it is.' "

Bernadette Fisher Wheeler, a *Newsday* reporter, hated Levitt's tiny, boxy houses on first sight. "Levittown was the last place on the planet I thought I would be living," she recalled. "But as it turned out, we moved there because the house was such a good buy." In the end, "we loved living there. I came into work and told Alan Hathway [her managing editor], I would be eating crow for the rest of my days."

In a 1996 memoir, David Beers quotes his mother describing her joy on becoming a Levittown "Pioneer." "We were thrilled to death," she recalled. "It was a whole new adventure for us. Everyone was arriving with a sense of forward momentum. Everyone was taking courage from the sight of another orange moving van pulling in next door, a family just like us, unloading pole lamps and cribs and Formica dining tables like our own, reflections of ourselves."[15]

Bill Griffith, who grew up in Levittown and later satirized the suburbs in the cartoon *Zippy*, confessed that for his parents, who grew up poor, Levittown "was a miracle." His mother "couldn't believe she owned her own house." They thought "they would never live anywhere but an apartment." They saw their community almost "through the eyes of someone . . . in love."[16]

The massive Long Island housing project that made so many people happy also made Levitt the largest and most influential homebuilder in the United States. He became the face of America's postwar housing boom and attracted the obsessive interest of national media outlets, most of which were headquartered in New York City. As *Fortune* magazine wrote at the time, "It is a poor week when Levitt houses aren't featured in at least one full-column story in the New York newspapers."[17] Between the late 1940s and late 1960s, virtually every major news outlet devoted a prominent story, often successive stories, to the creator of Levittown. *Time, Life, Newsweek, Esquire,* the *Saturday Evening Post, Business Week,* and countless others depicted Bill Levitt and his accomplishments in heroic hues. *Nation's Business* called him "a Hollywood image of the successful executive."[18] In July 1950, *Time* put him on its cover, and in 1998 it ranked him among the one hundred most influential people of the twentieth century.[19] The next year, *Fortune* made Levitt a finalist for "Businessman of the Century."[20] "It is often the case," the journalist Tom Lewis wrote, "that one person in an industry rises above the rest, accrues fabulous wealth, and so dominates the public imagination to become synonymous with the enterprise itself: Rockefeller in oil; Carnegie in steel; Ford in automobiles. In the newly emerging housing industry of the 1950s it was Levitt." This consensus figured prominently in David Halberstam's history of the 1950s, which devoted a chapter to the homebuilder: "If the first great business figure of the American century was Henry Ford, the second, arguably, was William J. Levitt."[21]

In focusing obsessively on the brash, media-savvy Bill Levitt, these stories largely erased his brother, Alfred, who designed the original Levitt homes. But Alfred himself endorsed this coverage. "Bill," he said, "can't draw a line on a plan, nor does he know how to build anything. But ... there wouldn't be any Levitt & Sons [without] the almost extraordinary talent that my brother has."[22] That talent was salesmanship and entrepreneurial vision, even if the personality behind them raised eyebrows. *Time*'s 1950 cover story called Bill "a cocky, rambunctious hustler with brown hair, cow-sad eyes, a hoarse voice (from smoking three packs of cigarettes a day), and a liking for hyperbole that causes him to describe his height (5ft. 8 in.) as 'nearly six feet' and his company as the 'General Motors of the housing industry.' " But the magazine admitted that Levitt's "supreme self-confidence ... is solidly based." He was "the most potent single modernizing influence in a largely antiquated industry." A slightly earlier article in *Harper's* also mentioned Levitt's "mournful, wide-open eyes" but credited him with "considerable charm and an engaging way of appearing to explain some of his own tricks of the trade. ... [He] is the firm's best press agent, salesman, and one-man lobby ... an example of what the London *Economist* has described as 'the new type of [American] business man.' "[23] *Fortune* declared that the firm Levitt led was "the best thing that has happened to the housing industry in this century."[24] *Architectural Forum* enthused that Levitt's "800 sq. ft. bungalow ... equipped with electric range, refrigerator, steel kitchen cabinets, washing machine, 18 ft. double-glazed window and two-way fireplace to sell for $7,990 is only the latest and most spectacular of the kind of impossibilities on which the Levitts thrive."[25]

In giving Bill Levitt most of the credit for the transformation of homebuilding and the ability to satisfy the huge postwar demand for a single-family house, these stories slighted the prewar researchers, government officials, and private builders who had invented and pioneered the mass-production techniques behind Levitt's success.[26] But his firm was the first to use these techniques on a mass scale, and its many innovations reoriented homebuilding after the war.

He encouraged others to follow in his footsteps. Builders could buy the Levittown architectural plans for five dollars per house, which, according to *Architectural Forum,* made "some of their houses . . . stud-for-stud copies of Levitt's." They wanted to copy Levitt's designs because, as *Fortune* put it, "the Levitt product displays better exterior design, better interior design, more mechanical improvements, and more all-around merchandise appeal than any other commercial house of its price."[27] The copycat builders included Frank Collins in Pennsylvania, Carl Freeman in Washington, D.C., Joseph Geeraert in Maryland, and many others. All of these builders priced their homes $500 to $2,000 above the Levitt prototype. Other postwar builders, particularly on the West Coast, didn't copy Levitt directly but undertook similar projects, in concept if not in scale.[28] The Levitt vision became the prototype of the postwar American suburb. *Architectural Forum* declared in 1949 that "never before in the history of U.S. building has one house type made such an impact on the industry in so short a time."[29]

But the Levitt house was not meant for everyone.

At first, Levitt rented and sold only to veterans of World War II, and army veteran Eugene Burnett and his wife, Bernice, were eager to buy in. "We got there and looked at the house, the model house," Burnett told a *Newsday* reporter in 1949. "I didn't see any Blacks. We were the only ones," and "everyone was staring at us." After inspecting the model, Burnett "walked up to the salesman and I said to him, 'Pretty nice house. I'm interested. Would you give me an outline of the procedure, how do I apply?' "

The Burnetts could afford to rent a Levittown home; Eugene was a post office employee and Bernice an office worker with a college degree. They were eager to get out of the city, especially since in Harlem, where they had grown up, "heroin had . . . posed its ugly head."

They "wanted to raise our children somewhere else." But there were positive motivations as well. "I was a ghetto boy who always lived in apartments," Eugene explained. "To see a plot of land and the outside of a house and this is mine and I can buy this . . . that's what I mean by beautiful."[30]

The Burnetts were far from the only African Americans wanting to flee Harlem. In public opinion surveys conducted some years later, 83 percent of Harlem residents said they would rather leave the area than try to find better housing in the community or have officials build new or renovated dwellings there.[31] What especially appealed to Bernice Burnett about Levittown were the "modern devices," the washing machine, electric stove, and roomy refrigerator included with each Levitt house. She loved the "airiness" of homes with large windows looking onto grass and shrubbery, not a gray streetscape and lines of row houses. "You could really dream."[32]

The desire for a "plot of land," a place of their own surrounded by greenery, was a sentiment hardly limited to African Americans. A great many white Americans wanted exactly the same thing. But when the Burnetts expressed interest in a Levittown home, Eugene recalled how the Levitt salesman "became very solemn, he looked me in the eye, braced himself and said, 'It's not me . . . but the owners of this development have not as yet decided whether or not they're going to sell these homes to Negroes.' "

"I will never forget that long ride back to Harlem," Eugene recalled. "How I didn't start World War III is beyond me. Because that was the feeling I had."[33] Although the salesman seemed to leave the door open, the Black veteran suspected that the decision to exclude African Americans had already been made. He found out later that Levitt's original leases included a "racial covenant," a statement requiring that the tenants of his homes agree "not to permit the premises to be used or occupied by any person other than members of the Caucasian race." Such covenants became unenforceable after the U.S. Supreme Court ruled in *Shelley v. Kraemer* (1948) that they violate the Constitution, but Levitt easily circumvented the decision. He simply deleted his "Negro ban" from his contracts but maintained the policy. "Levittown has been and is now progressing as a private enterprise job," he told the local *Levittown Tribune*. "It is entirely in the discretion and judgment of Levitt & Sons as to whom it will rent or sell."[34] Levitt's discretion and judgment told him to rent and sell only to whites, a policy he justified on business grounds: "I have come to know," he declared, "that if we sell one house to a Negro family, then 90–95 percent of our white customers will not buy into the community. . . . The plain fact is that most whites prefer not to live in mixed communities."[35]

Closed out of Levittown, the Burnetts bought a house in Ronek Park, a development sixteen miles east of Levittown and a longer commute to New York City. Ronek Park was advertised as having "no UnAmerican, Undemocratic restrictions as to race, color or creed," a promise that Bernice Burnett understood to mean "Whites wouldn't move there," given the availability of the whites-only Levittown close by.[36] As Bernice predicted, Ronek Park quickly became mostly Black. The new Black community was pleasant enough, but it was a fraction of Levittown's size and lacked many of its amenities. The lots were a thousand square feet smaller and didn't include the shrubbery that was standard with Levitt homes. There were no community swimming pools, ball fields, playgrounds, community centers, or "village greens" with convenient stores, as in Levittown.

The Burnetts' experience shows that African American families weren't barred from the suburbs, and in the postwar years large numbers took up residence there. But excluded from white developments like Levittown, they mostly ended up in segregated, all or mostly Black spaces, the places deemed ineligible for Federal Housing Administration (FHA) mortgage guarantees and the affordable interest rates and repayment terms that came with them. These precincts tended to be farthest from employment opportunities and located in unincorporated parts of Long Island, where the lack of local governments resulted in lax building standards, poor infrastructure and amenities, and, in some cases, the illegal conversion of single-family houses into multifamily rentals. Would-be suburban slumlords bought homes from owners unable to make their mortgage payments and turned them into "informal" housing for the poor, generally African American and Puerto Rican families.[37]

Levitt was doubtless right about his "plain fact" that most whites disliked integrated communities, but according to Kenneth T. Jackson, our foremost authority on U.S. suburbs, "there was such a demand for housing—they had people waiting on lines—that even if they had said there will be some blacks living there, white people would still have moved in."[38] By selling homes to African Americans, Levitt could have made a major contribution to racial equality and challenged other builders to follow his example. But as Doris Kallsman, a white Levittown resident, wrote, the G.I. Bill's mortgage guarantees, "meant for everyone, [were] a golden opportunity in this country, and we missed it."[39]

Not everyone who showed up at Levitt's openings was there to buy a house. Picketers from the American Labor Party protested Levitt's refusal to employ union laborers, while protesters from the NAACP denounced the company's refusal to sell to African Americans—and its hypocrisy in allowing the employment of non-white laborers and domestic help. Levitt would maintain his policy of racial exclusion in his New York, Pennsylvania, and Maryland communities until all new homes were sold. He could not prevent resales to African Americans, and a handful moved in. When the first Black family bought into Levittown, Pennsylvania, in 1957, it caused a bitter conflict with homeowners there. Only in Levittown, New Jersey (renamed Willingboro), were Blacks allowed to buy new homes, and this only because the state supreme court ruled against a Levitt lawsuit designed to keep his discriminatory policy in place.

Levitt stubbornly defended his racist policies. He was, he insisted, only following the FHA's rulings. The FHA, created under the New Deal along with the allied Home Owners' Loan Corporation, had long maintained urban segregation through redlining, the process of designating on color-coded maps the heavily Black neighborhoods deemed too risky for banks to issue mortgage loans. In these neighborhoods, colored red on the maps, residents found it difficult to purchase homes. Neighborhoods deteriorated for want of capital, and poverty became endemic. For suburban development, the FHA decreed that for the sake of stability, "it is necessary that properties shall continue to be occupied by the same social and racial classes." It recommended "suitable restrictive covenants" aimed at maintaining economic and racial uniformity. Government agencies thus made it easy for Levitt to exclude African Americans, and he took handsome advantage. In this way, too, Bill Levitt left his massive imprint on the built environment of postwar America. He created pleasant communities for white families of modest means, and most appreciated the experience, endowing it with warm, lasting memories. What commonly went unacknowledged in these white suburbs was that Black Americans didn't get to share the benefits, and that they would have good reason to view Levittown through a different lens.

Although the Levittowns and their clones mostly took shape as spaces for white people only, it's important to add that plenty of people, whites as well as Blacks, opposed this state of affairs. We will see that the NAACP and a variety of civic and religious groups used the legal system, state legislatures, and public protests, among other things, to dissolve racial barriers and create genuinely integrated communities.[40] Levitt faced his greatest challenges on the question of racial exclusion, and the efforts to integrate his various communities stand out as a key element of the Levittown story.

The postwar conflicts over the segregation and integration of postwar suburbia played out against the backdrop of a housing shortage that would endure well into the 1960s and that has reemerged today as an acute crisis of affordable housing. In the postwar decades, the paucity of decent places to live was hardly unique to the United States; it extended to Europe and elsewhere around the globe. As we'll see, Levitt responded to the shortage with a large Levittown on the outskirts of San Juan, Puerto Rico, and with several American-style developments in the exurbs of Paris, France. These overseas Levitt communities would do much to shape the suburbanization of their respective lands. The appeal of a suburban house and yard has hardly been limited to the mainland of the United States. As for Bill Levitt himself, a complicated individual who contributed to postwar life for good and ill, he loomed large in this country and abroad. Although largely forgotten today, Levitt's personal story can serve as both an inspiration and a cautionary tale.

1   Prelude to Levittown

THOUGH HE WAS loath to admit it, Bill Levitt (1907–1994) owed a large part of his success to his father, Abraham, and his brother, Alfred, a self-taught architect. Bill was the grandson of Louis Levitt, an impoverished rabbi who had immigrated to the United States from Russia, and his wife, Nellie, who had come from Austria. Abraham (1880–1964) was the youngest of Louis and Nellie's five sons. He quit school at age ten and educated himself, passing the New York State Regents exam at age twenty. He then skipped college and sailed through the New York University School of Law. At age twenty-two, he had his JD degree and was a member of the bar, specializing in real estate law. A few years later he married Pauline Biederman and fathered two sons, William and Alfred (1911–1966). The family lived comfortably in a four-story brownstone in Brooklyn's Bedford-Stuyvesant neighborhood, which was then heavily Jewish.[1]

Abraham was a tiny man with a philosophical bent. He admired the German philosopher Ernst Haeckel, who rejected the notion of free will and believed only in fate. Abraham favored his younger son, who like him was shy and intense with an artistic streak. Bill, with his self-confident air and eagerness to promote himself, resembled his mother, with whom he was very close. Bill went to PS44 and Boys High School in Bed-Stuy, where he played lacrosse and joined the swim team. He followed his father to NYU, taking a dual major in mathematics and English. But college wasn't for him; he dropped out after just over two years. "I got itchy," he told an interviewer. "I wanted to make a lot of money. I wanted a big car and a lot of clothes."[2] He would later claim he had graduated from NYU, but the school's alumni records say otherwise.

Shortly after leaving NYU, Bill went into business with his father; Alfred joined the family enterprise as well. Accounts differ about the origins of the family homebuilding industry, but it seems that in the mid-1920s, Abraham branched out from his practice of real estate law and developed a parcel of his own in Rockville Centre, a town in southwestern Long Island not far from the Queens border. He bought the property in partnership with several of his clients. Before they began to build houses, the municipality announced plans for a sewage treatment facility adjacent to the property. Levitt's partners panicked, and in July 1929 he bought them out. He figured he could screen off the facility, and in an effort to make something of his investment, he decided to build a house.

For this project, he enlisted his sons, Bill and Alfred, and created a company called Levitt & Sons. At age twenty-two, Bill was named president in charge of finance, construction, and merchandising, while eighteen-year-old Alfred, who loved to draw but had no architectural training, became vice president in charge of design. Abraham withdrew into semiretirement but advised his sons and specialized in landscaping their projects. Alfred dropped out of NYU and drew up plans for the house, a half-timbered, Tudor-style dwelling with two stories and six rooms. Based on the drawings alone, the Levitts quickly attracted one buyer, who bought the house for $14,500, and then a second. By the end of 1929, the firm had constructed eighteen houses and sold them all. Over the next two years, despite the nation's rapidly worsening economy, the Levitts built and sold several more dwellings and amassed the capital to purchase a fifty-acre tract bordering on the Rockville Links Country Club. They named this new development Strathmore at Rockville Centre, which to them connoted the British upper class. (There is, in fact, a Scottish Earl of Strathmore and Kinghorne as well as a Dublin County mansion called Strathmore built in the 1860s.) Alfred's second wife, Monique, a French dancer he met on a trip to Paris, later confirmed the British influence, saying that he fell in love with the Tudor style during a stay in England. She added that Abraham and Pauline gave Alfred the middle name Stuart in homage to the Stuart monarchs of the seventeenth century.[3]

The Levitts marketed their Strathmore homes to relatively affluent people, but at prices considerably lower than the going rate. In part, this was due to the deflation of the early 1930s and the era's high unemployment, which enabled them to pay workers modest wages. But it also resulted from economies of scale and efficient construction techniques. The Levitts cut costs by giving each of their houses a similar floor plan, using standardized materials, and designing façades that varied just enough to make similar houses look distinct. The Rockville Centre undertaking proved so successful that even as the economy tanked around him, Bill felt financially secure enough to marry his high school girlfriend, Rhoda Kirshner. In 1933, he became the father of William, Jr.

According to Abraham, Bill and Alfred made an excellent team. "Bill wouldn't be a success without Alfred," he told an interviewer, "and Alfred wouldn't be a success without Bill. Together they are terrific."[4] The young men didn't agree, and Bill would eventually push his father and brother aside. Long before he took that step, however, he became the public face of Levitt & Sons. His prowess as a salesman was such that even during the Great Depression, their homes were so much in demand that he decided to create a large development on the North Shore of Long Island, which had long been the exclusive domain of the ultra-rich. But as the Depression took hold and some estate owners suffered sharp declines in their fortunes, properties became available at favorable prices. In January 1934, the Levitts bought a forty-six-acre estate near the village of Manhasset, where they built 250 houses over the next two years. The houses sold quickly, and the Levitts plowed their profits into another plot of land, for which they planned three hundred dwellings.

The second batch of homes also sold well, and Levitt & Sons continued to buy land in Manhasset, including a one-hundred-acre parcel and manor house owned by Consuelo Vanderbilt, the daughter of William Kissam Vanderbilt, heir to the family fortune. The firm named this parcel after the heiress (Strathmore-Vanderbilt) and turned her mansion, redone in the 1920s to resemble a Louis XV château, into the clubhouse for the golf course built around it. By 1939, there would be four contiguous subdivisions, collectively named Strathmore at Manhasset. While building in Manhasset, Levitt & Sons also bought the Brokaw estate in the neighboring village of Great Neck, where they built 136 dwellings and called the development Strathmore at Great Neck.[5]

The Levitts wanted their North Shore projects to be communities, rather than mere housing tracts, and they endowed them with parks, ball fields, community centers, and, in one case, a country club. In Strathmore-Vanderbilt, the firm turned part of the Vanderbilt estate into the Strathmore-Vanderbilt Country Club, which Levitt deeded to the subdivision's homeowners. Its 150 families would benefit exclusively from the clubhouse, golf course, swimming pool, and tennis courts, while paying annual dues for their upkeep.[6]

In all these North Shore Strathmores, the Levitts preserved many of the area's mature trees while adding shrubs and other greenery. They built curving streets that meandered through Manhasset and Great Neck's gentle hills and instructed residents "to drive as though your child . . . may come rushing around the next corner."[7] These communities would be distinctly upscale, aimed at well-to-do professionals. To reinforce their air of exclusivity, all homebuyers in each subdivision had to be approved by a "membership committee" consisting of existing homeowners. "The company believes," a Levitt advertisement said, "that an undesirable class of people can quickly destroy the value of any neighborhood. Without being stupidly snobbish, a policy was adopted long ago to limit Strathmore to refined, American families." Their refinement came from being White Anglo-Saxon Protestants.[8] Although the grandson of a rabbi, Levitt barred Jews from the North Shore projects in an effort to assure his elite clientele of doctors, Wall Street lawyers, celebrities, and advertising executives that they wouldn't have to rub shoulders with unsavory people and the nouveaux riches. This, Levitt insisted, was purely a business decision; he was no self-hating Jew and made large donations to Israel and many Jewish charities.

Levitt priced his North Shore homes between $8,000 and $22,000 at a time when the average new house cost less than $4,000.[9] He traded on the North Shore's reputation as Long Island's Gold Coast, the enclave where America's wealthiest families, the Vanderbilts, Astors, Whitneys, and Morgans, built faux châteaus and elaborate mansions in the late nineteenth and early twentieth centuries. This was the place where F. Scott Fitzgerald's fictional Jay Gatsby longed for acceptance, and where New York's rich and famous spent their summers in the decades before the Hamptons came into vogue. Levitt's aristocratic pretensions didn't divert him from employing splashy marketing techniques, which he did with mounting success. In April 1937, he had one of his large new homes in Strathmore at Manhasset wrapped in six thousand square feet of cellophane topped with a red cellophane bow. A twelve-foot zipper down the middle gave entry to prospective homebuyers.[10] The stunt generated a huge amount of publicity, with pictures of the home featured in *Life,* the *New York Times,* and other publications.

The homes Levitt built on the North Shore were far more modest than the castles of the robber barons, but their storied location appealed to the "little rich" of the 1930s. So did their traditional English and colonial designs, high-quality building materials, name-brand fixtures, and top-of-the-line appliances (Kohler toilets, Armstrong flooring, GE refrigerators). By building twenty houses at a time and using standardized windows, doors, and other components, Levitt was able to price the homes at thousands less than their competitors. He gave buyers "swank at low cost," said the editors of *Architectural Forum,* adding that Alfred had "a flair for making houses look like twice the money in them."[11] All told, Levitt & Sons built, and quickly sold, about 1,900 houses on Long Island, along with a hundred more in upscale Westchester County, New York (Strathmore-in-Westchester), making it one of the nation's largest prewar homebuilders. The company had averaged more than two hundred houses per year at a time when just six firms nationwide were constructing as many as twenty-five homes annually in Levitt's price range.[12] Eighty-six percent of prewar builders put up two or fewer houses a year, and 60 percent built only one. In 1947, the editors of *Fortune* magazine called homebuilding "The Industry Capitalism Forgot."[13]

Fortune's comments echoed the argument made a decade earlier by A.C. Shire, the technical editor of *Architectural Forum,* who called U.S. homebuilding an "anachronism . . . highly resistant to progress, follow[ing] practices developed in the days of handwork [and] bogged down by waste and inefficiency."[14] The problem was that homebuilding had remained an artisanal enterprise with skilled craftsmen constructing houses pretty much the same way, and using the same methods, as they had for centuries. Most work was done by hand, and a new house required a bevy of workers, each with different skills:

carpenters, plumbers, roofers, excavators, electricians. The work they did was often meticulous, but slow and costly. The pace had picked up only marginally after the war—held back, *Fortune* said, by burdensome union constraints and an industry culture that required the extensive use of subcontractors and prevented builders from buying their materials wholesale. These constraints pushed up costs at every step, making the average house too expensive for the average buyer and doing little to dent the massive post–World War II housing demand. To meet this demand, *Fortune* called for much larger homebuilding firms with the capital to organize production on an industrial scale and the power to tame labor unions and impose more efficient practices. The article singled out Levitt & Sons as the most prominent example of a company doing what needed to be done.[15]

Even before the end of the war, Levitt anticipated the intense demand for affordable housing and developed a business model to meet it. In doing so, he could draw on discussions among professional planners, government housing officials, and other commentators that had been going on since the 1920s. Levitt also took note of prewar experiments in building housing using modern mass-production techniques, often to create communities located close to factories and other places of large-scale employment. Several of those experiments took place in California, which experienced huge population growth in the 1920s and 1930s and needed new, low-cost housing to accommodate it.[16]

Like these prewar California projects, the Levitt model was based on standardizing production so as to build affordable homes quickly and on a very large scale. The result was what Levitt called the Cape Cod, by which the company meant a boxy, 750-square-foot house with four and a half rooms—kitchen, living room, bathroom, and two bedrooms—on slightly more than a tenth of an acre. This basic dwelling closely resembled the "minimum house" developed by researchers in the 1930s and ultimately adopted by the FHA as its cost-effective prototype of a home that could be built quickly and inexpensively with industrial techniques. Those who designed this minimum house sought to use the square footage more efficiently by eliminating rooms used only part of the day and creating interior spaces that could work for multiple purposes. The first room to go was the dining room, occupied at most a couple hours a day. The basement was also dispensable, since it required costly excavation and provided no living space.

The heating and laundry equipment usually installed there was moved to the main part of the house. Foyers and hallways also wasted space. In advocating the minimum house, the FHA urged builders to eliminate "every square foot of space, every odd corner, every length of pipe, every pipe connection, every foot of lumber" that wasn't strictly necessary, even as it admitted that a homebuilder would find it hard to do all this and make a profitable, desirable house.[17] As the prominent journalist Robert Lasch put it, the builder would need to bring "together a variety of specialized skills and professions": expertise in "land acquisition" and the planning and layout of subdivisions, an architectural staff, construction engineers, and "financial experts to manage the loans."[18]

Nevertheless, the FHA and the Roosevelt administration did everything they could to create the conditions for private homebuilders to make their plans a reality. When Franklin D. Roosevelt assumed the presidency in 1933, the housing situation was dire. Even before the Great Depression, homebuilding was slow and costly, and being done at a grossly inadequate pace. When the Federal Reserve raised interest rates in 1928, residential housing starts began declining sharply, and by 1933 starts had plummeted by 95 percent. Worse, the economic depression prevented many existing homeowners from making their monthly mortgage payments, and by 1933 foreclosures had reached one thousand a day. Half of all mortgages were in default, adding homelessness and the fear of homelessness to the nation's economic disaster. Even those who could make their monthly payments found themselves underwater: the value of their homes had dropped so sharply that many people owed more than their houses were worth. President Herbert Hoover belatedly tried to address this situation, but his efforts failed to make a dent.[19]

One of FDR's earliest acts as president was designed to protect small homeowners from foreclosure. His Home Owners' Loan Corporation (HOLC), created in June 1933, provided government funding to refinance homes in danger of mortgage default and to enable those whose homes had already been foreclosed to buy them back. By June 1935, the HOLC had made $3.1 billion of mortgage loans to fully one-tenth of all owner-occupied, nonfarm residences nationwide. It bailed out more than a million homeowners.[20] These efforts succeeded by creating a new kind of mortgage that allowed homeowners to refinance their existing mortgages with new loans that stretched payments of principal and interest over twenty years (after World War II, this period would be extended to thirty years). Monthly payments would remain constant for the life of the loan, and at the end of the loan period, the house would be fully paid off and owned free and clear. Before this New Deal innovation, mortgages were granted for just five years or less, making for high monthly payments and excluding most middle- and working-class families from homeownership. Worse, mortgages would typically cover only 50 to 70 percent of the cost of a home, which meant that homebuyers had to come up with down payments of 30 to 50 percent.[21] And even with these large up-front payments, most mortgages were not fully paid off at the end of the five- or ten-year loan. Homeowners had to scramble for new loans to finance the unpaid portion. In good economic times, most people could secure new loans, but when a depression hit, millions found themselves in default.

When the Roosevelt administration created the HOLC, so many mortgages were in default that the government decided to minimize its costs and risk by concentrating on the properties valuable enough to make the rescue effort work. To assess the value of American homes, the HOLC created an elaborate procedure for appraising residential property and then trained an army of appraisers to apply these procedures uniformly throughout the country. Some of these appraisers went to work for private banks, which for the most part adopted the government standards for determining the value of a house.

According to these standards, there were four categories of homes, ranked from A to D and color-coded with A in green, B in blue, C in yellow, and D in red. The ranking of a house depended as much on the characteristics of the surrounding neighborhood as on the dwelling itself. The A, or green, category included new homes in "homogonous" areas "in demand as residential locations in good times and bad." "Homogonous" meant neighborhoods populated exclusively by "American business and professional men," which the HOLC understood to mean white and non-Jewish. Predominantly Jewish neighborhoods or those with an "infiltration of Jews" could at best be ranked in category B. These areas were deemed "still desirable" and expected to remain stable, although they were capable of no further improvement. Category C areas were "definitely declining," while category D, or red, had already hit bottom.[22]

Virtually all urban Black neighborhoods were placed in the red category, and "C" regions were graded next to last because the housing stock was older, and prices and rents were so low "as to attract an undesirable element."[23] The HOLC didn't invent the idea of categorizing neighborhoods by race, ethnicity, and class; realtors had long done this, on the self-fulfilling assumption that when Black families, even prosperous middle-class ones, moved into an area, property values would sink.[24] Realtors, like city and town officials, recognized that most white people didn't want Black neighbors, and that well-to-do white Protestants generally wanted to exclude Catholics and Jews. The HOLC enshrined these cultural prejudices as government policy. With the help of banks and realtors, it ranked every block of every American city and most suburban areas as green, blue, yellow, or red—drawing up color-coded "Residential Security Maps" that remained secret to the public but were made available to banks.

These maps make clear that appraisers valued nonurban lands more highly than urban ones. Near St. Louis, for example, the still-countrified town of Ladue earned a "green" rating because the area was "highly restricted," limited to "capitalists and other wealthy families." The appraisers noted that not "a single foreigner or negro [sic]" lived there.[25] The white, working-class precincts of the city didn't fare so well. They received a grade of C, while the mostly Black Lincoln Terrace earned a D in 1937, even though its solid, well-built bungalows were just ten years old. The neighborhood had been designed for middle-class, white homeowners, but Black families bought its homes instead. Despite being well-kept, the area was smudged in red on the local Residential Security Map after appraisers said it had "little or no value today, having suffered a tremendous decline in values due to the colored element now controlling the district."[26]

For HOLC appraisers, the mere presence of Black residents blighted a district and reduced its value to nothing. Even neighborhoods with only a few Black residents were generally given a D. Areas with Black inhabitants were guilty of two unpardonable sins: their racial identity and urban location. Although some city districts were graded A or B, suburban areas were much more likely to receive these ratings. The most extreme example was Newark, New Jersey, which didn't receive a single A.[27]

Despite its highly prejudiced ratings, the HOLC nonetheless issued some loans to neighborhoods ranked C or D. It was private banks that took the agency's ratings to heart: they generally refused to offer mortgages to residents of these areas. The worst offender, though, was another New Deal agency, the Federal Housing Administration, created in 1934. The FHA's main charge was to reduce unemployment by encouraging the construction of homes. It did this by insuring up to 90 percent of loans issued by private banks for both the building and purchase of single-family, detached dwellings priced at no more than $9,000.[28] The National Housing Act, the legislation that created the agency, committed the U.S. Treasury to repay banks for any losses incurred from delinquent loans. The FHA thus shifted the risk of making construction and mortgage loans from private banks to the federal government. With the government shouldering the risk, interest rates fell dramatically, making home purchases much more affordable.

What also made homes more affordable were the economies of scale the FHA achieved through a great innovation in the financing of home construction: government-guaranteed construction loans. In the past, a builder first had to get a bank to lend the money to erect a dwelling. Once the home was finished or well underway, he had to find a buyer who could qualify for a mortgage loan, which the purchaser would use to buy the house and thus enable the builder to repay his construction loan and earn a profit. This process does much to explain why most builders put up just one house at a time: they couldn't come up with the capital to construct several at once. (Other reasons had to do with the lack of mechanization, union rules, middlemen, and subcontractors who jacked up construction costs.)[29]

Title VI of the National Housing Act changed this by enabling a builder to request "commitments" from the FHA to insure a certain number of mortgage loans before any buyers had been secured. Levitt's initial "ask" for his postwar Levittown was for two thousand commitments, which he quickly received. These commitments then provided, in installments, 90 percent of the capital needed to build the two thousand homes. In effect, these commitments made Levitt (or another mass builder) the temporary mortgagee. He repaid the FHA mortgage only after rental income began to pour in or when an individual home was bought, earning him a profit of at least $1,000 on each $7,000 dwelling.

In the 1930s, with the country still in depression, these innovations bore only modest fruit. The full potential of the FHA's policies would not be realized until after the war, when the agency's work would be supplemented by what is commonly known as the G.I. Bill (the Servicemen's Readjustment Act of 1944), which enabled veterans to buy any house costing less than $9,000 with no money down. The FHA guaranteed the first 90 percent of the mortgage, and the Veterans Administration the other 10 percent. As Bill Levitt later said, "The only way we were going to get a volume of housing was to grant to the veteran, in effect, a one hundred percent mortgage. 'Cause he had no cash."[30] Together, the FHA and G.I. Bill revolutionized the financing of homebuilding, increasing the percent of American families living in homes they owned from 44 in 1934 to 63 in 1960. Homeownership has remained relatively stable since then, except for the late 1990s and early 2000s, when it briefly soared into the high 60s.[31]

Largely because of policies enacted in the 1930s, white Americans have benefitted from home ownership far more than African Americans. This was especially true from 1934 to 1960, but whites have maintained their homeownership advantage since then. The FHA stacked the deck in their favor in several ways. The agency wanted to minimize the risk that mortgagees would default on their loans by allocating its funds mainly to neighborhoods deemed to enjoy "relative economic stability" and "protection from adverse influences."[32] FHA officials assessed these qualities using the HOLC's color-coded maps, which told them that "yellow" and "red" neighborhoods, mostly located in urban areas, were unstable and unprotected. These neighborhoods tended to be densely populated, and their older structures were believed "to accelerate the transition to lower class occupancy."[33] Many of the red-colored or "red-lined" precincts that were ineligible for FHA-guaranteed loans were predominantly Black. Lacking a federal guarantee to repay a loan in case of default, most banks refused to issue mortgages to prospective homeowners in redlined areas.

The FHA officials' assumptions about the risks of lending in these areas had no basis. There was no evidence that people in yellow and red regions were more likely to default than those in green and blue ones. In fact, the evidence was the opposite: for loans issued by the HOLC, yellow and red areas paid up more reliably than green and blue ones.[34] But the FHA stuck to its conviction that the low-ranked precincts were doomed to decay and to house a poor, often Black population. This assumption quickly became a self-fulfilling prophecy. By refusing to guarantee loans in yellow and red parts of a city, the FHA discouraged investment there, not only home purchases but also new construction and renovation. The result was widespread urban decline, which motivated people with the means and the opportunity to leave for the greener pastures of the suburbs—or in Los Angeles and other geographically vast cities, to new developments in sparsely populated parts of town.[35]

From the start, FHA officials showed a preference for suburban development and for the outlying precincts of western and southern cities. Thanks to yellow- and redlining, most FHA-guaranteed funds went to the construction and purchase of single-family homes on unbuilt or sparsely built lands. The agency frowned on multifamily dwellings and generally wouldn't insure homes in neighborhoods that included stores, offices, or rental units. These preferences produced the suburban-style developments that mark the postwar landscape: subdivisions with owner-occupied single-family homes surrounded by grass-covered yards, with shops and businesses segregated into commercial enclaves or along designated commercial thoroughfares. The commercial strip, as distinct a feature of postwar suburbia as the housing development, is equally a product of FHA policies.

In case banks and developers failed to get the message, the FHA drew up plans for "typical American houses," all of which were suburban dwellings on individual plots, separated from one another and set back from the street.[36] These plans established minimum standards for construction and design, which was doubtless a good thing, and thus anticipated the "cookie-cutter" tract homes that Levitt and other developers would build after the war.

Not satisfied with encouraging people to leave cities for new suburban subdivisions or move into new suburban-style enclaves within city boundaries, FHA officials tried to shape the character of these developments. They did so by enshrining as federal policy the racial attitudes typical of white Americans, most of whom didn't want to live in integrated neighborhoods. It became FHA policy to prevent the jumbling together of "inharmonious racial or nationality groups." "If a neighborhood is to retain stability," the agency's Underwriting Manual declared, "it is necessary that properties shall continue to be occupied by the same social and racial classes." The best way to avoid social and racial mixing, the manual said, was to insert in property deeds "restrictive covenants" designed to exclude Blacks—and often Jews and other minority groups.

The agency kept careful track of the residential geography of African Americans and used this information to keep the races apart. The FHA, wrote its assistant commissioner in November 1948, "has never insured a housing project of mixed occupancy," because "such projects would probably in a short period of time become all-Negro or all-white." So committed was the FHA to this dogma that it refused to insure mortgages in a section of Detroit where an all-white community grew up around the edges of an all-Black community. The two groups' proximity to each other created an "inharmonious" community. But after a white real estate developer erected a high wall between the white and Black areas, the agency began to approve mortgage guarantees on the white side of the wall.[37]

The result of these policies was an American landscape shaped into doughnuts. The holes were the central cities, populated largely by dark-skinned and "ethnic" people, while the dough surrounding them consisted of all-white suburbs or residential enclaves. Inner cities increasingly shed their white, middle- and upper-middle-class populations, leaving core urban areas occupied by poor people unable to support quality schools and strong city services—leading to more white flight. White suburbs, meanwhile, could shower resources on everything from schools to sanitation to the repaving of streets.

Far from all African Americans lived in cities on the eve of World War II. Many still lived in rural regions or in Black enclaves outside the urban core. But beginning in the mid-1930s, African Americans who preferred to live outside cities or core urban areas had to elude obstacles erected by the FHA—in addition to the many other practices that would increasingly exclude them from desirable suburbs: informal racial restrictions, discriminatory zoning laws, and the prejudices of white realtors, builders, and local politicians. When Blacks took up suburban residence, they usually landed in segregated places without mortgage guarantees, having fled redlined neighborhoods like the ones in Camden and Patterson, New Jersey, where for decades after World War II there was not a single FHA mortgage. From 1934 to 1962, less than 2 percent of the government-backed financing for the construction and purchase of homes went to African Americans and members of other minority groups, and that tiny share of funding went mainly to dwellings in segregated areas.[38] Even in the 1960s, when African Americans, many with college educations and well-paying jobs, began to move in large numbers to the suburbs, it was still mainly to all-Black or mostly Black developments.[39]

This government-backed racial exclusion and steering to segregated enclaves authorized Bill Levitt to create Levittown, New York, as an all-white community. It also dovetailed with his prejudices. "Black people," he told *Esquire*'s Ron Rosenbaum, had "multiplied geometrically" in this country "until finally . . . they moved into the north [and] onto the same street we lived on in Brooklyn. Next to us a Black assistant D.A. moved in. Fearing a diminution of values if too many came in, we picked up and moved out. We then got into the suburbs, into building." He cited business reasons for keeping Black people out of his developments:[40] "If we sold to Blacks, Whites would not buy."[41]

The racism built into the FHA tainted what would otherwise be an innovative, highly successful project to facilitate the large-scale construction of affordable, desperately needed homes. World War II temporarily interrupted the process by redirecting building materials and labor to the military effort, making private housing construction difficult and halting the Levitts' prewar momentum. After 1941, their only recourse was to look to the government. Fortunately, the U.S. Navy wanted low-cost housing for its officers, and Levitt secured a contract to erect 750 tiny rental houses in Norfolk, Virginia, which contained the largest naval base in the United States. The navy wanted these dwellings within a year. Looking back on this project in 1977, Levitt said, "We realized that if we were to build as we had in the past, it would have taken us three or four years to do the job, so, of necessity, we had to dream up new methods." He didn't invent new techniques but adapted those pioneered by a few homebuilders on the eve of the war. Prominent among these prewar builders was Fritz B. Burns, a Los Angeles developer who had built 788 tract homes priced at just over $3,000. Another of Burns's projects, a wartime Los Angeles development called Westchester, consisted of 3,200 units intended for defense-industry workers. He cut costs and saved time by using precut lumber, specialized work crews, preassembled components, and standardized plumbing units.[42]

The Levitts clearly learned from this example, but the Norfolk dwellings were more attractive and less rudimentary than Burns's Los Angeles homes. They also displayed some innovations. The Levitts saved time and effort by painting ceilings and perimeter walls before installing room partitions. They framed an entire wall on the ground, raised it, and then connected it to other walls framed the same way, an approach that proved cheaper and quicker than the traditional method. Rather than use masonry foundations, they perched their houses on concrete slabs, which required less labor than the standard methods still used by Burns and virtually all other builders.[43] Another Levitt idea was to turn concrete burial vaults into septic tanks. "It used to take us half a day to do a septic tank," Levitt recalled. "We went to a manufacturer and showed him what a cinch it was to make a few changes in his product and turn out precast concrete septic tanks—née burial vaults—for us." Now they could install twenty on the same day.[44]

The navy was so happy with the firm's work—they'd built the 750 houses in ten months, instead of a year—that it requested another 1,600. "We learned more with every house we built," Levitt said, "and this second job was really a post-graduate course in mass production." It was there, in Norfolk, that "we began to grasp the principles of mass production."[45]

Having worked for the navy early in the war, Levitt joined it in 1944 and shipped out to Oahu, Hawaii, with the Seabees, the service's construction branch. With typical bravado, he claimed that rather than learning from the Seabees' vast experience, "It was the other way around." One of the Seabees' engineers, a Lieutenant Kamuf, who later went to work for Levitt, said his future boss spent his time overseas drinking and gambling and generally living it up. Levitt never saw combat.[46]

While Bill enjoyed himself in Hawaii, he, Abraham, and Alfred planned for the postwar phase of their business. Bill encouraged his father and brother to think big. In 1944, the Levitts began to buy tracts of farmland in Hempstead Plains, near the eastern end of Nassau County, about thirty miles from Manhattan. They took advantage of an infestation of the golden nematode, an agricultural pest that was strangling part of the potato crop in Hicksville and Island Trees. In 1934, Hicksville farmers had begun to notice that their potato fields were showing signs of stunted growth and root damage.

The parasite had hitchhiked onto truck and tractor tires and was spreading widely in western Long Island, then still a largely agricultural area.[47] By 1947, the golden nematode had blighted more than six thousand acres of farmland. Not all farmers were affected, but most worried that the value of their lands and crops would plummet. Their fears were exacerbated by a glut of potatoes grown elsewhere in the country.

Even without the golden nematode, the Levitts would likely have built their development in this part of Nassau County. They bought 60 percent of a key parcel of land from a holding company called the Merillon Corporation, which was unaffected by the nematode because the acreage consisted of grassland, not farmland. Thanks to Merillon and the arrival of military contractors such as Grumman Aircraft, Republic Aviation, and Liberty Aircraft, agriculture was declining in the area even before the potato blight. The bug simply hastened the transformation and made most remaining farmers eager to sell. A couple of real estate companies knew that Levitt & Sons was buying land in and around Hicksville and that it was interested in acquiring more.[48] The agents brought these highly motivated sellers to the firm's attention, and in 1946 and 1947, the Levitts purchased large tracts of inexpensive land.

In the 1950s, Bill Levitt would claim that he had decided, even before the war ended, to double down on the mass-production techniques learned and refined in the Norfolk project and build a huge development of low-priced, standardized homes to meet the coming vast demand for affordable housing. While the land purchases make clear that the Levitts intended to undertake a major postwar housing initiative, they didn't abruptly decide to transform their company from a builder of houses for the affluent to one aimed at the working and lower-middle classes. After the war, they continued to build new Strathmores, marketing 1,100 houses for $17,500 to $20,000 each. Meanwhile, they made slow and careful efforts to construct mass-produced, low-cost houses, a series of experiments designed to try different techniques and test what experts predicted would be a soft market. In 1946, they erected one thousand two-story Cape Cods on eight-thousand-square-foot lots (the Levittown lots would be six thousand) in Westbury, Long Island, just west of what would become Levittown. The price was $10,000, considerably more than the Levittown homes would cost. Next, the company built thirty-one dwellings in nearby Albertson to experiment with heating pipes baked into a cement floor. In another experiment, in Carle Place, the Levitts put up 191 tiny, two-bedroom Cape Cods that could sell for $7,000.[49]

The Westbury and Carle Place houses took longer to sell than the Levitts had hoped, and this trying experience, together with new government incentives favoring rental housing, made them proceed cautiously. In May 1947, the company announced a new two-thousand-unit development of tiny rental houses for veterans only. The 750-square-foot Cape Cods would be located in Island Trees, a farming community fifteen miles north of Jones Beach, the popular day resort that had made Robert Moses famous. For the Levitts, a company that had built more than five thousand homes since 1929, another two thousand represented a large but hardly revolutionary move. Only after they found themselves overwhelmed by hordes of people eager to rent and buy their dwellings did they make a full-fledged commitment to this new market.[50] When they did, their efforts set off a massive transformation that would change the face of Long Island, and then the nation.

2 Levittown, New York
Icon of Postwar America

IN 1947, AS he began building his Long Island development, Levitt took full advantage of a favorable political environment in which the federal government eagerly backed his company with enormous public resources. Between 1947 and 1950, Washington pumped $20 billion ($260 billion today) into the U.S. housing industry via government-insured, low-interest loans that mainly benefitted large-scale homebuilders like Levitt.[1] This public largesse enabled his company to raise the massive amount of capital needed to turn Long Island potato fields into by far the largest suburban community in the country. Without this government intervention, which moved the Bank of Manhattan Company to give him the largest line of credit ever offered to a private corporation, Levitt & Sons would almost certainly have remained a builder of modest, upscale developments like those he created between 1929 and 1939.[2] As Abraham Levitt told an interviewer in 1955, "Levittown could not exist without the FHA. Banks would not have loaned the money without the Federal Government insuring that the money would be repaid if anything happened. Some jobs are too big for private enterprise. The government has to step in and help private capital."[3]

The government did not, of course, have to help the Levitts garner huge profits; it could have built far more public housing than it did, or expanded the dual track of public housing and risk-free private homebuilding initiated during the New Deal. But the housing industry, realtors, and the U.S. Chamber of Commerce strenuously opposed public housing projects in favor of private development guaranteed by government-backed mortgages. After the war, when Republicans took control of both the House and the Senate, the new majorities tried to annul much of the New Deal social agenda.[4] Although they achieved only modest results, one of their most successful initiatives was to limit public housing. In a series of Senate hearings led by Joseph McCarthy, not yet the country's most infamous Cold Warrior, Republicans attacked public housing as socialistic. Bill Levitt served as one of McCarthy's star witnesses, and unsurprisingly he argued for "private" development rather than public housing.[5]

Before the war, public housing had mostly taken shape as urban apartment buildings, although the New Deal had produced one particularly successful suburban project, Greenbelt, Maryland, outside Washington, D.C., plus two smaller versions in Greenhills, Ohio, and Greendale, Wisconsin. The D.C.-area project provided housing for low-income families in a garden city environment composed mainly of low-rise rental units. It was small, serving just 885 families, all white.[6] Greenbelt's modest size suggests that even with sufficient political support, the government by itself couldn't have satisfied the massive postwar demand for affordable housing. This was especially true given that the overwhelming majority of Americans wanted to live in newly built single-family dwellings, a preference Levitt fully understood.[7]

Beyond the federal government's financial support, Levitt benefitted from the work, and effective subsidy, of local officials as well. In the 1920s and 1930s, Robert Moses, the New York building czar who created much of Long Island's infrastructure, laid out the parkways that ferried motorists from the eastern edges of New York City to the interior of the island. The Northern and Southern State Parkways brought Levittown close enough to the city to make it a bedroom community based on the private automobile, while other roads took Levittown homebuyers to the offices and factories of defense-oriented industries that had made Long Island their home.

Yet it would be wrong to say that these federal and local incentives were mainly responsible for Levitt's success. Plenty of New York–area builders could have taken advantage of what the FHA and VA, along with Joseph McCarthy and Robert Moses, had wrought. But it was Levitt who grasped these opportunities.

Levitt's firm proved to be one of the few that were capable of achieving the FHA's prewar goals. He successfully produced thousands of copies of the FHA's minimum house and rented them for just sixty dollars a month, with an eventual option to buy for $6,990. The company began taking deposits for these rental units in early 1947, and before any of the two thousand were started, they had applications for more than six thousand, the number the company would build over the next two years.[8]

Although the New York–based media exaggerated Levitt's originality, it was right to focus on the unprecedented size and scale of the company's operation. Not only did it buy up huge swaths of land and amass vast amounts of capital through government and private loans; it also consolidated a homebuilding industry that had traditionally been divided into dozens of players, each profiting from its contribution and thus adding to the house's cost. A middleman bought, say, lumber from a lumber mill and then sold it to the builder, marking up the price along the way. Such profit-taking was true of all the middlemen that builders dealt with, and the result, according to Bill Levitt, was that builders paid double the cost of manufacturing the materials they needed. This system produced a large number of businesses allied to homebuilding and spread profits and employment opportunities widely, but it ruled out the construction of houses that most Americans could afford.[9]

To eliminate these middlemen, Levitt created the North Shore Supply Company, a building materials dealer with just one customer, Levitt & Sons. In effect, Levitt became its own middleman, which enabled the company to purchase its supplies directly from the manufacturer while maintaining the fiction, although fooling nobody, that it was respecting long-standing industry practices. The ability to buy directly vastly reduced Levitt's costs and gave the company a huge advantage over its competition. And Levitt's purchases were massive. In 1950 alone, the firm consumed 57,600,000 feet of lumber, 1,500 miles of copper tubing, 12,770,000 square feet of Sheetrock, 24,084,000 square feet of floor tiles, 290,000 yards of cement, and 1,927,000 pounds of nails.[10]

Not content to dispense with middlemen, Levitt proceeded, after the war, to bypass the manufacturers of building materials by setting up manufacturing companies of its own, which again had Levitt & Sons as their sole customer. In 1948, Levitt bought three million linear feet of

The frames for Levitt houses arrived at the building sites in precut kits.
No saws were needed, only special nails made in a Levitt factory.
(Levittown Construction Photograph Collection, Special Collections
Department, Hofstra University)

trees in northern California and established its own lumbermill, the Griz-
zly Park Lumber Company, in the town of Blue Lake. From then on, it
"bought" all its lumber from the Blue Lake mill, where workers precut
the wood into framing kits for each Levittown house. Each workman
could precut the frames for ten houses every day. The framing kits were
transported by rail to a staging area just outside Levittown and then
trucked and forklifted to the individual homesites, where unskilled and
semiskilled men quickly assembled the frames, no saws required. Levitt
also built its own nail-making enterprise to supply this key ingredient at
cost. It invented a new kind of expansion nail that enabled it to use low-
cost gypsum siding instead of wood to sheath its houses. Another wholly
owned subsidiary made Levitt's concrete blocks.[11]

The company didn't have to create wholly owned enterprises for
each item it needed. Instead, it exercised informal control over several
specialized companies by making agreements with them to sell 100
percent of their products to Levitt. In exchange for guaranteed sales

in bulk, these companies charged Levitt considerably less than they would have charged other homebuilders. A New Jersey company supplied Levitt, and Levitt alone, with preassembled stairways and cabinets, while another made the homebuilder's standardized doors and windows. Even when Levitt couldn't become a manufacturer's sole customer, as with large companies such as General Electric and Bendix, the size of its purchases enabled it to order custom-designed items. Alfred Levitt convinced Bendix, for instance, to make washing machines with stainless steel tops that could serve as work surfaces in Levittown's ultra-compact kitchens.

These innovations dramatically cut the cost of building materials, and thus of houses. So did Levitt's construction techniques, copied from prewar builders and refined for the scale of the Levittown project. After careful study and experimentation, focused in part on the famous time-motion studies of Frederick Winslow Taylor and Frank and Lillian Gilbreth, Levitt broke the construction process into twenty-six steps modeled on the Fordist factory.[12] But rather than have stationary workers and a moving assembly line, as in an automobile plant, Levitt made his workers mobile. He organized them into twenty-six teams, each moving from one homesite to the next, performing one step of the construction process. Levitt preferred this method to the prefabrication of home parts in a factory, as some companies were doing. Prefabrication was more expensive than Levitt's methods and, given high transportation costs, wouldn't become cost-effective until much later.

Levittown became a huge outdoor factory, with much of the work done by machines. For the typical homebuilder, who constructed only a house or two each year, mechanization didn't make economic sense. But for Levitt, building several thousand homes a year, the investment in machinery paid off because it allowed the company to speed up construction and cut labor costs. Levitt bought a small fleet of trenching machines to excavate around the perimeter of each homesite, creating a cavity into which the concrete footings of the house were poured. The footings both supported the walls and strengthened the cement slab on which the house would stand. To keep costs and prices down, Levitt had eliminated basements despite substantial opposition from local governments, which wanted to maintain their existing building codes.

Nassau County's leaders, all Republicans, had no interest in diluting the sparse local population with an influx of Democrats from

New York City. When County Executive J. Russell Sprague toured Island Trees with Governor Thomas Dewey, he told the *Newsday* reporter Stan Peckham, "This is where that asshole Bill Levitt wants to
build these cheap little houses with no cellars."[13]

Local labor leaders supported the basement requirement as well,
partly to prevent jobs from being lost and partly to pressure Levitt to
drop his plan to hire only nonunion workers. Levitt retaliated through
newspaper ads urging veterans to attend a May 27, 1947, hearing before
the town board of Hempstead, Long Island, at which the basement issue
would be discussed. "Be at the public meeting," the ad urged. "If you
want a modern, comfortable, beautiful house as a rental within your
reach, you must be there. We're doing our part; you must do yours!"[14] In
advance of the meeting, *Newsday,* which ardently advocated the building
of Levittown in hopes of expanding its readership, published a slew of articles urging veterans to show up and support Levitt.[15] The response was
overwhelming. Between eight hundred and a thousand (depending on
who was counting) former servicemen packed the meeting hall and overflowed into the corridors surrounding it. Many wore their old military
uniforms, and their wives attended with babies in their arms. "I remember the crowds, the incredible crush of people," recalled Julia Konopasek,
a twenty-four-year-old Queens resident. "It was like electricity running
through the air. Everyone was there for one thing—to get town officials
to approve Levitt's plan."[16] During testimony by an "expert" on the necessity of basements, a veteran interrupted: "You want basements? I'm
living in a basement. It's my mother-in-law's." The crowd erupted in
applause, chanting, "We want housing! We want housing!" No one else
dared speak against Levitt, and the town counselors quickly caved. The
meeting was over in twenty minutes.[17]

Labor leaders also wanted to maintain the requirement that interior
walls be made with wet plaster rather than the new mass-produced
drywall (Sheetrock) panels that Levitt planned to purchase by the thousands, and they sought as well to retain a ban on paint-sprayers and
certain other power tools. Wet plaster was far more labor-intensive
than drywall, as of course was painting by hand. Backed by house-hun-
gry veterans and *Newsday,* Levitt pushed these long-standing requirements aside. The Nassau-Suffolk Building and Construction Trades
Council responded by picketing Levitt's building sites and threatening
to close down the operation. But after a brief work stoppage, members

of the Operating Engineers Local crossed the picket lines and went to work for Levitt, who promised to pay the equivalent of union wages and more. He largely fulfilled that promise but only by requiring longer workdays. As for why the nascent strike ended so quickly with no concessions from Levitt, it seems likely (although there's no proof) that Bill Levitt made a deal with the powerful Long Island union boss, William C. De Koning. In 1953, the labor strongman was convicted on charges of extortion and conspiracy for having promised hundreds of Nassau and Suffolk County building contractors to defang the many unions he controlled in exchange for payments into his welfare fund.[18]

After these victories, Levitt proceeded with his construction plans full tilt. *Time* magazine, like the rest of the New York–based press, was impressed. "Every 100 feet," *Time*'s reporter wrote, "the trucks stopped and dumped identical bundles of lumber, pipes, bricks, shingles, and copper tubing—all as neatly packaged as loaves from a bakery."[19] "Levitt houses," wrote the sociologist John Liell, "were assembled rather than built."[20]

But first, the building sites had to be prepared, a massive undertaking that involved laying sewer, drainage, and freshwater pipes underground, removing trees and other vegetation, and grading the land. Only then could the thousands of miles of asphalt, all-weather streets be laid out, a huge engineering operation in itself. With the streets in place, Levitt's fleet of cement mixers and other heavy equipment could finally rumble in, allowing the homebuilding to begin.[21]

Levitt had invested $200,000 in two dozen cement trucks, which made the concrete and poured it into the freshly dug foundation trenches and wood frames of each slab. Once a truck had lumbered on to the next homesite, a Levitt crew sank copper heating pipes into the wet cement. A mechanical trowel then smoothed and leveled the slab. By investing in cement mixers, trenching machines, and automatic trowels, Levitt reduced the labor cost of each slab to fifty-five dollars.[22]

The pipes buried in the slab would be connected to a heating and hot-water boiler, suspended from the kitchen ceiling to save space, that would provide the home's "radiant" heating. Heat would simply radiate up from the floor rather than from costly baseboard units or from ductwork stretched through the attic and into each room of the house. In any case, Levitt wanted to reserve his attics as "expansion space" for the house. The cost savings of radiant heating were immense, but problems began to surface, some immediately, others years later. On cold winter mornings, the twelve-inch asphalt tiles used as flooring became so hot that a barefoot person could feel as if they were walking on hot coals. Wall-to-wall carpet, which Levitt didn't include, or at least thick slippers were essential. As a kid growing up in Levittown, Pennsylvania, I had to hop from my bed onto a small area rug to avoid burning my feet on winter mornings. More serious problems surfaced later, when the radiant heating pipes sprang a leak, which they commonly did. Repairing or replacing them meant prying off the floor tiles and digging up the cement slab. Rather than undertake this expensive, disruptive repair, thousands of Levittowners, including my parents, shut down the radiant system and installed baseboard heating. Levitt's radiant heating kept initial costs down, but cost homeowners substantial sums in the long term.

Once the slab was fully dry, the framing crew appeared and put up the entire precut frame in a few hours. Another crew sheathed the roof in thinner-than-normal plywood, which also required relaxed building codes. Yet another crew covered the exterior with asphalt shingles specially developed for the Levittown house, using Levitt's proprietary expansion nails.[23] The next crew, in the interior, squeezed bags of insulation between the two-by-fours, and on their heels another crew came in to install the drywall sheets. Each sheet was four feet wide, and this width determined the house's dimensions, since it would have been wasteful to slice a board in two. Next, the doors and windows were installed, the prefabricated staircase hammered in, the walls spray-gunned with a special Levitt paint, the roof shingled on, and the cabinets installed. Most of the crews performing these steps consisted of Levitt subcontractors, small companies that were officially independent but worked exclusively for Levitt. By paying each subcontractor a fixed amount per house, the mother firm shifted the responsibility for controlling costs onto these subsidiary businesses, which had an incentive to work harder and more efficiently so as to increase their profits and potentially the wages of their workers. The latter tended to earn at least as much as their unionized counterparts, although by working longer hours. Using subcontractors in this way also absolved Levitt of the need to manage the bulk of his labor force and deal with any problems that arose.[24]

The crowning glory of the Levitt house was the gleaming white, fully automatic Bendix washing machine, installed by a worker whose sole task was to tighten the bolts that kept the appliance in place. Automatic washing machines were largely unknown in such modest homes, but Levitt had negotiated an excellent price, and he featured the appliance in his advertisements. Most Levittown buyers couldn't have afforded one, but when the cost was included in the rental amount—and later the amortized selling price—it seemed to be free.

Since Levitt's assembly line method enabled the company to work in different stages on dozens of houses at a time, some days might see thirty or thirty-five of them finished. The average daily completion rate stood at ten to twelve, still an impressive number, although commentators often pegged it at thirty or thirty-five. Some even claimed that a Levitt house was completed every sixteen minutes, or that the houses took just a few hours to build.[25] Still, to construct four thousand or five thousand homes a year, as Levitt did in 1948 to 1950, you have to work steadily and fast, enabling the completion rate to increase from year to year.[26] Such speed was made possible by standardized parts, precut lumber, mechanized equipment, and extreme division of labor. *Architectural Forum* estimated that the average worker on a traditional custom-built home "spends 25 percent of his time figuring out what to do next." For each Levitt house, "this percentage must be close to zero."[27] By November 1951, the firm had built 17,447 houses, as many as the city of Stamford, Connecticut, built in three hundred years. Unlike those in Stamford, the price of a Levittown house was within the financial reach of huge numbers of people, many of them unhoused or poorly housed. Levitt & Sons earned a healthy $1,000 profit on each dwelling.[28] Few if any of its competitors could match this achievement at an equivalent scale. "Any damn fool can build homes," Levitt declared in 1947. "What counts is how many can you sell for how little."[29]

The downside was the transformation of productive farmland into an endless looking glass of near-identical human boxes reproduced thousands of times. But millions of Americans wanted single-family homes separated from other homes by grassy plots, and Bill Levitt, the marketing mastermind of his firm, gave them exactly that, at prices many could afford. "The plain fact," Levitt declared, was that, "for many families, the choice lies between the so-called 'tract' house

The Levittown Cape Cod. (Photograph by Edward Berenson)

and none at all."[30] The Island Trees Cape Cod and its successor, the Rancher, proved to be good deals all around, and especially for the Levitt brothers. In 1949, Bill drew a salary of $300,000, a hundred times that year's average household income.[31] His salary would continue to rise, as would the profits from the four-year-long building project: roughly $20 million in 1951 dollars, or more than $240 million today.[32] Still, for all of Levitt's ingenuity as a builder and businessman, he could not have succeeded without massive support from the federal government. His great distinction was to take advantage of that support better than most other homebuilders, using it to provide thousands of good-quality homes for people of modest means— provided they were white.

With the construction of Levittown, Bill Levitt, the fast-talking salesman, became the face of the firm. But it was his kid brother, Alfred, a self-taught architect, who came up with the designs that made the firm's tiny houses appealing to working- and middle-class families. In

1936, at age twenty-four, Alfred took a sabbatical from the family homebuilding enterprise to study at the feet of Frank Lloyd Wright. The famous architect was building a dramatic modern house in Great Neck, Long Island, for the radical publishers Benjamin and Anne Rebhuhn—Benjamin had been briefly jailed for advocating birth control. Wright designed the dwelling in close collaboration with the couple, who loved the way the architect connected his homes' interiors to the natural environment. For the Rebhuhns, he designed a two-level structure shaped into a cross, punctuated with eighteen-foot windows that showcased the wooded property. He wanted the Rebhuhns and their guests to feel always surrounded by trees. To emphasize the connection with nature, Wright framed his tall windows and roof overhangs with red cypress and clad the house with horizontal planks of the same wood, which he neatly accented with weathered brick. (Alfred was horrified to see that he rejected 90 percent of the bricks delivered to the site.)[33] The architect repeated the red cypress motif inside the home, using it for the floors and ceilings. Like many other Frank Lloyd Wright houses, the Rebhuhn dwelling had no basement and was built on a slab. It had a carport rather than a garage. To enter the house, you have to walk the full length of the transept (library and living room); the front door opens into the center of the structure, where the transept intersects with the nave (living room, dining room, maid's room). Out back are a brick terrace and a badminton court.

Inside the house, the living room and library soar upward, two stories high. Wright installed floor-to-ceiling shelving in the library to accommodate the couple's ten thousand books. He designed a built-in twenty-eight-foot sofa for the living room and furnished the rest of the house with his own creations. To literally bring the outside in, he built the dining area around a live oak tree, which grew for decades until it perished when the house caught fire in the early 1970s. (The tree had to be carefully removed, and the roof and floor patched where it had stood.) The floor plan was open, the different spaces— living room, dining room, library, and kitchen—distinguished mainly by their custom-made furniture and floors at slightly different levels. A long fireplace, open on two sides, set the dining room off from the entryway and living area without the need for a wall. Upstairs, the home's two bedrooms connect to a balcony overlooking the living room. A servant's quarters was tucked behind the kitchen. When completed, in 1937, the dwelling cost $35,000, nearly ten times the price of the average Depression-era house.

Alfred Levitt, parked at the construction site every day, drank in every detail of the Rebhuhn house. He loved the open plan and was impressed by the two-sided fireplace that both separated and joined the entryway, living, and dining areas. He noted that the house sat on a slab rather than a basement and that it had a carport rather than a garage. Twelve years later, he would incorporate many of these design elements into the first Levittown houses ("Ranchers") built for sale rather than as rentals. (The original Levitt Cape Cod, built in 1947 and 1948 and then discontinued, owed far more to the FHA's 1930s "minimum house" than to Wright.)

In the Rancher, Alfred's interior featured an open plan with a dual-sided, Wright-inspired fireplace as the centerpiece both separating and joining its rooms. He nodded to tradition by including a hinged desk/bookcase between the kitchen and living room that, when pivoted 180 degrees, enclosed the kitchen and screened it from the entryway. Some homebuyers, Alfred reasoned, would find the Wrightian open plan a little too radical. But he did nothing to mute Wright's influence on his efforts to bring the outside in. Every Rancher featured a rear wall of twelve floor-to-ceiling, double-glazed "Thermopane" windows flanked by a glass-paned door. The picture windows' built-in insulation kept out the cold and proved no more expensive to build than a standard exterior wall.

Bill and Abraham wanted the Levitt ranch to have a garage, but Alfred insisted that it not accommodate a car. "Until people are decently housed," he declared, "I believe we have no moral right to house autos."[34] He would later change his mind, and even before he did, Levitt ads and friendly journalists made clear that homeowners could build a carport or garage along the Rancher's sixteen-foot, windowless side wall.[35]

Alfred's architectural innovations ingeniously adapted the modernism of Frank Lloyd Wright for the masses. "There is no point in trying to do something," Alfred said, "unless it can be handed out to the great masses of people as a cultural increase . . . a device by which a few thoughts of the progressive architects can be given to the public."[36] Buyers seemed to like this "cultural increase," which, according to the architectural critic Lester Walker, "meant the California good life—the beautiful, relaxed good life [embodied in] the California ranch."[37] They especially appreciated the open plan and picture windows, which made the tiny Levitt homes seem larger than they were. The tight twelve-by-sixteen-foot living room, separated from the kitchen only by the two-sided fireplace, gave the illusion of spaciousness, as did the window-wall through which homeowners could admire the six thousand square feet of grass, shrubs, and trees surrounding the home—even if these were identical to the grass, shrubs, and trees planted up and down every block. For many homebuyers, the illusion worked. "The thing about the window," said Vivian Montgomery, who bought a Levittown ranch in 1951, "is how it brings the outside in. You can sit here looking out at your garden, and you don't realize how small the room is."[38]

These illusions made no small contribution to the house's success. Important as well was Alfred's other major innovation: moving the kitchen from its traditional place at the back of the house to the front. Doing so saved money by shortening the sewer pipe leading to the cesspool and eventually the street. It also turned the kitchen into a command post for the wife and mother, who everyone assumed would be its main occupant. From the kitchen, mom would oversee the kids as they did their homework on the dining area table or played out front. She could quickly see who was at the door and welcome visitors. According to a 1949 Levitt ad, addressed to the husband, as if wives played no role in the buying decision, the kitchen "belongs" up front, "where it's just a step for your wife to answer the door, and where she can see who's there and what's going on."[39] The house's open plan served a similar purpose, allowing the wife to look past the two-sided fireplace into the living room or toward the opening leading to the two bedrooms. Alfred said he "decided to borrow from Frank Lloyd Wright and put in a fireplace as a central pivot of the plan. We plotted circulation around the chimney, which faced both the kitchen and the living room," and made it the "control station from which the housewife can easily reach any part of the house."[40] It was assumed that the wife and mother would be at home during the day, and that she wouldn't mind having no private space of her own.

The final inspirations from Wright were to include key elements without taking up space, and make the Levittown house transformable into a larger dwelling. The Rancher conserved space by eliminating hallways and building shelves and other storage spaces into closets, tucking them under the staircase, and burying them beneath the bathroom sink. For future expansion, the original Cape Cod and subsequent ranches featured a tall attic that could accommodate two tiny additional bedrooms. For those wanting more upstairs space, the second floor could be built out from the sharp slope of the roof to make it flush with the front of the house. To facilitate outward expansion, Levitt made the twelve rear windows removable. Taking them out would create an archway into a new room added to the back. The windows could then be reused.[41]

If Alfred was inspired by Wright, Bill looked to Henry Ford in his decision to refresh the product with a new model every year. And beginning in 1949, these models would be for sale rather than for rent. The 1949 Rancher sold for $7,990, with houses on corner lots going for $8,500. Comparable houses elsewhere cost at least $10,000.[42] The down payment for a Levitt house was ninety dollars, waived for veterans, with a monthly carrying charge (mortgage payment, taxes, water, and insurance) of fifty-eight dollars. This modest amount was considerably less than what the veterans lucky enough to find an apartment were paying in rent. The demand for homes to purchase proved even more ferocious than for Levitt's rental units. It led, *Architectural Forum* enthused, to "the most spectacular buyer's stampede in the history of U.S. housebuilding."[43] That stampede moved Levitt to buy more and more land, and each year to offer something new.

The 1950 version went full Frank Lloyd Wright and dispensed with the swinging partition. It bowed to popular demand (and Bill's wishes) by adding a carport; in 1950, virtually every Levittown family owned a car. Another key innovation was to endow the dwelling with a television built into the stairwell facing the living room—"built-in" seems to be a term invented by Bill Levitt. For the 1951 model year, the last in Levittown, New York, the homebuilder eliminated the television—by then most families had their own—and added one finished upstairs room.

The frenzy for Levitt homes continued until 17,477 were sold. By 1951, when Levitt's Long Island building spree was finished, the company had created a community of some eighty thousand souls, one of the largest outside New York's major cities. "It's been terrific," said

Levitt's 1950 model included a tiny television built into the stairwell. It was promptly dropped the following year. (Photograph by Edward Berenson, taken and reproduced with the permission of the Levittown Historical Society)

Levitt, gloating about the ferocious demand for his product. "I don't want any publicity on this," he told a bevy of journalists, though he knew they would give him just that.[44]

The people who flocked to Levittown were mostly couples in their twenties or early thirties with one or two young children. Most came from Queens, New York City's easternmost borough, but a fair number had migrated from elsewhere in the Northeast. Their incomes were modest and their ethnic and religious backgrounds diverse, except that none was Black.[45] Prospective inhabitants found out about Levittown through word-of-mouth, obsessive media coverage, and a growing cascade of advertisements in New York City and Long Island papers, including the *Levittown Tribune,* which Levitt created. Most were full-page ads with idealized renderings of the Levittown homes: artistically drawn Cape Cods and ranches surrounded by velvety lawns and mature trees while showing no neighboring homes. In reality, the houses were packed closely together, and the Levitt-installed greenery featured stick-like infant trees and baby shrubs on seeded but still muddy lots. The ads highlighted the low monthly cost of owning a Levitt home—fifty-eight dollars in 1949, sixty-one dollars in 1951—and the "free" community facilities, the swimming pools, ball fields, and "village greens," which later would be known as strip malls. These facilities weren't free, of course, since their costs were bundled into each mortgage and taxes were needed to maintain them.[46] Still, most suburban developments didn't include Levitt's amenities, and, at first, homebuyers appreciated them.[47]

Although Levitt described its Long Island development as a planned community, the planning was done on the fly.[48] Carle Place and the other Levittown prototypes convinced the Levitts that they could profitably build tiny houses to rent for sixty dollars a month and sell for between $7,000 and $8,000, but they had no idea what the overall demand for their homes would be. They proceeded cautiously, feeling their way into the unknown. "At the start we were somewhat fearful," Abraham Levitt recalled in 1955. "Levittown at that time was a long way out with nothing there but potato fields. So we took it easy, one step at the time, and bought enough land for . . . two thousand [houses] to start with. Building continued as houses sold well."[49] Alfred added, "We never knew from one year to the next how much more we could build so we never had an overall master plan."[50]

Originally, they bought enough land for two thousand houses, then four thousand, then four thousand more, and so on, until all seventeen-thousand-plus were built. Levittown thus took on an irregular shape, and the cost of building homes increased from year to year, not so much because the price of materials and labor went up, though they did to some extent, but mainly because the price of land rose sharply as the available acreage shrank and landowners took advantage of Levitt's hunger for their property. At the beginning of the project, Levitt paid $250 per acre ($35 per house); at the end, the price had risen to $3,750 ($535 per house).[51] Levitt would plan much more boldly and thoroughly when it built its second mass development, in Lower Bucks County, Pennsylvania, from 1952 to 1958.

The Long Island Levittown's lack of an overall plan distinguished it from the British garden city movement to which it has been compared. Announced by Ebenezer Howard in 1898 as an ideal(ized) alternative to the modern city, seen as too crowded, impersonal, dirty, and unhealthy, the garden city would unite the best features of the city and country by creating self-sufficient towns of about thirty thousand inhabitants. Each town would be surrounded by farmland and open rural space and have good housing, factories and workshops, shops and services, schools, theaters, and other cultural venues. Although most garden cities evolved into suburban enclaves dependent on nearby cities rather than self-sufficient communities—as would several "new towns" built after World War II—they were always more than mere housing developments.[52]

Levitt's Long Island community included no industry or other places of employment save for a few stores, and it relied heavily on the automobile for travel within the community and to jobs. Although Grumman Aircraft had employed Long Islanders since 1930 and other industries came to the island after the war, New York City remained the mecca for the white-collar workers who heavily populated Levittown in its early years.[53] Later, the development would be more working class, and as women joined the labor force, service jobs would play a larger role. But most Levittowners, even those employed in Nassau County, had to commute a significant distance to work. The Levitt advertisements and pro-Levitt press coverage largely ignored the lack of both local employment opportunities and public transportation. There was just one Long Island Railroad stop three miles from the Levittown core. Not until they moved into their new homes did many Levittowners realize they could not get by without a car. The purchase and upkeep of an automobile substantially raised their cost of living and revealed that the Levitt ads touting low monthly mortgage payments were deceptive, especially since property taxes, minimal at first, were destined to rise.

One reason for the increased taxes was to pay for schools. The existing primary schools in Island Trees in 1947 could accommodate only forty-seven students—and the new residents would soon require facilities for thousands. Levitt had made no provision for schools, but the firm agreed to sell at cost lands it owned to the three school districts that overlapped the new community. Each district then had to finance the construction of schools; six for kindergarten to sixth grade would be built by 1951, when Levittown was complete, along with several secondary schools. By 1957, the community's annual education budget exceeded $9 million, the sum needed to finance fourteen schools and sixteen thousand students. Property taxes that year were the second highest in Nassau County and caused Levittown's first major political conflict.[54]

Between 1945 and 1956, the tax rate in Levittown's District 5, which educated two-thirds of the community's students, went up 650 percent, from seventy-three cents to $4.74 per $100 of assessed valuation. Levittowners increasingly began to question school spending. Although most supported the school board and its policies on the grounds that a good education was worth the expense, a significant minority opposed the "progressive education" championed by the school board and thought the district should cut costs by focusing on the "Three R's" plus moral education. This divide on spending and educational philosophy reflected differences of income and, especially, religion. Jews tended to be liberal and middle class and to support the progressive majority, while Catholics, who were more often conservative and working class, favored the conservative minority.

These conflicts formed the backdrop of a cultural battle that erupted in 1954 over a minor element of the elementary school curriculum, a recording of "The Lonesome Train" (1943), a cantata about the transport of Abraham Lincoln's body across the country following his assassination. That October, the *Catholic World*, a small magazine published by a Catholic missionary society, claimed that the cantata was "patently loaded with Communist propaganda" because it presented Lincoln as a champion of working people. In reality, the song's portrayal of Lincoln was fanciful but hardly Marxist. The school superintendent, John Johnson, refused to ban it, but he faced a growing assault on the district's curriculum after a teacher circulated a mimeographed parody of the hugely popular 1954 Disney song "The Ballad of Davy Crockett," entitled "Davy Crackpot." Many parents condemned the parody for brazenly undermining "our children's respect for a patriotic figure" and felt it was communistic. So, they added, was "The Lonesome Train," which became a hot-button issue dividing conservatives and Catholics from liberals, Unitarians, and Jews.

The cantata became the main issue in the spring 1956 school board election and even took on racial overtones. When the Anti-Defamation League of B'nai B'rith, a Jewish organization, proposed a "Workshop on Human Relations" to soothe tensions, Fred Gerber, the leading conservative on the school board, declared, "I don't like the title 'Human Relations'—I'd like to ask them if they'll let their daughter marry a colored fellow and see what they'll say." This comment suggested that the "Lonesome Train" controversy evoked Cold War fears not only about communism but about racial mixing. Could too much reverence for Lincoln lead to calls for the integration of Levittown?

Gerber's conservatives won the election and immediately banned "The Lonesome Train." When Gerber tried to expand his majority in the election of 1957, liberals built an organization of five hundred members—conservatives called them "Commies with a capital C"—and retook the board majority after an acrimonious campaign. Despite this victory, Superintendent Johnson had had enough. He took a job in the state education bureaucracy in Albany, and his Levittown position remained unfilled for more than a year.

Even in victory, the liberals were forced to cut spending. Property taxes had become exceptionally high, driven not only by educational expenses but by the cost of maintaining the "public" facilities Levitt had built—the pools, playgrounds, ball fields and the like. Residents also had to pay for water, garbage collection, police, and fire companies, all of which further raised the cost of living in Levittown. And a huge new public expense loomed: a proper sewage system to replace the cesspools Levitt had built on the cheap, which now posed an environmental hazard. Residents also had to buy land for churches and synagogues (Levitt had donated some space for houses of worship, but too little) and pay to build them, a burden that didn't exist in long-settled communities.[55]

Between the costs of owning a car, property taxes, maintenance of public facilities, and many other obligations, being a homeowner in Levittown became a financial stretch for many people drawn to the community by the promise of a single-family home for sixty dollars a month. The result, as one real estate agent hyperbolically put it, was that "we're all hanging on by the skin of our teeth."[56] Some doubtless were, but even for those who could easily make ends meet, living in Levittown exacted other costs. Foremost among them was a three-hour round-trip commute to New York City, which (with the gendered division of labor) required many men to spend eleven- to twelve-hour days away from home. For women, it was the opposite: long days stuck in the house and in charge of the kids, often without a car. With no transportation during the week and no stores within walking distance, women had to do their shopping on weekends.[57]

This gendered division of labor existed because virtually all original Levittown households (98 percent) consisted of married couples, usually with one or two young children, and the cultural norm for middle-class people (and aspirants) was for the husband to be the wage earner and the wife to stay home with the kids.[58] Day-care centers and preschools were uncommon. With just one wage earner, family incomes were modest, which, of course, is why Levittown's low housing prices were so appealing.

In 1950, the average Levittown family income was $3,685 a year ($48,000 in 2024 dollars), slightly above the national average of $3,300.[59] Virtually all Levittown households earned between $2,750 and $4,700: no one was poor, and no one was rich. The average resident was a high school graduate with some college; men on average had one more year of education than women. And although 13 percent of Levittown women were college graduates, only 10 percent belonged to the wage-labor force. These educational levels, relatively high for the time, produced a largely male workforce that was more white collar than blue collar, although many of the former held modest positions. The largest occupational category was "clerks and kindred workers," which comprised a third of all employed Levittowners. "Skilled workers and foremen" constituted the next-highest category at 17.5 percent, with "semiskilled workers" (14.5 percent) and "professionals" (14.1 percent) close behind. "Owners, managers, and officials" (8.8 percent) and military personnel (6.9 percent) rounded out the group. In 1951, U.S. Movietone News, a leading newsreel company, portrayed the typical Levittown resident as representing "Mr. Average American." "He" was thirty years old, married, and the parent of a three-year-old and a seven-month-old. He owned a car and a radio and held a semiskilled job in manufacturing. No "she" was mentioned.[60]

Almost everyone in Levittown was young. Since Levitt originally rented and sold only to veterans, few of whom were officers, the adults' average age in 1948 was thirty-two for men and thirty for women. The modal (most common) age hovered slightly below the mean: twenty-nine for men and thirty for women. Just as rich and poor were nonexistent, so were young and old adults. Fewer than 5 percent of Levittown residents belonged to the fifteen to twenty-four age group, and just 2.7 percent were forty-five or older. This age distribution of adults produced a mass of babies and toddlers: nearly a third of the Levittown population was under five. Having babies was deemed Levittown's "major industry," and pregnant women epitomized the "Levittown look."[61] Yet the tiny Levitt dwelling had no room for large families: 70 percent had just one or two children. As one resident put it, "The Levittown house is a built-in birth control policy."[62]

The community's uniformity produced a raft of commentary, at first ironic but later absurdly serious, maintaining that Levittown's identical houses created a small city of cloned individuals and families. *Architectural Forum* opted for irony, commenting in 1949, "Like their houses, Levittown's inhabitants . . . have an eerie similarity. The men all look about the same age. . . . The women are pretty. . . . Each set of parents has exactly two offspring in tow, and the offspring are, respectively, exactly 32 and 36 in. high."[63] This light tone later gave way to exaggerated fears of Levittowns as mind-numbing factories of conformity and cultural listlessness. Lewis Mumford, an influential social critic and architectural historian, famously denounced Levittown and its copycat cousins as fostering "people of the same class, the same incomes, the same age group, witnessing the same television performances, eating the same tasteless prefabricated foods, from the same freezers, conforming in every outward and inward respect to a common mold."[64] Bill Levitt more or less agreed, except that he saw uniformity as a good thing. "It's not just our houses that are uniform," he wrote in 1958, "but the furniture and appliances we put in them, the clothes we wear, the cars we drive. This isn't something to grieve over. It's something to glory in. . . . The reason we have it so good in this country is that we can produce lots of things at low prices through mass production. And with mass production, of course, uniformity is unavoidable."[65]

Whether bad or good, uniformity struck a great many fifties commentators as what Levittown was all about. One of the most acerbic and ridiculous was the journalist John Keats, who outdid Mumford with his dystopian book *The Crack in the Picture Window* (1956). Keats's fictional protagonists, unsubtly named John and Mary Drone, joined millions of others in occupying "whole square miles of identical boxes . . . spreading like gangrene" across the United States. Their Levittowns are little more than "fresh-air slums . . . conceived in error, nurtured by greed, corroding everything they touch."[66]

Keats repeated these musings in an article for *Esquire* that was even more hyperbolic. "In these new worlds," he wrote, "men lose their identities to become nameless neuters, children lose their fathers and women lose their minds." Everyone suffers, but men suffer the most. They become "unmanned, intellectual castrates" who "seek the gray garments of conformity." During the day, when the men are gone, their housing developments morph into "homogeneous matriarchies" in which "the ladies band into hysterical leagues, organize the stuffing of the ballot box, elect and depose public servants with giddy abandon." When men return home from work, the wives "collar their husbands . . . drag them to the polls, give them their orders, and thus each woman votes twice." Since all the women are the same, there's no democratic competition, just one uniform horde. Their natural counterpart is the lemming, creatures that "live in developments—identical burrows all jammed together." Human lemmings "raise the same number of young, wear identical garments, have identical habits, work at the same tasks, have the same small talk and eat the same vile food day in and day out." Soon, "the entire population of Long Island," lemming-like, will desert their "identical picture-window boxes to rush across the toll road to Jones Beach," where they will fling themselves into the sea. "The Homo lemmus population of Long Island will be the first to go, because it was the first to appear."[67] The movie version of Mumford's and Keats's critique was the 1956 film *Invasion of the Body Snatchers,* whose suburbanites, already disturbingly alike, are replaced by pod-grown replicas even more conformist than the originals.

Invasion at least billed itself as science fiction; Mumford and Keats meant their works to be serious commentaries on real American life. The attention they received evoked a powerful counter-critique, often from popular magazines like *House Beautiful, House and Home,* and *Architectural Forum,* all fascinated by the Levittown phenomenon. James Gallagher, a *House and Home* reporter who lived in the development, wrote to *Harper's* in exasperation: "I am convinced that most stories about our megalosuburbia on Long Island are written from the Savarin Bar in Penn Station in Manhattan," based on nothing more than "an aerial photo, taken in 1951." Back then, before trees and shrubs had grown in, "the serried rooftops, with peas-in-a-pod houses as though in bas-relief against the barren potato fields," did indeed look "depressingly monotonous." But if "these amateur sociologists" actually traveled out to Nassau County, they might have noted how much better things looked at street level, where Levitt had designed subtle but important variations to relieve the monotony. The Levittown ranch sported four different elevations, varied setbacks from the street, and a rainbow of colors. And because the homes were made to be improved, by 1958, when Gallagher wrote his piece, "no two houses are alike on the outside, and even floor plans have only a familial relation to one another. . . . We have built up, back, front, sideways, even down." As for everyone being the same, if this was ever true, ten years on, "the toddlers [of 1948] are teenagers now," while newcomers were making the next generation of babies. What's more, old people had moved in, as "a great number of resales have been to families in their fifties and beyond."[68]

House Beautiful focused on the extent to which Levittown homes had been transformed in less than a decade. In a twelve-page article, "How Individuality Got a Second Chance," the editors included twenty-five photographs to show in detail how much Levittown now owed to its homeowners' creativity and individuality.[69] The photos documented "pushed out" living rooms, added bedrooms, remodeled kitchens, new garages, and patios out back, with privacy gained through trellises and climbing plants. In many cases, homeowners seeking to remodel their Cape Cods and ranches found inspiration in *Thousand Lanes,* a monthly magazine published in Levittown and filled with articles and advertisements intended to "instruct, inform, and entertain" residents with an eye to improving their homes.[70]

The transformation of the Levittown homes has been a motif of positive commentary almost from the beginning. In her seminal book on the community, the historian Barbara M. Kelly highlighted the process in her subtitle: "Building and Rebuilding Levittown."[71] Writers have focused both on the rebuilding of the houses and the maturation of the landscape. One common journalistic take is for the once skeptical or hostile writer to revisit the development and see it with new eyes. In a long 1964 feature for the *New York Herald Tribune,* Suzanne Gleaves wrote, "It's tough to find a single house that is still exactly the way it was the day it came off the assembly line. . . . The cosmetic effects of all this fiddling are debatable, but it adds a welter of new faces to Levittown's basic single countenance." On the inside, "Kentile flooring is gone in favor of hardwood," and houses now feature "sliding shoji screens, paneling, murals and scenic wallpaper, planters, indirect lighting and elegant kitchens." By this point in the article, Gleaves's skepticism has dissolved: "Anything [upscale] Fairfield County [Connecticut] has—

wrought-iron lampposts, wrought-iron name signs, fountains and wall ovens—Levittown has in excelsis."

As for the landscape, Gleaves juxtaposes two photographs: the first is that iconic aerial shot of naked Cape Cods rising from barren fields; the second, a new view from above showing houses nearly obscured by tall trees in full leaf. "From the air now, Levittown is identifiable not as an open wound on the land but as a green bower. It is difficult to spot a single roof in summer." Levittown residents, she adds, "look out of their remodeled houses on a landscape that represents a giant stride from the dreary apartments and drearier streets of the cities from which most of them escaped. 'This is where I want my children to grow up,' they say, and mean it so firmly that many of them do not move away when, economically, they are able to." She concludes that although nature and thousands of inhabitants have "failed to turn the ugliest duckling into a swan, it grew up into a very sleek and contented duck."[72]

Toward the end of her piece, Gleaves notes that mid-1960s Levittown now included people of all ages. She doesn't, however, mention the community's ethnic and religious diversity, a phenomenon that distinguished it from most older suburbs and urban neighborhoods, which tended to house people of the same racial, ethnic, and religious group.[73] In Levittown, Americans of Italian, Irish, and Polish descent lived side-by-side, as did Catholics, Protestants, and Jews.[74] In 1952, Levittown's largest religious denomination was Catholics, who made up 45.3 percent of the community, at a time when Catholics were 25 percent of the U.S. population. In New York City, Catholic inhabitants had reached 51 percent. Jews were even more overrepresented, with 15 percent of Levittowners identifying as Jews, about four times the percentage in the United States overall. (Jews were nearly 30 percent of the Big Apple's population.) As for Protestants, they accounted for 38 percent of the Levittown population, more than twice the Protestant representation of New York City (16 percent). Both figures were considerably lower than the Protestant population in the nation as a whole, which stood at 66 percent.[75]

Levittown's demographic characteristics changed over time. By the early 1960s, its population had grown somewhat older, less married, and more blue collar. In terms of religion, the community's Jewish numbers stayed about the same, while Protestants declined and Catholics increased. Since the majority (54 percent) of Catholics held blue-collar jobs, while most Protestants (55.6 percent) and Jews (62.5 percent) held white-collar jobs, these demographic developments reflect the community's shift toward the working class.[76]

Although Gleaves overlooked Levittown's ethnic and religious diversity, she did highlight the exclusion of African Americans, who at mid-century represented 10 percent of the U.S. population.[77] She was writing amid the civil rights ferment of the mid-1960s, and unlike most 1950s commentators, she was sensitive to the injustice of racial segregation. Levittown's "smattering of Negroes," she wrote, "estimated at less than 100 people," remains "astonishingly few in relation to the size of the project and the prices of the houses."[78] What she didn't emphasize was the consequences of the African Americans' exclusion. Whites alone profited from the ability to accumulate equity in a Levittown home and from the community's low crime rate, good schools, affordable recreation, decently paid jobs, and now-shorter commutes, as industry increasingly fled the city for the suburbs.

African American veterans and other homebuyers, like their white counterparts, understood the advantages of renting, and especially buying, a Levittown house. But as we have seen, those who tried to obtain one were unceremoniously turned away. Some in the community tried to resist these discriminatory practices. In June 1949, just as Levitt was beginning to sell its new ranch homes, a group of Levittowners, with the support of the NAACP and other organizations, created the Committee to End Discrimination in Levittown (CEDL). The immediate impetus for forming the group was Levitt's refusal to sell to four Black veterans. In one of those cases, Myrtle Archer, the mother of a World War II soldier, tried to buy a home for her son and was told, "We will not sell to a Negro veteran." Mrs. Archer asked to speak with Bill Levitt, who refused to see her.[79]

The other three African American veterans were not even allowed to enter the restaurant where home sales were taking place. In response, committee members staged a sit-in outside the restaurant and planned further actions against the company. They also demanded that the Federal Housing Administration "compel Levitt to rent and sell to Negro veterans or lose FHA guarantees on present and future projects."[80]

In the wake of these protests, Levitt announced in the *Levittown Tribune* that "Levittown has been and is now progressing as a private enterprise job, and it is entirely in the discretion and judgment of Levitt & Sons as to whom it will rent or sell."[81] In making this statement, Levitt was fully aware that he enjoyed the FHA's support. In November 1948, Thurgood Marshall, then special counsel for the NAACP, had met with Federal Housing Commissioner Franklin D. Richards to try to persuade him to withhold mortgage guarantees for Levitt homes until the company agreed to stop discriminating against Blacks. Richards refused. "I regret to advise," he wrote Marshall, "that I find nothing in the National Housing Act or in the Supreme Court Decisions to which you refer [mainly *Shelley v. Kraemer,* which declared racial covenants unlawful] which would authorize this Administration to refuse to insure mortgages on the ground suggested," meaning racial discrimination.[82] Shortly after this ruling, *Newsday* reported that Nassau County District Attorney James N. Gehrig said "he knew of no law" that could force a builder to sell to any particular buyer. When Levitt rejected the purchase applications of two Black veterans from New Jersey, Gehrig allowed the rejection to stand.[83]

New protests ensued. Levitt denounced those who opposed his whites-only policy as communists, and *Newsday*'s editors, eager to see Levittown succeed, echoed the sentiment: "Organizations which appear to be either Communist dominated or Communist inspired have been attempting to raise a racial issue at Levittown. The issue did not exist until it was fostered by people not immediately affected by it. Their only real motive seems to be to set race against race, and if possible, to bog down the Levitt building program, which means homes for thousands of people."[84] The local *Levittown Press,* also friendly to the Levitt organization, opined that Levittown faced "a question of color, but it's Red, not black."[85] Levitt and his allies would regularly accuse the firm's opponents of being communists, whether they were complaining about racial discrimination, rent increases, or antiunion policies. It made little difference that these opponents took pains to denounce communism and deny any ties to the movement. Most belonged to the NAACP, pro-labor organizations, or liberal synagogues and the B'Nai B'rith. Rabbi Roland B. Gittelsohn, who regularly criticized Levitt's discrimination against African Americans, declared himself equally opposed to communism and Jim Crow.[86] In response, the builder promised to soldier on "despite the skeptics and the professional critics and the communists."[87] The last, he added, could not have been Levittown homeowners, for "no man who owns his own house and lot can be a communist. He has too much to do."[88] Such sentiments created a bond between Levitt and Senator Joseph McCarthy, who had made a well-publicized visit to Levittown in August 1947.[89]

Levitt wasn't satisfied just to bar African Americans from renting or buying one of his homes; he refused to allow a Black person even to set foot inside, except as domestic help. When two white Levittown families invited a few Black children to play with their kids, Levitt initiated eviction proceedings against them. The white renters, Gertrude Novick and Lillian Ross, explained that they had "decided to have a little play group, an integrated play group, so we had families from Hempstead bring children in." Novick, who belonged to the Committee to End Discrimination in Levittown, wanted to make a point, though not without a measure of guilt. She admitted that she and her husband had rented their house in full knowledge of Levitt's racial policies, which they opposed. But "we really had no place to live," and her integrated play group was a small way to make amends.[90] Not only did Levitt move to evict the two families, the firm also retaliated against the CEDL by forbidding the organization to use the company-built Levittown Community Hall for its meetings.[91]

Despite Levitt's adamant rejection of any hint of integration, even a children's playdate, some African Americans managed move into Levittown. William Cotter, who headed the local chapter of the NAACP and had helped found the CEDL, rented a Levitt house in 1951. The homebuilder responded with an eviction notice, which Cotter challenged in court. After a two-year battle, Levitt prevailed, and the Cotter family had to give up their home. Although the Cotters enjoyed support from many of their neighbors, they received a steady stream of racist letters and angry phone calls from people who wanted them out. Eventually, the family found another house on the same street, a sublet from a white homeowner, and later succeeded in buying the property.[92]

A few other African American families secured Levittown houses, but the firm and its subsidiaries continued to fight integration and the political forces that promoted it. In February 1952, Adolph Ross received word that the lease on his Levittown ranch would not be renewed. Ross contended that he was being punished for his involvement in organizations opposed to Levitt's policy of racial exclusion. The Levittown Liberal Committee tried to shame Bethpage Realty, a Levitt subsidiary, into reversing its anti-Black discrimination: "Your attitude and action play into the hands of the enemies of this country [who] would like nothing better than an opportunity to prove that the Great American Democracy does not behave democratically."[93] When this effort failed, four hundred people gathered at Ross's home to protest the eviction. By this time, Levitt was preoccupied with his Pennsylvania project and had liquidated most of the firm's rental properties in the Long Island development. Bethpage Reality rescinded the eviction order.[94]

How Levitt liquidated its rental properties is a story in itself. In early 1949, after Levitt decided to build houses for sale and no longer for rent, the company discreetly announced its intention to get out of the rental business. It had originally built six thousand rental units, a few hundred of which were bought by their tenants, leaving Levitt with about 5,400. Slightly more than four thousand of these dwellings belonged not to Levitt & Sons but to the Bethpage Realty Corporation, whose stock, valued at about $5 million, belonged entirely to Abraham Levitt and his two sons. It's unclear why 1,400 rental units remained with the parent company; Levitt liked to keep its main homebuilding business uncluttered and generally devolved other aspects of its operations into wholly owned subsidiaries. Perhaps Levitt planned to sell these 1,400 houses to their tenants. A survey of the community showed that 28 percent of those who rented in 1947 ultimately bought homes in the development, many purchasing their original dwelling.[95] In any case, Bethpage served as landlord for 4,028 rental properties, worth about $30 million, all told, which the company had bought with borrowed money—mortgages amortized over twenty-five years. By the end of 1949, Bethpage had accumulated very little equity in these properties and still owed nearly the full amount.[96] The mortgage interest was no problem, since it was more than covered by Bethpage's rental income. But that income was taxed at a 50 percent corporate rate, and Levitt wanted to avoid this taxation. By selling the mortgages, the Levitts would receive immediate profits and cut their tax liability in half, since these profits would be taxed at the long-term capital gains rate of 25 percent.

In February 1950, the *Philadelphia Sunday Bulletin* reported that Bethpage Realty had sold the four-thousand-plus rental homes to the

Junto Corporation, a small Philadelphia nonprofit tightly connected to the city's patrician elite. Founded in 1941 by John Frederick Lewis, Jr., heir to a great Philadelphia fortune and leading patron of the arts, the Junto Corporation billed itself as a modern incarnation of the Junto Club, created by Ben Franklin in 1727.[97] Franklin intended the Junto to be a "club of mutual improvement" for self-taught artisans like himself as well as other "ingenious men," among them a shoemaker and amateur mathematician, a cabinetmaker, a runaway Oxford student, a scrivener, and a "gentleman of fortune."[98] The new Junto Corporation was also designed for adults who wanted to improve themselves, but unlike Franklin's closed circle of a dozen men, it would be open to everyone and feature practical, vocational courses. After the war, Junto turned to more academic pursuits. Its "lunch and learn" program, said Junto's executive director, Henry Klein, "was a noble experiment to let the poor secretary listen an hour and run back to work." The "poor secretary" perhaps felt condescended to, and the experiment failed. The school then "picked up instead the college-educated, slightly bored housewife who shops in town," offering her courses on Shakespeare, the Dead Sea Scrolls, and the New Math.[99]

By the late 1940s, Lewis had withdrawn from active leadership of the Junto Corporation, which now had as its presiding officer an advertising executive named Philip Klein. Through his Wall Street connections, Klein got wind of Levitt's desire to sell its rental properties, and together with the Junto board president, Albert A. Owens, paid Bill Levitt a visit sometime in mid-1949. The homebuilder knew neither man, but he may have been impressed by their ties to Philadelphia's cultural elite. Still, any business arrangement between Levitt and Junto would be highly unusual. Levitt & Sons was a powerful multimillion-dollar corporation, while Junto was a shoestring nonprofit with an endowment of $13,000. But Klein and Owens were eager to expand their operations and take advantage of their tax-exempt status, which they believed allowed them to buy and sell real estate without incurring any tax liability. Bill Levitt also saw tax advantages: income from a deal with Junto would be taxed at the capital gains rate.[100]

On December 24, 1949, Klein and Owens, officers of a company with essentially no assets, took out a five-day "weekend loan" of $1.5 million ($19.5 million today) from the Fidelity-Philadelphia Trust Company. The loan would serve as a down payment to Abraham,

Alfred, and Bill Levitt for the purchase of Bethpage Realty, whose selling price was $5.1 million. The bank made this loan on the strength of the two men's signatures and the promise of repayment with Bethpage Realty assets that Junto did not yet own. "The bank," Klein said a few months later, "had confidence in our integrity."[101] The loan documents do not exist in the Junto archives housed at Temple University in Philadelphia, so we can't know the details of this unusual financial operation.[102] But according to reports in the press, which widely covered the deal two months later, the transaction unfolded in the following way: the Levitts received the $1.5 million down payment and promptly transferred the entire Bethpage treasury, worth $5 million, to Junto. The nonprofit then dissolved the Bethpage board of directors and named Owens its new president and Klein its secretary-treasurer. Two of the three other newly installed Bethpage directors were officials of the Junto Corporation.[103]

At this point, the new Bethpage owners used the realty company's treasury, which now belonged to them, to pay off the $1.5 million bank loan and the remaining sum owed to the Levitts, less $250,000 to be paid later, for the purchase of Bethpage Realty. This was a circular transaction in which Levitt & Sons used Junto to transfer $5 million in liquid assets from its subsidiary, Bethpage Realty, to the parent company. In doing so, it offloaded 4,028 mortgaged properties onto Junto's balance sheet while claiming the transaction as a long-term capital gain, which was taxed at 25 percent instead of the prevailing 50 percent corporate rate. They also got rid of the rental units, whose income would have been taxed at the high corporate rate for years to come. In exchange, Junto, being tax-exempt, got the entirety of the mortgage income (though it did have to pay state and local taxes). Since the overall value of the houses in this deal amounted to some $30 million, it may have been the largest residential real estate transaction in history. Junto, a tiny Philadelphia educational institution, became one of the biggest landlords in the world—the owners of 40 percent of the housing stock in Levittown, New York—without paying a dime.[104] Real estate experts predicted that Junto would realize a net income of $75,000 a year ($980,000 today) from its new rental properties, and the actual figure may have been higher.[105]

Klein and Owens seem to have presented their Levitt/Bethpage deal to the Junto board only a week before it closed.[106] Since the minutes of this meeting are missing from the Junto archives, we don't know how board members reacted. We can surmise it was controversial, though, from a subsequent special meeting for which the minutes exist. After all, the Levitt arrangement took the educational organization far outside its normal realm. Typical transactions for its adult education courses had involved tuition payments of ten or twenty dollars and small honoraria to teachers. It would have been surprising had no board members raised questions about plans to borrow a seven-figure sum, take on a housing inventory worth $30 million, make payments on a twenty-five-year mortgage, and collect rental income to the tune of $260,000 a month.

Board discussions in subsequent meetings show that Junto remained tied to Bill Levitt and that the Bethpage Realty Corporation continued to manage the Levittown properties, now with an absentee governing board headquartered in Philadelphia. For all intents and purposes, Junto became a subsidiary of Levitt & Sons, complicit in its policies. Minutes from January 4, 1951, refer to "a letter from the Friends' [Quakers'] Race Relation Committee," which called "attention to the fact that there are no Negro families in Levittown." The minutes indicate no reaction to this statement and reveal instead that Junto took handsome advantage of its new rental income. It bought a five-story building in downtown Philadelphia, took over a small junior college for women, and contributed to other charitable organizations. Leaders of the schools division were unhappy with Junto's new identity and warned of trouble to come.[107] That trouble arrived in June 1954, when a congressional committee announced it was investigating Junto (and Levitt) for having claimed, without justification, a tax exemption for its profits in the Levitt deal. By then, however, Junto had sold its Levittown properties to a Philadelphia real estate broker, who quickly found buyers for all 4,028 houses.[108] Nothing came of the congressional investigation.

With the disposal of its rental properties, Levitt ended its role as landlord, which had moved it to intervene heavily into the life of the community. We have seen that Bill Levitt not only refused to rent to African Americans but evicted tenants who so much as socialized with them. He believed his all-white policy would prevent his development from becoming "undesirable." Even so, he was sensitive to the widespread belief among journalists and cultural critics that his community of low-cost houses would become a slum. To counter this perception, he issued several decrees designed to keep properties looking neat and clean. Upscale communities had long done the same.[109] The company required renters and homeowners to mow their lawns at least once a week; those who failed to do so would have their grass mowed by Levitt employees and be billed for the service. Laundry could be dried only in the backyard (Levitt provided washing machines but not dryers) using umbrella-style circular drying racks, which had to be folded when not in use. Long clotheslines were forbidden, and no drying could take place on weekends. Since just about everyone assumed that washing and drying was the wife's responsibility, the 10 percent who worked outside the home during the week had to take care of this task early on weekday mornings. To show off the community's neatly mowed lawns, Levitt forbade fences, which Bill considered ugly. Without fences, outdoor activities unfolded in full view of the neighbors. Nothing stopped kids from taking shortcuts to school, the pool, and play areas by cutting through nearby yards and carving footpaths everywhere.[110]

These rules policed the division of labor by gender and enforced a common postwar vision of family life. Wives were expected to do the laundry during the week and husbands to mow the lawn on weekends. The house's interior was the woman's responsibility, the outside the man's. When not doing chores, wives, husbands, and children spent time together, since except for the two bedrooms, no one had a separate space. In prewar suburban homes—and plenty of urban ones—men enjoyed time alone in the garage or the den, while children retreated to play areas in the basement. The enclosed kitchen at the back of the house gave women a measure of separation. In Levittown, families squeezed into the kitchen for meals and watched TV together in the living room. The culture of the 1950s emphasized nuclear families and togetherness, and the Levittown house's design fortified both.[111]

After Levittown ceased to be a rental community, and especially after the Levitt firm moved its operations to Lower Bucks County, Pennsylvania, these rules were relaxed. But Levitt's policies on racial exclusion continued unchanged. When individual homeowners put their houses on the market, they essentially never sold to African Americans, whether by individual choice or in response to community pressure. Real estate agents steered Black buyers—and there were plenty in the prosperous 1950s—away from Levittown and toward majority Black areas on the island's south shore, especially the towns of Roosevelt, Freeport, and Hempstead. Brokers hid listings from African Americans interested in Levittown and other all-white places and quoted falsely high prices to further discourage racial integration. These steps were consistent with the Code of Ethics devised by the National Association of Real Estate Boards (NAREB), which required that "a realtor should never be instrumental in introducing into a neighborhood a character of property or occupancy, members of any race or nationality, or any individual whose presence will clearly be detrimental to property values in the neighborhood." After the U.S. Supreme Court ruled racial covenants "unenforceable" in the *Shelley v. Kraemer* decision of 1948, the NAREB excised the phrase "members of any race or nationality" from this code, but realtors almost everywhere stayed true to the original version. In 1953, Levittown, now fully built and home to a population of over seventy thousand, was the largest community in the United States with no more than a handful of Black inhabitants. In 1960, it housed a grand total of fifty-seven Blacks; two decades later, the number had fallen to forty-five—this despite a growing African American middle class and a raft of legislation barring discrimination in housing. The creation of Levittown and other postwar mass housing projects, which together added far more single-family homes to the nation's housing stock every year than had existed in total a half-century earlier, vastly deepened the racial segregation that had long been a feature of American suburban life.[112] The building of Levitt's next community, in Pennsylvania, would make the problem worse.

3 The Loss of Innocence

IN THE FALL of 1950, Harry A. Kalish, Bill Levitt's attorney and a founder of Philadelphia's most prestigious law firm (now named Dilworth Paxson), called the homebuilder with some private intelligence: the United States Steel Corporation intended to build a huge plant in Lower Bucks County, Pennsylvania. The factory would be nestled in a bend along the Delaware River six miles from Trenton, New Jersey, the state capital, and twenty-five miles from Philadelphia, then the third-largest city in the United States. The Pennsylvania location appealed to U.S. Steel executives for its ample available space close to the huge East Coast markets and for the ability to send oceangoing vessels up the Delaware to its location. Traditional midwestern sources of iron ore had been depleted, and steel companies now had to ship iron in from Venezuela, where large deposits had been discovered.[1]

Although the original plans called for a small facility, the demands of the Korean War, which broke out in late June 1950, soon gave U.S. Steel the incentive to create a much larger plant—the largest of its kind, Kalish told Levitt, to be built all at once. When finished in July 1953, the Fairless Works, named after the company's president, Benjamin Fairless, would include two blast furnaces for smelting pig iron, nine open-hearth furnaces for converting the iron into steel, a mile-and-a-half-long finishing mill, a hot strip mill, pipe mills, immense warehouses, and a one-thousand-yard-long dock along the Delaware

River. The huge plant would employ more than six thousand people and transform the sparsely populated farmland of Bucks County into a center of industry closely connected to the Philadelphia economy.[2] Levitt, seeing it as too good an opportunity to pass up, immediately began to buy farmland adjacent to the embryonic works. On this land, Levitt would build a second Levittown nearly as large as the original one, only this time the community would be fully planned in advance.

Bill and Alfred had not intended to create a second mass housing development right away, or perhaps ever. As they were completing their seventeen-thousand-plus homes on Long Island, Alfred drew up plans for a much smaller Long Island project whose dwellings would be priced between those of the prewar Strathmores and those of Levittown. The new venture, which Alfred called Landia, would result in just 1,750 houses, each with about 1,200 square feet of living space and priced at $13,000. There would be roughly 6,500 inhabitants. The Levittown homes were much smaller, 750 to 800 square feet, and considerably less expensive; the Strathmore dwellings covered 1,750 to 2,000 square feet and cost up to $22,000.[3]

Landia was designed as a fully planned community modeled on the New Deal's Greenbelt experiment, but for a relatively affluent middle class. There would be a shopping center, day-care facility, pools and other recreational amenities, train station, and parks. Land would be set aside for churches and synagogues, a town hall, and community center. A thirty-acre "industrial area," Alfred wrote, would be "an integral part of the community, but . . . separated from the rest of Landia by a wooded shelter belt."[4] The light-industry firms invited to Landia would provide some local employment, but more importantly, they would pay property taxes, reducing the tax burden on homeowners. Those in Levittown had no such financial help.

Streets would be designed to keep through-traffic away from residential areas and to ensure that cars moved slowly to protect children at play. Kids would walk to school on wide sidewalks, and parks and public facilities would be a stone's throw from most residences. A new train station would make it unnecessary to drive to jobs in New York City, although the community would be close to major Long Island parkways for those who preferred private transportation.

Landia never got beyond the drawing board, in part because of restrictions on building materials due to the Korean War, but mainly because the Levitts decided to throw all their energies into a new, much larger project in Pennsylvania. There, on land adjacent to the new steel mill, the community planning intended for Landia could be applied writ large to a second Levittown with seventeen thousand mass-produced, affordable houses, built according to the same principles and techniques as in Levittown, New York.

In early 1952, the federal government helped persuade the Levitts to abandon Landia in favor of another Levittown by lifting the Korean War restrictions it had imposed on homebuilders. The government took this step shortly after Kaiser Metal Products announced plans to double the size of its Bucks County plant to coincide with the installation of U.S. Steel's Fairless Works.[5] Thanks to these giant new complexes, Levittown was dubbed a "strategic area" for homebuilding. Bill Levitt, who had begun buying up land before the new designation, saw the Lower Bucks County site as virgin territory. "We are where Long Island was 40 years ago," he told *American Builder* magazine. Bucks County "has been unexploited. The sky's the limit!"[6] This was typical Bill Levitt hyperbole, but the new site was in some ways superior to the original one. It was closer to Philadelphia than Levittown, Long Island, was to New York City. The Pennsylvania location had two train lines and two highways heading into the city, instead of just one each for its Long Island counterpart.

The company had amassed a huge reservoir of capital, enjoyed great borrowing power, owned millions of dollars' worth of labor-saving building machinery, and had a wealth of experience to lean on—making the huge new development a manageable risk. One of the Levitts' biggest mistakes on Long Island had been to vastly underestimate the desire for their houses. They originally planned two thousand dwellings but quickly found themselves with six thousand eager renters and buyers, and then six thousand more. They thus built Levittown, New York, piecemeal, always behind demand and unable to plan the community as a whole. Levitt responded as best it could, and often creatively, with new home models sporting attractive features, but in many ways the development seemed jerry-built and improvised.

In Levittown, Pennsylvania, the firm resolved to avoid its earlier mistakes by securing in advance the land for the entire development and planning it from top to bottom. "We learned a lot on Long Island," Bill Levitt said, "and every bit is going to be applied in the new town." Alfred was more forthright: "On Long Island, we never knew from one year to the next how much we could build so we never had an over-all master plan. Today we are taking the bull by the horns."[7] Once they got started, Bill's hype artistry kicked in. His Pennsylvania project would be the "biggest pre-planned community since Pierre L'Enfant laid out Washington," as well as the "most perfectly planned community in America."[8] This was hyperbole, of course, but Levitt's boasts contained a grain of truth.

Over a six-month period in 1951, Bill Levitt bought essentially all the land destined for Levittown, Pennsylvania, first offering $1,000 an acre for property that had been selling for $400, then raising his average offer to $1,500. At the end of six months he had acquired 150 farms, covering eight square miles, and spent about $10 million ($121 million today).[9] (U.S. Steel had already bought four square miles of farmland in the area.)[10] The Levitts then spent another $4 million preparing the site, which involved grading and getting rid of the trees. Keeping the area's many mature oaks, maples, and beeches, Bill said, was "not good for production."[11] The company then invested $2 million in a sewage disposal plant and $750,000 on a water pumping and filtering station, something private builders rarely did. But as a sparsely populated rural area, Lower Bucks County lacked the infrastructure to support a suburban city of Levittown's projected size, and the four municipalities included in Levitt's land purchases had nothing like the resources needed for these projects. "Here in Bucks County," Levitt recalled two years into the project, "we found local services on the level of 1900. . . . There was no water, no sewers, no highway department, no adequate police [and] fire departments—we had to start from scratch."[12]

Beyond sewage treatment and water purification, Levitt had to burrow water mains and sewer lines beneath the surface before streets were roughed in. Eventually the company would spend $8 million on trees, shrubs, and grass. "No other man in history," wrote the editors of *Fortune* magazine, "ever had so much money to spend on decorative vegetation."[13] All told, the company spent some $30 million ($363 million today) on land purchase, preparation, and landscaping plus infrastructure, dividing the costs among some seventeen thousand houses.[14] "By the time the snow flies in 1954," wrote *Fortune* two years earlier, "Levittown, Pennsylvania will be worth about $200 million [$2.4 billion today]," adding, "no other commercial builder has ever set up objectives one-third so ambitious."[15]

Although the Levitts believed they were operating on virgin territory, in fact the area destined to become Levittown would be superimposed on four existing municipalities—three townships and a borough. One of those jurisdictions, Middletown Township, planted itself squarely in the way of the Levitts' plans, rejecting the firm's lot sizes as too small. Levitt countered that larger plots would make the houses too expensive and petitioned for a change in the zoning rules. As he had done on Long Island when local regulations stood in his way, Bill whipped up opposition to the local authorities, enlisting lawyers, the state legislature, the local media, and potential homeowners. One meeting of the Middletown zoning board grew heated: the chairman called Levitt a "usurper of municipal authority," to which Bill responded by calling the chairman a "demagogue." The chairman became so incensed that when a spectator made a pro-Levitt remark, he rushed across the room, intending to pummel the man, and had to be restrained by the crowd. It may be no coincidence that at exactly this time, the state legislature passed a law allowing a township to annex land from a neighboring municipality if a majority of landowners agreed to the shift. When it became clear that Middletown could lose a sizable chunk of land to nearby Bristol Township, Levitt got his way. He did have to agree, however, to set aside more open space for parks and recreation than he originally planned. But in the end, a few local officials accustomed to overseeing sparsely populated farmland proved no match for the powerful, well-connected Levitt corporation, with its legal talent, experienced executives, public relations expertise, and support from ordinary people who wanted a Levitt-built home.[16]

Levitt also had to deal with labor organizations unhappy with his antiunion stance. As construction began in May 1952, members of the Philadelphia Building and Construction Trades Council, AFL, defied a court order banning mass picketing and surrounded the building site. They hurled rocks at workers driving in and started fights with others coming to work on foot. Order was restored only after the local sheriff called in the state police. Levitt obtained a new injunction drastically limiting the number of pickets allowed near the site, but not before the union succeeded in halting construction for several days. Ultimately, however, the AFL activists gave up, and the building resumed its whirlwind pace.[17]

The Levitts had mapped out eight "master blocks," each with a school surrounded by three or four neighborhoods, which they called sections.[18] When the development moved from the drawing board to reality, the master blocks largely disappeared, and the forty sections became the community's organizing framework. As on Long Island, all streets in each section began with the first letter of the section name itself. So the Thornridge section included Timber Lane, Tulip Lane, Thimbleberry Lane, and many others beginning with *T*. It took some creativity to come up with so many names. A main thoroughfare, in this case Thornridge Drive, circled each section, keeping through traffic away from most residential streets, which curved gently or sharply to prevent cars from moving fast and potentially endangering the children who often played in the street. For added safety, there were no four-way intersections, and children rarely had to cross a through road to get to school.

As in Levittown, New York, providing public schools proved a huge challenge. Levitt set aside land for schools and offered to build some of them, but local officials rejected the offer because they wanted to have control over the size and design of school buildings as well as their cost. During the resulting delays, early residents with school-age children had to contend with large class sizes and double-header school days so that a single building could accommodate twice its usual number of students. It was only because many families' children had not reached school age that the existing school districts were able to manage the overcrowded conditions. When the new schools were ready, officials named them for prominent Americans, including two, Walt Disney and President Dwight D. Eisenhower, who flew to Levittown for the dedications of their namesake buildings, shadowed by armies of reporters.

Although Levitt didn't construct the schools or houses of worship, the lands Bill had reserved for these institutions were crucial; as with the schools, churches and synagogues went up quickly. The fifties were a time of high religious identification and attendance, with 51 percent of respondents to a 1957 Gallup poll saying they had attended a religious service in the previous seven days. The Levittown numbers wouldn't have been as high, mainly because the community originally had no religious institutions, but by the end of the decade, Jewish, Catholic, and Protestant denominations had together spent more than $7 million ($74 million today) on churches and synagogues.[19]

As school districts and religious organizations erected buildings on Levitt land, the company provided elaborate recreational facilities—Olympic-size swimming pools, ball fields, and playgrounds—just as in Levittown, New York. The original cost of using these facilities was ten dollars per household per year, a better deal perhaps than even the homes themselves, which Bill Levitt dubbed "the most house for the money."[20] Levittown was to be a *community,* not just a development. Pools and ball fields would do a great deal to foster that community, and the schools, churches, and synagogues would do even more. The public spaces that these facilities provided turned what could have been an atomized collection of family units into something much greater than the sum of its parts.

As a community, Levittown needed stores, and instead of Long Island's decentralized "village greens," which didn't succeed, the Levitts planned a huge sixty-five acre, $25 million ($293 million today) "Shop-o-Rama," a spacious mall with supermarkets, multistory department stores, drugstores, clothing shops, and other necessities. The Levitts began building the mall in 1952, simultaneously with the first houses, and finished it less than three years later. In the meantime, with no grocery stores nearby, milkmen, mobile bread vendors, frozen food sellers, even potato chip trucks—the 1950s versions of the horse-and-buggy peddlers of an earlier era—enjoyed a captive market.[21]

As the Shop-o-Rama was being built, retailers competed fiercely to get in; the number of applicants for leases was ten times the available space.[22] The Levitts had selected a central, easily accessible location, and in the absence of public transportation, surrounded the stores with an immense, six-thousand-car parking lot. Inside the uncovered space, stores fronted on wide pedestrian walkways shaded by mature trees. Since malls had not yet become commonplace, the Shop-o-Rama attracted hordes of people and served as Levittown's "downtown," a place for socializing as well as shopping. It included a community center, movie theater, restaurants, and soda fountains. Alfred Levitt saw the Shop-o-Rama as a space for wives freed by Levitt conveniences from full-time housework: "Thanks to the number of appliances in our house, the girls have three hours to kill every afternoon. They want to find some excitement, and they prefer to do it even with their grocery shopping in the main retail district," the Shop-o-Rama.[23]

It doubtless didn't occur to Alfred that Levittown's women might have had other options beyond the kitchen and shopping mall, but in the early years, the overwhelming majority of Levittown's women didn't work outside the home. More than a few, isolated at home during the day and often distant from relatives and old friends, found the Shop-o-Rama a haven amid a Levittown life that could be lonely and bleak. One resident, Mary Robins, was often unhappy as a pioneer in the new development and experienced the new mall as a gift: "The shopping center came, and that was the most wonderful thing."[24]

When it opened in 1955, the Shop-o-Rama was the largest shopping center between Trenton and Philadelphia and attracted people from the entire region.[25] (It would later succumb to competition from enclosed malls.) In its early years, it was home to parades, carnivals, circuses, beauty contests, and baseball games on the neighboring ball field. It became an obligatory stop on political campaigns. In 1960, both John F. Kennedy and Richard M. Nixon held rallies there, and both drew huge crowds, especially Kennedy, for whom more than one hundred thousand people, the largest gathering in Bucks County history, somehow squeezed into the parking lot.[26] The election that year marked the transformation of Lower Bucks County from rural Republican stronghold to reliable Democratic terrain, thanks to Levittown's large Roman Catholic population and unionized steelworkers.[27]

In the 1950s, the United Steelworkers Union was a relatively progressive outfit. It expected that about 7 percent of its workers at the Fairless plant would be Black and insisted that African Americans be allowed to buy homes in an integrated Levittown and the adjacent Fairless Hills, a community of four thousand prefabricated houses built for its employees by a subsidiary of U.S. Steel.[28] Bill Levitt, however, persisted in barring Blacks, using the same justifications as he had in New York: "I have come to know that if we sell one house to a Negro family, then ninety to ninety-five per cent of our white customers will not buy into the community. That is their attitude, not ours. We did not create it, and cannot cure it. As a company, our position is simply this: we can solve a housing problem, or we can try to solve a racial problem. But we cannot combine the two."[29] He added that as a private builder, he had the right to sell to whomever he chose.

The 1948 Supreme Court decision in *Shelley v. Kraemer* prevented him from including a racial covenant in his deeds, but Levitt could instruct his salespeople not to do business with African Americans. The company tried to be discrete about its discriminatory policies, since it faced anti-discrimination pressure not only from the steelworkers' union but from the NAACP, the Quakers, and a few other religious organizations. Still, potential Black buyers were turned away and potential white ones assured that no integration would take place. When Charles R. Allen, Jr., a journalist for *The Nation,* posed as a prospective Levittown buyer anxious about having Black neighbors, "the salesman lifted a reassuring hand." Listen, he said, "strictly between you and me—and believe me, we sell to whites only, mister."[30] Another journalist, Allen Ward, confirmed Allen's report. When Ward called the Levitt sales office to ask whether Blacks would be allowed, the agent replied, "The people moving in don't want Negroes here." Ward then spoke with a new Levittown homeowner, who said to him, "It sure is wonderful . . . no niggers are allowed to buy homes there." This view seemed typical of the new residents. The editor of the then-weekly *Levittown Times* told Ward, "The anti-Negro feeling is pretty strong," with letters to the editor favoring an all-white Levittown by a margin of more than two-to-one.[31] Allen added in his piece that just as white buyers were to be shielded from Black neighbors, upper-middle-class executives would not have to rub shoulders with factory laborers. Each Levittown "section" would have only one kind of house, and the cheapest, middling, and most expensive homes would be segregated from one another.

In the first phase of the new development, Levitt focused on the middling house, dubbed the Levittowner, a one-thousand-square-foot (twenty-five-by-forty-foot) dwelling on a seventy-by-one-hundred-foot lot. It sold for $9,990—a "remarkable bargain" enthused *House and Home*—which veterans could buy with no money down and monthly carrying charges of sixty dollars.[32] At the model homesite, the company also displayed a considerably larger and more expensive ($16,900) Country Clubber as well as the Budgeteer, a tiny, 750-square-foot rental property for sixty-five dollars a month. No one wanted to rent the Budgeteer, and Levitt didn't build any. Perhaps he never intended to build any rental homes but felt obliged to display one. That's what FHA and VA officials wanted, although in Congress, Senator Joe

Bill Levitt (*left*) showing off the frame of his "Levittowner" model. (Special Collections Research Center, Temple University Libraries, Philadelphia, Pennsylvania)

McCarthy advocated homeownership as a bulwark against communism. By pricing the monthly rental for the Budgeteer, not a market-friendly name, above the monthly mortgage for the considerably larger Levittowner, Levitt guaranteed minimal demand for the Budgeteer. He also guaranteed that the government would relent on rentals and allow him to make his Pennsylvania project a community made up entirely of homeowners.[33]

Beginning on December 8, 1951, when Levitt opened the model homes for inspection, demand for the Levittowners was ferocious and unrelenting. Much of it came from young couples crammed into tight Philadelphia row houses, often shared with a parent or two, or into small, uncomfortable apartments. Some fifteen thousand to fifty thousand people descended on the development's model homes; 3,500 were

Potential buyers besiege Levitt's model homes. (Special Collections Research Center, Temple University Libraries, Philadelphia, Pennsylvania)

sold in the first ten weeks and then 1,600 a month, more than three times the rate of Levittown, New York, where home sales had smashed records at the time.[34] To juice the demand, Levitt took out full-page ads in a dozen New York– and Philadelphia-area newspapers, while generating a huge amount of free publicity from an army of journalists who, consciously or not, contributed to the advertising blitz. Their stories about the opening of Levittown, Pennsylvania, focused on the traffic jams that trapped prospective buyers for hours, the huge lines of people snaking through the model homes, and the crush of onlookers standing four deep inside the Levitt showroom. "It was clearly [the area's] biggest day," wrote *House and Home,* "since some local boys, assisted by General Washington, defeated the British . . . at the Battle of Trenton."[35]

The interiors of the model homes had been elaborately staged by Beatrice West, a prominent Manhattan interior decorator. The Levitt showroom, which displayed every element of the Levittown house, from the made-for-Levitt floor tiles and wall paint to the name-brand kitchen appliances, seemed like a high-tech World's Fair exhibit on the look of modernity. Visitors could peer into a miniature dollhouse version of the homes yet to be built and imagine their own future house. Thousands were desperate to plunk down their deposits.[36] The reports of avid buyers sound exaggerated today but were generally true. "The crowds were enormous," Mary Remis told the sociologist Chad Kimmel. The sales agent "just pointed to what was available. We had no idea what type of Levittowner it was gonna be, but you know, for a hundred dollars down, how could you complain?"[37] (Levitt actually required no down payment for veterans, just a $100 deposit, which buyers often mistook for a down payment.) Remis and thousands of others on tight budgets were intent on escaping the city. "The idea of green grass and open space," Larry Franklin told Kimmel, "was to me, paradise!"[38]

Many didn't have the $100 deposit, and journalists reported that salespeople accepted uncashed VA checks and even watches to be redeemed when buyers had the money.[39] Bill Levitt told reporters he was ecstatic about his success, as his firm exceeded the sales records of his New York development.[40] He was happy to have registered yet another commercial success, but his ambitions went further than that: he wanted to become famous for shaping the way people lived. "I'm not here just to build and sell houses," he told Penn Kimball of the *New York Times*. "To be perfectly frank, I'm looking for a little glory, too. . . . I want to build a town to be proud of."[41]

The houses, he added, might all resemble one another, but this was a small price to pay for their value and the way of life they made possible. Besides, Levittown, Pennsylvania, would be "the least monotonous mass housing group ever planned in America."[42] From his rented local headquarters in a charming old Bucks County farmhouse, the homebuilder declared the traditional, handcrafted dwelling obsolete. When Kimball admired the farmhouse's "ornate molding and broad baseboards," Levitt replied, "It isn't fair to ask the public to pay for things they don't need and can't afford. Imagine asking a modern housewife to clean this place." Imagine, a Levitt underling added, "sticking your own wife way off in the country like this, all by herself," as if men decided such things on their own. Bill Levitt clearly believed he knew best what men as well as women wanted, or rather that he would decide what's best, and they would not only go along but be happy about it. "Market research stuff," he opined, "is bunk. People need to be shown. Ask a woman if she wants a door on the kitchen. She says she [does]. Then you build a kitchen the size she can afford, and she complains of claustrophobia. . . . We don't have to take the door off because she complains. We don't put it on in the first place."[43]

As always, there was a measure of truth in Levitt's bluster, but his company actually did a fair amount of informal market research, and he and his firm were sensitive to what people wanted. In designing Levittown, Pennsylvania, Levitt responded to critics of the visual monotony of Levittown, New York, by giving each of his Pennsylvania models three or four variations and several different color schemes, along with varied setbacks from the street. When it became clear that homebuyers wanted more space than the New York Levittown offered, the firm made its Pennsylvania houses more spacious and gave them three or four bedrooms. Bill Levitt also eavesdropped on potential homebuyers as they paraded through his model homes and visitor center, and regularly acted on what he heard. Two years into his Pennsylvania project, he undertook a monthlong survey of buyers' wants and needs.[44]

As in Levittown, New York, the combination of Levitt prescriptions, buyer preferences, and especially the firm's ability to deliver "a lot of house for the money" made for satisfied customers; many saw their spanking-new home as "a miracle." Fran and Bill Calkins had been stuck in a Camden, New Jersey, walkup apartment that cost them $100 a month, a third of Bill's take-home pay. Struggling with a bad back, Fran winced as she trudged up and down two flights of stairs carrying wet laundry, tricycles, and a playpen. "After five years of marriage," the *Ladies' Home Journal* reported, "their total savings were $150." But with a government check and bit of spare cash, they had enough to get into a new Levittown, Pennsylvania, house, which they couldn't quite believe. "Ours, all ours!" Bill exclaimed to the *Journal*'s writer. "Life seems beginning for us at last," added Fran, described in the piece as "a long-legged beauty of twenty-nine with a lovely figure and strawberry-blond hair," who proudly "showed off her new home, gleaming with brass and furniture polish."[45] With articles like this, who needed paid advertising? Still, Levitt continued to fill newspapers with ads. As in the New York Levittown, stories abounded of newcomers to Levittown, Pennsylvania, who couldn't find their houses at night in the months before streetlights went in, and of fellow "pioneers" who banded together to fix broken-down cars, give one another rides, and watch each other's children.

Some buyers came from Levittown, New York, drawn to the Pennsylvania project by the larger, more comfortable houses on offer. The original Bucks County "Levittowner" was 25 percent larger than the Long Island ranch, on a lot that was one thousand square feet bigger. This was the house my parents bought in the spring of 1953 and occupied in August. Pictures of the house—and me as a toddler clinging to my parents in front of it—show a low, rectangular structure sitting on a slight rise above the street and unadorned by grass, shrubs, or trees. This was typical of the Thornridge section's barren early landscape.

The front door stood in the middle of the house, recessed into a small vestibule barely large enough for a welcome mat. As you entered, the dining area was just to the left and a coat closet to the right. The dining area, which didn't exist in the Long Island Cape Cods and ranches, featured two banks of floor-to-ceiling windows and just barely fit a table for two adults and two or three kids. Window coverings made of basswood, a common tree in the northeastern United States, came with the house. The same basswood formed a stiff curtain separating the dining area from the kitchen, which featured an L-shape of white metal cabinets and name-brand appliances. My parents never closed the curtain and soon took it out. Without it, the dining area extended the tight kitchen and made both seem larger; the two rooms together measured just 160 square feet. There was a small refrigerator and electric oven on the far wall and a sink along the front wall of the house. The opposite wall accommodated the washing machine and oil burner. Levitt featured the well-appointed kitchen in many of its ads, emphasizing the modern GE electric stove and oven, the included GE refrigerator, the compact York-Shipley oil burner for heat and hot water, and the built-in Bendix washer. The company kept the costs of these appliances down by ordering huge numbers of them at heavily discounted prices. Above the appliances and below the stainless steel sink stood eighteen bright-white metal cabinets and drawers, adding to the kitchen's "modern" look. There was, however, very little counter space, so food had to be prepared on the dinner table or the oil burner's flat metal top. Levitt ads ignored the kitchen's lack of space, portraying it as the homemaker's "command central," the place where she could prepare food, do laundry—"no more running down to the basement"—and supervise the children. During the day, with the kids at school, Mom could step from the kitchen directly into the carport through the house's side door. From there, she could easily race off to the supermarket in time to have dinner ready when her husband came home.[46]

Between the kitchen and living room stood the central and most distinctive feature of the house: a red brick hearth that marked the boundary between the food areas and living room while creating an open plan—more open than the Levittown, New York, ranch—à la Frank Lloyd Wright. Alfred Levitt had achieved this openness by extending the hearth only partway into the dining area, leaving no barrier between it and the living room. The fireplace was open on three sides and shielded only by a see-through screen. From the dining area or living room you could look through it into the other room. Above the fireplace were four stepped ledges that led up and back to the exposed chimney. Behind the chimney were two bookshelves, which my parents filled with a twenty-volume set of the *Collier's Encyclopedia* and several volumes of *Reader's Digest* condensed books—the only books we owned for many years.

The upper bookshelf, which held the encyclopedias, sat about two feet below the ceiling, leaving an open space between the kitchen and living room and further connecting these parts of the house. The Levitt hearth echoed the one in Wright's Rebhuhn house, and although modern in form and function, it recalled centuries-old homes whose interior space centered on a large stone or brick structure used for heating and cooking. Reinforcing the Levittowner's open plan were the black-and-white-streaked asphalt tiles that visually connected the kitchen and dining area to the living room. The living room was also connected visually to the backyard via a wall of insulated windows. In another version of the Levittowner, the window wall faced the front yard and the street.

On entering my parents' house, you could head left into the dining area and kitchen, go straight into the open living room, or turn right into an L-shaped hallway that led to the bathroom and three bedrooms. The bedroom windows, positioned at shoulder height so

The Levittowner's open plan was designed to foster family togetherness.
(Special Collections Research Center, Temple University Libraries, Philadelphia,
Pennsylvania)

dressers could be placed under them, had sashes that slid from side to
side rather than up and down. The master bedroom shared a wall
with the lone bathroom, a tight space just barely big enough for the
tub, sink, and toilet, all made by reputable companies and, like the
house itself, designed to last. The only structural problems were the
radiant heating coils, which sprang a leak, and the asbestos siding,
which faded and developed stains as the rusting nailheads bled onto
the panels.

As our family grew, my parents added on to the house, a common
practice in all the Levittowns. The easiest addition was to enclose the
carport, which, for us, became a bedroom, laundry room, and storage
room. When my grandfather died and my grandmother moved in with
us, my parents built on again, this time behind the house. The new addition contained a master bedroom and family room/sun porch with

windows lining the two exterior walls. Later, there would be other improvements, some more visible than others: a tiny powder room in the coat closet next to the front door, a new heating system, vinyl siding to spiff up the exterior, and a waist-high counter between the kitchen and dining area. The counter separated the kitchen without closing it off, maintaining the sight lines of the original design.

My parents moved to their Levittown house with just some odds and ends of furniture they'd acquired as they moved from my mother's hometown of Philadelphia, where my father went to college and dental school, to his hometown of Massena, New York, and then to Camp Breckinridge, in Kentucky, while my father served, once again, in the army during the Korean War. When they finally bought furniture, they chose spare, Scandinavian-style pieces made of lightly stained natural wood that fit with the open plan of the house. They were doubtless influenced by the modernist interior decoration displayed in Levitt's model homes, as well as by magazine and newspaper articles that told readers how to dress up their homes.[47] The sofa, armchairs, and cabinet that housed the alcohol my parents never drank all hovered above the floor on thin, six-inch wooden legs to emphasize their airy lightness, and that of the rooms they unobtrusively filled. Scholars have found that at mid-century, professional people and others with college educations preferred modern furniture to traditional styles, and my parents conformed to this observation—unlike working-class people, who often preferred heavier, solid-looking objects with bright colors and shiny surfaces.[48]

Even if people's furnishings differed, in our neighborhood, as in every other neighborhood in the development, all houses were the same model, the Levittowner, although there were significant external variations. The house next door was flipped relative to ours by ninety degrees so that the front windows and door were perpendicular to the street—ours faced it—and opened onto a sloped-roof carport a few feet from our carport. The two carports served as buffers between each dwelling's living quarters, allowing a measure of privacy that both families welcomed, given the absence of fences, which Levitt had forbidden in an effort to foster neighborliness and clean sight lines from the street. Our carport also had a sloped roof, which extended the roofline of the rest of the house and made it look larger than it was. Some versions of the Levittowner had flat-roofed carports, which created a different look. There were six distinct exterior colors, and no two houses in a row were ever the same color. Our asbestos siding was gray, the neighbor's pinkish. A further source of visual variation was the slightly varying setbacks from the street. These external differences, together with the Levittowner's ampler living space compared with its New York predecessors, moved the architectural critic Lewis Mumford to grudgingly admit that the Pennsylvania development offered "a superior interior design" and "a great deal of value for the price."[49] He deemed it a modest success. Since for efficiency Levitt offered no optional extras, as car manufacturers did, each house was identically priced, save for those on larger corner lots, which cost $500 more.

My parents bought one of the spacious corner lots, and for us kids the exterior spaces were at least as important as the interior ones. In spring and summer, we played baseball so often in the backyard that we etched a diamond into the turf and made it impossible for grass to grow. In winter, we played touch football in the street with the hordes of kids who lived on the block. When we got a little older, we walked the block or so to the elementary school, where we played basketball and stickball, and swung unsupervised on the gymnastics equipment cemented into the ground. This was dangerous, but parents mostly didn't interfere.

Parents also let kids ride their bikes all over town, and once we were ten years old, the Levittown Public Recreation Association allowed us to ride to the nearest swimming pool and spend the day there without our parents. Bicycling to the pool, which took about ten minutes, we saw two other styles of houses, one less expensive than ours, one more expensive. By 1952, with the building of Levittown, Pennsylvania, the demand for affordable suburban homes was no longer so strong that Levitt could get away with building just two models, as in Levittown, New York.[50] In my part of town, the less expensive model was the Rancher, an updated version of the New York Levittown model that sold for $8,990 and had two bedrooms plus an unfinished attic. The Rancher could be built even more quickly than the Levittowner, because Levitt's subcontractors had years of experience with the design. The new iteration seemed roomier than the original, since it squeezed more living space out of the same overall dimensions by eliminating hallways and the fireplace, opening the stairwell, and moving the heater and washing machine from the kitchen to the bathroom. Levitt kept down the price of the Pennsylvania Rancher by eliminating exterior sheathing; the stiff sheets of asbestos cement siding (Colorbestos, invented for Levitt by Johns-Manville) were nailed directly to the studs. For families needing more space, the unfinished attic could be converted into two

The Rancher, Levittown, Pennsylvania's most economical house. (From the Collection of the Mercer Museum Library of the Bucks County Historical Society)

The Jubilee, Levitt's model with a finished, two-bedroom second floor. (From the Collection of the Mercer Museum Library of the Bucks County Historical Society)

additional bedrooms and a second bathroom for just $2,100. If you were a do-it-yourselfer, the materials cost just $600.[51] The Rancher sections of Levittown housed a fair number of steelworkers; many of my friends' fathers worked at the U.S. Steel plant.

The more expensive dwelling we passed on the way to the pool was the Jubilee, a one-and-a-half-story structure originally priced at $10,990, about the same as the Rancher, with a professionally finished upstairs. The Jubilee came with four bedrooms, two downstairs and two upstairs, plus two bathrooms and an attached garage. Like the Levittowner, it had an open plan, although the kitchen was somewhat more enclosed. From the outside, it looked a lot like the original Levittown's Cape Cod, but with an added garage. It was, the Levitts said, "the most traditional house we have built since the war."[52]

Everyone in my elementary and junior high schools came from the sections with Levittowners, Ranchers, and Jubilees. But at our synagogue, I met kids from the more prosperous "Country Clubber" sections of town, which Levitt advertised as suitable for "executives" and situated farther from the steel mill than any other section. In this westernmost precinct of the development, Levitt preserved a number of mature trees to lend the area a more established air and allow some houses to be secluded from their neighbors. When people moved into the Country Clubber sections, they were greeted with leafy greenery and shady privacy rather than the treeless landscapes of the more modestly priced sections.

To their credit, the Levitts didn't intend the poorer parts of town to remain barren. The company seeded every lot with grass and planted fruit trees, white pines, and willow trees in every yard, along with shade trees bordering the street. Levitt also graced every yard with an assortment of evergreens and flowering shrubs. Father Abraham had made himself the landscaping specialist, and in the Levitt-owned *Levittown Times* he instructed new homeowners, many of them former city dwellers, in the art of caring for the plants, grass, and trees his company had installed. He also taught people in person. Here, as in Levittown, New York, Abraham was driven around the development in a big black limousine, from which he'd emerge regularly to grab a garden hoe or planting trowel from the homeowner and show her or him how to manage the lawn.[53]

The Levitts claimed to have spent $8 million on landscaping, including 170,000 evergreens, 250,000 flowering shrubs, 51,000 fruit trees, and 600,000 pounds of grass seed.[54] Their admirable goal, mostly realized in the decades to come, was to leaven the uniformity of their endless expanses of tract houses—or at least to disguise it—with a significant dose of nature, albeit one planned and installed en masse, like their houses. Nature, however, didn't always cooperate. In the early years, successive plagues of "Japanese" beetles descended on the area and devoured many of the newly installed plants.[55]

Residents of the Country Clubber sections with preserved trees on their lots didn't have to wait decades for their saplings to mature. Still, in my part of town, old, wooded areas remained—not on individual properties, but around the fringes of the neighborhood. My parents had chosen a lot with a thick woods right behind our backyard, and beyond the woods was a deep-water former quarry. A metal fence went up around these areas after kids drowned in another quarry close by, but we burrowed under and climbed over the barrier to retrieve errant baseballs and play in this forbidden, somewhat magical domain. We also played in a wooded area on the grounds of our local elementary school, and in a larger woods a ten-minute walk away. Our neighborhood wasn't typical, since it sat on the eastern edge of the development, next to lands Levitt hadn't purchased, but other border areas also benefitted from their proximity to the parts of Lower Bucks County that Levitt had left undeveloped.

Thanks to Levitt's agreement with Middletown Township, the Country Clubber sections retained more wooded areas and unbuilt lands than other parts of the development, and the firm planted twice as many evergreen shrubs and three times as many flowering perennials as in the rest of the community.[56] The 1954 Country Clubber looked like an enlarged version of my parents' house, with its recessed front door in the middle, a six-paned, doubled-glazed picture window on the left, and three narrow, shoulder-high sliding windows on the right. A low, flat-roofed two-car shelter jutted out from the left side of the house. The Country Clubber had twice the square footage of our Levittowner, if you count the second floor, which was built under a sharply pitched roof that was finished on the inside with knotty pine. The ceiling was so low that an adult could stand only in the middle of the upstairs space. Pictures show a Ping-Pong table pushed up against the sloped ceiling-wall, limiting its use to children. Placing a bed flush with the sloped ceiling-wall allowed a sleeper to get in and out only on one side. As *House and Home* generously put it, "Furniture placement demonstrates how space under slanting ceiling, while lacking headroom, is . . . perfectly usable."[57] Still, there were eight hundred square feet of more or less usable space upstairs, including a recreation room, bedroom, and bathroom. Natural light came in only on the two sides of the house and through a dormer in the back.

The Country Clubber would evolve dramatically over the remaining years of construction in Levittown. The 1955 model harked back to the original 1952 design, the one whose production was halted in the face of opposition from Middletown Township. The new version measured 1,530 square feet on the ground floor, with another seven hundred feet of expansion space under the eaves of the tall, unfinished attic. Unlike the 1954 model, it no longer looked like an oversized Levittowner. The 1955 Country Clubber had an L shape, with two bedrooms jutting out from the front righthand side. The third bedroom occupied the right rear corner, separated from the large master bedroom in the front by two back-to-back bathrooms, one of them belonging to a master suite. The front door led to a largish foyer that opened onto a spacious living room, dining room, and kitchen, which boasted a washer and dryer. The house retained the Levitt open plan, except that the kitchen was mostly enclosed and large enough for a table. The left side of the structure sported a huge two-car garage, and the dwelling occupied a twelve-thousand-square-foot lot. In later versions, the house came with a finished second floor and a dishwasher.[58]

Despite being more prosperous, age ranges in the Country Clubber sections resembled those of the community as a whole. Levittown, Pennsylvania, like its Long Island cousin, was very young. In 1953, the population consisted mainly of married couples who were thirty years old, give or take, with one or two children mostly under age five. Just 4 percent of the community was past forty-five. In terms of religious affiliation, the Pennsylvania Levittown also mirrored the New York one with its overrepresentation of Catholics (39 percent versus 25 percent nationwide) and Jews (15 percent versus 4 percent) and underrepresentation of Protestants (41 percent versus 62 percent).[59] People of Italian, Irish, and Slavic heritage lived alongside Protestants originally from northern Europe. It was a "white ethnic" place, more heterogenous than most American communities.[60]

Everyone, kids as well as adults, was very much aware of the hierarchy of houses—and therefore incomes—in the development. The new Levittown was more stratified by income than the original one, since it had a much wider range of home prices. And while Bill Levitt and others regularly boasted that there was "no other side of the tracks" in Levittown, Pennsylvania, in reality the Rancher sections tended to be working class, often steelworkers, while the Country Clubber areas housed the middle and upper-middle class.

The working-class and upper-middle-class houses also sat on opposite sides of the community. Their children attended different schools and often different houses of worship. Levitt's greatest mistake in Pennsylvania, besides his exclusion of African Americans, may have been the decision to build only one kind of house in each section. Doing so made construction more efficient, but it produced sharp status distinctions and made some parts of the community more desirable than others. The prosperous residents, one working-class resident maintained, "absolutely hated the steelworkers. They just thought we were scum."[61] Levitt would not repeat this mistake in the next Levittown, built across the Delaware River in New Jersey.

Neighborhoods like mine, with their middling Levittowner models, were more socioeconomically diverse than either the Rancher or Country Clubber sections. Working-class and middle-class families lived side by side, though few could be considered upper-middle class. The two men directly across the street from us were professionals, one an engineer, the other an airline navigator and former navy pilot. My father was a dentist with mostly working- and lower-middle-class patients. Since no one had dental insurance, his fees seem almost comically low by today's standards. Our next-door neighbor was an electrician, and several men on our street worked in the steel mill. Most women were full-time homemakers, including some with professional training. The woman diagonally across the street had a nursing degree but wasn't employed; she had four young boys at home. One female neighbor was a musician who gave piano lessons at home.

Levittown's income disparities were exacerbated by other inequities in the community and by the division of Levittown into four distinct municipalities: Falls, Middletown, and Bristol townships and Tullytown Borough. Falls Township benefitted enormously from the presence of the Fairless Works, located entirely within its bounds. The gigantic factory complex added substantially to the township's tax base and gave homeowners there the lowest tax rates in Levittown. Because the Middletown Township part of the development consisted solely of Country Clubbers, it enjoyed a strong tax base of relatively prosperous homeowners. The non-Levittown parts of Bristol and Tullytown ranked among the poorest in the region, and the Levittown areas included Levitt's most modest homes. These were the least affluent parts of the development, and homeowners there had to make do with fewer services and more sparsely funded schools. The disparities among its parts did much to prevent Levittown from incorporating as its own distinct municipality. The wealthier, more industrial townships refused to share their advantages with the less favored parts of the development. For this reason, the huge Levitt-built community, which would have been the tenth-largest city in Pennsylvania, remained a political backwater lacking in statewide political influence and the resources that would have come with it.

Building in Levittown, Pennsylvania, proceeded over the six-year period from 1952 to 1958, during which Levitt made many modifications to his homes. In 1954, the company added a one-car garage option to its basic Levittowner and created pricier and cheaper versions of the Country Clubber. In 1957, the company introduced two wholly new models, the Pennsylvanian and Colonial, both priced at about $15,000 and providing some 1,500 square feet of living space. Both models dropped the modernist innovations of the earlier homes. Inside, the open plan was gone, and from the outside both looked like generic, two-story structures that could have been postwar suburban dwellings anywhere. As the housing market softened after the mid-1950s, Levitt reverted to the more traditional designs desired by the slightly more prosperous people who bought these larger, three- or four-bedroom homes.[62] By then, unlike a few years earlier, the proliferation of Levitt-like developments had given homebuyers a great deal of choice.

The most traditional house of all those built in Levittown, Pennsylvania, was the Colonial, which Bill Levitt described as "a two-story with a lot of new ideas and old-fashioned solid comfort."[63] Like the classic American home that inspired it, the Colonial placed all the public areas downstairs and all the bedrooms upstairs. It was the only Levitt model with no first-floor bedrooms—the Pennsylvanian had two on the first level and two on the second—and the only one with a formal dining room. The Levitts built only a few hundred Pennsylvanians and Colonials, but they would serve as dress rehearsals for the much larger number that would be the mainstays of the next Levittown in New Jersey.

Levitt's completion of the Pennsylvania community in 1958 marked the transformation of a region still largely rural and agricultural in 1950 into an industrialized, quasi-urban landscape. In the process, an area that had always been almost exclusively white, Protestant, and Republican became nearly as ethnically and religiously diverse, although not as racially diverse, as nearby cities. By the late 1950s, Lower Bucks County not only housed the huge Fairless Works and Levittown, but also other firms—Kaiser-Fleetwings, which employed seven thousand in manufacturing aircraft parts, National Steel, the huge Rohm & Haas chemical plant, the Rubber Supply Company of Morrisville, and Minnesota Mining and Manufacturing—plus the U.S.

Steel–built housing development Fairless Hills. The farms that had existed there since colonial times almost entirely disappeared as the area's population rose by 177 percent between 1950 and 1960, making Lower Bucks County one of the fasting-growing regions in the country.[64] But even years later, the memory of the farms remained alive as homeowners regularly found asparagus stalks sprouting in their lawns and even piercing through asphalt driveways.[65]

Local elites were divided about this massive change. Some extolled the cascade of jobs and opportunities, while others lamented the loss of an (idealized) rural life, and with it the sturdy yeoman farmers who had tilled the soil since the time of William Penn, the Quaker leader who founded Pennsylvania in 1682. A study by the sociologists Marvin Bressler and Charles Westoff showed that two-thirds of local political and civic leaders approved of the changes taking place, while one-third disapproved. Those favorable to the area's industrialization and urbanization typically said things like, "More money will be spent here in any twelve months than has been spent here in the last ten years" and "We'll finally get a city sewage system in the area." As a journalist for the *Bucks County Traveler* put it, "many sections of the county would give almost anything to have a Fairless Works in their backyard."[66] Perhaps the most ecstatic comment came from a local bank president: "This will be the greatest thing that ever happened around here. . . . It will mean a lot of prosperity, new businesses, new homes and tremendous development."[67]

Those opposed to the development of Lower Bucks County objected to the "big" housing developments, "big" industrial installations, and "big" demographic changes. They expressed concerns about traffic, congestion, and the threat to their tranquil life. Even the leaders favorable to U.S. Steel worried about the influx of industrial workers, especially after U.S. Steel announced a willingness to hire African Americans. Virtually all of the leaders surveyed expected a significant increase in the number of Blacks, who represented just 2.9 percent of the Lower Bucks County population in 1950. Most of the African American newcomers were drawn to the new industrial jobs, and half of the leaders in question said that the growth of the Black population would cause problems involving housing. They feared, rightly as it turned out, that most white residents were not willing to live in the same community as Blacks. "There will be too many Negroes coming in here for my tastes," one of Bressler and Westoff's informants said.[68]

The local elites also expected to be surrounded by far more lower- and working-class people than they were accustomed to. The leaders who favored industrialization claimed to be unworried about this influx, since the existence of Levittown and Fairless Hills would allow most to become homeowners, guaranteeing a high degree of stability in the community and the relative absence of bad actors. They appeared to agree with Bill Levitt's dictum, "No man who owns his own house and lot can be a communist."[69] The elites opposed to industrialization, by contrast, worried that the new factory workers would be a "hard-drinking, free-spending, rough crowd."[70] They also feared that as union members, the workers would be Democrats, which would dramatically change the area's political valence, and not for the better. Although local leaders expressed substantial opposition to the changes underway, those with the most power, mainly a handful of wealthy individuals with influence in local, state, and national Republican politics, strongly endorsed them. The money and jobs that would pour into the region trumped the political shift toward the Democrats, which in that time of broad consensus didn't worry them terribly. The power elite's support helps explain the area's rapid, smooth transformation from a rural backwater to what some, referring to Germany's potent industrial region, called the "Ruhr Valley of the United States."[71]

Bressler and Westoff did their study of Lower Bucks County elites before the Fairless Works and the huge Levitt development were complete. Once the steel mill was fired up and the new houses multiplied, local responses showed far more wariness, even hostility, than before. In 1953, a group of businessmen complained to U.S. Steel executives about air and water pollution, and the Morrisville Borough Council tried to limit smoke from the blast furnaces, only to be told that such limits were impossible. Residents of the area criticized the Fairless Works for fouling the Delaware River and subjecting them to "smoke soot and obnoxious odors."[72]

People also objected to the visual damage that the ultra-rapid industrialization had caused. As one resident wrote, "Along with the tremendous growth of the County has come an unplanned, chaotic patchwork of building and development that has dug deep scars into the face of the County. . . . The once beautiful view that stretched for miles has now been . . . destroyed by wasteful suburbicide." Even Bill Levitt, one of the culprits, complained that random commercial development had turned the county's roads into "the worst eyesores in the entire Northeastern United States."[73]

Levitt had elaborately planned his housing development, but he could not control what got built around its edges and along the county and state roadways that predated Levittown and cut through its expanse. But even though it was local officials who had failed to regulate what became a chaos of commerce, Levitt regularly took the blame. Non-Levittown residents routinely denounced him in public meetings, threatened to sue him, and in one case tried to punch him during a dispute. They blamed him for populating the area with "trailer trash," "undesirables," and "just a lot of rubbish hauled in overnight." In 1954, the Falls Township board entertained a citizens' petition designed to bar liquor sales in cafés, saloons, and restaurants, so as to keep the township from being "filled with elements foreign to our ideals." To blunt this avalanche of criticism, Levitt brought in a public relations firm to deflect the blame and restore some goodwill. Its success was modest at best.[74]

Underlying the criticism was a belated realization that the region's character had changed for good. Not only had the land been shorn of crops and trees, and the air and water degraded, but colonial-era homes and buildings had been bulldozed to make way for the steel mill and the thousands of Levittowners, Ranchers, Jubilees, and Country Clubbers. These new structures, critics said, lacked the character of the old edifices, which were now sorely missed. History, long ignored or taken for granted, was (re)discovered, and locals wanted what remained of it to be preserved. The charming village of Fallsington, founded by Quakers in 1690 and now squeezed between Levittown and the Fairless Works, sprouted historical societies and strict zoning laws designed to keep suburban and industrial encroachment at bay. In 1953, some five hundred "concerned citizens" formed Historic Fallsington, Inc., dedicated to protecting "the village that time forgot" from "development in the adjacent Levittown and Fairless Hills," which "threatened to end" its eighteenth-century character "forever."[75] Fallsington would stay largely intact, but as a tiny island in a sea of sprawl.

Even as locals grew increasingly hostile to the massive development, most of those who bought the original Levitt houses in 1952 and

1953 seemed pleased with their status as Levittown homeowners. When interviewed by a team of New York University sociologists in 1953, 77 percent of the Levittown residents surveyed gave their new community the highest possible rating. Healthy majorities deemed Levittown a desirable alternative to cities, a "suburban oasis," and an appealing planned environment. A troubling corollary of these positive responses were the racist attitudes they revealed. Majorities extolled the new community as a refuge from Black people, and when Bill Levitt faced criticism for excluding African Americans, many leapt to his defense.[76]

Beyond these early assessments of life in Levittown, questions by journalists on the community's tenth, twentieth, thirtieth, and subsequent anniversaries show that residents continued to enjoy living there, while recent interviews with people who grew up in Levittown suggest that they retain fond memories of the community. There are no randomly sampled public opinion polls, so we lack a precise picture of Levittowners' views, but at the very least, we can see that journalists, often prejudiced against the community, regularly gave the development positive reviews and had no trouble finding community members willing to do the same.

"What is Levittown like today?" asked the editors of *Bucks County Traveler* five years after the first residents moved in. "Even its most grudging critics," went the answer, "will admit that it's in pretty good physical shape ... for here in the country is everything a city needs—and none of the grime." This view reflected the era's antiurban bias, but it was grounded in the reality of Levittown's success. Every Levitt-built house had sold quickly, and resales were brisk. A genuine community had taken shape. People came together in the fifteen rapidly constructed houses of worship, in the dozen new schools, in the five community swimming pools, in the ball fields and playgrounds that attracted adults and children alike, and in the huge state-of-the art shopping center. Hence the article's conclusion: "After five years, Levittown shapes up as a vigorous, youthful, growing community." Critics still "rant about the drabness, the sameness, the mediocrity, and the cracks in the picture windows [but] Levittowners see only a few smudges that can easily be wiped away."[77]

In an article marking Levittown's twentieth anniversary, the *Philadelphia Inquirer* asserted that "time has proved the critics wrong in their predictions that a community serving one economic group with homes and streets monotonously the same would create cultural and intellectual uniformity." The paper quoted Marvin Bressler, the Princeton University sociologist who had coauthored the 1954 study of Levittown and lived in the development for ten years in the 1950s and 1960s. "The intellectual attacks on Levittown are foolish," Bressler said. "On its most basic level it comes down to this: It is more pleasant to live in your own house with trees and grass than to live in a row house without trees and grass. People just don't lose their individuality because their house happens to look like their neighbors'."[78] This comment echoed that of Columbia sociologist Herbert Gans, who had lived in Levittown, New Jersey, and wrote the 1967 book *The Levittowners,* which became the most famous study of the Levitt developments.[79]

Yet the *Inquirer* found Levittown, Pennsylvania, far from perfect. African American families continued to feel unwelcome, and for good reason, although the community now had a small Black population and was diverse in other ways—resales had allowed a tiny number of non-whites in. Traffic choked the surrounding arteries, and crime had gone up. Levittown lacked a real downtown and business district, which might have enabled it to evolve with its population. The community had been conceived for young couples with small children, and the teenagers who now lived there had too little to do. Still, its houses had retained their appeal, especially since so many had been remodeled and expanded, making them far more different than in the early years. At the lower end, Levittown dwellings remained affordable for working people. The article concluded on a positive note by quoting a couple who had lived there since the beginning: "We couldn't afford an apartment, but with mortgage payments of $63 a month, we could manage." Even with their two teenage children, "We like it here . . . I can't see a reason in the world why we'd ever want to move."[80]

For Levittown's twenty-fifth anniversary, the *Inquirer* entitled its article "The Levittowners Outlast Their Critics." The piece again turned to Gans, who had written, "Levittowners have not become outgoing mindless conformers; they remain individuals, fulfilling the social aspirations with which they came. . . . Levittown permits most of its residents to be what they want to be." This description seemed to fit Philomena Dougherty, one of the first residents in Levittown, Pennsylvania. Installing her young family in the development, she had

found it "really beautiful—it was revolutionary . . . exciting." Levittown houses, the article added, "remain in demand," even though—
and here was the lone sour note—"the community doesn't seem to be
as friendly" as in the past.[81]

Levittown's twenty-fifth anniversary attracted a fair amount of attention, including from the Rutgers sociologist David Popenoe, who
interviewed a representative sample of the community's inhabitants.
What he learned echoed the journalists' more anecdotal findings. Despite a few concerns, mainly about teenagers and drugs, the residents'
attitudes toward Levittown are overwhelmingly positive. "You have
everything you need, and it's near work and the big cities," went a
typical comment. If Levittowners were to move, it would never be to
a city but to another suburb with houses like their own, only larger.
The working-class families Popenoe interviewed seemed especially
content, since in Levittown they could afford a middle-class life.[82]

The residents who were unhappy with their Levittown lives tended
to be working-class families with four or more children and relatively
low incomes. To make ends meet, the husband often worked two jobs,
while the wife, lacking a second car, was "stuck at home," lonely and
bored. Since the publication of Betty Friedan's *The Feminine Mystique*
(1963), this lonely, alienated housewife had come to seem omnipresent
in the American suburbs, but Popenoe found just two or three women
in his sample who "fit into this category," and only one a "serious
case."[83] Instead, he discovered several "dependent" women, either wid-
ows or divorcées. They were financially insecure and isolated but not
unhappy with the neighborhood. One interviewee "thinks the world of
Levittown; she never wants to live anywhere else." Another, despite her
difficulties, "likes Levittown very much, especially her neighborhood
and neighbors. . . . She would deeply regret having to move."[84]

Even the community's teenagers, the least content of Popenoe's interviewees, mostly found Levittown "nice" or at least "OK." They
liked that it was shielded from "gangs or problems like the city." Still,
about a quarter of them reported being bored and having "nothing to
do." Their parents generally dismissed these attitudes, saying their
kids "just don't want to do" the things available to them. But many
teenagers felt these activities were too structured and too likely to re-
volve around the school. The happiest ones were those involved in
competitive sports or active in their churches and synagogues.[85]

These anniversary "check-ins" continued to interest journalists and sociologists alike. For Levittown's thirtieth anniversary, the *Inquirer* commissioned a long piece by David Diamond, once a child in the community. Entitled "The Children of Levittown," the article collected the memories and other testimony of nine people who had grown up there. "I think there were three black kids in our whole school system," recalled Anita Gevinson. "We figured there were only three in the whole world." Gevinson, who became a Philadelphia radio personality, also remembered that there were no poor people. But like the others Diamond interviewed, she "felt their lives had been made more interesting—even better—by growing up in Levittown." Claudia Peluso, an aspiring actress in New York City, retained the ethos of suburbia even while living in Greenwich Village. "I was spoiled," she said, "by the newness of the houses," and she felt "there was something wrong in buying a place that was built for someone else." A New York co-op wasn't for her: "They don't even have front yards."[86]

The most remarkable thing about Diamond's article, however, is the number of people he found who credited Levittown with broadening their worldview. Sylvester Micir, who had lived in a Croatian enclave in Pittsburgh before his father took a job at the Fairless Works, said that Levittown exposed him to "different nationalities, to different cultures, to different ideas, to different religions. . . . You get to be a little more well-rounded." Barbara Schwartz Kopans, a press aide to Michael Dukakis, then the governor-elect of Massachusetts, grew up entirely in Levittown and credited the place not only with giving her a "good political sense," but the ability to understand her urban counterparts. She "was able to relate to the people who lived in Boston a lot better than the other people on [Dukakis's] staff who grew up in a homogeneous community where they were all well-educated and their friends were all well-educated, and all their friends were rich." Michael Riccardi, a real estate and insurance broker, said that "in the city you find there are more ethnic-type related neighborhoods," whereas in Levittown, "you have people who came from an Italian section moving next door to a family who came from a Polish section. [Now] I think I can generate relationships with almost any type of person." As if in answer to Lewis Mumford, who extolled the richness and sophistication of urban culture while condemning Levittown as a cultural wasteland, Riccardi found that the suburban community broadened him, while the city had closed him off. Diamond's interviewees didn't seem to recognize—or care—that Levittown's diversity encompassed class, religion, and ethnicity, but not race.[87]

The two dozen interviews I did with current and former Levittown residents for this book echoed much of what journalists have reported, while adding some illuminating details.[88] Virtually everyone I spoke with had nothing but positive memories of their early years. Those memories have doubtless shaded into nostalgia, with the difficult times smoothed over. Comparing their experiences to those of their children, they often judged their children's lives to be more difficult and complicated than their own. But this nostalgia is not the longing for a "lost paradise," as the historian Peter Fritzsche claimed in the epilogue of an essay collection on Levittown, Pennsylvania. Everyone I spoke with knew that Levittown had been grounded in racial discrimination, and that when its pure whiteness was threatened, residents made a violent effort to expel the Black interlopers. What former Levittowners expressed was not a longing for paradise but a different phenomenon that Fritzsche evokes, a lost innocence. Levittown was a place where (white) kids could grow up in blissful ignorance, inhabiting a suburban world free of the dangers and complications that plague even affluent suburbs today, to say nothing of the urban neighborhoods their parents had long since abandoned.[89]

George Strachan, Jr., born in 1948, moved with his parents five years later to the least expensive and most working-class part of Levittown.[90] His father had landed at job at the Fairless Works a year earlier and lived in a rented room for a year while waiting for his Levittown home to be built. In the meantime, George, Sr., returned as often as he could to Johnstown, Pennsylvania, where he and his father had labored in the coal mines. When a Levittown Rancher finally became available, George bought one for $8,999 and installed his wife and two young sons there. The former coal miner had joined a parade of young men from the mines and mills of western and northern Pennsylvania. They marched east and south looking for safer, better work in the new Fairless plant and the other industries springing up around it.

George, Sr., who lacked a high school education, began as a laborer and gradually worked his way up thanks to U.S. Steel's apprenticeship program, which trained ambitious employees in the skills needed to hold better-paid jobs. He became a millwright, or mechanic who serviced the mill's machines. His wife eventually got a part-time position at the Educational Testing Service (ETS) in Princeton, New Jersey. Few of the women recruited by ETS owned cars, so the firm sent a bus to the Levittown Shopping Center to transport them to work. Mrs. Strachan's modest income made a big difference in the family finances.

George, Jr., like his younger brother, Bill, was a good student and natural athlete. What he liked best about Levittown was its ball fields, pools, and competitive Little League baseball teams. In 1960, he played with members of the Levittown team that won the Little League World Series.[91] "There was something magical about Levittown," he told me. It felt safe because "there was no bad side of the town," and "the safety of the community gave kids a freedom that youngsters don't have today." Kids rode their bikes all over town and played outside with little supervision from their parents. The only firm rule was that you came inside when "the streetlights went on."

For George, Levittown represented the "American dream," although he recognizes that the community could have limited his horizons. Everyone around him was blue collar, often without a high school diploma, and his neighborhood gave him no models of social mobility. "The only college-educated people we ran into were our teachers." This changed in high school, where he encountered kids from affluent families whose parents had been to universities and had professional jobs. "That's when I realized things could be different," he said—that he too could go to college, at least in theory; his family lacked the money to pay for it. But by working summer jobs at the steel mill, he made enough to pay his way through Penn State, earned the credentials for a career in business, and ultimately started his own financial services firm.

George was nine years old when the first Black family moved into Levittown, and though he had followed the newspaper coverage of the racial strife that followed, "I don't remember being aghast." He didn't know any Black people and had no sense of the barriers they faced. "When I worked at the steel mill, that was the first time I'd ever talked to any Black people." As an adult, he came to see the injustice of excluding African Americans from the community that had done so much for him, the son of a coalminer and steelworker. "If it wasn't for Levittown and the things I was able to experience there, the friends I made, the education I got, I wouldn't be where I am today."

The large numbers of Catholics and Jews in Levittown may be why Andrea Eisenberg, who grew up in a Jewish family, never experienced antisemitic hostility. There were plenty of Jews, but more important, the Catholics in her neighborhood accepted her just fine. Andrea's parents moved to Levittown just after it opened in 1952. She was three years old and remained in the community until she went off to college. She remembers those childhood and adolescent years as a "fruitful time." She felt "free and safe." "I could do anything I wanted, and that was OK." She loved the neighborliness of Levittown, with its interconnected backyards and strong ties among the families on her street. Most of all, she "felt privileged, even rich." When she later found out what her dad earned, "I said, 'You're kidding me.' It was so low. I thought we were upper-middle class." This must have been because "Levittown had a feeling of overall equality. . . . We all kind of seemed the same. There were no big shots." Everyone's parents were just starting out in life, so "maybe that helped with the equality thing." This equality applied to her gender as well. "I was a girl in the fifties and sixties, but I didn't think there was anything I couldn't do."[92]

Dennis Bauer, having moved to the development as a five-year-old in 1954, still lives there, as do his son and grandchildren.[93] Bauer still enjoys living in Levittown, although it has changed a great deal. The most dramatic transformation is doubtless the closure of the steel mill after a quarter-century of decline. When the Fairless Works of U.S. Steel opened in December 1952, the company president, Benjamin Franklin Fairless, touted it as an advanced, ultramodern plant "that will go on for 50 or perhaps 100 years to come, pouring steel into the ribs of our nation and wealth into its economic veins."[94] In reality, the new "integrated" mill, which collected iron smelting, steelmaking, and steel fashioning in one massive enterprise, would soon be obsolete.

U.S. Steel's Fairless Works were built around a familiar technology— gas-fired, open-hearth blast furnaces—that had been standard for decades. European and Japanese firms, however, had invested in the highly efficient "basic oxygen" furnaces pioneered by an Austrian steel manufacturer in 1952, which worked by injecting pure oxygen into molten iron. What an open-hearth furnace could produce in six hours, a competitor using the new method could make in forty minutes.[95]

In the 1950s, when the world market offered little competition, U.S. Steel survived despite the lag in technology because its production capacity was by far the largest in the world. But Japan invested heavily in oxygen furnaces, and eventually the top Japanese steelmaker, Nippon Steel, left its American counterpart in the dust. In 1974, U.S. Steel's sixty-seven furnaces, most still using open-hearth technology, produced a total of thirty-one million tons of steel. But Nippon Steel, with only twenty-five furnaces, made forty-five million tons—four times as much per furnace as U.S. Steel.[96] Even in the face of this competition, U.S. Steel was slow to adopt oxygen converters—slower than not only Japanese firms but other American ones as well. It was just as slow with other innovative technologies. By the late 1970s, U.S. Steel had become a dinosaur.[97]

Throughout the 1960s, when the hot American economy provided plenty of demand for its steel, U.S. Steel executives shrugged off their failure to adopt the new technology. The company regularly expanded its workforce at Fairless, growing it from six thousand in 1960 to just under ten thousand in 1973. But that year's Arab oil embargo vastly increased the price of petroleum and moved Americans to buy smaller cars, many of them made in Japan, which used less steel. Demand for steel dropped just as inflation made it costlier to produce. The Fairless Works found itself in an especially precarious position because all of its facilities had been built in 1951 and 1952, which meant, as U.S. Steel's chairman would eventually tell Congress, that the plant suffered from "terminal obsolescence," and the cost of modernizing was prohibitive.[98]

The layoffs began in 1975. The first wave cost 2,300 jobs at Fairless, and as demand for steel fell through the early 1980s, the hemorrhaging continued. Between December 1982 and January 1983, 165,000 American steelworkers lost their jobs, 3,500 of them at the Fairless Works. At that point, U.S. Steel proposed to shut down the blast furnaces and open-hearth furnaces at Fairless and import thick slabs of steel from a Scottish company. Fairless's hot strip mill would then transform the slabs into rolls of finished steel to be used in cars and other products. But the deal with the Scottish steelmaker fell through, and Fairless continued its downward path. Another seven hundred people lost their jobs in June 1984, leaving the plant with just one iron-producing blast furnace and four open-hearth furnaces in service, down from two and nine, respectively. A long strike in 1987 yielded a contract that prevented more layoffs, but only temporarily. In 1991, now operating under the name USX, the company shut down all iron- and steelmaking at Fairless, laying off another two thousand. Only eight hundred jobs were left, a manpower reduction of over 90 percent in less than twenty years. Only the hot strip mill and a couple of other operations remained. These massive cuts, as the company euphemistically put it, were "restructuring actions . . . intended to enhance USX's future market competitiveness."[99] But competitiveness remained elusive, and by 2001 the plant employed just one hundred people.[100]

The once-mighty complex continues to limp along, with nearly as many people employed in tearing it down and undoing decades of environmental degradation as in its last industrial activity: galvanizing steel sheets made elsewhere. In December 2020, U.S. Steel (the old name was restored in 2001) sold much of the Fairless site to a company that plans to turn it into a hub for e-commerce with warehouses and other facilities.[101] Here as elsewhere, deindustrialization has turned into Amazonization, with well-paying union jobs giving way to poorly compensated, nonunionized warehouse work.

The long decline of the Fairless Works was traumatic for a great many Levittown residents. When earning good wages at the mill, even those without high school diplomas could buy Levittown houses, support families, and even send children to college. But those who were laid off had trouble finding paid work. Eighty percent of those dismissed in 1991 remained unemployed a year later. Fred and Gabriela Kruck, who had both worked at the plant and made $65,000 between them, had to sell their Levittown house in 1992 to pay two years' worth of back property taxes. Dick Wilson, laid off in 1991 after working at Fairless for thirty-one years, told a journalist, "I thought it was my birthright—be white, dumb, work in the mill, buy a Levittowner."[102] Even though he struggled to find a new job, he was better off than some because his house was paid off, and unlike people hired after the early 1970s, his union benefits included lifetime health insurance and a monthly pension check. Many others had been laid off before Wilson, and by the early 1980s, workers with their eyes open knew the future was bleak. "I must have lived in fear of losing my job for at least the last twenty or fifteen years," said Bob Oestreich. "It was a real slow process, watching it go down."[103]

U.S. Steel wasn't, of course, the only victim of deindustrialization in the vicinity of Levittown. Most other factories, so vibrant in the

1950s and 1960s, also began to stumble in the 1970s, when the problems of foreign competition and obsolete U.S. technology were made worse by energy shocks. Gasoline and other petroleum prices soared, squeezing companies' profit margins and increasing the pace of layoffs. As working people lost their jobs, the energy crisis added insult to injury by raising the prices of heating oil and especially gasoline.

These problems deeply affected suburbs like Levittown, where virtually every household depended on its cars for shopping, transporting children, and going to work—if family members still had jobs. The oil shocks of 1973 and 1979 exacerbated the stagflation of the decade and created a nationwide wave of anger as motorists stewed in long lines at service stations. Not infrequently they found that the gasoline had run out before their turn at the pump. Independent truckers who owned their rigs may have suffered the most from the cost and scarcity of fuel.

In Levittown, Pennsylvania, anger over gasoline prices exploded into the nation's largest protest against the energy crisis.[104] On June 23, 1979, a small army of locally based truck drivers called attention to the situation by parading at a snail's pace through Five Points, the busiest intersection in the development, known for having gas stations on all five of its corners. The event made the local news, and hordes of Levittown residents came out to Five Points to support the truckers and vent their own anger over the price and scarcity of gas.[105] At first, reporters covering the protests found a festive scene, but by six thirty in the evening, when all of the Five Points gas stations had run out of fuel and closed early, the demonstration took a sharper edge. One truck driver parked his eighteen-wheeler in the middle of the intersection, intending to block all traffic. Local police ordered the driver, William Brown, to move his rig, but instead, he climbed on top of his cab and began haranguing the crowd, now comprising a thousand people lining all sides of the intersection and spilling into the street. Officers soon pulled him off his truck and shoved him into a squad car. When the policemen seemed to handle Brown roughly, the crowd began to chant, "Police brutality, police brutality." More officers arrived, including members of Philadelphia's K-9 corps, and began to move people off the streets, provoking a hail of soda bottles and beer cans from the protesters. Police gained control of the situation only after making twenty-five arrests.

A gas shortage demonstrator stands in front of a burning car during a riot at night, Levittown, Pennsylvania, 1979. (Glasshouse Images/Alamy Stock Photo)

The officers' success in restoring order was short-lived. The next day, about one hundred young people flocked to Five Points to continue the protests. They dragged an old sofa into the intersection and created a "beer-party atmosphere," as a local reporter put it, openly drinking alcohol and smoking weed.[106] At one point, revelers pushed an old Ford Torino into the intersection and set it ablaze. They did the same to a van parked at one of the gas stations, which a small group had looted and trashed. Someone poured stolen motor oil onto the car fire, which erupted into a cloud of smoke.

The scene had become a "combat zone," according to reporters, and now a sizable police force, swathed in riot gear, joined the fray. Swinging their billy clubs, they bashed dozens of people, many of them bystanders only there to watch the action. Officers stopped cars inching through the intersection, smashing their windshields and pulling drivers onto the street. This time, police arrested 120 people while sending another one hundred, including some police officers, to the hospital. The next night, with a curfew in place, the protests subsided, though not completely. For days, passing motorists and their passengers rolled down their windows and yelled, "You pig" at the police.[107]

The "Levittown Gas Riots," as journalists dubbed them, made national news. Interviews and letters to the editor revealed much sympathy for the truckers. A twenty-one-year-old man interviewed by the local paper said he opposed the crowd's vandalism but added, "Gas protests may be the only way the federal government would pay attention to the average people. . . . If this is what we have to do, we have to do it." Another interviewee worried about heating her home the following winter, while a third lambasted Pennsylvania governor Dick Thornburgh, who she said "couldn't care less for the people and the problems and hardship [politicians] cause." One Levittowner wrote to the local *Courier Times* saying the country should be "shut down" for a day to show the government "how angry we are" and that "we're tired of being robbed and we won't stand for it anymore."[108]

Such populist anger helps account for the failure of President Jimmy Carter's bid for reelection in 1980 and the rise of Reaganite conservatism. A fair number of Levittowners became "Reagan Democrats." But as a community, Levittown managed to weather the catastrophic job losses of the 1970s and 1980s. People grew accustomed to two-income households and lower-paid employment in the service sector—big box stores, hospitals and medical centers, school districts, and government—now the largest source of jobs in Bucks County.[109] Houses in the development remain affordable to working- and lower-middle-class families, although many struggle. Longtime Levittowners find the community less child-centered and less neighborly than before. Memories of difficult times remain.

Anita Getz's family arrived toward the end of Levitt's building spree in the Pennsylvania development.[110] They came to Levittown because they thought West Philadelphia was becoming unsafe and the schools were declining. Their longtime Jewish neighborhood was attracting African American families, and the Jews were leaving en masse. In Levittown, Anita loved the public pool in summer and ice skating on Lake Caroline in winter. She hung out with the many kids on her street and stayed outside in every season until the streetlights came on. Not everything about growing up in Levittown was good: she found herself bullied at school, mainly for being Jewish. But those memories faded, and after she and her husband, also a child of Levittown, had lived for a time in northern Pennsylvania, she said to him, "Let's go home." They bought the house that had belonged to her best friend's parents. Anita knows lots of people who are moving back to Levittown. You can still buy a good house for not too much money.

But they returned to a different place. There are far fewer young kids and more older adults like Anita. The surrounding areas have become densely commercialized, and the stores and restaurants she knew growing up have been replaced with big box outlets and chain eateries. The malls have emptied out. There are fewer Jews in Levittown, and both synagogues have moved to new, more elaborate facilities for congregations that are dispersed around Lower Bucks County. Each year, Anita hesitates to put a lighted menorah in her window during Hanukkah but ends up doing it anyway. Despite the changes, she still enjoys Levittown and plans to stay, but not permanently: she and her husband will eventually retire and move to Florida.

4 The Racial Explosion

"NIGGERS HAVE MOVED into Levittown," the mailman yelled up and down Deepgreen Lane. He'd just learned that Bill and Daisy Myers, an African American couple, had bought the house at number forty-three. It was August 1957, and no Blacks had ever lived in the community. Within hours, a huge crowd of angry white Levittowners gathered outside the Myers home. Soon they began screaming epithets and hurling rocks. Several crashed through the front picture windows, the shards covering the floor. When Bristol Township police officers finally showed up, they found themselves unable to contain the mob. After the protesters returned for a second day and again could not be dispersed, the sheriff telegraphed the Pennsylvania State Police, writing, "The citizens of Levittown are out of control."[1]

In the spring and summer of 1957, Daisy and Bill Myers, like thousands of other young couples, were looking to buy a house they could afford. They had two small children plus a newborn and needed three bedrooms and a yard. Bill, a veteran of World War II, held a degree from a Virginia university and earned a modest but steady income as a refrigeration technician at a firm in Trenton, New Jersey. Daisy, also a college graduate, was a schoolteacher before taking leave to start her family. Bill and Daisy had met in Virginia in 1948 and married two years later.

Bill wanted to live close to his job, and Levittown, Pennsylvania, was just six miles away. After living in a mostly Black enclave in Bristol

Township, the Myerses fell in love with a Levittowner almost identical to the one I grew up in. Even the gray-streaked asbestos siding was the same. The house faced the street horizontally, four rooms wide and two rooms deep, and featured a rectangle of six large picture windows that extended from floor to ceiling and allowed the summer light to illuminate the open interior. There was just one problem: Levittown had been conceived as an all-white community, catering to young families eager for a suburban life free of urban ills and offering racial exclusivity on the cheap.

In 1957, when the Myerses looked into Levittown, Bill Levitt was still building new houses—the development would be finished a year later—and still instructing his sales agents to ignore people like Daisy and Bill. Their only possibility was to buy a "used" house from an individual homeowner rather than the Levitt company, but even this was next to impossible. There was huge community pressure not to let Black people in.

This pressure made life increasingly difficult for Philadelphia's rapidly growing African American population. By the late 1950s, the postwar housing shortage had been alleviated for whites but had become, if anything, even worse for Blacks. It was a nationwide problem, but particularly bad in and around Philadelphia. Between 1946 and 1953, only three-tenths of 1 percent of new homes built in the region were available for African Americans to buy.[2] The 140,000 new dwellings built in these years, epitomized by Levittown, went up almost entirely in the three suburban counties surrounding Philadelphia and its suburb-like northeastern fringes—all places that, with few exceptions, barred Black homeowners. The new developments enabled white people to escape the city's cramped, increasingly run-down dwellings, while Blacks found themselves confined to redlined urban neighborhoods or, at best, to modest row houses in somewhat more prosperous areas being abandoned by whites. As long as Philadelphia remained an industrial town with decent jobs for African Americans, these formerly white-owned homes gave Black Philadelphians a relatively high homeownership rate.[3]

But this wouldn't last. In the early 1950s, city-based industries began packing up and following the new housing developments to the suburbs. New companies coming into the area set up shop outside the city, as U.S. Steel did with its huge Fairless Works. With manufacturers shunning the city and suburban developments closed to Blacks, many found themselves unemployed; in the mid-1950s, the jobless rate for African Americans in some parts of the city reached 40 percent. These neighborhoods sank into poverty, their inhabitants crowded into homes whose number could not increase. With persistent unemployment, the tax base shriveled, leaving growing numbers of African Americans with underfunded schools and evaporating city services.[4]

Under these circumstances, it was crucial to make suburban housing available to African Americans near where jobs were available, and the NAACP devoted a great deal of time and effort in the 1950s to making this happen.[5] The urban historian Thomas Sugrue has argued that "the battle against housing discrimination—in Levittown and elsewhere—was perhaps the most consequential of the entire history of civil rights in America."[6] No objective, except perhaps school integration, was clearer to the NAACP than this, which is why it had already focused on ending housing discrimination more than a decade before the Myerses began looking for a suburban home.

In 1945, at the NAACP's request, President Harry S. Truman had the FHA remove from its Underwriting Manual the model language for racially restrictive covenants that it had written for all properties with mortgages insured by the agency. Three years later, after the U.S. Supreme Court's *Shelley v. Kraemer* decision barring such covenants, the NAACP succeeded in having the FHA revise its regulations to say that it would not insure any mortgage on a property with a "recorded" racial covenant. The NAACP then asked that all relevant federal agencies refuse to insure mortgages on properties from which African Americans had been excluded in practice, even without explicit covenants. This the agencies refused to do. The NAACP then turned to Congress, but as an internal NAACP memorandum put it, "Innumerable attempts to get legislative edicts from the Congress protecting the rights of minorities to secure housing where there is some kind of governmental involvement have . . . failed." The government's inaction meant that "the racial restrictions imposed by real estate operators, home builders, mortgage financing institutions, property owners' associations, and prejudiced home owners . . . provide an almost insurmountable barrier to the minority group homeseeker."[7]

In the wake of this inaction, the NAACP and its allies in liberal organizations and the labor movement turned to grassroots organizing, followed by meetings with homebuilders. In December 1951, as building in Levittown, Pennsylvania, was getting underway, the NAACP attorney Constance Baker Motley organized a meeting with Bill Levitt and leaders of the United Steelworkers Union, the Philadelphia Housing Authority, and the Urban League. Levitt made it clear from the start that he hadn't changed his mind on integration. He would not, Motley said, "take a chance on admitting Negroes and then not be able to sell his houses." Union leaders proved more sympathetic to fairer housing opportunities but made no commitments. U.S. Steel executives, while also expressing sympathy, announced that the Fairless Hills housing development being built for their workers would likewise be an all-white community. In frustration, NAACP officials turned to President Eisenhower, Vice President Nixon, and Pennsylvania governor John Fine, arguing that Levitt's policies were undemocratic and un-American and gave America's Cold War enemies a propaganda advantage—all to no avail.[8]

The lone avenue left was the courts, and with Levittown, Pennsylvania, going up practically overnight, the NAACP's Legal Defense Fund, led by Motley and Thurgood Marshall, filed suit on behalf of six African American veterans who had been prevented from buying homes there. Their targets were Levitt and the administrators of the FHA and VA. The suit, filed in January 1955 in the U.S. District Court for Eastern Pennsylvania, argued that because the U.S. Supreme Court had invalidated racial covenants and the FHA and VA had revised their regulations accordingly, Levitt should be required by law to sell to Blacks. This was especially true in that his company depended on government-backed mortgages to market its homes— which meant, the NAACP attorneys maintained, that Levitt was being aided by the government to such an extent that "his action could be interpreted as the action of the federal government." Motley and Marshall also argued that because Levitt was building not only houses but roads, sewers, sidewalks, streetlights, schools, and parks, the company was creating a de facto city and thus acting as a representative of the Commonwealth of Pennsylvania. Levitt was therefore subject to the due process clause of the Fourteenth Amendment, which forbade racial discrimination. Levitt's attorneys countered with various technical and procedural arguments and denied that the company had anything to do with either the federal or state government.[9]

The court sided with Levitt. Reliance on FHA- and VA-insured loans, it ruled in March 1955, did not "result in making Levitt and Sons, Inc. of New York the government of the United States or a branch or agency of it, nor [is] the government of the United States the builder or developer of the Levittown project."[10] Levitt was a private entrepreneur, and laws and constitutional requirements that applied to governments did not apply to him. Moreover, "Neither the FHA nor the VA has been charged by Congress with the duty of preventing discrimination in the sales of housing project properties." The NAACP was therefore asking the court to make law, "which can only be done by Congress."[11] The NAACP had, of course, turned to the courts precisely because Congress and the president had refused to act. But the district court's ruling was so unequivocal that Motley and Marshall decided it would be futile to appeal.

The two attorneys turned instead to cases of discrimination in public housing where they had better chances to win. They kept an eye on Levittown but ceded the initiative for integration there to the Quakers, a religious group that had been active in Pennsylvania's antislavery and civil rights movements since the seventeenth century. Rather than force integration through the courts or legislation, Quakers wanted to gradually seed African American families into white communities. They hoped to show that whites and Blacks could live harmoniously together without making whites feel threatened by their efforts. They could assuage white fears, the Quakers thought, only if the Blacks who moved into places like Levittown seemed "inoffensive," meaning economically and culturally middle class. Quaker activists clearly brought their own class and racial prejudices into the effort to integrate Levittown, but beyond the NAACP, no group did more to open Levittown to Blacks. In 1952, the American Friends Service Committee (AFSC), the Quakers' activist arm, quietly began searching for white Levittown homeowners willing to sell to African Americans, and African Americans interested in buying into the development.[12]

The AFSC, together with the new Human Relations Council of Bucks County, allied itself with local liberals, leftists, and progressive religious congregations for the integration effort. The group included two well-known novelists who lived in Bucks County, James Michener and Pearl Buck. In a 1955 memo, Jane Reinheimer, director of the AFSC's Housing Opportunities Program, explained that her organization had "been concerned for some time with patterns of segregation in Levittown [and] wanted to secure the establishment of more open patterns."[13] The Quakers and their supporters had no trouble finding Levittown homeowners willing to sell to Blacks, but locating "acceptable" Blacks was much harder. One after another, those with the right attributes declined the Quakers' invitations. Some found the idea of moving into a potentially hostile white community too risky; others preferred living with Black neighbors, and still others found the financial challenges too daunting. Finally, after several years, the Quakers and their allies found Daisy and William Myers, who seemed perfect.

Daisy was born in 1925 and had grown up in a middle-class Black neighborhood in Richmond, Virginia. Her father held a steady job with the Richmond, Fredericksburg & Potomac Railroad, and like the teachers, mail carriers, doctors, and lawyers who lived there, her parents owned their home. In a book about her experiences in Levittown, she wrote that the family's personal circumstances were relatively comfortable, but life in Richmond was "all Jim Crow." All "public places, gatherings, and conveyances were segregated." She "attended segregated schools, rode in the back of the trolley, could not eat in most restaurants, or sit at food counters."[14] She enrolled in an all-Black college, Virginia Union College, majoring in sociology and education, and then taught in an all-Black school.

The world of Jim Crow was so utterly familiar that she "had not thought about the race problem while . . . growing up." She didn't fully realize how constrained she had been until she moved north to enroll in a graduate program at NYU. "New York was [a] breath of fresh air," a "Promised Land" where Blacks and whites freely associated with each other, and Blacks enjoyed freedoms unimaginable in Virginia. An illness in her family took her back to Richmond, where she enrolled in the Hampton Institute, now Hampton University, a historically Black institution whose most famous student was Booker T. Washington. She found a teaching job at a school on the Hampton campus, and there met Bill Myers, a native of York, Pennsylvania, who had come to Hampton on a basketball scholarship. Bill had served in Europe for two years during the war and briefly taught at Hampton after finishing his degree.[15]

Bill hated the Jim Crow regime, and although Daisy wanted to stay near her family in Virginia, the couple moved in 1951 to Bill's hometown, York, Pennsylvania. They tried to buy into a white neighborhood, were turned down, and eventually settled in a racially mixed part of town. Daisy found a job as a substitute teacher in an all-Black school and then was hired full-time as a social worker in a local agency. When her supervisor retired, the agency named her acting supervisor, but before long, Daisy said, she was asked to train an inexperienced white person for the supervisor's job. She quit and returned to teaching. When Bill lost his job in York, they decided to move to the Philadelphia area, where new opportunities seemed to beckon. They settled in Bristol Township's Bloomsdale Gardens, a Black enclave, and Bill found work in Trenton.[16]

Bloomsdale Gardens was perched on the edge of what would become Levittown, and as the development grew, the couple came to know it well. Daisy belonged to two organizations that often met there, the Levittown League of Women Voters and the Bristol Township Recreation Board, and both Bill and Daisy had friends and acquaintances in the community. They belonged to an "informal discussion group" run by Quakers, Daisy wrote in her memoir, and "it was at one of these meetings in the early spring of 1957 that the idea of moving to Levittown was first mentioned." Someone asked Bill, "Do you know a nice Negro couple that would like to move to Levittown?" "Pretty soon, Bill said, 'Why not us?' "[17]

At the time, Daisy and Bill didn't know that the Bucks County Human Relations Council had spent years looking for a Black family interested in moving to Levittown. Once the Myerses came forward, they were summoned to a series of meetings to look into their suitability. "They pried into our lives so extensively," Daisy wrote, "that one would wonder if they were going to *give* us a house instead of us having to buy it." Even after being "put through the third degree," she saw that some members of what she privately called the Committee to Discuss the Successful Move-In of a Negro Family remained hesitant. Perhaps various neighborhoods should be canvassed, someone suggested, to "see if a Negro family would be acceptable." Daisy and Bill shot that idea down: "We have always felt that Negroes have too long been expected to ask permission for what they deserve." Other committee members worried that a Myers move-in would produce panic selling, but that notion seemed strange to Daisy, since Levittown was "already integrated in a way": it included "Puerto Ricans,

American Indians, and Asians" as well as some mixed-race couples.[18] While she doubtless exaggerated the existing racial diversity, her belief on this score gave her hope that she and Bill wouldn't face too much opposition when they took possession of a Levittown house.

But first they needed to find a house for sale. One materialized when Irv Mandel paid a visit to his next-door neighbors, Bea and Lewis Wechsler, and asked if they would object to his offering his home, which had languished unsold on the market for two years, to a "Negro Realtor."[19] The Wechslers, as Mandel must have known, were not only unlikely to object but sure to embrace the idea. Before the war, they had been active in a variety of left-wing organizations, possibly including the American Communist Party. After the war, in which he had served overseas, Lew became an activist social worker; Bea had been a leader of the Bronx Tenants Council, which agitated for rent control and housing integration. When their second child was born, they decided to move to the suburbs and found Levittown, Pennsylvania, appealing. "We loved Levittown," Lew wrote. "With the trees and shrubs growing steadily, it looked beautiful. There were lots of other kids for ours to play with."[20] What troubled them about their new community was Levitt's unwillingness to sell to African Americans. Bea joined the Bucks County Human Relations Council to help remedy that situation, and Lew took an active role in the local Democratic Party.

Their activism made them aware of the effort to find Black families interested in Levittown, and white homeowners willing to sell to them.[21] They didn't, however, want to play too visible a role in that effort, for fear that amid the raging Cold War, opponents of integration would accuse them of communist subversion. But Mandel's proposal to sell to a Black family placed the Wechslers in the thick of the process. They met with the Quaker leaders spearheading the integration initiative and then with the Myerses. Since Mandel was unwell and living in Philadelphia, it was the Wechslers who showed Bill and Daisy the house. It was exactly what they wanted, and Lew agreed to broker the deal. But Mandel got cold feet, fearing that his father-in-law, for whom he worked, would fire him for selling to Blacks. Lew got the Quakers to assure Mandel that if he lost his job, they would find him another.

The only remaining issue was the down payment: about $2,000 against a purchase price of $12,150, the balance to be paid with an

FHA-backed mortgage loan. The Myerses didn't have $2,000, and several banks refused to lend it to them. Then, with the Quakers' help, the couple found a wealthy New York woman who agreed to advance them $1,500, with no interest and no deadline for repayment. This was enough, and Mandel and the Myerses readied the sale. To avoid stoking opposition, the protagonists agreed not to publicize the deal in advance, although Bill and Daisy told trusted friends about their impending move, and Quaker and other religious figures quietly prepared the way. On July 9, 1957, the Faith Reformed Church held a panel discussion on "Fair Housing in Bucks County" at which attendees were asked how they would react to a Black family moving in next door. No one said they would use violence to oppose it, but no one seemed eager to have a Black family close by.

Although Quaker leaders had been trying for years to find a Black family to break Levittown's color bar, the American Friends Service Committee did not play any official role in the deal.[22] Two members of the Falls (Quaker) Meeting, Samuel Snipes and Peter von Blum, helped plan the logistics of the move, but were not involved in the sale itself. The two men wrote that they deliberately kept the AFSC and the Bucks County Human Relations Council out of the picture, believing that at least one key figure in these organizations "would not be helpful" (emphasis original), especially "if things became tense." Now that a Black move-in was actually happening, it seems that certain leaders were having second thoughts. Daisy Myers thought the same thing. Von Blum and Snipes had more confidence in the Council of Churches and in the ministers with whom they had discussed the Myerses' move in advance; these ministers, they believed, were "ready to play a helpful role."[23]

That help would be crucial in the days to come. Shortly after the mailman alerted neighbors on August 13, 1957, that a Black family now lived on their street, groups of people began to congregate in front of the Myers house. More arrived when the afternoon paper, the *Levittown Times*, landed on residents' lawns with the headline, "First Negro Family Moves into Levittown."[24] Alarmed, Lew Wechsler went outside to gauge the situation. He heard one disturbing comment after another: "The NAACP bought the house for the nigger as a test case" and "No one wants them here; let's drive them out." Wechsler told one man, "The Myerses have the same right to buy a house as I do." The neighbor responded angrily, "You should be ashamed of yourself! Our houses are worth only half of what they were yesterday." Lew heard the line about plummeting value repeated, and as more people arrived, the crowd grew agitated. One of his friends urged him to go back inside, saying, "It could get rough here."[25]

By early evening, one hundred or so cars from outside the neighborhood had glided in and parked on streets surrounding the Myers home at 43 Deepgreen Lane. One man knocked on the Myerses' door and demanded to know who had sold them the house and why they had bought it. Bill declined to answer. As the crowd continued to grow, Bill and Daisy packed their three children into their car and drove back to their old home in Bloomsdale Gardens, accompanied by a police car summoned to assist them.[26] Some of their supporters stayed in the house to protect the property and monitor the protests. By eleven thirty p.m., the crowd had grown to at least two hundred—some news reports said five hundred—and stones began to fly toward the Myers house, shattering two of the six front picture windows. Just before midnight, fifteen Bristol Township police officers arrived. They tried to move protesters away from the house, and when some resisted, officers began making arrests.[27] "We went there to uphold the tenets of the laws," police chief John R. Stewart later told reporters, "and to disperse the crowd which had become a boisterous and milling mob."[28] The crowd finally dissipated in the wee hours.

The following day, August 14, the press arrived en masse. The Human Relations Council of Bucks County tried to use them to calm Levittown residents. Its chairman, Reverend William Warren, said the Myerses were simply "average, middle class citizens like the rest of us." Although many residents worried that their presence would change the character of the community, he added, "It is extremely unlikely that Negroes will ever move into Levittown in large numbers." Levittown, Long Island, had just fourteen Black families a decade after its founding, so "it is both illogical and unsound to believe that neighborhoods in Levittown will change in the same manner that they have in parts of Philadelphia." The Myers family, in other words, would not compromise Levittown's standing as a white community. This statement, while sympathetic to Bill and Daisy, hardly served as a wholehearted endorsement of integration, but it was consistent with the Quakers' efforts to find "suitable" African American families for Levittown. Just not too many of them.[29]

Police officers inspect the Myerses' shattered front window. (Special Collections Research Center, Temple University Libraries, Philadelphia, Pennsylvania)

Journalists streaming into Levittown noted Warren's words. Those from the Philadelphia papers—the *Evening Bulletin, Inquirer,* and *Daily News*—arrived first, along with reporters for African American journals. The national and international press soon followed, as did television cameras and film crews. The racial "incident" in Levittown became a media sensation, focused on the individuals involved—the Myerses, their most visible opponents, police officers, and key politicians. Daisy and Bill were photographed extensively inside their new home or standing in front. These pictures show a young, light-skinned African American couple, pleasant-looking and unexceptional. Daisy is modestly dressed in a light-colored blouse and dark skirt. She's wearing glasses, her hair pulled back and away from her face. She is stout in the middle, having just given birth to her third child. Bill is tall and thin, with short hair and a small moustache. It's summer, and he's wearing a white polo shirt and light-gray pants.

Daisy and Bill Myers. (Special Collections Research
Center, Temple University Libraries, Philadelphia,
Pennsylvania)

Journalists mostly interviewed Bill, although it became clear that
Daisy was the more experienced public speaker. When asked why he
moved to Levittown, Bill responded straightforwardly: "I feel that I
have the right to live where I choose. I selected my Levittown home
because it fits my family."[30] He denied being "sponsored" by the
NAACP, as his opponents falsely claimed, and presented himself and
his wife as an ordinary couple with no agenda except to have a normal life.

A normal life in Levittown is precisely what the growing number of
protesters didn't want the Myerses to have. When they returned to
their new home around four thirty p.m. on Wednesday, their second
day in possession of the dwelling, they were greeted by another crowd

of protesters who had been there since the morning.[31] More than one thousand cars cruised through the neighborhood, many times more than the usual number. So many cars came in that earlier, at three thirty, police officers had closed all entrances to Dogwood Hollow, the Levittown section surrounding the Myerses' street. But by then, so many people had parked in the area that the crowd again swelled to several hundred. It grew even larger after the police withdrew at nine p.m. Officers soon returned to disperse them. They arrested two for disorderly conduct after they ran from house to house trying to keep the protest going.

Around ten p.m., two groups of about one hundred people each, having been ordered by police to leave Dogwood Hollow, converged on the emergency meeting of the Bristol Township Commissioners then underway. Members of both groups demanded that the commissioners "do something" to prevent the Myerses from taking possession of a Levittown house and remaining in the community. When the commissioners responded that they lacked the authority to do that, protesters shouted them down and made such a ruckus that the meeting could not continue. It adjourned at eleven p.m. With the ranks of protesters at the Myers home continuing to grow, the Bristol Township police chief and commissioners instructed the county sheriff to wire the governor requesting the intervention of the state police. "Chief of police says the citizens in Levittown are out of control," the telegram began, and he requested "the aid of the state police." The local police, the sheriff added, could not contain the crowd, which had stormed into the commissioners' meeting and "made threats against the Constitution . . . and say they are going to take things in their own hands if [the commissioners] do not act." A mass meeting was about to take place, and the sheriff feared "there will be real trouble after the meeting." Only the "presence of the state police" could ensure that the anti-Myers protests "can be quelled without blood shed [sic]."[32]

The state police moved in quickly, but they struggled to control the mounting number of protesters. Shortly after the troopers arrived, Myers opponents burned a cross in front of the Walt Disney Elementary School, a short distance from the family's new home. The flaming cross was eight feet high and made of bamboo and rags soaked in kerosine. Meanwhile, hundreds of protesters spent the hot August evening in a continuous "picket line" in front of the house. Some of the picketers left the area to join a hastily called meeting intended to pressure the Myerses to leave. Some six hundred people gathered in the parking lot of the Veterans of Foreign Wars building after they were prevented from coming inside.

James Newell, an electrician and Levittown resident who had helped organize the meeting, emerged as the leader of the group, which named itself the Levittown Betterment Committee. Newell was a large, imposing man with a rugged face and military-style flattop haircut. A widely reprinted photograph shows him from behind, towering over a densely packed crowd, his hands in the air holding up an improvised megaphone. In the face of calls to "burn them out," Newell advocated "peaceful and legal" methods to get the family to leave, although he was unclear what those methods would be. A groundswell of voices shouted down one participant's proposal that the residents of the Myerses' neighborhood take a vote on whether the family should stay or leave. The group then endorsed by acclamation a ten-member executive committee named and led by Newell. The committee's first act was to assign several people to go house-to-house, collecting signatures on a petition to oust the African American family. Reverend Ray L. Harwick, who would soon lead the pro-Myers group, witnessed Newell's meeting and described it as "an atmosphere of hate."[33]

The Myerses held firm. "I still intend to move in as soon as the house is ready," Bill told reporters. He added, though, that "if I feel there is some danger involved, I might have to reconsider."[34] He had reason to be concerned. With reporters besieging the house and phone calls, mostly hostile, coming in day and night, the couple would need experienced help to defend them and help them shape the story they wanted to tell.

On the second day of agitation, Stephen J. Remsen, who directed the Philadelphia branch of the Jewish Labor Committee (JLC), received a call from the regional director of the AFL-CIO, to which the JLC belonged, urging him to install himself in Levittown and help organize the pro-Myers forces. The JLC's mission was to help trade unionists combat "job discrimination, segregation, and intolerance."[35] Arriving at the Myers home, Remsen "found a mob against the move-in and a wonderful group of completely disorganized do-gooders decrying the violence against the Myers family."[36] Remsen immediately

James Newell, leader of the Levittown Betterment Committee, harangues an anti-Myers crowd. (Special Collections Research Center, Temple University Libraries, Philadelphia, Pennsylvania)

began organizing them into a pro-Myers Citizen Committee for Levittown. Meeting at the William Penn Center, the Quakers' historical home, the group issued a statement expressing "regret" over "the unfortunate action directed as a protest against the arrival of the William Myers family," and asserting that "racial and religious bigotry have no place in our community."[37]

The statement was a start, Remsen said, but he worried that there was no full-time professional "public relations man," saying, "The irresponsible elements of course are news. The decent people are not."[38] Together, Remsen and Tom Colgan of the American Friends Service Committee pushed aside "certain elements we did not care for [who] were counselling the Myers family." Next, the two men "pressured the people who were suspect as either communists, crackpots, or controversial to get out of the picture." Remsen was doubtless referring to Lewis Wechsler. After spending time with Bill Myers, he and Colgan decided Bill "is definitely not a Commie." It's extraordinary that anyone could have thought he was, but Cold War paranoia was such that even he had to be cleared. Another Jewish organizer, Albert Vorspan of the Union of American Hebrew Congregations (UAHC), an arm of Reform Judaism dedicated to liberal causes, ran a security check not only on Bill and Daisy but on both sets of their parents, ultimately declaring all of them "absolutely 'clean.' "[39] Remsen and Vorspan clearly believed that even a hint of radicalism would have made the Myerses impossible to defend.

Once the Myerses were declared "clean," Remsen tried to line up support for the family from local labor unions but had "a terrible time." The union leaders and members "were some of the most irresponsible lilly-white [sic] mobsters." Finding that no one wanted to side publicly with the family, Remsen asked national union leaders, who were much more sympathetic to integration, to put pressure on them. This effort succeeded to some extent, especially with the United Steelworkers, which published a strong statement against racial violence and for the Myerses' right to live where they chose. Remsen claimed that after this statement was issued, several union members who had participated in the protests dropped out.[40]

One obstacle to lining up support for the family was the refusal by the editor of the *Bristol Daily Courier and Levittown Times,* the widely read local paper, to criticize the anti-Myers protesters or even oppose their violence, cross-burnings, and harassment. The *Trenton Evening Times,* also read in Levittown, did editorialize in favor of the Myerses' right to live in the community and against their neighbors' racial prejudice, which the paper called "Levittown's Shame," writing: "This demonstration of racial antagonism reveals an unseemly and repulsive aspect of life in a community whose people enjoy many superior advantages. Something better in the way of tolerance was to be expected of them. Instead, several hundred men, women, and children gathered at midnight to stone the home of a man and his family of whom they know nothing except their color, which they do not like."[41]

The Philadelphia papers mostly echoed these sentiments, as did the African American press around the country. Meanwhile, the pro- and anti-Myers forces continued to organize themselves, with the latter developing a far stronger presence. At best, the Citizens Committee of Levittown mustered seventy-five people at its meetings, while the anti-Myers Levittown Betterment Committee consistently drew between five hundred and 1,200 to their boisterous outdoor gatherings. The

Citizens Committee was by far the more timid of the two, arguing that the Myerses had the right to live in Levittown, but failing to take an unequivocal stand in favor of integrating the community. This was doubtless because such a stance was unpopular—even within the Citizens Committee, some believed in "separate but equal" housing for whites and Blacks.[42] Perhaps more important, many of those who supported the Myerses' right to live in the community kept their views to themselves. "We never received widespread community support from the silent sympathizers," Daisy wrote. Their "default gave the impression that the masses of Levittowners were behind the actions of the Betterment group."[43]

The Betterment Committee, by contrast, made its opposition to racial integration perfectly clear. "We the citizens and home owners of Levittown, Pa," read its petition, signed by hundreds, "protest the mixing of Negroes in our previously all white community. . . . Negroes have an equal opportunity to build their own community of equal value and beauty without intermingling in our community."[44] African Americans, of course, had no such equal opportunity because virtually all government-backed mortgages went to white homebuyers. The only dissension within the anti-Myers ranks was over the use of violence. Most of those who attended Betterment meetings backed Newell's call to oust the Myers by "legal" means, but a minority wanted to go further. One protester threatened to "shoot [Bill] down on sight."[45] And even as he rejected violence, Newell encouraged his followers to keep up the pressure on the Myers family by boycotting merchants and delivery people who served them and by gathering in large numbers outside their house, setting up the possibility, even the likelihood, of clashes with the police. Newell also did nothing to discourage the harassing phone calls and letters that jangled the Myerses' nerves day and night.

Those opposed to the Myerses believed they had the right to live in a "closed community," and that by moving into Levittown, Daisy and Bill Myers had violated this right. Members of the Betterment Committee maintained that the presence of even a single African American family reduced their property values, because like Bill Levitt, they thought white people would no longer want to buy into the community. "Every time I look at [Bill Myers]," one of his neighbors said, "I see $2,000 drop off the value of my house."[46] Such views were grounded in racist stereotypes, but Myers opponents were doubtless right to worry about their home values. If many white people decided to flee the community, prices would drop as the supply of available dwellings went up and demand from potential white buyers went down. In the 1950s, most white homebuyers did not want to live in an integrated development, however minimal the presence of African Americans. Their choices were shaped both by anti-Black prejudice and a rational assessment of the real estate market.

Although the Betterment Committee noted the fears about property values, it focused more on general white worries about living among Black neighbors. It issued a statement urging readers to ask "residents in any suburb . . . why they left negro [sic] sections in Philadelphia. These people and Mr. Myers agree that white communities are preferable to Negro. . . . We want to protect our families and bring our children up in a trouble-free community."[47] One member of the Betterment Committee told a reporter that people didn't want African Americans in Levittown "because of all the crime and violence that happens where colored people live."[48] Behind such statements was the fear of losing the status they believed they had gained by living in an all-white community. Becoming a Levittown homeowner represented upward mobility; but if Blacks moved in, their white neighbors would no longer be upwardly mobile. As one of the Myerses' neighbors put it, "A lot of people moved to Levittown to get away from colored people."[49]

Many expressed their anger and hostility directly to the Myerses in letters and phone calls. In her memoir, Daisy mainly acknowledged the great many supportive letters and calls she and Bill received, but Lew Wechsler's account quotes many of the ugly letters in full. One letter read: "I am yet to see a colert [sic] person ever to indanger [sic] himself in defense of a Jew. Now I can see why the Jew is hated, they do not stick to [their] own. . . . It is about time that they wake up and mind there [sic] own business. . . . The collard [sic] have more land and wealth than any other people, unless we try to keep our identity we will be swalowd [sic] up by them."[50] Another missive, addressed to "Mr. Lewis (I love Niggers) Wechsler," expressed the fears of miscegenation that surfaced after the Myers family arrived. "I only hope as long as you like them, someday the nigger Mr. Myers [sic] son falls in love with you daughter and she has a nigger baby then you can all be one happy family."[51] While most of the nastiest material came anonymously by mail, Lew heard some of it voiced directly. You are "nigger-loving Jew bastards," one protester said to his face. This, he wrote, "was quite a shock; we had not had a hint of anti-Semitism in the four years we have lived in the neighborhood."[52]

Protesters led by Newell maintained a nearly continuous presence in front of the family's home. A photo in the *Philadelphia Bulletin* shows people standing shoulder-to-shoulder, four deep, across the narrow street from the residence. Children are sitting in front, with the adults behind them. A half-dozen police officers, stationed on the Myerses' front lawn, face the crowd.[53] On Saturday, August 17, with the protests showing no sign of subsiding after four days, Bristol Township officials decided to ban all gatherings of more than two people, and the Pennsylvania State Police, now in charge of the situation, told Newell that no large outdoor gatherings would be permitted near the Myers home. The Betterment leader gave this information to the six hundred protesters gathered there that evening, but instead of dispersing, they paraded slowly past the dwelling. State troopers tried to keep them moving, and when some balked, the officers prodded them with their batons. One man became unruly, and a trooper bashed him with his nightstick. A news photographer captured the incident; his photograph, published the following day, showed a blood-soaked protester being taken into custody, the eighth to be arrested since the protests began.[54]

Although most physical violence had come from the police, one priest used his Sunday sermons to "regret exceedingly" that "Levittown citizens have used violence in an attempt to settle the dispute over the William Myers family's residence in Levittown." A Presbyterian minister expressed "disappointment and concern over the reported disorder," while the Congregationalist pastor urged "calmness and peace." The clergymen focused on violence and disorder rather than the underlying issue of racial integration, which no one advocated from the pulpit that Sunday.[55]

At the start of their second week in Levittown, Bill and Daisy still hadn't spent a night in their new home. They would sleep there for the first time that Monday night, August 19. Remsen of the Jewish Labor Committee and Colgan of the AFSC moved in with them and would remain overnight as witnesses and friends.[56] Bill and Daisy had

Crowds gather in front of the Myerses' home to protest their presence.
(Special Collections Research Center, Temple University Libraries, Philadelphia,
Pennsylvania)

kept their month-old infant with them but sent their two oldest children to stay with relatives in York until the protests calmed down. But they only intensified. On Monday, some four hundred people defied Bristol Township's ban on gatherings of three or more and parked themselves in front of the Myers home, yelling and cheering.

With dozens of reporters, TV cameramen, and newsreel photographers thronging their home demanding interviews, Colgan, an experienced public relations professional, organized a press conference for Monday evening. Major local and national newspapers and TV networks were represented, and although it is unclear whether foreign journalists were present, European and Latin American outlets covered the Levittown strife and decried the bigotry on display. *Pravda*, happy to publicize any example of American racism, joined the barrage of criticism from abroad.[57]

At the press conference, Bill did most of the talking, with his wife, Remsen, and Colgan standing by. Myers told the press, "I intend

to stay in my Levittown home unless there are unforeseen developments." He didn't say what those might be. "All I want is a chance to
be a good neighbor." He emphasized his status as a veteran and asserted that, like any American, he had the "right to live where I
choose." He had bought the house in a private transaction with the
previous owner, who had put the property on the market, and he
claimed to have benefitted from no outside support or financing. This
was true in that the AFSC had not brokered the sale, as it later would
for other Levittown houses involving African American buyers. But
Bill neglected to mention that he and Daisy had been vetted by the organization, or that Lewis Wechsler had arranged for the sale and
helped secure some of the financing. As for the protests, then in their
seventh day, Bill said that they had caused his family a "great strain,"
but that the ban on meetings was unjust. "They certainly have a right
to meet, as I have a right to live where I choose." Daisy then stepped
up to the microphone to thank the many people who had offered their
support and magnanimously expressed her belief that "the crowds
gathering outside are not indicative of the feeling of most of the people in Levittown."[58]

The Levittown Civic Association, a local organization that predated
the Myers affair, proposed to test Daisy's belief by conducting a poll of
Levittown residents to see how many wanted the family to stay. It
doesn't seem to have done the poll, but it did hold a debate at a local
high school over the Myerses' right to be in the community—suggesting that the anti-Myers position could be valid. As they had done
from the beginning, members of the Betterment Committee dominated
the debate, turning the session into yet another protest against the
Myers family.[59]

Meanwhile, the crowd that had gathered near the Myers home
clashed with state police officers trying to disperse them. Protesters
began to throw stones at the troopers, hitting one of them and knocking
him to the ground. The two dozen officers then waded into the throng,
bashing people with their clubs. One woman collapsed in shock, and a
man had his head split open. As officers began making arrests, people
chanted, "Gestapo," "Brutes," "Dictators," "Women beaters," and,
"This is America!" Even with troopers wielding their clubs, several
dozen demonstrators refused to leave the area, remaining there until
nearly two a.m.[60]

The following day, James H. Paul, the self-proclaimed Republican leader (other Republicans disputed the label) of Falls Township, published an extraordinary quarter-page paid advertisement in the local newspaper. Entitled "Protest," the ad denounced "the vicious outburst of brutality brought upon the people by the Pennsylvania State Police Troopers in . . . a peaceful demonstration against the invasion of our community by the Negro." In Paul's view, the police and the Myers family were entirely to blame for the unrest. His statement concluded by addressing "Mr. Myers" directly: "Look around you at the violence and disruptions in a once peaceful suburban community caused by your moving here—and go back where you came from."[61] Although Levittown was trending Democratic, this raw statement starkly expressed a significant hostility among white Levittowners, Democrats and Republicans alike, to the prospect of including African Americans among them. So did another paid advertisement a few days later: "Many people in Levittown have indicated that one of the major factors considered in reaching a decision to buy here was the all white population. Let us keep it that way."[62]

With no reliable polls, we don't know how pro- and anti-Myers opinion broke down, or what percentage of community members were indifferent to the situation. What's clear is that the anti-Myers forces mobilized their supporters far more effectively than their opponents, and that the Betterment Committee and its allies successfully created a rumor mill that was damaging to Daisy and Bill. Those rumors were evident in a short documentary by Dan Dodson, an NYU sociologist, shot during the Myers strife.[63] Dodson interviewed about a dozen people on camera, all of whom, whether pro- or anti-Myers, testified to the omnipresent rumors. The main one was that outside groups—the NAACP, the communists, and the Jews—had backed the Myerses in a deliberate attempt to force integration on a community opposed to it. Another rumor held that Bill and Daisy were "professional integrators" who had forced themselves on other all-white neighborhoods. Still another claimed that Bill actually worked as a dishwasher, not as a refrigeration engineer, as the pro-integration forces claimed.

Beyond these rumors, those among Dodson's interviewees who opposed the Myerses were all sure that their presence would reduce property values and that integration would inevitably lead to mixed marriages and miscegenation. "The whole trouble with this integration business," a thirtysomething woman told Dodson, "is that, in the end, they probably will end up with mixing socially. Their aim is mixed marriages and becoming equal with the whites." Another woman warned that if Blacks and whites "live near each, they're not going to think anything of marrying together." Pretty soon, said another, "My neighbor will be having a Negro son-in-law or daughter-in-law." It was the fear of such mixing that moved these people to choose Levittown. "One of the main reasons I moved there," said one woman, "is because it was a white community."[64]

Dodson doesn't say how he chose his interview subjects, so we have no idea how representative they were. It seems likely, though, that those who spoke on camera represented the opposing sides reasonably well. As for Dodson himself, his narration made clear that his objective in making the film was to foster integration, and he created an information packet to accompany the film so that teachers could use it effectively in their classrooms, and community organizers in their neighborhoods.[65] Dodson made no pretense of objectivity; he wanted to change hearts and minds.

So did the Jews and Quakers who had resolved to help the Myerses. Vorspan of the Union of American Hebrew Congregations joined Remsen and Colgan in the public relations effort for Bill and Daisy, who were besieged by the media and inexperienced in dealing with journalists. "It is impossible," Vorspan reported, "to describe the pressures of newspapers, magazines, television, radio, etc. upon us: we served as the buffers between the mass media and the Myers family." Concerned that reporters were too focused on "the drama of the mob," he wanted to change the subject. "My primary effort was . . . to shift the focus of attention from the mobs to the positive developments and forces, including the support of all three faith groups, the work of the Citizens Committees, the kindness displayed to the Myers by many families right in Levittown." But given the superior numbers of the anti-Myers forces and the daily drama of their demonstrations and clashes with the police, Vorspan admitted to being only "partly successful."[66] The pro-Myers activists, small in number and mostly limited to discussion and debate, just weren't very newsworthy. Still, as a representative of a major Jewish organization, Vorspan was proud of the Jews' role in supporting the Myerses. He quoted Reverend Harwick, head of the pro-Myers Citizens Committee of Levittown, as admonishing his congregation—most of whom took the other side—that the "best Christians in town are the Jews." Vorspan recognized, however, that Levittown's racial strife had led to "a sharpening of inter-faith lines and divisions," with Jews and Quakers on one side and Catholics on the other. "The newspapermen who visited the homes near the Myers found the fiercest bigotry in Catholic homes, the most support of Myers in Jewish homes."[67] Even so, Catholic clergymen publicly supported the Myerses' right to live in Levittown, as did their Protestant counterparts, although few Christians other than Quakers came out publicly in favor of integration.

Meanwhile, the anti-Myers protests showed no sign of subsiding, although not everyone came to Dogwood Hollow with the intention of pushing the family out. Some were curious and wanted to observe the situation firsthand. Robert King, age fourteen in August 1957, rode his bike across town to take a look.

> We heard about those riots going on, and we went down there. We were on an adjacent street. It was pretty intense. An awful thing. I remember it was a pretty good crowd. Of all kinds. Police began to disperse the crowd. I was standing between two houses. Policeman saw a number of us standing there and went running toward us. I ran my butt off, running through backyards. Some zigs and zags. And I got to the next street over. There was a couple standing there, and they saw me running. The woman said, "Get in the house." I went in the house until it quieted down. And I said thank you very much.[68]

The couple was rightly worried about the boy's safety. On Tuesday of the Myerses' second week in their new home, the state police decided to keep protesters away from the residence. Troopers took up positions along the curb of Haines Road, a through-street two blocks from the house, and refused to let the crowd surge across the road toward Deepgreen Lane. The officers also stopped every driver who tried to enter Dogwood Hollow, allowing only those who lived in the section to proceed. These traffic stops produced verbal clashes and two arrests.

After darkness fell and troopers continued to prevent protesters from moving toward the Myers home, the crowd's hostility grew more intense. By nine p.m., protesters formed "a solid wall across

Officer Thomas Stewart crumples to the ground after being hit in the head by a rock. (Special Collections Research Center, Temple University Libraries, Philadelphia, Pennsylvania)

Haines Road, stretching at least 50 yards long and about five persons deep."[69] At nine thirty, the crowd surged toward the row of twenty-five officers wielding billy clubs. When the troopers pushed them back, rocks began to fly. One hit state police sergeant Thomas Stewart just above his right ear. He crumpled to the ground unconscious. A close-up photograph published in the *Bristol Daily Courier* shows him flat on his back, his arms stretched out to the side. His eyes appear to be closed. His hat lies upside down next to him. A *Philadelphia Bulletin* photo shows him lying hatless on the ground, with one arm covering the wound on his head. Another officer stands over him, still holding his club.[70]

Seeing the officer fall to the ground, the protesters took off, with the rest of the troopers giving chase. No one was caught, and no further arrests were made. Stewart was rushed to the hospital, where doctors diagnosed him with a concussion and sewed up his lacerated ear. The felling of an officer moved the state police to ban all further gatherings near the Myers home. Reporters were also kept away, and Bill and Daisy announced that they would give no more interviews or press conferences. Newell, for his part, condemned the stone-throwing but promised to hold a meeting the following evening to keep his movement going.[71]

As Newell searched for a place to gather—a local fire company had refused the use of its facility—the police tightened its cordon around the Myerses' section. For the first time in nine days, no protesters gathered nearby. But those hostile to the Myerses announced their continued presence by burning a cross—the second since the family's arrival—in front of a local elementary school.[72] Denied a meeting place, Newell agreed to debate Reverend Harwick during a regular meeting of the Kiwanis Club, a popular service organization. My father, who belonged to the club, witnessed the debate and left it all the more convinced that the Myerses had the right to live in Levittown and should be left alone.[73] This was also the position of our family's rabbi, William Fierverker, who linked his Conservative synagogue with the other Jewish organizations advocating for the family. Fierverker drafted a resolution supporting the Myerses, which was endorsed by the 450-member congregation over the objections of "a small, opposition minority."[74]

The rabbi's resolution didn't urge the integration of Levittown, and it's unclear whether such a resolution would have passed. The pro-Myers forces believed the family had the right to live in Levittown, but they most likely assumed—and probably desired—that the development remain mostly white. At the Kiwanis Club meeting, Harwick said the Citizens Committee of Levittown had "adopted a completely neutral stand on integration" and simply wanted "to achieve an atmosphere that will permit rational discussion of the issue." Newell said he was all for rational discussion and wanted a "peaceful solution," but peace would "only be achieved when Mr. Myers gets out of Levittown." Even a single Black family was one too many. The Betterment Committee leader claimed he harbored no prejudice and that, growing up in Durham, North Carolina, he had been "close friends with many Negroes." But he claimed to know that Blacks lowered property values and that "82 per cent of the unwed mothers in Philadelphia are Negroes." He also said he had taken a poll in one section of Levittown (he would not say which one) and found that 97 percent wanted the Myers family out of the community. Getting them to leave, he added, "would discourage other Negroes in the future."[75]

By Wednesday, August 21, with the police having stopped the mass protests, the anti-Myers forces turned to other tactics. They launched a rumor that the NAACP had given the Myerses $18,000 to buy their house, a notion that Bill, along with the NAACP, categorically denied.[76] During a press conference Wednesday evening, as he dismissed the rumor, Bill added that some people had indeed offered him money—not to buy the house, but to sell it. He had just been offered $15,000, which would have given him a profit of $3,000, or 25 percent in a week, but he turned the offer down. Rumor had it that Bill Levitt himself had made the offer, but it had actually come from Bucks County assistant district attorney Paul R. Beckert, the Republican candidate for district attorney.[77] Beckert said he represented two unnamed individuals eager to make a "quiet deal" to prevent future violence.[78] According to Daisy, he had told Bill that "it would be best for all concerned if [he] accepted the proposition and moved away. The offer was presented in the tone of a mild threat."[79] But the Myerses were determined to stay, bolstered by a growing number of letters of support, including one from Jackie Robinson.[80]

Their determination led to harsher tactics. Myers opponents tried to get local merchants and delivery people to boycott the family, threatening that large numbers of Levittowners would refuse to patronize them if they continued to serve the newcomers. Several gave in to the threats, as did the Fire Association Insurance Company, which cancelled the Myerses' coverage. Another tactic was to send caravans of cars up and down Deepgreen Lane with Confederate flags flapping from their radio antennas and horns and radios blasting at night. A group led by Betterment Committee member Eldred Williams took over a vacant house immediately behind the Myerses' and played loud, racially charged music ("Dixie," "Old Black Joe") constantly and beamed bright lights at night to keep the family, already sleep deprived with a new baby, from getting rest. Williams hoisted a Confederate flag above the roof.

Other forms of harassment included naming a dog "Nigger" and walking in front of the Myerses' house, loudly calling its name; throwing firecrackers into their yard; banging the mailbox on the edge of their property; phoning Bill and Daisy at all hours threatening to bomb their house and harm their children; and walking or driving on the Myerses' street playing musical instruments excessively loudly or screaming racist taunts.[81] A more subtle form of harassment, from people ostensibly on their side, consisted of intrusive questions about their finances, political beliefs, feelings about interracial marriage, and a supposed "master plan" for the integration of Levittown. Of all these questions, the two Daisy found most offensive were: "Have you given any thought to moving back to a Negro community because of local publicity?" and "If a poll of residents showed we were not wanted, would we move?"[82]

The Myerses' opponents also harassed the Wechslers next door for supporting the family. They received constant menacing phone calls, endured antisemitic slurs, were called "nigger-lovers," and found their children unwelcome in neighbors' homes. Someone burned a cross on their lawn.[83] Altogether, five crosses were burned at different locations following the Myerses' arrival, including one spiked with blank cartridges that exploded in the heat.

Beyond the Myerses and Wechslers, several others who had helped Daisy and Bill move to Levittown and supported them afterward suffered serious consequences. Irving Mandel, who had sold his home to the couple, lost his job after his employer learned of the sale. Hard as they tried, Quaker activists could never find him another; already in poor health, he died shortly afterward. Peter von Blum, a Friends stalwart who had assisted the Myerses, suffered an exodus of clients from his civil engineering firm, which he soon had to close. Yet another Myers supporter, Reverend Fred Manthey, found himself abandoned by his flock and was sent elsewhere by the Congregationalist Church. When a reporter for the *Philadelphia Tribune,* the city's leading African American newspaper, visited Levittown for a story, an anti-Myers person told her to "get out of Levittown; you don't want to get hurt."[84]

Amid the harassment and threats, which continued well into the fall of 1957, the state police withdrew its officers, and the local police stopped protecting the Myers residence. The absence of crowds, police officials said, made their officers' presence unnecessary. Bill and Daisy were unconvinced; to replace the absent police, Quakers organized a "citizens' guard" to patrol the property and deter attacks. My father joined the citizens' guard, a risk that terrified my mother.[85] Along with the Friends, liberal Protestant and Jewish organizations, together with the Steelworkers Union and other labor organizations, maintained public support for the Myerses and soothed tensions in the community. Reverend Harwick spearheaded a Declaration of Conscience to be signed by "all who wish to stand up and be counted for religious morality and decency in our community." Harwick and others were deeply disappointed that the *Bristol Daily Courier and Levittown Times,* having elaborately and competently covered the racial conflagration, never editorialized on the Myerses' behalf. The owners may have thought they would lose subscribers if they took a stand.[86]

Local officials may also have feared the loss of citizens' support, since they refused to intervene against the ongoing harassment of the Myerses and their friends. Especially glaring was their failure to prevent a series of cross-burnings in late August and early September, including one on September 22 at the home of the Quaker activist Peter von Blum. To try to end the harassment, which now included homemade bombs and threats to blow up homes of Myers supporters, Bill and Daisy decided to travel to Harrisburg, the state capital, to seek help from the top. Pennsylvania governor George M. Leader had taken a strong stand against racial discrimination and in favor of their right to live in Levittown, so why not appeal to him and his attorney general, Thomas McBride? On September 24, Bill and Daisy, the Von Blums, and Tom Colgan met with McBride—Lewis Wechsler said he and his wife were excluded because of their leftist politics.[87] The attorney general promised to help, and shortly after the meeting he reassigned state police troopers to the Myers home, on the grounds that the local police weren't adequately protecting them. He was doubtless moved to act quickly after two more racist incidents took place—a cross-burning on September 24 that singed the home of car dealer John M. Preston, who had sold a new Mercury to Bill and Daisy, and the defacement of the Wechsler home with Ku Klux Klan symbols the following day. A note taped to the Prestons' window read, "Beware! Keep your Big Mouth Shut. The KKK has Eyes. We know your every move." A poster pasted to the Wechsler home showed a demonic black creature trying to grab a white woman in a revealing dress, above the caption "Conquer and Breed." Someone had spray-painted "KKK" next to it. A few days later, a smoke bomb went off between the Myerses' and Wechslers' houses, and several Betterment members repeated their threats to blow up or burn down any Levittown house sold to Blacks, including the Myers house.[88]

Finally, no doubt at McBride's behest, state and local police arrested Howard Bentcliffe on October 16 for defacing the Wechslers' home. Bentcliffe insisted he hadn't acted alone and that a large organization, together with a KKK klavern, was behind him.[89] By "large organization" he could have meant the Betterment Committee, some of whose members may have sympathized with the Klan, but the existence of a klavern seems unlikely. On October 22, after ten weeks of demonstrations, violence, harassment, threats, and intimidation, McBride issued a detailed complaint against Williams, Bentcliffe, Newell, and five others and requested a preliminary injunction against any further anti-Myers activity. The Bucks County Common Pleas Court granted the injunction the next day. Williams and Bentcliffe were arrested (the latter for the second time) for malicious mischief and conspiracy—specifically for having burned crosses, damaged property, and harassed people with Ku Klux Klan propaganda.

The men went on trial three months later. Two police officers, an FBI agent, and three of their victims—Wechsler, Von Blum, and Preston—testified against them. Both men had confessed to the policemen who arrested them that they had planted the flaming crosses and the Klan posters, but in court they pleaded not guilty. On the witness stand, the arresting officer testified that Williams, a gas station attendant, admitted his guilt and said that the stash of Ku Klux Klan literature, posters, and membership applications found in his car belonged to him. Williams had also told the officer that, at Bentcliffe's request, he had made a cross out of pine boards wrapped with rags soaked in kerosene. "I wanted this cross to be strong," he said, "so that teenagers would not get blamed." Williams's lawyer countered that making a cross didn't constitute malicious mischief under Pennsylvania law.[90]

Bentcliffe, a liquor store clerk, didn't appear with an attorney and insisted on representing himself. As he approached the bench intending to call a witness, he suddenly collapsed to the floor, apparently unconscious. A doctor called to the scene thought Bentcliffe might have suffered a heart attack, and his wife confirmed that he had a heart condition. After the physician deemed it unsafe to continue the proceedings, the judge declared a mistrial.

Williams's trial resumed a week later, and he was quickly found guilty and assessed a $100 ($1,000 today) fine. Bentcliffe received a three-week respite and then was also found guilty, fined $250, and given a year's probation. The judge told him, "You should go to jail, but because of your health you are getting this break."[91] The following August, the same judge, Edwin H. Satterthwaite, issued a permanent injunction against Williams, Bentcliffe, and five others (one defendant had been dropped from the complaint), barring them from harassing the Myers family. Satterthwaite said the five men and two women had engaged in "horror-inspiring secret machinations or burning of crosses, implied threats of KKK intervention and malicious defacing of property by vile and opprobrious posters."[92] Although the actual punishments were mild, the judge's words made clear that in 1958, Pennsylvania authorities, from the governor to a local judge, meant to block public expressions of racial hatred and make it possible for African Americans to live in communities formerly intended for whites only.

Those words, however, did not amount to a clarion call for racial integration, and Levittown, Pennsylvania, would not open its doors to more than a few Black families at a time. The Myerses stayed there not quite four years, selling their house in June 1961 to Henry and Rochelle Ford, an African American couple with two young boys. The deal was brokered by Friends Suburban Housing Inc., which specialized in sales to Blacks in the Philadelphia suburbs.[93] Henry Ford, formerly a star college football player who was drafted by the Cleveland Browns in 1954, taught high school math in the Levittown area and became a much-admired local figure. "They say that time heals all wounds," opined the *Philadelphia Daily News* in January 1965, "although some leave a scar. Like the scar that was left on Levittown 6½ years ago from a wound inflicted by racial violence. . . . The wound healed slowly [but] all traces of any scar were removed yesterday when the Levittown Junior Chamber of Commerce announced its outstanding young man of 1964."[94] Ford was that man; he later went to work for Pennsylvania governor William Scranton.

The *Daily News*'s optimism was premature. Levittown clearly had changed since that violent summer of 1957, but it had not become an open place. In 1964, of the seventeen-thousand-odd families in the development, only twenty-five were Black. (In 2022, just 4.9 percent of Levittowners identified as Black or African American.)[95] The low African American numbers stemmed not only from the reluctance of white Levittowners to accept them as neighbors, but also from the community's negative reputation among Blacks. The African American press had extensively covered the fierce reaction against the Myers family, and if, for white America, it was overshadowed by the nearly simultaneous school integration crisis in Little Rock, Arkansas, many Black Americans had the Levittown incident seared into their memories.[96] Some two decades after the cross-burnings and the hostile crowds shouting for the Myers family to get out of town, an African American senior colleague of mine said he had initially been suspicious of me because I came from Levittown. Still, memories fade, and even apparently committed racists can change their minds. James Newell, the former leader of the Levittown Betterment Committee, admitted in 1965 that after living with Henry Ford as a neighbor, he thought "integration has worked out far better than we anticipated."[97]

Daisy and Bill Myers had prepared the way for Henry and Rochelle Ford, but at great cost to themselves. Daisy noted that none of those who harassed them received more than a judicial slap on the wrist, and during her four years in Levittown she experienced "both friendliness and bigotry still in our daily lives." The friendliness was gratifying; the bigotry hurt. After Daisy took her kids to the public swimming pool for the first time, a neighbor advised her not to return: "They are lying in wait for you, and it would be awful for those kids of yours to be hurt."[98]

Despite genuine friendships and a steady decline in hostility toward the Myerses, it still seemed the community would never fully accept them. "We realized years ago to our sorrow," Daisy wrote in 1960, "that the housing market above all else stands as a symbol of racial inequality. No matter how renowned, wealthy, or prominent, the Negro cannot buy in a free and open market."[99] After leaving Levittown they moved to Harrisburg and then back to York, where they both did very well. Daisy took a job as a sixth-grade teacher and Bill, once again, as a refrigeration engineer. Daisy became a guidance counselor and finished her career in education as a school principal. After retiring from that position, she became an assistant to a U.S. congressman, serving with him until 1999.

She started to keep a journal of her harrowing Levittown experience shortly afterward, and in a meeting with Pearl Buck, the novelist encouraged her to turn it into a memoir. She finished the text in the early 1960s but kept it in a drawer for forty years. In retirement, she joined a writing workshop whose leader helped her make it a book. "What happened to me and to my family," Daisy wrote in 2004, seven years before her death, "prepared us for who we are now—stronger human beings. The Myers family has not only survived but thrived while seeking a part of the American dream: to have a comfortable home. No one should ever be punished for that."[100]

5 Integration and Its Discontents

IN JANUARY 1955, the NAACP heard rumors that Bill Levitt had purchased a large swath of land in Burlington County, New Jersey, just across the Delaware River from his Pennsylvania development and twenty miles from Philadelphia. The news was alarming, since the civil rights organization had been unable to prevent Levitt from barring African Americans from his New York and Pennsylvania projects. The rumors were soon confirmed in a *New York Times* article reporting that Levitt had acquired some 3,500 acres of farmland in Willingboro Township.[1] Harry Kalish, the same Philadelphia lawyer who had alerted Levitt to U.S. Steel's Pennsylvania plans, had been helping him to quietly buy up land in Willingboro since early 1954.

Kalish had enlisted a local attorney and part-time judge named Alexander Denbo and a local real estate broker, Robert Bloomer, to buy as much farmland as they could get, without mentioning that Bill Levitt was behind the purchases. "When Kalish visited me," Denbo recalled twenty-five years later, "he did not tell me I was working for Bill Levitt. . . . It wasn't until six months later that they put me in a car and took me to Levittown, Pennsylvania to meet the man I was working for."[2] Levitt wanted to avoid what had happened in Lower Bucks County, where land prices went up once it became common knowledge that he wanted a huge expanse there.[3]

Although the Pennsylvania development was only half finished and Levitt wouldn't start building in New Jersey for at least three years, NAACP officials thought it imperative to intervene immediately. They had had little success in getting the courts to bar discrimination in privately built suburban developments; their new goal was to have the New Jersey state legislature step in.[4] But with Levitt seemingly focused on Pennsylvania, New Jersey legislators had little motivation to act quickly.

This situation left Levitt free to plan his new community largely unconstrained by outside forces. The firm also benefitted from the political geography of south-central New Jersey, which was much more favorable than the complicated terrain the homebuilder had found in both Long Island and Lower Bucks County. Rather than sprawl over four municipalities and several school districts, as in Nassau and Bucks counties, Levittown, New Jersey, would be contained within a single political jurisdiction. Levitt essentially bought the entire township of Willingboro, acquiring more than 90 percent of its land.[5] He also arranged for the jurisdiction's largest town to be hived off into a neighboring township so that just six hundred people, most of them small farmers, remained in Willingboro.[6] The result, for Levitt, was essentially virgin territory, five thousand acres—not 3,500, as originally reported—of mostly open fields with a smattering of houses, some dating back to the first Quaker settlements in colonial times.

One of the farmers approached by Levitt's representatives was J. Cresswell Stuart, whose family had owned land in the area for generations and who belonged to the township's tiny political elite. One day, Stuart recalled years later, "a big black Cadillac car" glided onto his property, and man riding shotgun asked, "Did I know of any farms for sale?" It eventually became clear that "they were going to buy the whole township," and Stuart himself would sell most of his property to Levitt. Dozens of other farmers willingly, even eagerly, sold out to Levitt because he offered them top dollar, between $1,000 and $3,000 an acre. "The little [forty-acre] farm that was next to us," Stuart said, "she got $90,000. Couldn't turn that down." Even if there had been opposition to Levitt's plans, the local officials, mostly modest farmers who ran the town's affairs part-time, were no match for the experienced, wealthy, and well-oiled homebuilding firm. Yet despite the lack of resistance, Bill Levitt kept these sales confidential.

Stuart reported that although he and a few others "had a thousand meetings with the Levitt organization," no records were kept. "Everything was word of mouth. Noting written down."[7] Stuart told an interviewer that "Levitt has also been playing a cloak and dagger game," giving him and other leaders bits and pieces of information but withholding that material from other elected officials. When Stuart's colleagues learned of his privileged, if unwanted, relationship with Levitt, they became convinced that he and his friends were acting in cahoots with the firm against the community's best interests.[8] The homebuilder shrugged off these local conflicts and mostly operated as he saw fit. Now that Levitt & Sons belonged entirely to him— his father had retired, and Alfred had left the company in 1954 and sold him his shares—his independence as a businessman and community planner was complete.

Without Abraham and Alfred, Bill relied on the input of a handful of executives, but he alone made the decisions. The New Jersey community would be an improved version of the Pennsylvania one, and even more thoroughly planned in advance. It would have a new water supply and sewage system, along with roads, shopping centers, parks, playgrounds, and pools. Unlike in the first two Levittowns, Levitt decided not only to set aside land for schools but also to build them himself, with the cost spread over the entire community through small increments added to the price of each house. By financing the schools this way, he hoped to avoid, at least for a time, the steep property taxes that had brought negative publicity to the first two Levittowns.[9]

Levitt's biggest innovation in New Jersey was to jumble together his three different models from least expensive to most expensive throughout the community. In each section, a four-bedroom Cape Cod ($11,990) sat next to a single-story Rancher ($12,240) or to a two-story Colonial, some with three bedrooms ($13,990), and others with four ($14,490). To add to the street-level variety, each model was given two different elevations and a range of exterior colors. Most of Levitt's executives opposed the mixing scheme because it increased building costs, but Bill insisted on this change, hoping to silence the criticisms by Mumford and others of the earlier Levittowns' visual monotony. "We are ending once and for all the old bugaboo of uniformity," Levitt declared. "In the new Levittown, we build all the different houses . . . right next to each other within the same section."[10]

The introductory prices of model homes in Levittown, New Jersey. (Willingboro Public Library, Willingboro, New Jersey, Local History Collection)

Mixing the different houses together, he added, represented the "most important step forward in volume housing" and would "remove the curse of standardization."[11] Levitt also wanted to avoid the Pennsylvania development's segregation by class, also the object of critics' ire and disdain. The views of these critics had seeped into the mass media, and Levitt feared that their criticism would harm sales, especially since he intended Levittown, New Jersey, to be more upscale than his earlier mass developments.

While trying to persuade their boss not to mix home models in the new community, Levitt's executives also urged him not to call it Levittown. Existing Levittowns had received so much bad press that the new community needed a different name to set it apart and make it more desirable to the middle- and upper-middle-class buyers the firm wanted to attract. But Levitt insisted on keeping his name on the New Jersey development, and in a 1959 referendum he narrowly got the early homebuyers to agree. Four years later, however, they voted to change the name back to Willingboro, a gesture of defiance that Bill would never forgive.[12]

With Alfred gone from the company, Bill commissioned the highly respected modernist architect Richard Neutra to design the new homes.[13] In the 1940s, Neutra had created a widely admired housing project in Los Angeles, along with dozens of spare, low-slung apartment buildings and single-family homes, many with huge floor-to-ceiling windows to let in the California light.[14] The sketches Neutra made for Levitt reveal five large front windows, additional windows on the side, and a flat roof that protrudes beyond the house's external walls. Neutra's appealing designs continued the modernist aesthetic Alfred had imbibed from Frank Lloyd Wright, but Bill ultimately rejected them. He worried that the plans departed so much from FHA-approved models that the agency wouldn't back them with guaranteed mortgage loans. Levitt also thought Neutra's design would be too expensive to build and that homebuyers' architectural tastes had become more conservative, as had his own.[15] The modernism of the Pennsylvania community's "Levittowner" now seemed too avant-garde. Instead, the third Levittown would turn to generic-looking Cape Cods, ranches, and large two-story colonials adapted from a precursor built in small numbers toward the end of the Pennsylvania project. There was little distinctively "Levitt" about the Colonial, which was doubtless what Levitt and his buyers wanted. He intended to maximize sales with a lowest-common-denominator design that would allow buyers to imagine they were moving into a solidly middle-class suburb rather than a Levittown. This also partly explains why the Levittown name was quickly dropped.[16] Alfred had hoped the New York and

Pennsylvania Levittowns would give homebuyers an appreciation for modernist architecture; in Levittown, New Jersey, Bill had no cultural or aesthetic ambition and only wanted to register the strongest possible sales to as affluent a clientele as he could attract.

To sell those houses, Levitt advertised incessantly and wrote some of the ads himself. Buyers would get the "best house for the money," better even than the earlier Levittown homes, along with ready-made schools and the other amenities for which Levitt communities were known. The firm advertised in the Philadelphia papers and also in the *Levittown Times,* a new paper created at Levitt's urging by the Calkins newspaper family, which had bought the *Bristol Daily Courier* and the *Times* of Levittown, Pennsylvania, and would eventually merge them into the *Bucks County Courier Times.* With the creation of the New Jersey *Levittown Times* in 1958 (later renamed the *Burlington County Times*), Bill Levitt had the local papers on both sides of the Delaware River in friendly hands.[17]

As with the earlier Levittowns, the ads spurred hordes of people to visit his model homes. Once there, prospective buyers were greeted by friendly men in conservative business suits who had been trained not to pressure anyone. But they politely screened out people who looked unkempt or acted strangely. As an experiment, one man deliberately showed up unshaven and shabbily dressed; the representatives declined to deal with him. When he returned a few days later well-groomed and nicely turned out, he immediately received an application. Levitt representatives also ran credit and employment checks to make sure a prospective buyer wasn't heavily in debt, chronically unemployed, or otherwise unable to make the monthly payments. The employment and income standards were modest, since Levitt was a high-volume operation and the mortgages were backed by the FHA. Still, because he meant Levittown, New Jersey, to be more upscale than the earlier developments, Levitt wanted to avoid homeowners who would struggle to live there.[18]

Levitt presented the New Jersey Levittown as more exclusive than the Pennsylvania one, and in many ways it was. He eliminated the $9,000 Rancher prevalent in the first-built sections of Levittown, Pennsylvania, and priced the three-bedroom, single-story model $2,500 higher than in Pennsylvania, although he gave the New Jersey house two hundred additional square feet and added a garage instead of a carport. When this house sold only modestly, Levitt modified it by adding a family room attached to the kitchen, a larger dining area, and sliding glass doors, bringing the square footage to 1,400 and the price to $13,240.[19] These changes eliminated the modernist open floor plan still featured in the original but didn't prevent *American Home* from ranking it in 1961 among the "6 Best Homes for the Money." The Levittown, New Jersey, ranch, wrote the magazine's judges, was "one of the best mass-produced houses . . . an exceptional value." It had "an appealing design and a workable floorplan," which "mother will especially like" because "from the kitchen she has a commanding view of both the back and front yards."[20]

Some houses in the new community cost the same or even less per square foot than their predecessors in Pennsylvania. And one of the New Jersey houses, the four-bedroom Cape Cod, was priced lower ($11,990) than its Pennsylvania counterpart ($14,500). To realize this cost savings, Levitt cut 180 square feet of living space but kept the same number of rooms and the one-and-a-half-story structure.[21] The two-story, four-bedroom Colonial cost the same in each community ($14,490), but the New Jersey version was two hundred square feet larger. Levitt called the Colonial "our runaway best-seller"; it was popular because "it's frankly traditional, and right now that is the way the market is swinging." Buyers also liked having some amenities that didn't exist in the New York or Pennsylvania Levittowns: a family room in addition to the living room; a separate dining room and laundry room; a dry-walled garage; walk-in closets; and two and a half bathrooms. For those who wanted an even larger house, Levitt added, for the 1960 model year, a 2,170-square-foot dwelling costing $20,990. It had four bedrooms, three full baths, a family room, a formal dining room, and a larger kitchen with a dishwasher and garbage disposal, as well as a built-in TV antenna and a two-car garage with room for a washer and dryer.[22]

Levitt's original plan for Levittown, Pennsylvania, divided the huge development into several subcommunities, each with its own school, shopping, pool, and recreational facilities. He never fulfilled these intentions because the crazy quilt of municipal and school jurisdictions made it impossible to fashion coherent subcommunities. The New Jersey Levittown didn't have that problem, and Levitt proceeded to create ten largely self-contained neighborhoods, or "parks," each

Drawing of Garfield Park for a Levitt sales brochure. (Willingboro
Public Library, Willingboro, New Jersey, Local History
Collection)

with 1,200 to 1,500 houses centered around a company-built school.
Levitt planned to surround the school with recreational parkland
including a pool, playgrounds, and basketball courts. These subcommunities, he said, would be "large enough to justify extensive
facilities [but] small enough so people won't feel they are lost in the
mob or dwarfed by vastness."[23] Another advantage of dividing the development into distinct parks, he said, was that schools could be used
as community centers on evenings, weekends, and in the summer,
while the pool and playing fields could accommodate school recesses
and athletic events.

Levitt wanted buyers in his new community to feel they were moving into a residential park, not an anonymous stretch of identical
mass-produced houses. He also wanted the existing Levittowns' many
detractors to perceive the new project as better than its predecessors.[24]
Endlessly sensitive to criticism, he was determined to refute the pum-
meling he took from architects, urbanists, and cultural critics by emphasizing his interest in building livable, desirable communities, not

mere houses. His chief counsel, Ira Goldman, told the sociologist Herbert Gans, who took up residence in Willingboro, that Levitt craved prestige and accolades and fervently wished to be recognized for making a major, even unique, contribution to American society. Levitt argued—and Gans would later agree—that Levittowns did not engineer conformity, monotony, or dullness, and that the Levittown environment shaped its inhabitants very little; far more important were the characteristics, habits, experiences, and traditions they brought with them from their pre-Levittown lives. And once in Levittown, homeowners decorated their homes, and later remodeled them, according to their own tastes. They were of course influenced by ambient cultural trends, but they would have imbibed these influences wherever they lived.[25]

If Levitt failed to convince many critics, he apparently impressed President Dwight D. Eisenhower, who told Nikita Khrushchev that he should visit Levittown, Pennsylvania, when he toured the United States in 1959. Levitt couldn't have been more pleased and bragged about the distinction. Khrushchev didn't come, but in 1961, a delegation of Soviet officials toured the New Jersey development. They were impressed in many ways but felt the houses could never withstand a Russian winter.[26] Still, Levitt loved the official recognition. According to Goldman, he wasn't motivated by money—he had long since made more than enough, though he did want to make a profit every year—but by a drive for "prestige, adulation, and the feeling of leadership in the housing industry. He also wants respect and prestige for the Levitt family name."[27]

Levitt had no interest, however, in the major innovations that many professional planners would have liked to see. When they suggested that he could use land more efficiently by building row houses and small apartment buildings, he responded that he constructed single-family residences, period. He also declined to set aside land for industry and commerce, except for the inevitable shopping centers.[28] But he would later change his mind about that.

Levitt announced his plans for Levittown, New Jersey, at a Washington, D.C., press conference on June 5, 1958, during which he said he would build one thousand homes by the following February; sales would begin immediately. Down payments would range from $350 to

$500 and monthly carrying costs from $83 to $101.[29] When he opened the floor for questions, journalists immediately asked whether he planned to sell homes to Blacks. "Our policy on that," he responded, "is unchanged. The two other Levittowns are white communities."[30] He again instructed his sales agents not to sell to African Americans and to assure white buyers that the new community would bar Blacks.[31]

Civil rights organizations in New Jersey had been afraid this would happen, and by the time Levitt announced the Willingboro project, the state legislature had already barred the housing discrimination he planned. In June 1957, the New Jersey legislature amended its existing (1945) anti-discrimination statute to prohibit discrimination in housing guaranteed by mortgages financed by federal agencies. This amendment was aimed explicitly at Levitt, whose business model relied on FHA-backed mortgage loans. The law gave the New Jersey Division Against Discrimination (DAD), a branch of the Department of Education, the right to investigate and rule on complaints of housing discrimination.[32] This legislation placed New Jersey ahead of its neighboring states in civil rights and responded to a very recent history of racial discrimination in the Garden State. Several elementary schools in Burlington County, which included Willingboro Township, had remained officially segregated until the early 1950s, and segregation persisted for another decade in some public restrooms and restaurants, and at Holiday Lake, a beach area on the edge of Willingboro.[33]

With the new anti-discrimination legislation in place, on March 31, 1958, the DAD director warned Levitt that racial exclusion in Willingboro could violate the law and requested a meeting with him. Levitt didn't respond, although Ira Goldman, his general counsel, eventually contacted the DAD director and agreed to meet with Harold A. Lett, the DAD's assistant director and chief of enforcement. The get-together didn't take place, however, until the day after Levitt's June 5 announcement that Blacks would be barred from Levittown, New Jersey. At the June 6 meeting, Goldman told Lett that, in his legal judgment, New Jersey's anti-discrimination law didn't apply to the Willingboro project.[34]

Shortly after this meeting ended in failure, two African Americans, Willie R. James, an army warrant officer based at nearby Fort Dix, and Franklin D. Todd, a control analyst for the Bristol, Pennsylvania, manufacturer Rohm & Haas, tried to buy homes in the new development.[35] After being turned away, they filed a complaint with the DAD. Behind the scenes, the NAACP leaders Roy Wilkins and Thurgood Marshall had been communicating with Levitt executives and believed "the Levitt organization is trying to work something out."[36] A Levitt officer met with the two men, but nothing came of the discussion. In the meantime, New Jersey senator Clifford Case, a Republican, asked the FHA not to insure mortgages in Willingboro until Levitt eliminated his whites-only policy; the agency didn't comply. The New Jersey Assembly responded to the FHA's inaction by voting unanimously on June 16, 1958, to warn William J. Levitt that "discrimination will not be tolerated within the borders of this state."[37] A few days later, Lett traveled to Willingboro to meet with Levitt and Goldman. Recalling the meeting some years later, he said the homebuilder "was adamant there would be no integration in Willingboro."[38] Lett left the meeting resolved to back James and Todd's anti-discrimination complaint and quickly ordered the Levitt organization to treat their home purchase applications like any other. The American Jewish Congress, the Jewish Labor Committee, and four other national Jewish organizations joined the NAACP, the ACLU, and the New Jersey Committee Against Discrimination in Housing in supporting Lett's efforts.[39] The Jewish organizations issued a statement calling Levitt's whites-only policy "a desecration of democracy and the basic ideals of the Judaic heritage. . . . We deplore the fact that instead of using your unparallel [sic] opportunity to advance democratic living, you have chosen instead to entrench even more deeply the institution of racial ghettoes."[40] Over the next several months, another twenty-two African Americans applied to purchase homes in Willingboro. None of them received a response.[41]

Despite the forces arrayed against him, Levitt insisted on fighting the discrimination complaints. In July 1958, his attorneys filed a suit in the New Jersey Superior Court, arguing that the legislation granting the DAD authority to rule on housing discrimination complaints violated the New Jersey constitution.[42] The attorneys also maintained that even if the law were constitutional, its prohibitions didn't apply to Levitt & Sons. The company received no housing funds from government agencies, and only companies that did needed to obey the state's anti-discrimination law. The DAD responded that because the

FHA backed the mortgages contracted by Levitt's buyers, his company did, in fact, receive public housing assistance. Levitt's counterargument was that the FHA had no direct dealings with their company but instead made private arrangements with individual homebuyers. Those arrangements were not covered by the New Jersey anti-discrimination law. These were dubious arguments as best, but Levitt was convinced he would prevail, as he had in the past.[43]

As the suit began its journey through the superior court, a process that would take nearly a year, a young Philadelphia couple, Herbert and Iris Gans, joined the throng of people trooping through Willingboro's three model homes. Herbert was a sociologist teaching at the University of Pennsylvania. Although he and Iris genuinely needed a house, his objective in choosing Willingboro was to study the community as a participant observer, interviewing fellow residents, attending town meetings, and gathering information by distributing questionnaires.[44]

The Ganses arrived at the Levitt sales office on the evening of June 30, 1958, just three weeks after Bill had announced the advent of his third Levittown. After waiting in line for an hour and a half, Herbert and Iris were asked what model they wanted and given three possible sites. They picked the four-bedroom Cape Cod, the least expensive of the dwellings on offer, and learned that their house would be ready on October 16, just three and a half months later. Herbert was intent on being an original Levittown, New Jersey, homeowner, and he got his wish. He wanted to observe the community's development right from the start.[45] Gans found the homebuying experience "much like going through an auto showroom," for "buying a Levitt house is like buying a car." Levitt offered fewer models than the typical car dealer, but the Levitt house-buying process, like the car-buying process, was designed to get buyers to choose a higher-end version. "The differences between the cheapest and more expensive models loom large," Gans wrote, "while the price difference, when expressed in $ per month, is small."[46]

When the Ganses took title to the house and saw it finished for the first time, they were disappointed. "It looks rather less well built than the model we saw," Gans wrote, "and sits closer [than expected] to the next house."

> The walls are very thin, as is the bathtub, which looks ready to cave in when you bounce around. The rooms are nicely sized, but the planning still leaves things to be desired. . . . The kitchen layout, of

which Levitt is proud, has many faults. . . . The cabinets are too high for a 5′ wife, there is waste on top of cabinet space and not enough work space in other quarters. The stove looks to me to be dangerous with kids around; the electric cooking coils are quite exposed.[47]

Like Levitt, Gans assumed that the kitchen would be the wife's domain.

Gans knew that he had been spoiled by his previous living quarters, and that other Levittown inhabitants might be less critical of their new homes. "This is mass production at its ultimate," he wrote, "but at a lower quality than we are used to. Perhaps we have been living in converted upper income homes too much." He used the phrase "low quality" again and again to emphasize what's lost with mass production: "The house reminds me of the [$]1.19 steak shops; the higher income food is provided at low cost, but that explanation is too simple. . . . People are buying for space as well as suburb; they are getting better housing, and a poor steak is better than a fancy hamburger to most." Still, despite these criticisms, which Gans recognized reflected an upper-middle-class perspective, he admitted that "we are not dissatisfied with the house; it will be comfortable, and the sunsets are so magnificent that they make up for many things. Also, once we get used to the tinny-ness, the earlier standards will be put in escrow."[48]

During his and Iris's first weeks in the community, Gans observed that neighbors weren't eager to invite one another inside their homes; since most were in considerably larger houses than their earlier ones, furnishing them would take a while, and many didn't want to display partially—or shabbily—furnished interiors. In the meantime, it was understood that "the front lawn is your indication to the outside world as to what kind of a homeowner you are." This realization moved Herbert and Iris to reseed and fertilize the fledgling grass Levitt had planted and make sure it grew: "So now we are busy watering our lawn twice a day." Working on the lawn, the sociologist discovered, was the best way to get to know his neighbors and to learn a workable suburban code of conduct. "Neighbors on all sides wave to you when you are outside; this is a friendly but impersonal way of recognizing and saying hello. But otherwise, contact among adults is sharply restricted," at least at first. Later, the Ganses would develop fuller relationships with their neighbors.[49]

Bill Levitt congratulates Lee and Joan Mount, the first people to close on a Levittown, New Jersey, house. (Willingboro Public Library, Willingboro, New Jersey, Local History Collection)

Gans made a point of getting to know the couple credited as the first to occupy a Levittown, New Jersey, house. Bill Levitt massively publicized this first family, welcoming the family in person and inviting newspaper and TV reporters to immortalize their possession of a new Levitt home. For the homebuilder, this was a great "business stunt," but for the family, and especially their children, it would be something to remember. The couple was excited to watch the house being built. They "came to look at their house going up all the time," Gans wrote, "and took movies." He understood the filming as "a personalizing of mass production. They can watch their house go up, see how it's built, what it looks like inside out—much like a custom house purchaser, though they have no say on changes."[50]

Gans wanted to learn as much as possible about all aspects of the new community and was naturally interested in the highly fraught racial question. He happened to land in Willingboro amid the anti-discrimination struggle and eventually wrote the best account of its contours in a final chapter of *The Levittowners,* his classic book about Willingboro's development and early years.[51] After speaking with Levitt executives, Gans concluded that the homebuilder's motives were primarily economic, that they excluded African Americans because "the immediate integration of the new Levittown would hurt sales to whites." The executives claimed that "our firm is liberal and progressive, but we don't want to be singled out or used as the firm which should start the other builders off. If there is no other builder who can keep Negroes out, we will not do so either . . . we don't want to lose millions by being the first."[52]

Gans was not unsympathetic. "There was some justification," he wrote, "for the charge that they were being singled out." The Division Against Discrimination focused on Levitt because it was the largest homebuilder in the East. The DAD's leaders believed that if Levitt had to integrate, other builders would follow suit. And if integration proved costly, Levitt's company was wealthy enough to absorb the losses. Also, since Levitt had come to symbolize suburbia in the 1950s, all eyes would be on him. Forcing him to integrate would be a major, visible win for civil rights.[53] Gans was too charitable toward Levitt, who had defended his policy of racial exclusion by slurring integration advocates as "communists." Levitt also resisted pressure from pro–civil rights Jewish groups and fended off a series of legal challenges from the NAACP—and was, of course, fully aware of the racial strife to which his policies had led in Levittown, Pennsylvania.

The homebuilder's son told Gans, in strictest confidence, that he wished he could sell to African Americans. According to the sociologist, when he asked how exclusion worked, Levitt, Jr., replied, "If anyone had Negroid characteristics or was defined as a Negro by the credit agency, he would be rejected." But if somebody "could pass freely, they would probably let him." Levitt had sold homes to Chinese Americans, Puerto Ricans, South Asians, and others. African Americans alone were singled out.[54]

In discussing the situation with other Willingboro residents, Gans found that "the majority of Levittowners were uncomfortably ambivalent about integration. Some were hostile and threatened to move or to protest violently." Working-class people who had fled the influx of African Americans in Philadelphia were especially likely to feel this way, "fearful that the same mass invasion of lower-class Negroes would occur in Levittown, confronting them with a sudden and visible decline in property values and status." Gans found that a much smaller group, "principally Jews, Quakers, and Unitarians," strongly favored integration. Still, the majority of Levittown residents neither strongly opposed nor favored integration, although those in this middle camp tended to worry that lower-class, rather than middle-class, Blacks would move in. Members of this group were concerned that their sons and daughters would date, and perhaps marry, African Americans as they became integrated socially into the community.[55]

Gans's extraordinarily rich field notes make clear that it wasn't just working-class people who were deeply hostile to living near African Americans. Charles and Loretta Vansciver, a well-to-do couple whose families had lived in the area for generations, said that they didn't want their children to go to school with Black kids or share public swimming pools with them. Charles didn't even want prosperous African American doctors and other professionals in the community, telling Gans that "if a Negro lived next to him, either he or the Negro would have to go." Charles admitted to feeling some shame about these attitudes, but Gans also noted that he "gets quite angry about the idea of Negroes trying to move into Levittown." He was especially exercised over the prospect of white women being attracted to Black men, especially those of wealth and status. Gans suspected that Charles hadn't fully accepted the presence of Jews and Italians in his previously all-Protestant town. Willingboro's young mayor, Malcolm Kennedy, confirmed these suspicions about Vansciver's religious bigotry and said other old-timers shared them.[56] As for Loretta Vansciver, she claimed to be less prejudiced than her husband; growing up, she had been exposed to a "better class of Negroes" and had some Black friends. Still, she didn't want white and Black children to attend dances together or swim in the same pools.[57]

Despite such attitudes, Gans reported only minor strife over the prospect of integration, even after Levitt began to lose in court. In July 1959, the New Jersey Superior Court, Appellate Division, ruled that Levitt's "contention that the housing in question is not 'publicly assisted housing accommodation' . . . is without merit." The court also found that the Division Against Discrimination had the legal authority to "enforce the laws of this State against discrimination in housing built with public funds or public assistance."[58] To head off hearings before the DAD and the negative publicity they would generate, Levitt appealed to the New Jersey Supreme Court. He hoped to delay a definitive ruling as long as possible in order to sell hundreds of homes to white people in the meantime. One of Levitt's lieutenants told Gans that the discrimination "case would be postponed over and over again until ¾ of Levittown is [filled] up and then it is too late."[59] But in February 1960, the higher court affirmed the appellate court's decision. It stayed the ruling, however, after Levitt announced his intention to appeal to the U.S. Supreme Court.[60]

Levitt didn't harbor much hope that the U.S. Supreme Court would overrule the New Jersey courts—it ultimately refused to hear the case—and he decided to allow the integration of his new community to proceed without waiting for a ruling to come down.[61] To his credit, but also to avoid negative publicity, he resolved to make integration proceed with a maximum of public support and a minimum of racial strife. He was determined to avoid another Myers situation, which he feared would scare off white buyers, but his desire to make integration work seemed genuine once he was faced with a fait accompli.

Levitt began by hiring as "integration consultants" Harold Lett, the African American second-in-command at the DAD, and his wife, Alene Simpkins, the supervisor of leasing and occupancy at the Newark Housing Authority. Lett and Simpkins then hired a white educator and human relations specialist to handle home visits with Willingboro's white residents.[62] They did so, Lett said, in hopes "there would be less likelihood of irresponsible rumor flowing from home-visits and passage through community streets by this person, than if a Negro were chosen to make such initial contacts." The Letts agreed to work with Levitt after he signed an agreement giving them access to relevant company documents, covering their expenses, and promising to reconsider all home purchase applications submitted by potential African American buyers to date.

The three integration consultants met with a key local clergyman, who agreed to help spearhead their efforts. Next, they sat down with the Willingboro police chief to make sure that his troopers would enforce the law and guard against any violence arising in response to Black families moving into the community. "The young, career-minded Chief of Police," Lett wrote, "made it clear that recent racial conflict in the Pennsylvania housing development was sufficient warning to him that alert and unbiased law enforcement was his only alternative." The third step was to get together with the publisher and editor of the two local newspapers, to encourage them to avoid "language or story emphasis that could heighten racial fear or prejudice," as the *Bucks County Courier Times* had done when the Myerses moved into Levittown, Pennsylvania. Lett and Simpkin's final step involved the creation of a Human Relations Council charged with handling any objections to integration or how it was conducted.[63]

The Human Relations Council was asked to identify community members who might foment racial conflict, and to make sure the police chief kept an eye on them. The council called this effort "operation hothead."[64] The consultants then met with the entire Levitt sales force to explain the enormous change in Levitt policies concerning sales to African Americans. In that meeting, the salespeople were urged not to "raise the issue of race" with potential homebuyers and to keep track of all comments and questions about Blacks or integration during their interactions with clients. It turned out that only 11 percent of buyers showed any interest in the racial composition of the community, and just 1.7 percent held "uncompromising views in opposition to racial inclusion." Four percent registered "minor notes of disapproval" of integration, while 2.4 percent wanted assurances that they wouldn't have Blacks next door.[65]

Gans wrote that the Letts, the council, and the Levitt company agreed to screen the early African American homebuyers to make sure they were solidly middle class. They assumed that whites wouldn't object to Black neighbors whose economic status equaled theirs and who shared their values. But in his report on the integration process, Lett didn't mention any screening, and in a 1973 interview he denied that it had taken place. It may be that screening was implicit rather than formal, since the FHA was insuring mortgages only for people with middle-class incomes.[66]

With the Levitt salesforce, police chief, and newspapers on board and a Human Relations Council in place, the most delicate remaining task was telling the two thousand white families already living in Willingboro that the community they thought would be whites-only would now accommodate Blacks. Local political officials, fearful of alienating voters, were unwilling to bear these tidings, so Lett and

Simpkins persuaded some two dozen local clergy to announce the integration plans from the pulpit on the same weekend. By speaking in unison, the religious leaders would prevent segregationists from converging on one congregation or pressuring individual clergymen to oppose the new plans. By all accounts, this approach worked almost to perfection.[67]

Despite the united front from the clergy, Levitt and his consultants remained nervous about white people's willingness to buy homes in an integrated community. Salespeople were instructed to place no more than one African American family per block and never to allow Black buyers to select homes next to each other. The idea was to avoid the perception that Blacks were "taking over" any part of the community, which might have led to Black and white sections of town, and thus to the failure of integration—an outcome Levitt officials, clergy, police, and local politicians wanted to prevent at all costs. Lett later maintained he'd had no knowledge of the effort to "scatter" African Americans around the development.[68]

Levitt officials also devised the idea of giving African American buyers the first choice of lots in each of Willingboro's "parks." The most desirable lots were those that bordered on woods, creeks, or open, unbuildable land, because these offered more privacy. White buyers were then given the option to buy an adjacent lot with a similar degree of privacy. It turned out that 80 percent of white buyers preferred these more private lots, even though it meant living next door to a Black family. This process resulted in neighborhoods that included both Blacks and whites, with white families always the overwhelming majority.[69]

These efforts allayed white fears about declining property values, at least in the short term, but not their worries about cross-race socializing, interracial dating, and marriage. The Human Relations Council held a meeting to air these concerns, which appeared to subside somewhat—in part because there was virtually no socializing across racial lines. The first Black families bought Willingboro homes in July 1960, but by 1964, only fifty were living in the community, a number that nonetheless dwarfed the combined total of the Levittowns in New York and Pennsylvania.[70]

There were several reasons so few Blacks took advantage of the newly integrated community. The most important was that real estate agents generally refused to show African American buyers resale houses—ones whose original owner had put them on the market. And white resellers, not wishing to anger their neighbors, mostly refused to consider Black purchasers. Those neighbors—many of whom were servicemen and -women at Fort Dix and McGuire Air Force Base, who might have to move at any time—often reminded the sellers that when they were trying to sell their own houses, having Blacks close by would compromise their ability to do so.[71] When Harry Kendall, a jazz musician and newspaper reporter, decided to move from South Philadelphia to Willingboro, he found he could not buy the house he wanted. "The white people on that street," he told a journalist, "got together and told [the seller] not to sell to me, because I was black." When he went with his wife and six children to look at another house, "the white people come out on the street, looking all around, and I could see the hostility." Kendall eventually managed to buy a Willingboro house, and his family remained in the community for decades. He became president of the Kinsmen, an organization for Black men in the development. One of the group's goals was to ease new Black homeowners into the community: "So a black guy would move in, we go over, sit down and talk to him about what to expect."[72]

Despite these problems, Gans deemed the integration of Willingboro a qualified success, a reasonable conclusion at the time. Compared to the United States as a whole, where integrated suburbs remained vanishingly rare, the New Jersey Levittown stands out for its ability, even if by court order, to include African American families. No violence or demonstrations marred their arrival in the community, and vocal opposition was muted and rare. This wasn't because white Willingboro residents suddenly became committed integrationists. What made Willingboro different was the existence of strong anti-discrimination state laws and courts willing to enforce them. Neither New York nor Pennsylvania had such laws when their Levittowns were being built. The New Jersey laws forced Levitt to drop his whites-only policy, and he decided that since integration was going to happen, it should unfold as smoothly as possible. Above all, Levitt wanted to avoid another situation like the one that greeted the Myerses in his Pennsylvania development, which had given Levittown a bad name both among white segregationists, who now saw Levittown's whites-only promise as unreliable, and among more liberal-minded people unwilling to live in a community known for racial antagonism. Levitt wanted to disassociate Willingboro from both sides of this controversy and even had one of his top executives personally welcome the first Black family to buy a home, although he himself didn't join him.

Harold Lett and Alene Simpkins, both of whom had experience and stature in the civil rights community, helped Levitt's integration effort a great deal, as did clergymen, the police, and the local press. The clergy's moral authority discouraged overt racism, while the police and press worked to keep residents calm. Important as well was the relatively high status of the African Americans who bought into the community. Many were doctors, lawyers, and military officers with higher average incomes than many of the white residents. The Black newcomers' status was not so high as to evoke resentment, but high enough to reassure whites about their own status.

Several of these newcomers came from Fort Dix and the McGuire Air Force Base, just seventeen miles away. Prominent among them were Willie James, who brought one of the original anti-discrimination lawsuits against Levitt, and Drs. Thomas Mayfield and Cleophus Robinson, both jet pilots and Tuskegee Airmen. Other early African American residents included Bill and Evelyn Lewis, parents of the Olympic runner Carl Lewis; Dr. Conrad Bell, Willingboro's first Black physician; and Dr. Charles Williamson, a surgeon trained at the Duke University Medical School. David Jackson, a graduate of Howard and Temple universities, became Willingboro's first Black elected official when he joined the school board in 1965. Judge Marie Bell, the wife of Conrad Bell, became Willingboro's first Black mayor. Although far from all of the early Black homeowners were as accomplished as these women and men, most were college graduates, and some had earned graduate and professional degrees.[73] Still, their numbers remained small during Willingboro's first decade, and this may be the main reason for the absence of racial strife.[74]

A long *Wall Street Journal* report of December 1970 expressed optimism about the community's racial situation. "There's ample evidence," the article declared, "that integration is indeed working in this small chunk of suburbia despite some occasional setbacks." The reporter noted that "often, when the first Negro family moves into an all-white suburb, the result is unpleasant," citing Levittown, Pennsylvania, as well as Warren and Dearborn, Michigan, where "first arrivals were harassed so much they finally gave up and moved out." Even in Willingboro, the state supreme court had had to order Levitt to "open its doors to a black family." While there was no violence in the new Levitt community, "the earliest black families found themselves the targets of suspicion."[75] Still, the effort to avoid concentrating African American families in certain neighborhoods quieted the early tensions, as did efforts by Black home-owners to avoid provoking their white neighbors. As head of the local NAACP, Willie James had wanted to boycott local stores for failing to employ African Americans, but "most blacks in Willingboro refused to go along with me and were appalled by such tactics."[76] Instead, the Kins-men, the Black men's organization, met quietly with local store owners, who agreed to hire more African American youths. Black adults made a point of participating in community organizations, joining the planning commission, the Kiwanis club, local churches and garden clubs, and serving as Little League coaches. Two were elected to the school board.

Despite these positive developments, the *Journal* reported, "there's still plenty of prejudice." Some white residents refused to frequent the town's public pool because Black families used it, and interracial dat-ing disturbed both Blacks and whites, especially when Black boys dated white girls, which was far more common than the reverse. Be-cause of this imbalance, "black girls feel themselves jilted and are de-cidedly hostile about it." A "rap session" intended to soothe these and other grievances resulted instead in a physical attack by fifty Black girls on a small group of white girls. In general, though, vio-lence was rare. When a white man slurred two African American teenagers, the situation was peacefully resolved in court. The *Journal* article ended on a positive note, concluding that the longer a school had been integrated, the better Blacks and whites got along. The peaceful coexistence it described reflected a town in which African Americans made up just 12 percent of the inhabitants. The situation would change when they began arriving in larger numbers.[77]

Although Levitt accepted integration in Willingboro—and also in two other, more upscale New Jersey communities he built in the early 1960s—he never embraced racial equality. His next large develop-ment, planned for Bowie, Maryland, in the suburbs of Washington, D.C., took advantage of Maryland's lack of anti-discrimination laws and barred Blacks.

In Willingboro, however, the legal battle receded from view as African Americans gradually moved into the community. But now Levitt faced an unprecedented problem: slow sales. Willingboro homes had sold briskly from 1958 to 1960, but then they began to level off. Levitt actually lost money in 1961 for the first time in the company's history.[78] The homebuilder blamed the slowdown on integration—"We had no violence or picketing, but our sales ground to a halt."[79] He had long held that racial integration would harm sales, but in the early 1960s, other factors were at work. The postwar baby boom was ending, the market had stabilized, and prospective buyers were no longer clamoring for houses months before they were built. For white people, the postwar housing shortage had been quenched thanks to Levitt's firm and its growing number of imitators. Most important, there had been two recessions, in 1958 and 1960–61, the first lasting eight months and the second ten months.[80] Both downturns resulted from the Federal Reserve Bank's decision to raise interest rates, which in turn bumped the interest on a thirty-year mortgage to 6 percent— up from 5 percent in 1957.[81] As unemployment rose and mortgage rates increased, Americans bought fewer houses. Levitt had no choice but to slow the building process in Willingboro. After he had sold some three thousand Willingboro homes between June 1958 and June 1960, the next three thousand took him until 1964. Instead of the seventeen thousand Willingboro homes originally planned, he constructed just eleven thousand, and selling them all took a full fourteen years. In Levittown, New York, 17,500 houses had been gobbled up in four years, and in Levittown, Pennsylvania, a nearly equal number had taken just six.

Americans were still moving to the suburbs in the 1960s, but more slowly than a decade earlier. Despite the smaller numbers and the putative end of the baby boom in 1964, Willingboro's demographic characteristics in its early years resembled those of the first two Levittowns—young couples with small children. Nearly 80 percent of the adults were under forty, with most in their late twenties to late thirties. In 1960, the median family size was four (two adults and two children), but one-fifth had three children and another 11 percent four or more. One-third of all Willingboro kids had not reached age five, and adolescents were rare. As for the new residents' socioeconomic status, 18 percent of the men were professionals, 56 percent were white-collar employees, and 26 percent held blue-collar jobs. Most worked in factories, stores, offices, and research facilities in and around Philadelphia and Camden, New Jersey. Twelve percent belonged to the armed forces, many as air force pilots. Some had retired from the service and now piloted commercial airplanes. Nearly half of the male residents had attended college, with 27 percent having completed a bachelor's degree, while 28 percent of the men lacked a high school diploma. Women's educational levels were similar, except for a somewhat lower number of college degrees. The median family income stood at $7,125, considerably higher than the $5,600 median for the country as a whole.[82] The $7,000 income translates to just $74,600 in 2024, but it bought far more house in 1960 than today because inflation in housing prices has been much greater than for most other things.

Although early Willingboro residents were relatively well-educated and earned more than the national median, Gans ranked them as largely lower-middle class. They had mostly attended community colleges and state universities rather than elite schools, and the professionals' occupations leaned far more toward teaching and social work than medicine and law. Still, about 10 percent of the original inhabitants were upper-middle class. If the white-collar people stood at the lower end of the middle class, the blue-collar ones ranked in the upper echelons of the working class, with jobs in highly skilled trades or as factory foremen. These blue-collar people saw themselves as middle class and wanted their children to pursue white-collar careers.[83]

In their religious affiliations, the original Willingboro residents resembled their counterparts in the first two Levittowns, with Catholics (37 percent) and Jews (14 percent) overrepresented and Protestants (47 percent) underrepresented relative to national averages. Willingboro's religious makeup resembled that of Philadelphia.

The relatively slow sales of homes in Willingboro after the initial burst told Levitt that the market for low-end houses was being exhausted. No longer could the company make huge profits by selling thousands of dwellings at rock-bottom prices. To compensate, Levitt built increasingly larger and more expensive homes. By 1968, his least expensive house cost $18,000 new, and the most expensive $21,000. The range in 1959 had been $11,900 ($14,000 in 1968 dollars) to $14,990 ($17,500 in 1968). The 1968 Willingboro homes were larger and included more amenities, but they were 21 to 31 percent more expensive in inflation-adjusted dollars. As with his prewar homes, Levitt gave these new dwellings English-sounding names: the Gramercy, the Kensington, the Buckingham, the Gladstone, and the Overbrooke. They had three or four bedrooms, family rooms, dining rooms, and enclosed garages—attributes lacking in New York and Pennsylvania Levittown homes. Levitt advertised the new Willingboro homes as featuring "luxury details" such as "handsome wood cabinets," "glamorous bathrooms," and "luxuriously paneled walls."[84] The designs, however, were uninspired, with faux columns in front, brick veneer facing, shingled siding, or both. One model was an L-shaped ranch, but most of the others were boxy two-story structures fronted with white columns that looked pretentious rather than functional. The houses sold, although gradually. And the golf course Levitt built to accompany the new homes didn't speed things up.

By the time the last houses were finished, in 1972, Willingboro had lost many of its blue-collar homeowners. In 1970, three-quarters of Willingboro households earned between $10,000 and $25,000, while in the country as a whole, 42 percent earned $10,000 or more. In median family income, Willingboro ($13,125) stood 37 percent above the figure ($9,586) for the country overall.[85] The community's integration in the 1960s clearly didn't lower its socioeconomic status, and homes there appreciated in value by 8 percent a year, considerably faster than the general U.S. rate.[86] In addition to the deliberate efforts to keep racial tensions at bay, its inhabitants' relative economic comfort may have helped as well. Willie James, who lived in Willingboro with his wife, Bernice, and their four children from 1960 to 1974, said his kids "didn't face discrimination." Lee Isackson, an early white resident of the community, told reporters, "It was normal for us to have friends of different races."[87] But as the number of African Americans grew in the 1970s, race relations began to deteriorate.

Beginning in 1972, when African Americans reached 12 percent of the population, fights between Black and white high school students became chronic. "We were having so many problems in the schools," Harry Kendall said. "Black boys and the white boys, they were at each other's throats. So we had a meeting at the high school. We let everybody speak. These white guys came in, they were in hoards [sic], and they occupied the entire back section of the auditorium. And every black kid who came up to talk, these grown white men would

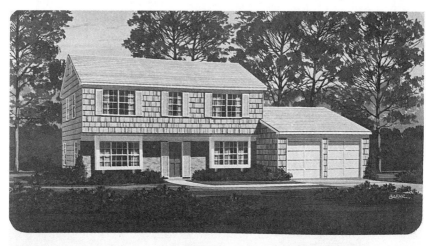

THE GRAMERCY This is the nine-room colonial home in Garfield Park North! The wide reception foyer opens at one side on a 22-foot living room with windows in three walls. On the other side is the formal dining room and, off the foyer, an attractive guest powder room.

The remaining area across the back of the house includes a large 17-foot family room for TV, snacks and all kinds of family fun. The extra-large kitchen is equipped with lovely wood cabinets. The two-door refrigerator-

freezer, automatic wall oven, and countertop range are all by General Electric. There are also such luxury details as a stainless steel sink, stainless steel range hood, even a chopping block work area!

Next to the kitchen, there's a separate breakfast room with sliding glass doors to the back lawn. Beyond that is the laundry, equipped with G. E. washer and matching dryer. There's also an attached two-car garage.

Upstairs you'll find four big bedrooms and two complete baths. Both baths have ceramic tile floors, built-in vanities,

and wall-wide illuminated mirrors. Plenty of closets—nine in all, including two seven-footers—plus extra storage space over the garage, accessible with pull-down stairs.

The Gramercy is pre-wired for telephone installation and television antenna outlets. Grounds are completely landscaped with a variety of shrubs and trees. All this—and more!—is included in the price. There are no closing costs. Fireplace or oversized lot available at additional cost.

PLANS AND LANDSCAPING SHOWN AND DESCRIBED ARE APPROXIMATE AND SUBJECT TO CHANGE.

The Gramercy was the "Colonial" in Levittown, New Jersey. (Willingboro Public Library, Willingboro, New Jersey, Local History Collection)

yell 'em down."[88] Meetings like this didn't help, and fights between Black and white students continued. During a dance at Memorial High School, a rumble among eight hundred Black and white students spilled out into neighboring streets. Parties regularly turned into interracial brawls, and other violent incidents piled up.[89] What worried local educators and town officials nearly as much as the fights was the students' self-segregation, both in and out of school. In the high school cafeteria, students sorted themselves into separate Black and white sections, with very little interracial mingling. A white girl reported that when an African American boy started calling to ask her out, her mother made it clear to her that "If I wanted to go out with him, fine, but don't bother coming home."[90]

Willingboro officials became so concerned that they asked the town's Human Relations Commission to examine the racial dynamics and issue a report with proposed solutions.[91] The basic problem, the

commission found, turned on "a number of incidents involving situa-
tions of provocation, confrontation, and occasionally violence among
individuals and groups. These incidents, many with racial overtones,
have involved youths, parents, police and innocent bystanders." The
causes included "a white mentality grounded upon historical prejudice and a fear of blacks [and] a black mentality wherein a feeling of
longtime repression and subjugation is mixed with that of excessive
rebelliousness and hyper-sensitivity to deliberate or unintentional racial slights." These problems were exacerbated by "over-reaction on
the part of some police officers [and] poor quality of reporting by the
local press," including "incomplete sets of facts, misquotes, and in-
flammatory editorializing." To address these problems, Willingboro
needed a better-paid and -trained police force, "viable police-commu-
nity relations programs," and the ability to reprimand "policemen
who engage in racial epithets."[92] What is surprising about the report
is that although it deems parents and the press partly responsible for
the racial strife, its proposed solutions focused entirely on the police.
The commission also overlooked the lack of summer and after-school
jobs in the community for African American teenagers.

Whatever the inadequacies of the Human Relations Commission's
report, Willingboro officials and civic leaders kept trying to make integration succeed. They added African Americans to the police force;
hired better-educated officers, white and Black; and gave them sophis-
ticated training. When an African American family sued a white
neighbor in federal court for harassment, Willingboro Township officially joined the case on behalf of the Black family.[93]

These efforts, though relatively successful, foundered on the shoals
of the real estate industry, whose agents increasingly steered African
American homebuyers toward Willingboro while discouraging them
from looking in neighboring communities, which remained lily-white.
When an African American reporter for the *Philadelphia Inquirer*
posed as a potential homebuyer from New York, brokers located
twenty miles from Willingboro persistently steered him there. "I've got
the feeling you're going to love Willingboro," enthused one agent, adding, "Willingboro is approximately 20 percent black. I'm sure that kind
of thing is important to you." When the reporter asked for other possibilities, the agent kept steering him back to Willingboro. At a different
agency, the broker took him to an all-Black section of Burlington

Township, and when the reporter asked for other options, he was told, "Well, I can show you some homes in Willingboro."[94]

As growing numbers of African American families moved in, whites began to flee, spurred by "block-busting"—efforts by real estate agents to get white homeowners to sell in a panic. Valerie Gladfelter, a former chair of the Human Relations Commission, told a journalist that she would commonly get "three, four, five calls a week from realtors— usually after several black families moved in—to see if I wanted to sell my house." A white Willingboro homeowner told the *Philadelphia Daily News* that whenever a Black family bought into his block, he received letters from realtors saying he should sell before prices drop. A Black resident said he got a stack of letters urging him to tell his (Black) friends about the good bargains available in the town.[95] The realtors' efforts worked. Between 1970 and 1973, the Black population of Willingboro jumped from 11 to 18 percent, while the white numbers dropped by more than 5 percent.[96] A prominent real estate agent claimed that 80 percent of sellers had put their homes on the market because they believed "the whole town was for sale, and they didn't want to be caught in any bind."[97] The local tax assessor responded that Willingboro's sales volume, always high with so many homeowners in the military, hadn't risen much and that home values were appreciating normally. What was changing was the town's racial makeup.

When Reverend Ernest Lyght, a Black minister, became pastor of the Church of Good Shepherd in the mid-1960s, most of his parishioners were white. By 1974, only a handful of whites remained. Still, in the mid-1970s, Willingboro hadn't reached a tipping point, and hope remained that what one official called its racial "Camelot," a moment of successful integration, would persist.[98] When Willie James visited Willingboro in 1974 after having moved to Rhode Island, he found "much more mingling between the black and white students, more children walking home together, more black and white families at the shopping centers together."[99] In the high school, however, white and Black students continued to self-segregate. At dances, the disk jockey alternated between rock and soul; Black kids sat out the rock songs, and white kids sat out the soul.

To preserve and nurture what social integration there was, town leaders, both Black and white, tried to protect Willingboro's fragile racial balance from the real estate predators. In 1974, the year Willingboro's population reached its peak, the township banned "for sale" signs in an effort to stem white panic. Local realtors claimed that the ordinance violated their First Amendment rights and sued the township in court. As the case proceeded through the judicial system, African American families continued to move in and white families out. And not only that: separate Black and white sections of Willingboro began to emerge as African American families clustered in the oldest, least expensive homes, all located in the original parks (Buckingham and Pennypacker) built in the late 1950s and early 1960s. Some of these properties had been poorly maintained, and their value appreciated slowly, if at all. Levitt had placed different home models next to one another in an effort to avoid segregation by social class, as had been the case in Levittown, Pennsylvania. But because he built increasingly expensive homes in the newer sections of Willingboro, class segregation occurred anyway—and to a large extent turned into racial segregation as Black families bought into the original parks, which increasingly received derogatory nicknames like "Little Africa."[100] It was in these areas that racial steering and block-busting took their greatest toll. Still, because their wealth grew substantially in the 1960s, with Black families' median income doubling between 1960 and 1970 and a growing Black middle class tripling their incomes, African Americans also bought into the newer, more expensive parks.[101] For these families, Willingboro was extraordinarily attractive; it featured all the benefits of suburbia—single-family homes with ample yards, good schools, public parks and recreational programs, and relatively low crime rates—while also providing non-ghettoed Black community life. And because so many African Americans already lived there, new Black homeowners faced little of the harassment that was common when they moved into white suburbs. Racial steering and individual choice meant that both segregation and integration took place in Willingboro, especially after 1970. This situation seemed highly positive to many African American residents, but many whites saw the clustering of lower-income Blacks as ominous. Even as African Americans remained well below a third of the population, some whites felt that Blacks were becoming the majority in town.

It's unclear whether banning "for sale" signs did anything to stem white flight, but in any case, in 1977 the U.S. Supreme Court ruled the ban an unconstitutional violation of free speech.[102] The signs returned, and Willingboro homes sold briskly, far more to Blacks than to whites. During the 1970s, the African American slice of the town's population grew from 11 to 37.8 percent. In the 1980s, it expanded again, reaching 56.1 percent in 1990. Of the ninety-seven towns of ten thousand or more people in suburban Philadelphia, Willingboro was one of just two (the other was Yeadon, Pennsylvania) that flipped from majority-white to majority-Black during the 1980s.[103] This transformation resulted not only from racial steering and block-busting, but also from frankly illegal actions by realtors. In the early 1980s, seven Willingboro-area real estate agents were convicted of falsifying the FHA and VA mortgage applications of scores of African American homebuyers, many of them from Camden and Philadelphia. The realtors faked the documents required to quality for government-insured loans, collected their 6 percent commissions, and installed families in houses they couldn't afford. This was not only illegal but tragic for homebuyers desperate to escape blighted urban neighborhoods, for whom the large homes and lush yards of the Levitt development seemed a dream come true. But they had nowhere near the incomes required to make their mortgage and tax payments, and their houses were soon foreclosed on, leaving the federal government on the hook for the fraudulent loans. Other Black families then bought the foreclosed properties at deeply discounted prices, dramatically lowering home values in Willingboro relative to those in neighboring white communities. White people had long harbored the fear that racial integration would lower their property values; thanks to racial steering, block-busting, and outright fraud, those fears came true, although there was nothing inevitable about it.

This was a sad development for the white Willingboro residents who remained in the community because they believed in integration or because they couldn't afford to move. African American residents also suffered from the slack appreciation in value, but the growing numbers of Black middle-class homebuyers who aspired to suburban life had fewer choices than their white counterparts. Much of white suburbia remained wary, at best, of integration, and all-white communities did their best to keep African Americans out. The fair housing legislation of the late 1960s only hardened white resistance to having Black neighbors.[104] As Colandus Francis, chair of the Camden County NAACP, put it, "A lot of black people don't want the hassle of moving into an all-white community."[105] With so few options, many found Willingboro an appealing choice. It was accessible financially, and the presence of a thriving African American community made it socially desirable. The schools, known for their relatively high quality, were another attraction. In 1992, three-quarters of Willingboro's graduating seniors, 80 percent of them Black, said they were going to college, a number that compared favorably with the surrounding, mostly white townships.[106]

In the three decades from 1970 to 2000, Willingboro's schools became almost entirely Black. The 2004 district census revealed a student body that was 90 percent Black, 5 percent Hispanic, and 4 percent white. In the mid-1970s, whites had made up 75 percent of students, but after the turn of the twenty-first century, Willingboro became one of just four school districts in all of New Jersey to be 90 percent or more Black. And this despite an overall Willingboro population that remained 25 percent white—the African American population reached 67 percent in 2000.[107] Many of the whites were older and no longer had school-age children, and other white families sent their kids to private or parochial schools. "Once a public school is perceived to be a minority school," said Rutgers historian Wayne Glasker, "Caucasian parents flee the school system."[108]

This was especially true of New Jersey, whose schools were among the most racially segregated in the country. In 2002–3, two hundred of the state's 593 school districts were at least 90 percent white; seven were 100 percent white. In the southern New Jersey counties of Burlington, Camden, and Gloucester, which had a total of 102 school districts, more than a third of the forty-five thousand African American students attended school in just three districts: Camden, Willingboro, and Winslow. What these imbalances meant for Willingboro's students is complicated. On one hand, many students liked attending an all-Black school. "We all have the same things in common," said Victoria Harris, a high school junior. A senior, Tammy Meyers, expressed a common view: "Why would you want to go to a school where you would be treated differently?"[109] But on the other hand, scores on standardized tests, especially in high school math, had dropped sharply. Only 36 percent of students showed "proficiency" in math, as compared with the overall state proficiency rate of 69 percent—the overall rate was 81 percent in English language arts.[110] In 1990, when the high school was already 80 percent Black, 84 percent scored "proficient" or better in math and 82 percent in reading and writing. By the early 2000s, SAT scores were disappointing as well. In 2002–3, the average Willingboro SAT score was 860 for reading/writing and math together, 158 points below the state average of 1018.[111]

Still, test scores are just one, often inadequate, indicator of school success. On the other side of the ledger, the Willingboro district enjoyed a 93 percent graduation rate (versus 89 percent statewide), and 71 percent of graduating seniors planned on higher education (versus a state average of 63 percent).[112] Half planned to go to four-year colleges. The high school boasted an award-winning academic team, competing in an intellectual decathlon for young scholars, and students commonly said they wouldn't have done as well in a mostly white setting. "I can come to school without worrying about racial problems," noted a high school senior headed to Hampton University in Virginia, a historically Black institution.[113]

Student perceptions of their school are clearly important, but administrators, school board members, high-achieving students, and parents had concerns. A senior heading to Brown University told the *Philadelphia Inquirer,* "I don't think the education here is enough to be able to go out and compete. . . . The teachers have no choice but to lower their standards to meet the students." A veteran teacher said the district "seems to be spiraling down."[114] One reason was inadequate funding. In New Jersey, the electorate votes on a proposed school budget each year, and by 2004, the Willingboro electorate had defeated sixteen of the previous seventeen budgets, including those that didn't raise property taxes. These defeats strongly suggested a lack of confidence in the school district and the school board, whose members had been sharply divided for years over funding and the quality of district administrators. One result of this strife was an unusually high teacher turnover rate, with huge numbers of early retirements and resignations. "They just get frustrated," said a longtime Willingboro teacher who served as president of the local teachers' union. He also cited poor training, unstable school leadership, and a school board "splintered by internal disputes."[115]

Not only was the school board rent internally, but beginning in 2005, the board majority and school superintendent were at daggers drawn.[116] In July, the board, in a split vote, suspended the superintendent, whom it blamed for financial mismanagement. He then sued the school board president, who was facing charges of having illegally solicited campaign contributions from district employees. Other administrators were also suspended, and they sued as well. In early 2006, board members revealed that the district had accumulated $9 million in debt; to pay it down, they would have to close schools, lay off teachers, and dramatically raise property taxes. A furious public blamed the deficit on mismanagement by the administration and board and denounced the budget cuts and tax increases in a series of meetings. When the board proposed a bond issue to address part of the debt, the electorate voted it down by almost three to one.

Multiple investigations ensued, and the state commissioner of education sent a sharply worded letter criticizing the school board. District leaders then turned to the state legislature for relief. In March 2006, the assembly and senate approved a ten-year, no-interest bailout loan to be monitored by an official from the state education department. But even with the loan, residents were asked to swallow a property tax increase of 50 percent. Voters overwhelmingly refused, rejecting the proposed budget yet again. The ongoing budgetary standoff between the voters and the school district would further compromise the quality of the schools.

The school district's financial problems can't be attributed to poverty in the community; Willingboro remained solidly middle class. In 2004, the median household income exceeded the national figure by $20,000, or nearly 50 percent.[117] Where Willingboro lagged behind, like most Black communities, was in household wealth, which for most middle-class Americans is concentrated in home equity. Home values in Willingboro, as in other mostly African American neighborhoods, sagged in relation to white communities of equal median income. In the United States as a whole, for every dollar of income in 1990, white homeowners on average possessed $2.64 of house. Black homeowners possessed $2.16 of house, or 18 percent less. Economists have labeled this gap in home values relative to income a "segregation tax."[118] In Willingboro, the segregation tax was even higher, at 23 percent; nationwide, the greater the degree of racial segregation, the greater the segregation tax.

As we have seen, Willingboro became a majority-minority municipality in the 1980s, and since then it has continued to lose white homeowners and gain Black ones. In the 1970s, the community had seventy-seven white homebuyers for every one hundred Black home-buyers; in the 1980s, the number of white homebuyers per one hundred Black homebuyers sank to fifty-six; by 1990, the number was less than forty.[119] By comparison, in the Philadelphia metropolitan region as a whole, 84 percent of homebuyers in 1990 were white. The more whites fled Willingboro, the more other whites stayed away. With fewer people interested in owning a home there, prices stagnated or rose much more slowly than in white areas with similar median household incomes. On the positive side, the lower home prices enabled Black families to buy into the community, but this pattern added to the racial imbalance, and thus to the community's segregation tax. The Black-white imbalance has continued to grow since 1990, reaching nearly 73 percent Black and 17 percent white in 2010, making the segregation tax even steeper.[120] Willingboro's middle-class families, both white and Black, have accumulated less household wealth than white families with similar incomes living in mostly white neighborhoods.

The school strife and budgetary problems of the early 2000s have given Willingboro a negative image in the press, much of it undeserved. Journalists regularly exaggerate the amount of crime. Dysfunctional school boards are not uncommon in New Jersey and elsewhere, but in reporting on Willingboro, journalists link this problem to low test scores while overlooking other measures of student achievement. The lived reality for most Willingboro residents is much more positive. It offers large, well-equipped homes for reasonable prices; a thriving Black community with robust religious congregations; excellent shopping nearby; and proximity to Philadelphia and New York City. Willingboro is far from perfect, and it highlights the persistent obstacles to racial integration, as well as what those obstacles have brought about: the wealth gap between white and Black families, the racial inequalities in access to good housing, and the educational disparities that limit opportunities for African American youth. Still, for many families, Willingboro remains a good place to live.

For Levitt & Sons, the slow sales of Willingboro homes revealed the need for a new business plan. No longer would the company construct one huge development at the time. Instead, it decentralized, planning developments in several places simultaneously. Between

1960 and 1975, Levitt communities sprouted in Maryland, Virginia, northern New Jersey, eastern Long Island, and abroad—Puerto Rico, France, and Spain. Most of the new projects were relatively small— hundreds to a few thousand houses—although those in the suburbs of Washington, D.C., and San Juan, Puerto Rico, ultimately resulted in nine thousand to eleven thousand single-family dwellings.[121] The new approach quickly righted Levitt's financial ship: the company's first net loss in 1961 gave way to large profits every year for the rest of the decade.[122] The Paris and Puerto Rican ventures were the boldest of the new regime, but the Levitt development in Bowie, Maryland, just beyond the D.C. Beltway, proved to be a rare example of relatively successful suburban integration.

6 Levittown Goes Upscale

CONSTANTLY ON THE hunt for new suburban lands to buy and develop, Bill Levitt profited handsomely from a gruesome Long Island homicide—which *Life* magazine dubbed "The shooting of the century"—and subsequent murder trial involving Ann and William Woodward, one of the elite North Shore's most prominent couples.[1] In the aftermath, Levitt acquired a huge Maryland estate that had belonged to the disgraced family. A few years later, it became a nine-thousand-home development known as Belair, a community that would achieve an unusually high level of racial integration.

At about two a.m. on October 31, 1955, a night watchman on a three-hundred-acre estate in Oyster Bay, Long Island, heard two gunshots in rapid succession. He ran toward the sound, which seemed to come from the bedroom of William (Billy) Woodward, a wealthy banking heir and racehorse owner who had bought one of the estate's buildings as a weekend retreat. As the watchman peered into Woodward's window, a local policeman arrived and broke into the home. There, he found the heir's wife, Ann, cradling her husband's lifeless naked body.

Ann later told police that there had been evidence of a prowler on their property in recent days. Her story rang true to the detectives questioning her, since someone had recently broken into several North Shore homes. For protection, Ann and William had decided to arm themselves with shotguns, which they kept handy in their separate bedrooms. Those who knew the couple reported that their marriage had long been in trouble, and household employees regularly witnessed fierce, abusive verbal battles between them.

Billy belonged to an old money New York family whose wealth and standing came not only from banking and real estate but from Maryland's nationally famous Belair stables, the home of three Kentucky Derby winners and the mid-1950s horse-racing star Nashua. Ann's background was the polar opposite. She came from a poor Kansas family that became even poorer when her long-estranged parents got divorced. To escape her dysfunctional household, she decided to try her luck in New York City, and through her sexy good looks landed jobs in theater and radio. She became known as "the most beautiful girl in radio," a label not meant to be ironic.[2] Rumor had it that Ann met Billy's father, William, Sr., while working as a showgirl and began an affair with him. The father may have introduced Ann to his son, and in any case, the pair married in 1943. Billy's mother had opposed the match and openly scorned Ann's lower-class roots, but the young wife wanted nothing more than to be accepted by New York society. She succeeded, for a time.

Unfortunately for her, Billy treated his marriage vows lightly and had multiple affairs with other women—and, according to some accounts, with men as well. Ann twice hired private detectives to trail him and document his infidelities. Billy, too, employed private eyes to catch his wife in the act. By the late 1940s, Billy had had enough and demanded a divorce, to which Ann refused to agree. The marriage limped along unhappily for years.

On the evening of October 30, the couple attended a party at a nearby estate for the visiting Duchess of Windsor. Partygoers reported that Billy drank only moderately, and Ann, a teetotaler, not at all. It appears that after the couple returned home, they retired to their respective bedrooms. Ann told police, and later a grand jury, that she heard their poodle barking and thought a prowler had broken in. She grabbed her twelve-gauge, double-barreled shotgun and rushed into the hallway outside her room, where she pumped two charges into a shadowy figure just a few feet away. As the second shot went off, she realized to her horror that the suspected intruder was her husband. This, in any event, formed the substance of her testimony, although the details changed somewhat during the police and grand jury investigation. Billy seems to have been less worried about intruders than his wife, since he had emerged from his room unarmed and unclothed. Perhaps he always slept naked, but it was the end of October, and the weather was cool. Did Billy and Ann have sex that night, or was another woman or man in his room?

Ann's story about a prowler on her property appeared to be confirmed when local police arrested a burglar named Paul Wirths, who said he had entered the Woodward mansion on the night of the shooting. When the dog started to bark, Wirths said, he ducked into a closet where he found a safe, but then hightailed out of the house after hearing the gunshots. The local authorities found his story believable, since a hall closet did contain a safe. This detail may also have influenced the grand jury, which declined to indict Ann after just twenty-five minutes of deliberation. Billy's mother, however, was unconvinced, and she hired her own investigator to look into the case. In the end, she decided not to pursue it, hoping to shield the family from further negative publicity. But to no avail; New York's high society believed Ann guilty of murder and gossiped incessantly about her.

The New York–area and national press gave this story elaborate coverage, and later, Truman Capote and Dominick Dunne would write lightly fictionalized versions of the tale.[3] Capote's story, published in *Esquire* in 1975, portrayed a thinly disguised version of Ann as a cold-blooded killer and appeared to confirm the view, widely held in New York society, that she had gotten away with murder. After reading the story, Ann sank into a deep depression from which she never recovered, committing suicide that October by swallowing a cyanide capsule. Dunne's novel, *The Two Mrs. Grenvilles,* came out a decade later. Tragically, both of her sons killed themselves as well, one in 1976 and the other in 1999.[4]

Billy's demise, coming just two years after the death of his father, also a highly successful horse breeder, left no one to manage the family's Belair Stud racing stable, with its champion racehorses and 2,300-acre estate. The property featured a renovated twenty-six-room mansion dating from the mid-eighteenth century and included twenty other dwellings, barns, and miscellaneous structures. The executors of Billy Woodward's will—one a family business manager, the other the CEO of New York's Hanover Bank—quickly disposed of the stud farm and horses and put the estate up for sale in September 1956. A

month later, a New York realtor named William Zeckendorf announced he had agreed to buy the property for $1,187,000, $63,000
less than the asking price.[5]

A Maryland judge voided the deal, however, after it became clear
that Bill Levitt and another developer, Norman L. Adolf, had offered
substantially more for the estate, $1.5 and $1.4 million, respectively.
Levitt was willing to bid generously for the property because of its
beauty, horse-racing pedigree, and ties to American aristocracy—it
had originally belonged to Maryland's colonial governor, Samuel
Ogle. Above all, he was drawn by its proximity to Washington, D.C.,
just twelve miles away, and the excellent highways that linked it not
only to the nation's capital but also to Baltimore (eighteen miles
away) and Annapolis (twenty miles).

Levitt sued to block the sale to Zeckendorf, as did Adolf and the
guardian of Billy and Ann Woodward's two sons, who argued that
the executors had not acted in the boys' best interests. Levitt told the
judge he "got hot under the collar" when he reflected that Zeckendorf's original bid had been just $750,000, half of what the home-
builder had offered. Zeckendorf quickly raised his offer to $1.1
million and ultimately to $1,187,000, which met the asking price, he
claimed, since no real estate broker's fee would be deducted. Zeckendorf also argued that it would be somehow dangerous to negotiate
with another bidder while his offer was on the table. This was a
strange argument, and the judge didn't buy it.[6] The Woodward executors, he ruled, had "failed in their duty" to obtain the highest possible
price for the Belair estate. The best offer was Levitt's, which he had
raised to $1.75 million. On August 27, 1957, the homebuilder's big
black limousine rolled onto the Woodward estate, where he personally took possession of his hard-won property.[7]

Three years later, Levitt announced ambitious plans for a new development on the Belair lands. The project, initially consisting of
3,500 homes, would be smaller than his Levittowns and aimed, he
said, at "professional and middle-class families" in search of housing
near Washington and Baltimore. The new community would be fully
planned to avoid the unsightly "helter skelter" development that supposedly characterized the D.C. suburbs to date, as well as the "rash of
hot dog stands [and] Christmas tree of neon lights" that had produced
"the national disgrace that lines most of our nation's highways."

Blaming "a handful of promotors" for this disgrace, Levitt emphasized that his new community would be "properly zoned, properly
codified, properly safeguarded against this type of blight." Stores
would be confined to commercial areas, mainly shopping centers, and
housing codes would ban the tangle of TV antennas, electrical wires,
clotheslines, and chain-link fences that supposedly marred his competitors' projects. He planned to conceal TV and FM receptors inside his
dwellings, making Belair "about the only community in the civilized
world that won't require a single TV antenna."[8] Beyond this, he
planned to keep streetscapes free of wires by placing telephone poles
behind houses. Confining fencing to backyards would keep front
yards open and uncluttered. Each dwelling would be set back from the
street and surrounded by elaborate landscaping. Instead of bulldozing
trees, as he did in his first two Levittowns, he would leave a great
many standing. Levitt routinely touted his beautification efforts, as if
to contradict the many critics who accused him of filling the pristine
countryside with suburban sprawl.

Levitt began building on the Belair property in the fall of 1960,
opening model homes in October. To simplify the development's administration as well as his building activities, he engineered to have
Belair annexed to the tiny village of Bowie (pronounced "boo-we"), a
decaying railroad hamlet of just one thousand souls, most of them African American and poor. The annexation would place the new development within a single municipality and enable Levitt to control it at
first and his homeowners later on. Bowie's Black population would be
overwhelmed by the white, well-educated families moving to Belair,
whose leaders would quickly confiscate the name Bowie and relegate
the old Bowie to an afterthought. Between 1960 and 1970, Levitt
would acquire several parcels adjacent to the original Belair property,
ultimately creating one of Maryland's largest cities.[9]

As sales were slowing in Levittown, New Jersey, the opening of
model homes in Bowie recapitulated the frenzy of interest last seen
nearly a decade earlier, in Levittown, Pennsylvania. With typical hyperbole, Bill Levitt declared Belair "the biggest opening in the 30 years I've
been with our firm." In fact it didn't match the beginnings of his New
York and Pennsylvania developments, but as the *Washington Post* reported, "Crowds estimated between 20,000 and 30,000 flocked to the
showing of model homes along Route 50 [where] cars were backed up

1½ miles waiting to get into the parking lot at the site."[10] The following weekend, prospective buyers stewed in a four-mile-long traffic jam that never seemed to abate, and newspaper photos showed long lines of people waiting to troop through the model homes. A week after the homes went on sale, three hundred buyers had secured one with a deposit, although their move-in date was still more than a year away. By then, 1,500 homes, worth $20.4 million, would be sold.[11]

Buyers were enticed not only by the Levitt homes' ample size and reasonable prices but also by the savvy interior decoration by Alice Kenny, Bill Levitt's former secretary, now his second wife. Kenny had devised a conservative mélange of "early American" and sedately contemporary furnishings. The *Washington Post*'s critic aptly described the interior designs, with their Federal-style furnishings, as "calculated to appeal to those of conservative but discerning taste." One early homebuyer found the model homes "just like heaven."[12]

Another mélange of early American and contemporary styles graced Levitt's sales brochure, whose cover featured a decorative "Belair at Bowie Maryland" sign. As the archaeologist Julie Ernstein shows, the brochure's cover foregrounded the Belair sign, with its Federalist references, generic colonial imagery, and, of course, the name Belair, which explicitly connected the new development with the area's aristocratic horse culture of the recent and distant past.[13] The sign borrows key features of Federalist furniture, especially the breakfront cabinet, writing desk, and dining table, mimicking the curved decorations on the breakfront top as well as the spindly legs of the writing desk and dining table. Perched between the sign's curlicues and replacing the cabinet knobs is what appears to be a pineapple, often a symbol of colonialism and perhaps of the British empire. The sign also refers to Levitt & Sons' history and visually connects that history to enduring elements of the American past—not only Federalist furniture but the greenery and generic steeple that evoke timeless village life. But situated in that village are three Levitt houses, representing the modern comfort of updated traditional American homes (Cape Cod, colonial, ranch) and inviting potential buyers to imagine themselves benefitting from twentieth-century conveniences while enjoying a tranquil country life. As Martin L. Rize, one of Levitt's chief landscape designers, put it, "We wanted to create a country atmosphere because when people were buying out here, they thought they were buying into the country."[14]

The cover of a Levitt sales brochure for Belair, with a Federalist-accented sign and references to a countrified past, updated with modern Levitt homes. (Archives of the Belair Mansion)

To reinforce that genteel atmosphere, Levitt kept intact two long rows of stately tulip poplar trees that, since colonial times, had framed the long allée (driveway) leading to the Belair Mansion, which he restored and modernized. The allée was incorporated into the development's main street, Belair Drive, and the tulip poplars now graced the front yards of those fortunate enough to buy houses on this stretch of the road. The allée dated from the eighteenth century, but the rest of the property had changed a great deal as the successive owners improved the mansion and its grounds. A half-century before Levitt bought the Belair estate, the Woodwards had hired the famous Beaux-Arts architecture firm Delano & Aldrich to design a Colonial Revival garden and tennis courts. That firm had just finished Kykuit in Sleepy Hollow, New York, the property that became the Rockefeller family's main estate. In the early 1960s, Levitt turned the garden and tennis courts into the Belair Bath and Tennis Club, a facility reserved (with a membership fee) for residents of the development. Beyond these elements of the estate, Levitt preserved other trees and planted new ones, along with a variety of shrubs (azaleas, laurels, rhododendrons) native to the region—all intended to enhance the new development's country flavor and its associations with an idealized Anglo-American past. He gave the streets names like Belair Drive, Tulip Grove Drive, Stonehaven Lane, Shetland Lane, and Buckingham Drive.[15]

These historical associations and manufactured nostalgia doubtless helped sell houses. But his Bowie success came mainly from his reputation for producing quality houses at reasonable prices, a reputation nurtured by the popular media. Beyond the free publicity, Levitt undertook a massive advertising campaign. The weekend of the Belair opening, the firm ran six full-page advertisements in the *Washington Post, Evening Star,* and *Baltimore Sun.*[16] The early ads announced "a fabulous new community" in which "the price we <u>say</u> is the price you <u>pay</u>," emphasizing the absence of hidden costs, extra charges, and unpleasant surprises: the listed price for each model was firm. "A long time ago," the ad copy read, "Levitt decided there's only one right way to sell a house: *include everything in the quoted price.*"[17] Another ad referred to a *Harper's* magazine article that deemed "a Levitt house . . . the biggest bargain on the market," with prices 40 percent below those of houses built with traditional artisan methods.[18] Yet another advertisement told "A Little Story. About a Big House. At a Tiny Price!!!"[19] These themes were repeated again and again, along with assurances that Levitt salesmen never pressured anyone. They didn't need to, because buyers could have "a home of your own for just $116 a month," a home that's "fun to own," "easy on the budget," and better than traditional ranches and colonials ("We just don't make 'em the way they used to").[20] One ad showed a street sign that read, "You are entering BELAIR. Population: Happy!" There, readers could find "your 'Dream House.' " The "you" was pictured as a smiling white couple, the wife a pretty blonde in a white sleeveless dress, the husband tall and handsome in a suit and tie.[21]

Advertisements cannot, of course, create a market where none exists. Levitt's strong Belair sales benefitted from the pent-up demand for middle-class housing after successive recessions in 1958 and 1960. This was especially true of the growing Washington, D.C., area, where large numbers of people drew solid middle-class incomes working for the federal government. Once the recessions ended, thanks to looser monetary policy and fiscal stimulus, nearly a decade of robust economic growth ensued. More Americans than ever possessed the means to fulfill the "American dream" by purchasing a home in the suburbs.[22]

Advertisement for Belair at Bowie in the *Washington Sunday Star*. (Library of Congress Chronicling America Collection, public domain)

Like Levitt's New York, Pennsylvania, and New Jersey homes, the ones in Belair would sit atop cement slabs rather than a basement. The Maryland dwellings would be larger than his New York and Pennsylvania ones and similar in size to those under construction in New Jersey. But the Belair lots would be at least 30 percent bigger than those of the New Jersey Levittown.[23] The largest Bowie lots measured twelve thousand square feet or more, making them at least twice the size of the original Levittown, New York, lots. Like the last-built Pennsylvania Levittown dwellings and virtually all of the New Jersey ones, the Belair homes appealed to middle-of-the-road architectural tastes. They featured conventional façades sheathed in cedar or asphalt shingles or covered with brick or stone facing, rather than the utilitarian, quasi-modern siding of the first two Levittowns. Behind those traditionalist façades, however, lay up-to-date features such as central air-conditioning, dishwashers, wall ovens, and modern heating systems.[24]

The visual message Levitt meant to convey was that with Belair, he had left Levittown behind. Gone were the rows upon rows of nearly identical houses. As in Levittown, New Jersey, Levitt decided to place different models next to each other and to vary the houses' colors, rooflines, setbacks, and lot sizes. To add to its upscale appeal—Belair was the first Levitt community intended exclusively for a middle- and upper-middle-class clientele—the homebuilder left a great many green spaces and trees intact, including, as we have seen, a canopy of two-hundred-year-old tulip poplars that shaded the long entrance to the property's eighteenth-century manor house. Levitt restored the mansion and turned it into his firm's local headquarters; later he would donate it to the new community, which made the mansion its town hall.[25] Belair would sport Levitt's customary recreation facilities—swimming pools, ball fields, playgrounds—and his Bath and Tennis Club added a measure of snob appeal.

With this upscale veneer, Levitt targeted white-collar homebuyers—federal government employees, professional people, and other office workers from the prosperous triangle of Baltimore, Annapolis, and Washington, D.C. Even so, a Belair house was relatively inexpensive. "The Best House for the Money," proclaimed Levitt's ads, and the slogan was more than hype. In February 1962, *American Home* magazine dubbed the Belair Country Clubber the "Best Home for the

Money" in the southern United States, and homebuyers echoed the theme. "It's a lot of house for the money," said Air Force captain William M. Quinn shortly after moving in.[26] Richard and Barbara Mills told an interviewer they had bought into Belair because it was "extremely affordable." Joe and Helen Clark said no other builder provided central air-conditioning at a comparable price, and Sharon and Ronald Nelson bought their Bowie home because the monthly mortgage installments were lower than the rent they'd been paying. Asked what drew him to a Belair house and why he stayed, Don Kinsley replied, "Where [else] would you have all this?"[27] Reporters for the *Washington Evening Star* endorsed the sentiment, deeming Belair's "price per square foot . . . the lowest in the D.C. area."[28]

The first swath of houses ranged in price from $14,990 to $21,990, and by 1963, when the development's original sections were about half complete—new sections would be added later—average prices had gone up only slightly. The entry-level four-bedroom Cape Cod now sold for $15,990, the one-floor Rancher for $16,500, and the four-bedroom Colonial for $18,500. The deluxe Country Clubber topped out at $24,990. The Cape Cod required just $590 down and $118 a month; the Country Clubber, $2,290 down and $176 a month. In 2024 dollars, the lowest-priced Belair homes would cost $165,000, the most expensive, $258,000. Even allowing for inflation of nearly 1,000 percent, Belair's 1963 prices were a bargain compared to actual 2024 home values, which averaged $514,000 in Bowie.[29]

For these prices, the Belair models were roomy, intelligently conceived, and well equipped. Their modest cost, wrote the *Evening Star,* didn't come "at the expense of design."[30] Levitt, moreover, continued to improve each model as production proceeded from 1961 to 1968. Thanks in part to these improvements and to a blizzard of advertising, Levitt ultimately built 7,500 homes, nearly double the number originally planned.[31] A full-page ad in the *Washington Post* proclaimed, "People are buying Levitt homes faster than we can build them and they're willing to wait." The claim was largely true, and the ad explained it on three grounds: "outstanding value," "more room where you need it," and "a community that's fun to live in."[32]

There was such pressure to turn out houses quickly, that, at first, Levitt built them too fast, finishing eighty a week. The cycle "from bulldozer to moving van" took just eighteen weeks. Some of the construction was subpar, and Levitt had to make a number of repairs after his homebuyers had moved in. But to his credit, his crews fixed the problems, and they didn't recur.[33] Meanwhile, the ads continued relentlessly. Belair was a community "where children can run and play in the sunshine—in safety."[34] Other ads assured potential buyers that Levitt homes were "built to last a lifetime" and "needed little or no upkeep." That made them a "sound investment," especially since "no builder is better known than Levitt and Sons."[35]

Even the original, unimproved Bowie houses were considered an excellent buy in a Washington-area market that Levitt called "value-starved." At a time when just half of new houses nationwide had two bathrooms, all of the Belair models featured at least two. Every Belair dwelling sported a one- or two-car garage, dedicated laundry room, and, perhaps most innovatively of all, central air-conditioning. This feature was still relatively rare in the United States and a huge asset in the humid climate of Washington, D.C. Unlike the earlier Levittown models, all Bowie homes had a separate dining room and no fewer than three bedrooms. Their large master bedrooms featured en suite bathrooms, an amenity then mostly limited to "luxury" homes. Save for the compact Cape Cod, they all featured a foyer or entryway, which enhanced privacy by preventing family members or visitors from walking directly into a living space.

Most Bowie models also included a "family room" distinct from the living room. The former was intended to be "active and casual," the latter "quiet and formal."[36] Increasingly, the TV sat in the family room, a space for children, and was banned from the living room, a space mainly for adults. The family room, which replaced the often damp and poorly lit basement recreation room, was descended from the "social kitchen" of urban working-class homes, often the center of family life. Levitt and other postwar mass builders mostly abandoned this feature in favor of tiny kitchens connected to a dining "area." But American women, who did most of the cooking in the postwar decades, seemed dissatisfied with a cramped space good only for preparing meals and demanded larger kitchens. At first, Levitt and his counterparts simply expanded the kitchen to accommodate a table and chairs, but they soon added a lounge area connected to the kitchen, which enabled moms to keep an eye on the kids while they

THE ARDSLEY

THE BELAIR VERSION of the classic Cape Cod has a story-book charm all its own! Outdoors, it's a delight to the eye, with professional landscaping emphasizing the fine design. Indoors, the efficient use of space is amazing! From the 23-ft. sheltered porch through to the back lawn, there are more and bigger rooms than you'd believe possible.

There are four bedrooms, two on each floor, with a complete bath and linen closet on each floor. The master bedroom is exceptionally spacious - 17' x 17' 3"!

Beyond the generous 23-foot living room, you'll find a dining area-family room that opens to the back lawn. The adjoining kitchen is a homemaker's dream, with handsome, hand-rubbed wood cabinets, and plenty of counter space. Kitchen equipment includes a wall oven, a counter-top push-button range and 12.9 cu. ft. refrigerator—all by GE; and such luxury details as stainless steel sink, stainless steel Puritron hood, even a chopping block!

Just off the kitchen, in the separate laundry-utility room, there's a GE washer and matching dryer. Closets are plentiful, and there's extra overhead storage space in the attached garage. And for rainy-day comfort, the garage may be entered directly from the house!

The Ardsley is centrally air conditioned by Westinghouse, pre-wired for telephone installation, and equipped with Jerrold TV System. And everything's included in the price of the house, even the land. If desired, a two-car garage is available at additional cost.

The Ardsley, Belair's Cape Cod. (Archives of the Belair Mansion)

prepared the family meals. This lounge area evolved into a "family room" often connected to the kitchen. In the larger Belair models, the family room became its own large space, which allowed access to the kitchen but was no longer part of it.[37]

Of the four Belair models, the Cape Cod hewed closest to the original Levittown, New York, design. It had a steep-sloped roof, rear kitchen, and two first-floor bedrooms. Unlike the original Cape Cods, the Belair version came with two additional bedrooms and a bathroom in the half-story upstairs. Having upgraded the Cape Cod, a project already begun in the Pennsylvania and New Jersey Levittowns, Levitt turned to the ranch house, which first appeared in New York as a slight modification of the Cape. In Levittown, Pennsylvania, the ranch evolved into the immensely popular "Levittowner," a thousand-square-foot single-story home with three small bedrooms. In Belair, the single-story Rancher, Levitt's "Fun House," was one of the community's most sought-after homes.[38] Its main innovation, premiered in New Jersey, was its shape as an upside-down L. The left side of the

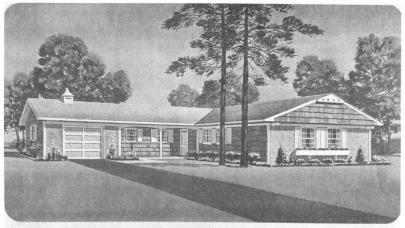

THE DEVON

THIS IS THE BIG RANCH HOUSE at Belair... 7 rooms on a really grand scale, with extra space built-in at every turn! From the 21-ft. sheltered porch, you enter a wood paneled foyer with guest closet. Beyond the foyer, there's a huge living room plus attractive dining area. The U-shaped kitchen has its own breakfast alcove, and beyond it, there's an enormous family room with another paneled wall, and sliding glass doors that open to the back lawn. There's a separate laundry room and an oversized attached garage, accessible from the house.

In the sleeping wing are three spacious bedrooms. The master bedroom has a private bath of its own, and there's another complete bath in the hall. It all adds up to a lot of living space – all on one floor! The up-to-the-minute kitchen is fully equipped with handsome, hand-rubbed wood cabinets, stainless steel sink, stainless steel Puritron hood, even a chopping block! Appliances are all by GE and include push-button counter-top range, automatic wall oven, 12.9 cu. ft. refrigerator, washer and matching dryer. The baths both have ceramic

tiled floors and tiled bath areas, and full-width, illuminated wall mirrors. One bath also has a built-in vanity, the other an oversized stall shower. The house is centrally air conditioned by Westinghouse, and the grounds are professionally landscaped with many trees, shrubs and other planting materials. And everything's included in the price of the house, even the land! If you want a fireplace or two-car, side-entry garage, these are available at additional cost.

The Devon, Belair's L-shaped ranch. (Archives of the Belair Mansion)

house faced the street horizontally and contained a one-car garage, laundry room, kitchen-family room, and a small porch. (A revised version would add a family room between the garage and eat-in kitchen.) The vertical part of the L, which extended toward the street, created a separate sleeping wing by placing all three bedrooms and both bathrooms in the front part of the dwelling. Behind them was a large living room/dining room combination, screened from the entryway by two back-to-back closets.[39]

Although the Capes and Ranchers proved popular, Levitt's more affluent buyers wanted a full-fledged two-story home, a "colonial" in the parlance of suburban design. Levitt had built some two-story dwellings before the war but mostly abandoned them after the war, focusing on one-and-a-half-story Cape Cods and single-story ranches. He had only contempt for the new split-level dwelling, which many 1950s and 1960s builders deemed an efficient use of space, since it fit three half-levels into a small, low-rise footprint. Levitt called the split an "abomination," a hybrid structure with the disadvantages of a multistory house—especially the need to climb stairs—without the privacy and sound advantages of completely separate floors.[40] This is why he kept building Cape Cods and ranches while many of his competitors embraced the split. But as postwar homebuyers grew more affluent and wanted larger, more traditional homes, he tiptoed back to full two-story models. He built a few hundred of them at the end of his Pennsylvania project, in 1957–58, and made them his largest New Jersey dwelling. In Bowie, the Colonial, advertised as a "Dream House," quickly became the most sought-after model, giving upwardly mobile families access to a "classic" American home.[41] The Colonial's front door opened onto a large center-hall foyer, which led to the living room on the left, dining room on the right, and powder room straight ahead. The family room, kitchen, and laundry faced the back, while a garage jutted out in front. The second story contained three or four bedrooms and two baths.[42]

The largest and most expensive Bowie model was the Country Clubber, which in an earlier incarnation served as the most elite home in Levittown, Pennsylvania, but which Levitt skipped in his New Jersey development. Belair's Country Clubber stretched fifty-seven feet from left to right and contained some 2,300 square feet of living space. A cross between a Cape Cod and a ranch, it was divided into three wings—a two-bedroom, two-bath wing on the left, a living-dining-family room wing in the middle, and a utility wing (two-car garage, laundry, and storage room) on the right. The middle wing rose high enough to accommodate two bedrooms, a bathroom, and two sizable storage spaces on the partial second floor. In February 1962, *American Home* featured the Country Clubber on its cover, as one of the six houses in the nation it considered "best for the money" based on their "good design, efficiency, workmanship, and materials." The Levitt model, *American Home* declared, "has everything a builder's house should have and many desirable features that some custom houses do not have." Its central air-conditioning, common to all Belair models, was "unbelievable . . . at this price," as was the "amazing package [of] 9 trees, 16 shrubs, and a big lot."[43] The Country Clubber wasn't the only Belair model to achieve such recognition. *Good Housekeeping* praised all of the Bowie homes and cited Levitt & Sons for "Excellence of Architecture Design, Land Development and House Planning, and General Advancement of the Arts of Better

THE GLADSTONE

The Gladstone, Belair's Colonial. (Archives of the Belair Mansion)

Home Building." The American Institute of Architects gave Levitt its Merit Award for two of the five Belair models.[44]

Despite the accolades, the Country Clubber didn't sell well at first. But sales improved markedly when Levitt created a special section of the development, quickly dubbed "snob hill," in which every house was a Country Clubber.[45] In this, the homebuilder imitated his second Levittown, which grouped the Country Clubbers in an elite section of town. In Bowie, this grouping was especially odd because it reverted to the uniformity for which Levitt was endlessly criticized early on, and which he was anxious to correct in Willingboro and most of Bowie.

If he had trouble selling Country Clubbers at first, his efforts to market a $30,000 "manor house" failed completely. He quickly dropped this ultra-large model. Despite this setback, Levitt drew the solid middle- and upper-middle-class clientele he sought. A 1969 survey by the Greater Bowie Board of Trade identified residents of the Levitt development as "well-educated, affluent people," far above the local or national norm in income and social class. Eighty percent had attended college, with 57 percent holding bachelor's degrees and 33 percent graduate degrees. In the surrounding Prince George's County as a whole, the respective percentages of degree holders were 16 and 11. Bowie's incomes matched its educational attainment. At a time when the U.S. median income stood at $8,389, 91 percent of Bowie residents earned more than $10,000, and 57 percent more than $15,000. The average household income in the city was $17,000, while a small elite earned twice that. Nearly half of those with jobs worked for the federal government, and another 7 percent belonged to the U.S. military. Only 34 percent worked in private industry. Since few jobs existed in Bowie itself, most employed people commuted to work, usually in Washington, D.C.[46]

As in the other Levitt communities, most women, although often well-educated, didn't work outside the home, but devoted their time to raising two or three or more children. Women were, however, highly active in the community, and they appeared anything but complacent about their roles in family and society. A local women's paper, the *Journal des Femmes,* an anglophone publication despite the title, became a forum for debate. Some writers held that women should devote themselves to home and family, while others maintained that wives should have careers, even if only to keep themselves interesting to their husbands. The dominant view in the *Journal* was that women should work part-time once their children entered school.[47]

For many families, that would be a while: most kids were young during the development's first decade. So, relatively speaking, was the community as a whole, though not as young as the New York or Pennsylvania Levittowns in their early days. In 1969, one-third of Bowie residents were aged twenty-seven to thirty-four, and 50 percent were thirty-five to forty-nine. For most of them, Belair was their first experience of homeownership, and, early on at least, few seemed discontented. Most said they planned to stay in Bowie for at least seven years; when residents left, it was mostly because their companies had transferred them out of town.[48]

Levitt's success in Bowie moved him to expand the development by purchasing an eight-hundred-acre Jesuit property in 1962 and some lakefront land five years later.[49] He also built a series of smaller, more upscale developments elsewhere in the Washington, D.C., region, including projects in Montpellier, Columbia, Crofton, Wheaton, and Upper Marlboro, Maryland, plus Loudoun County and Fairfax, Virginia.[50] These developments' houses resembled those built in Bowie, although some came with even more amenities, and a few developments included townhouses and optional basements.[51] Levitt constructed so many houses in the capital region that by the end of the 1960s, wrote the *Washington Post,* the company had "left a profound mark on the contours of the Washington suburbs."[52]

But his accomplishment, here as elsewhere, came at a huge social cost: persistent racial exclusion. Despite a growing African American middle class eager for suburban homes, Levitt maintained his all-white policy in Bowie, even after being required to sell to Blacks in Levittown, New Jersey. He cited "custom and precedent" as reasons to bar African Americans from Belair. Customarily, he said, Maryland homebuilders didn't create integrated communities, so neither would he. It would be "economic suicide" to sell to Black families when all other developers in the region did not.[53] African American individuals and organizations rejected this argument, which they had heard before, and quickly challenged Levitt's ban before the Federal Housing Administration.

In December 1962, Karl Gregory, an economist at the Bureau of the Budget, sent a formal complaint to the FHA over a Levitt's salesman's refusal to accept his deposit on a Belair home. Gregory's complaint cited President John F. Kennedy's recent executive order prohibiting discrimination in the rental and sale of housing supported by federal agencies. Levitt responded that the president's order applied only to FHA mortgage commitments made after November 20, 1962, and that all of the FHA's commitments to his company had come before that date.[54] When another Black homebuyer, Dr. Norris G. Mann, a physician who worked for the Food and Drug Administration, was also turned away from Belair, Levitt said, "We are not in violation of any law . . . nor are we violating the President's executive order." He was right on the letter of the law (but certainly not its spirit), and the FHA said so to both Gregory and Mann. Levitt added, "To sell a house to a Negro family will not really solve anything basic. It would, however, put this company at a crippling competitive disadvantage in relation to other builders who do not sell houses to Negro families and who are not apparently subject to public pressure to start doing so."[55] He told journalists he believed in a "universal open-occupancy policy," but only if all major developers abided by it.[56]

In June 1963, the newly formed Belair Citizens' Association addressed the question of integration in its first election for president. There were three candidates, one supporting integration, another opposing it, and a "moderate" somewhere in between. The moderate candidate, a career coast guard officer, won the contest with a platform that urged the association to "display only a passive interest" in integration, and maintained that the Levitt "policy at this time represents the best interests of the community." In other words, he did not favor integration but would not fight it either. After the election, he called it "inevitable."[57] Since other association offices were held by firm opponents of integration, there was little chance the organization would take any steps to open the community to African Americans. The same was true on the municipal level. In the mayoral contest of 1964, the pro-integration candidate came in third, as Bowie voters elected the anti-integration Republican (by one vote), even though Democrats held a two-to-one advantage in registered voters.[58] One prominent lawyer and longtime resident of Old Bowie suggested that the push for integration came from outside the community: "We don't have any trouble with our Negroes. We have some of the finest Negroes you'll find anywhere."[59]

But some of those African Americans belonged to major anti-discrimination organizations, and those organizations, along with African American newspapers, persistently rejected Levitt's rationale for barring Black buyers. They argued that, as the head of the country's largest and best-known homebuilder, he should use his company's prestige and economic clout to lead the effort to end racial exclusion. In August 1963, the local chapter of the Congress of Racial Equality (CORE) began to picket Levitt's Belair sales office, promising "to continue peaceful demonstrations every weekend until Mr. Levitt changes his policy."[60] One of the picketers was Persis Suddeth, an early Bowie-Belair resident who said she wanted to "break the ring of segregation around D.C."[61] Counterdemonstrators carried signs reading "Keep 'em White" and "Integration Stinks."[62]

In mid-August, eighteen Episcopal ministers joined the CORE protestors, saying, "Christian duty demanded support of CORE [against] Levitt's sales policy which is morally intolerable."[63] Other local clergy urged Levitt and other builders "to accept their responsibility" to reject racial exclusion. To emphasize their protest, the Episcopalians refused Levitt's offer of free land for a new church. The local Presbyterian clergy, meanwhile, tried to sell three Belair homes it owned to African Americans, but without success. They then polled local homeowners on the question of integration and claimed a majority of their sample supported it. Resales to Black homebuyers, however, remained rare. Still, the Bowie Human Relations Council quietly prepared for the community's eventual integration by creating a twenty-step program to prevent panic selling by whites and block-busting by real estate agents.[64]

In response to the pro-integration protests, Levitt closed Belair's model homes and obtained a court injunction against the demonstrators. When CORE members refused to back off, police arrested eight protestors. A standoff persisted until local officials promised to negotiate with Levitt in an effort to lift the racial ban.[65] It's unclear whether the homebuilder agreed to any talks, but compromise from him seemed unlikely. He continued to tell reporters that his company "will integrate, or not integrate, solely on the basis of what is good economically."[66] Altogether, seventeen protesters, four Black and thirteen white, ended up in jail, charged with trespassing and other violations. During their trial, in February 1964, defense attorneys argued that Levitt's policy violated the Constitution, while their clients had acted to uphold it. The state's attorney said that while he personally opposed Levitt's discriminatory policies, the protestors "had no right to go into this [model] home . . . to interfere with the economic livelihood of Levitt & Sons." The jury convicted the demonstrators after deliberating for just thirty minutes.[67]

Not only did Levitt refuse to sell Belair homes to African American buyers; he also displaced about fifty Black farmers from Bowie lands he intended for a new subdivision. The developer agreed to move the farmers' extremely modest dwellings elsewhere, but he made clear that African Americans would be barred from this formerly Black-owned terrain.[68] At the same time, Levitt ignored the needs of the mostly low-income Black families who had made up about half of Bowie's population before the Levitt development was annexed to it. The dilapidated Black neighborhood, known as Huntington, was split in two by the Penn Central Railroad (later Amtrak). The sewage system Levitt had built for Belair didn't extend to Huntington, where ancient septic tanks commonly overflowed and deposited their smelly, toxic contents into basements, streets, and the Patuxent River. In 1970, the city of Bowie finally agreed to connect Huntington, but the project was held up for years by political and bureaucratic obstacles.

The Reverend Paul Thompson, vicar of St. James Episcopal Church, excoriated the municipality for allowing raw sewage to seep into his basement, endangering his parishioners.[69]

Thompson's counterpart at Trinity Lutheran Church, which had branches in old Bowie and new Belair, confronted other forms of racial prejudice, hostility, and incomprehension. Though old Bowie was half Black, the church was entirely white. In June 1969, the Lutheran pastor, Kenneth Beachboard, was approached by a group of doctors, dentists, and other healthcare workers about opening a well-baby clinic, a dental clinic, and perhaps also a general medicine clinic in a church annex used for Sunday school classes. Since Bowie had no medical facilities, these clinics would fulfill a pressing need. At first, members of the congregation voted narrowly to approve the facilities, but they reversed themselves after finding dirty diapers and hypodermic needles in the building. Members of the medical staff said they didn't realize there would be no trash pickup and quickly disposed of the refuse themselves. But the damage was done. "We were cross-examined," said Terry Bohrer, who had spearheaded the clinics' creation. Church members "asked me . . . 'can you guarantee that the Sunday school children won't contract ringworm or lice' and 'Would you disinfect after each session?' " He added, "I couldn't believe this was happening in Bowie. I've never seen [such] prejudice before." The well-baby clinic ultimately found another location, but the other two clinics had to be abandoned.[70]

The opposition to having African Americans in the community didn't prevent white Bowie residents from "reverse-integrating" Bowie State College, a historically Black institution that had had no white students before Levitt's development opened. The whites were mostly Belair women interested in studying part-time, and in the 1963–64 academic year they made up 20 percent of the student body. The historically Black elementary school on campus became so popular among Bowie residents that its white enrollment reached 40 percent.

As for Belair's relatively upscale homes, not until 1968, after Prince George's County outlawed housing discrimination and Congress passed the Fair Housing Act, would Levitt sell a Belair home to an African American family; a few resales had brought a handful of Blacks to the community before then. Like the New York and Pennsylvania Levittowns, Levitt's Bowie development would long remain overwhelmingly white, an island of whiteness within increasingly Black Prince George's County. This situation would foster racial strife in the years to come.[71]

Meanwhile, Levitt's footprint in Bowie continued to expand. In September 1968, with Belair at Bowie reaching its full complement of 7,500 homes, his firm announced the opening of Belair Village, a new subdivision just to the south. Two months earlier, Bowie voters, most of them owners of Levitt homes, had approved a referendum to annex the new Levitt development to the city, potentially doubling its size and making it one of the largest municipalities in Maryland. Bowie had counted just one thousand people less than a decade earlier.[72] Belair Village would begin with a few thousand single-family homes, but Levitt also planned a large number of townhouses. This move away from purely detached homes built on Levitt's experiments in France and Willingboro. The single-family homes would be relatively expensive for a Levitt development, $22,000 to $30,000, but still "the most home for your money."[73] The townhouses, which were more like garden apartments, would sell for $17,000 to $22,000. Most were narrow two-story dwellings with a living room, family room, and kitchen on the ground floor and two or three bedrooms upstairs. One model had just one story and two bedrooms and, uncommonly for Levitt, these units would include an optional basement.[74]

Though annexed to the city of Bowie, Belair Village would be a separate community, with its "downtown" hugging a lakeshore, a private members-only swim and tennis club, and the usual Levitt complement of ball fields, playgrounds, parks, and land set aside for schools, churches, and synagogues. Along the lakeshore there would be shops, a gazebo, children's zoo, bandshell, outdoor amphitheater, and boating pavilion, all designed to evoke the charms of traditional small-town life, but with the comforts of a fully equipped modern house. One Levitt ad showed a dad in a rowboat with his young (blonde) daughter sitting beside him. Mom, also blonde, watches them from the shore with a picnic basket by her side. The caption reads, "Country living—with all the conveniences."[75] Other advertisements for the new development urged readers to buy a home before inflation pushed prices and interest rates higher. All the ads emphasized Levitt's reputation for building quality dwellings at reasonable prices.[76]

Such an idyllic picture of Levitt living had found its antithesis, as we have seen, in criticism of the developments' conformity, blandness, and lack of culture. One particularly hyperbolic version of this critique appeared in the 1967 German documentary *Suburbia USA*, about Belaire at Bowie.[77] The film begins with Malvina Reynolds's catchy song "Little Boxes," recorded by Pete Seeger in 1962, which was written about a California development but often applied to Levittowns and calls the houses "ticky-tacky" and "all the same." The film follows one Belair family for two weeks and records them at the breakfast table, the women preparing meals and supervising housework, the kids heading to school, and everyone dutifully attending church. The suburban space is depicted as almost completely devoid of men and "dominated by women," which the film presents as a bad thing: the "feminine mystique" leads to the erasure of men, as "The few minutes at the breakfast table are often the only time father and son spend together in twenty-four hours" and "The woman is the center of everyday life." In school, all the teachers are women, and "outside of school all the adults that kids come into contact with during the day are most likely women," a situation "some sociologists think . . . could be detrimental for an adult life."

Perhaps worse than the domination of women, according to the film, is "standardization in suburbia: everyone experiences pretty much the same thing every day." "One meets every week in the same group of friends, eats the same food, drinks the same drinks, and has the same conversations. Only the hosts rotate." Culture is nonexistent: "These communities are too small to be able to afford a library, concerts or theater," and "In suburbia, intellectual life is at its lowest level." Other than its swimming pool, "Belair has nothing more to offer—like most developments."

Neither Levitt nor his buyers were deterred by such critiques, and his output kept expanding. The 7,500 dwellings Levitt planned to build in Belair Village were nearly as many as he had in Belair, which would have made this development considerably larger than the one in New Jersey and only slightly smaller than the two original Levittowns. But this never happened. The new Belair project ultimately added only another 2,500 units, some of which would be plagued with shoddy workmanship and homeowner complaints.[78]

Still, Bowie became the largest municipality in Prince George's County and, in 1980, the city with the tenth-highest median income in the United States.[79] That was the peak of its affluence. Its size and prosperity fell in the 1980s as the many children who had grown up there left for college, marriage, and jobs. Most didn't return to Bowie because rental apartments were nonexistent and the few townhouses were relatively expensive. By then, Bowie's single-family homes had become too costly for first-time homebuyers, and in any case, few homes went on the market. Their original owners paid such low monthly mortgages that they had little incentive to sell; any new home would cost considerably more per month. After skyrocketing between 1960 and 1970, Bowie's population declined slightly over the following decade. Many of those who remained were in their fifties and up, and the lack of young people forced six of its schools to close. In their place came funeral parlors and senior centers. The once-Democratic city turned Republican, voting overwhelmingly for Ronald Reagan in 1980 and electing a conservative mayor.[80]

What would ultimately save Bowie, though not without major conflict, was the influx of prosperous African American families who, like their white counterparts, wanted to live in a spacious suburban house surrounded by green lawns and safe streets. By the 1980s, Prince George's County had become a haven for Black families eager to escape Washington, D.C. Many were comfortably well-off, and by 1990, African Americans constituted 52 percent of Prince George's population, setting it on a path to being the wealthiest majority-Black county in the nation.

Prince George's County had long displayed a rich African American history. Today's Bowie State University, a historically Black institution, traces its roots back to Baltimore in the immediate aftermath of the Emancipation Proclamation, when it was known as the Baltimore Association for the Moral and Education Improvement of the Colored People. Its Baltimore quarters were cramped and inadequate, and funding from the Maryland state legislature allowed school leaders to purchase a 187-acre tract in Bowie in 1910. The school became primarily a teacher-training institution in the 1920s, sending generations of instructors into Maryland's segregated schools. In the 1960s, it grew into a liberal arts college; two decades later, with the addition of STEM programs, it joined the state university system, its student body still mostly, but not exclusively, Black.[81]

Beyond Bowie State, Prince George's County was the home of several African American churches, all-Black schools, Black farming communities, and Black municipalities dating back to the early twentieth century. In 1950, 12 percent of the country's population was African American.[82] By the 1960s, Washington, D.C., had developed a sizable Black middle class that could afford houses outside the district's limits. Many flocked to Prince George's County. The more Black families took up residence in these suburban communities, the more whites moved out. By the 1970s, African Americans had become the majority in the parts of the county inside the D.C. Beltway, and by the early nineties, a majority in the county as a whole. When African American families began to move into Bowie, and especially into new subdivisions surrounding the Levitt development, the white population became anxious. What especially upset the whites was a federal judge's 1972 order desegregating Prince George's schools through busing. The decision was hugely controversial and sparked a hostile reaction, although the many busing opponents took pains to say their position wasn't racist.[83] When the busing plan was confirmed, a number of white parents pulled their children out of the public schools, but most grudgingly swallowed the desegregation order.[84] Although Bowie's residents couldn't prevent school busing, they had the power to reject a subsidized housing plan that year by voting the mayor who had advanced it out of office. Bowie's new mayor cancelled the project, ensuring that its housing stock would remain solidly middle class—and its population almost entirely white.[85]

That white population—94 percent of Bowie in 1990—had aged and stayed put, happy with the low mortgage payments and proximity to Washington and Baltimore. There were few Belair houses for sale.[86] But after Levitt stopped building there in the late 1970s, new subdivisions with far more expensive homes went up within the Bowie city limits. These houses, some of which sold for $350,000 to $400,000 by 2000, were mostly bought by Black families. The median home in the District of Columbia that year cost $157,000, and the median home nationwide, $135,000.[87] Between 1990 and 2000, Bowie's Black population mushroomed from 6 percent to 30 percent, as the city annexed the new Black subdivisions to increase its tax base.[88]

A variety of housing options enabled working-class Blacks to move into the county, but most of the African American newcomers were solidly middle class, with a wealthy upper crust. Many were drawn to Prince George's by its "critical mass of middle-class blacks," "the significant black presence" in its communities. As David Ball, a Washington contract administrator, told a *New York Times* reporter, "I really wasn't interested in moving into an all-white neighborhood and being the only black pioneer down there. I don't want to come home and always have my guard up."[89] Another African American resident said, "I like being with Black people who think like me."[90]

The influx of Blacks to Bowie substantially raised the city's median family income and created a rare situation in which a U.S. municipality's Black residents were wealthier than its white ones. "If you drive through Bowie and see a big house," Jason Fenwick, a Black lawyer and resident of the city, told the *Wall Street Journal*, "chances are an African American owns it. If you see a small house, there's a 70 to 80 percent chance a white owns it." Fenwick added, "It used to be that whites didn't like you because you're dirty, you don't work, you're poor. Now I have more money than you, more education, a bigger house—and you still don't like me."[91]

As Prince George's County became a Black enclave, African Americans assumed leadership positions as mayors, school superintendents and principals, businesspeople, and community activists. In 1994, Wayne K. Curry, an African American lawyer, became the first non-white politician to be elected the county's chief executive.[92] By 2000, the county's Black population had reached 62 percent, the white population down to 24.[93] Thanks to Belair-Bowie's island of whiteness, the city of Bowie remained more white than Black, but even there the African American population had grown by a factor of five since 1970. This rapid growth put many of Bowie's white inhabitants on edge.

In the late 1990s, the city's quiet racial resentment exploded into the public sphere. In June 1997, after a series of interracial fights among the students, someone set three crosses ablaze in front of Bowie High School. By then, Bowie's schools were 40 percent Black, and the high school had named its first African American principal. White parents increasingly criticized the new principal, Patricia Brooks, for failing to discipline rowdy students and for lax standards in general. Brooks saw things differently: "It was about power and who had it and who didn't."[94]

The split between Black and white parents over the principal led to a further shift in power relations in 1999, when a Black group ousted the all-white leadership of the PTA. Relations continued to deteriorate from there. When Prince George's County's superintendent of public education, an African American woman, cut the Bowie schools' budget and transferred the funding to poorer, blacker districts, white Bowie residents publicly protested the decision. "There's a feeling of reverse discrimination against us," declared a member of Bowie's all-white school board.[95] "We can't stand in line," said another white parent, "while they serve the rich African Americans and then the poor ones inside the Beltway and then, if there's something left over, *if*, then we get it."[96]

The protests became more vehement when a new high school opened in a neighboring, predominantly Black community to relieve the overcrowding there. Bowie schools were just as packed. Referring to Bowie's overcrowding during a tense, standing-room-only special community meeting, a white parent objected to a plan to temporarily bus students from a neighboring town to Bowie: the city, she said, didn't need "that element."[97] Blacks at the meeting were offended by the remark, which understandably sounded racist to them, although the individual who uttered it denied any racist intent. Not long afterward, someone scrawled racist epithets on the exteriors of Black-owned homes and the sides of nearby cars.

The *Wall Street Journal,* along with other newspapers, sent a reporter to Bowie after someone sprayed "KKK" in huge red letters on the garage of Jason Fenwick's next-door neighbor. This incident especially infuriated Bowie's Black residents, also unhappy about the cuts to their school budget, but who didn't see the reduction as having to do with race. Plenty of whites agreed that the cuts weren't racially motivated and tried, along with Black friends and neighbors, to soothe the tensions. Conciliation became difficult, however, when some white residents began to demand that Bowie secede from Prince George's County and join the mostly white Anne Arundel County next door. Secession was pure fantasy, but the idea convinced many Black homeowners in Bowie that their white counterparts would never accept them. Fenwick and others decided that the whites ought to leave, not through secession but individually. "I get no benefit from white Bowie," he said. "Why don't they just move—like they do in other communities when Blacks move in?"[98]

The issues that had galvanized Bowie's Black-white conflict, school quality and inadequate resources, were serious concerns for both communities. As a majority Black area, Prince George's County hadn't attracted the number and quality of businesses that would have rushed to white areas of similar wealth. This meant lower property tax receipts and underfunded schools, especially since when it was majority-white, the county had voted to impose caps on homeowners' assessments.[99] Stagnant revenue left Bowie's schools overcrowded and under-resourced. For want of cafeteria space, students were forced to eat lunch in shifts and often standing up. School libraries had to be converted into classrooms, and computers dated from the 1980s. Test scores dropped.[100]

Fortunately, the revenue situation was about to change. In 1999, a long-vacant parcel of land once owned by Levitt drew the interest of major shopping center developers as well as national chain stores and restaurants. Target, Kohl's, Staples, Sports Authority, Pier 1 Imports, and other stores soon opened in or near Bowie. So did Applebee's, TGI Fridays, Lone Star Steakhouse, and a full complement of fast-food places. "At first there was disbelief," said a major commercial developer, "because Prince George's County has been traditionally more rural and blue collar. . . . The retailers were very skeptical about the vibrancy of the market. Now . . . they are experiencing terrific success."[101]

They finally understood that although the area was heavily African American, it was affluent and growing. Bowie's population increased from forty thousand to fifty thousand between 1990 and 2000 and seemed poised to grow further. "Because of its population and education profile," said a spokesman for Borders bookstore, "we found [Bowie] to be an attractive community." Lest people think development would be limited to big box stores and shopping mall restaurants, a key developer made it clear that "We will not have a discounter value orientation. We are . . . negotiating with some very popular, high-quality both department and specialty stores."[102]

As Bowie became more desirable, African Americans continued to move in, and they gradually assumed more leadership positions. In the elections of 2002, two African American candidates were elected to the city council, marking the end of the white monopoly; a third of the council members were now Black.[103] In 2003, whites still made up 62 percent of Bowie's population, and African Americans 31 percent. But by 2010, the Black proportion exceeded the white, 48.7 percent to 41.4, with other categories, including "two or more races," totaling

10 percent. Bowie had become a majority-minority city, although still with a sizable number of whites. The two dominant races, however, were only moderately well integrated spatially. The Levitt-built areas (Belair and Belaire Village) remained primarily white, the more recently annexed parts of the city mainly Black. Even so, 20 to 25 percent of the Levitt section had become Black, and many whites lived in the majority Black parts of town.[104]

Between 2010 and 2020, Bowie's population grew from 54,727 to 58,329, largely from a further influx of non-white families. Much of the growth since the 1980s resulted from annexation of heavily Black subdivisions that had nearly doubled the city's area. The 2020 census revealed a population that was 32 percent white and 56.4 percent Black. The Hispanic/Latino numbers had increased, as had those who belonged to two or more races. The white population had declined in both relative and absolute terms, with the overall number of white inhabitants dropping by four thousand even as Bowie's total population rose by 3,600. Still, the white population fell much less steeply than in Willingboro, and Bowie maintained a measure of racial integration, in part because the relative wealth of the African America residents narrowed the class barriers that usually contributed to white flight.[105] Bowie didn't, however, elect its first Black mayor until 2019.[106]

Today, the community feels unusually integrated, as Blacks and whites seem to frequent the city's many shopping centers in equal numbers. The Levitt development remains more white than Black, but according to longtime residents, 25 to 30 percent of homeowners there are African American.[107] Overall, the Belair sections seem calm, quiet, and neatly trimmed, with no lawns unmowed or houses in need of paint. Mature trees shade the streets, and green spaces and woods punctuate the rows of houses. The whole development feels spacious, with none of the cramped, congested feel of the New York and Puerto Rico Levittowns. It takes an expert eye to see that it's made up of copies or variations of houses in the Pennsylvania and Willingboro Levittowns. Most Bowie homeowners have replaced Levitt's original asbestos or cedar shingles with aluminum or vinyl siding and have built additions, enclosed garages, and added landscaping. Some façades now sport bay windows and brick or stone veneer, while wooden decks protrude from the backs and sides of the houses. A great many dwellings have been remodeled on the inside, especially in the kitchens and bathrooms, where cabinets, appliances, and fixtures have been updated. Homeowners have painted over Levitt's original gold-speckled, cream-colored walls and replaced his asphalt floor tiles with wall-to-wall carpeting or shiny oak planks. Some have removed interior walls to create the open plan that Levitt largely abandoned after Levittown, Pennsylvania.[108]

As for Bowie as a whole, there's no real downtown; instead, stores and restaurants are concentrated in shopping centers built along highway-like boulevards. There is little street life. Most streets lack sidewalks, unneeded since this is entirely a car culture. One of Bowie's greatest virtues is the apparent satisfaction of its residents, many of whom have lived there for decades or have bought their parents' homes and moved back in as adults.[109] The other key virtue, rare in the United States, is a relatively successful racial integration in which Blacks and whites share a community and make it work reasonably well.

7 Bill Levitt in Paris

"FRANCE IS IN the same position today," declared Bill Levitt at a Paris press conference in 1964, "that Long Island was in fifty years ago." The demand for housing was such that his homebuilding company "can't afford not to go there."[1] He had a point. The building of single-family houses, what the French call *maisons individuelles* (separate houses) or *pavillons,* had stagnated since the end of World War II, and much of what existed consisted of rickety shacks erected by the homeowner in areas with virtually no infrastructure of roads, sewage systems, or zoning rules.[2] The few commercially built single-family homes produced after the war were mostly constructed one by one using expensive artisanal methods.[3] This was the case despite the overwhelming desire for detached homes among French families of all social classes. In poll after poll, beginning immediately after the war and continuing, by then, for almost two decades, 70 to 80 percent of French people said they wanted to live in a single-family home surrounded by greenery and not attached to neighboring homes. They wanted a living room, two or more small bedrooms, and fully equipped bathrooms and kitchens, even if it meant living in a mass-produced tract dwelling like those Levitt offered.[4]

What Levitt got wrong was the notion that the French building industry lagged behind the American one. While they largely neglected single-family homebuilding after the war, French builders didn't neglect modern, technologically advanced construction techniques. In many ways, their methods were more mechanized and arguably more modern than Levitt's. It's just that to alleviate the country's severe shortage of adequate housing, French leaders had prioritized large-scale housing projects using prefabricated, factory-made components that were standardized and easily reproduced. While the United States built Levittowns, France built huge housing complexes on the suburban fringes of Paris and other major cities. French officials and leading architects and engineers saw their country's existing stock of single-family suburban dwellings, most jerry-built on unplanned tracts, as a model to avoid.

In rejecting the single-family home, French elites had been influenced by the avant-garde architect and urban planner Le Corbusier (Charles-Édouard Jeanneret), who proposed to populate French cities with apartment towers and complexes composed of standardized units. But Le Corbusier designed and built only a few such projects, most notably Marseille's Cité Radieuse, a 337-unit building suspended on concrete pylons that seemed too radical for most traditionally trained French architects and urban planners. His general ideas, however, like those of other proponents of the "international style" (Mies van der Rohe, Walter Gropius, Adolf Loos), seeped into the work of more mainstream practitioners.[5] Postwar French planners, many of them influenced by socialist ideas, wanted working people to be renters rather than owners, for fear that homeownership would make them "petit-bourgeois" or "bourgeois" and turn them against collectivist, working-class values.[6] Levitt agreed, though from the opposite political perspective: he saw homeownership as a bulwark against communism.

Even if their construction methods were more advanced than those of the U.S. housing industry, French builders didn't apply them in earnest until nearly a decade after the war—unlike the United States, where Levitt and other mass builders went to work right away.[7] The French needed first to reconstruct the buildings and other infrastructure destroyed during the war, and then create the elements of a modern industrial economy—the factories, banking system, transportation and communication networks that, before the war, had been underdeveloped relative to other Western countries.[8]

While these priorities were perhaps understandable, the leaders' delay in dealing with the housing situation made a dire situation catastrophic. Nearly two million homes had been damaged or destroyed during the war, and the postwar baby boom made the housing deficit all the more acute.[9] In 1945, 7 percent of France's forty-one million people had no home—compared to a U.S. homeless figure of 4 percent. Even more than in the United States, much of the housed population in France squeezed in with relatives and packed themselves into tiny substandard units with three or four times their intended number of inhabitants. Others lived in abandoned railroad cars, squalid hotels, war-ruined buildings, or in the growing shantytowns that ringed major cities, especially Paris. By the mid-1960s, forty thousand people, many of them immigrants from North Africa, huddled on the outskirts of Paris in makeshift structures that mostly lacked heat, light, and sanitary facilities. During severe winters, people were regularly found frozen to death.[10] And the houses that existed were far more rudimentary than those in the United States. In 1946, 48 percent of French homes had no running water, 80 percent lacked an indoor toilet, and 80 percent possessed neither a bathtub nor a shower. Just 10 percent of households possessed running water, a toilet, and bath or shower in their unit.[11] Nearly 20 percent of French dwellings lacked a kitchen, and of those that had one, half were equipped only for simple meals.

These conditions saw virtually no improvement until after the mid-1950s, when huge housing complexes, *grands ensembles,* began to go up throughout the country and especially in the suburban ring around Paris, where the housing shortage was especially dire. The population of the French capital grew by nearly 30 percent between 1954 and 1968, even as slum clearance dramatically reduced the amount of inhabitable space. The only place to build large numbers of affordable dwellings was in the suburbs, whose population quickly dwarfed that of the city itself. The largest of the new suburban complexes, warehousing as many as fifty thousand each, mushroomed in sparsely populated peripheral towns like Sarcelles, Massy-Antony, and La Courneuve.[12] Although these projects were privately built, the French government effectively controlled them, playing an outsized role in their financing and organization, setting standards for the size and cost of apartments, and determining the construction methods to be used. The new apartment towers and blocks relied on mass-produced, prefabricated components such as floor-to-ceiling concrete panels with the windows already built in. The panels were made of reinforced concrete, not steel, because the companies contracted to build

The *grand ensemble* at Massy-Antony (today Massy-Opéra), France, begun in
1959 and destined to contain more than nine thousand apartments. (Direction
Régionale et intérdepartementale de l'environnement, de l'aménagement et des
transports [DRIEAT])

them had long championed concrete-based construction. Since the
government's objective was to build "massively, quickly, economically," as the official literature put it, the new buildings featured few
internal or external adornments and looked very much alike. The ultimate example of this approach was the *chemin de grue,* a construction system that used cranes mounted on railroad tracks to stack
identical prefabricated apartment units alongside one another down
the length of the tracks, creating long, narrow structures that seemed
built from huge, hollow Legos.[13]

The government officials, engineers, and architects who designed
and built the projects, along with the social scientists who endorsed
them, were proud of these developments for engineering better lives
and greater social equality. As the architect Marcel Lods put it, the
designers' goal was "to teach them [French people] how to live."[14]
They would manufacture national solidarity by eliminating class
differences over the use of residential space. Working-class people

had traditionally seen the kitchen as the center of family life, while middle-class families gathered in a living room, reserving their kitchens for the homemaker or the servants. In an effort to unite the two classes, the standardized housing units of the *grands ensembles* built middle-class habits into their designs.[15] These cultural initiatives would yield mixed results at best, and government efforts to impose unwelcome modes of living had people of both social classes dreaming of a single-family house all their own.

By the numbers, however, the effort to build mass housing was wildly successful. By 1958, France was creating three hundred thousand new dwelling units a year, and between 1953 and 1975, the beginning and end, respectively, of the government's mass construction project, France would increase its number of dwellings by 61 percent, from thirteen million to twenty-one million units.[16] As uniform and uninspiring as the new units were, they all included the basic amenities—running water, complete kitchens, and full bathrooms—that the overwhelming majority of French homes had lacked. Still, despite this major achievement, not everyone was housed, and the Parisian shanty-towns persisted into the 1970s.

French people quickly took their new amenities for granted and began to focus on the *grands ensembles*' downsides. They were ugly, monotonous, noisy, and so crowded that privacy seemed lost. At first, the towers and medium-rise slabs were surrounded by ample green space, which made the stark concrete exteriors less oppressive. One architect, Émile Aillaud, managed to avoid the flat rectangular boxes and towers that characterized most *grands ensembles* with his La Grande Borne project, a series of low-rise, curved structures that undulated around courtyards filled with greenery. But as more projects went up, the green spaces shrank, leaving the ugly, uniform buildings packed tightly together with little greenery in between. Often, the complexes sat far away from public transportation—this was especially true of La Grande Borne—and there were few stores, bakeries, and other services close by. Even schools required a trek, and playgrounds and ball fields had been largely forgotten.

In the Paris region, most of the *grands ensembles* were erected on the wrong side of the Boulevard Périphérique, the multilane, limited-access beltway circling Paris and cutting off the suburbs from the city. The *périphérique,* built between 1958 and 1973, isolated the residents of the *grands ensembles* in a no-man's land, neither country nor city. They could glimpse the beauty of Paris mainly on TV. Eventually, schools and stores would go up inside the complexes, and a regional rail system would arrive. But none of these services matched what was available in Paris itself.

Despite these inequalities and inconveniences, residents of the complexes nonetheless found them "acceptable" or "satisfactory," mainly because the new housing was at least better than what they had before.[17] Still, there were complaints, and journalists, few of whom lived in the towers, took them up with a vengeance, especially in the case of Sarcelles. Writers competed to trash the massive, fifty-thousand-person development as a "vertigo of technology," "human silo," "termite heap," and "dormitory city." In his book *Vivre à Sarcelles* (Living in Sarcelles), Jean Duquesne was especially hyperbolic, condemning the project as "this great barracks, this concentration camp where we are locked in rabbit cages."[18] Psychologists invented a mental condition called Sarcellitis to describe the supposed effects of living in these new habitats. The syndrome was said to affect women in particular. One writer asked:

> How does Sarcellitis begin? First the women cease to be interested in their housework. You visit them at five in the afternoon and the beds aren't made yet. From indifference they pass to disgust, from disgust to hatred. ... The sick ones are conscious of their state, which doesn't help. "I'm well housed, but when I go outside, I can't stand it. This uniformity frightens me like a concentration camp." ... Sarcellitis, total disenchantment, indifference to social life, insurmountable boredom, ending in nervous depression in benign cases, and suicide in acute cases.[19]

In 1961, Christiane Rochefort published a novel, *Les petits enfants du siècle* (Children of heaven), whose adolescent narrator, Josyane, comments ironically on the gulf separating the projects' monotonous life from the government hype touting them. "At night," Josyane says, "the windows would light up and inside there were only happy families, happy families, happy families. Going by, you could see them beneath the lightbulbs, through the picture windows. One happiness after another, all the same as twins, or a nightmare."[20] Josyane doesn't live in Sarcelles, and when she first sees it, she is stunned.

And I thought I lived in the projects! But this was THE Project, this was the real Project of the Future! Buildings and buildings and buildings for kilometers and kilometers and kilometers. All alike. In rows. White. And more buildings. Buildings buildings buildings buildings buildings buildings buildings buildings buildings buildings. Buildings. Buildings.[21]

Despite this criticism, the government maintained its focus on *grands ensembles* into the 1970s, persisting in the belief that whatever they said, French citizens were better off in these large projects. For government officials and a great many architects and social scientists, single-family dwellings produced an excessive individualism, isolating people from one another and wrecking the solidarities that had supposedly existed in traditional urban neighborhoods, and which they hoped to recreate in the *grands ensembles*. Never mind that those solidarities had been exaggerated and that the projects' residents, far from forging alliances, often hated their neighbors. Observers on the left admitted that working-class solidarities might be diluted because the proletariat were sharing their housing complexes with lower-middle- and middle-class people. But this was still better than letting them become proprietors of *maisons individuelles*.[22]

Although elite voices persisted in condemning single-family dwellings, a countercurrent of opinion began to develop in the 1960s. One of the earliest of these voices was Raymond Berrurier, the ambitious, energetic mayor of Le Mesnil-Saint-Denis, a tiny village of 1,200 souls twelve miles southwest of Versailles and twenty-four miles from Notre-Dame. Berrurier was elected mayor in 1938 and remained in that position until his death, thirty-nine years later. He leveraged his post to accumulate other offices along the way: vice president of the General Council (legislative body) of his *département* (state); vice-president of the association of mayors of France; and general secretary of the Council of European Communes.

Berrurier's village occupied one of the shrinking number of rural spaces in a greater Paris increasingly pockmarked by *grands ensembles* and "new towns." Originally designed to be part rural and part urban, these had become small cities in their own right. Le Mesnil-Saint-Denis stood a stone's throw from Saint-Quentin-en-Yvelines, which in 1968 already housed fifty-one thousand people and today encompasses a quarter million. Berrurier hated the *grands ensembles* and new towns and fiercely championed rural communes like his own, whose very existence he believed was under threat. "We are facing an evil," he wrote in the early 1950s, "that has afflicted the entire West, namely the stagnation and soon the death of thousands of rural communes . . . and the disorderly and monstrous growth of cities that overwhelm and crush the individual, sacrificed in barracks 10, 15, 20 stories high."[23] Despite his apocalyptic language, Berrurier realized that to protect his village and keep it vital, he had to meet modernity halfway. So he spearheaded an effort in the mid-1950s to develop some 150 acres of unbuilt land in the commune with single-family and low-rise housing.

Until 1926, this piece of land had belonged to an eighteenth-century château whose owner, a former mayor of Le Mesnil-Saint-Denis, sold it to a developer, the Société anonyme foncière et immobilière (SAFI, the Land and Real Estate Corporation), which divided it into two thousand tiny lots to be resold one by one, as was customary at the time. The lots sold slowly and only a few houses were built before the Great Depression and World War II halted further transactions. The houses were mostly of extremely poor quality, having been hastily erected by disreputable firms or the owners themselves. They had no electricity until 1957, no running water until 1962, and no paved roads until 1966. It was the commune that finally installed those amenities, at considerable cost to its tiny base of taxpayers.[24]

Berrurier was desperate to improve these blighted properties, which, he feared, harmed the community's reputation and also the ancient château that anachronistically loomed behind them. In 1952, he arranged for the commune to buy the château and the surrounding parkland for just $16,000 ($190,000 today). The commune would gradually repair and restore the once-elegant building, turning it into a new town hall and an elementary school. But the SAFI still owned the rest of the château's former lands—some 150 acres—and although it took steps to develop it, progress was slow and eventually petered out In 1958, Berrurier's town council voted to expropriate the holding, but the tiny commune lacked the funds to back up its decree, which in any case the SAFI challenged in various venues.

While these events unfolded, Bill Levitt opened an office in Paris, where, in 1962, he dipped his toe into the waters of French real estate development by constructing two apartment buildings. He also announced in a news conference that he planned to build single-family homes in the Paris suburbs.[25] "France today," he told *Business Week*, "is like the U.S. right after World War II. There's an enormous need for housing there, and no one to put it up."[26] While this wasn't true of housing in general, Levitt was right about single-family home construction. He was well aware that more than 12 percent of dwellings in the Paris region were more than a century old and that still, in 1962, a fifth lacked running water, a fourth were officially overcrowded, and half had no private bathrooms. Even with the new *grands ensembles*, France was still plagued by a shortage of decent housing, and those with modern amenities were especially scarce.[27]

Berrurier, fully attuned to this situation, wouldn't have missed the Levitt news, which doubtless moved him in November 1962 to contact a representative of the Gretima Company, an affiliate of the newly created Levitt subsidiary Levitt-France.[28] There's no record of Gretima's answer, but it's clear that Berrurier also contacted Bill Levitt, who responded favorably. In late December, the mayor wrote Levitt a long, quasi-philosophical letter expressing the hope that Levitt might want to create his modern development in Le Mesnil-Saint-Denis, which had wanted one for so long.[29] "We don't want simply to build houses," Berrurier wrote, "which is something anyone can do, even well on occasion." Instead he wanted to "create a genuine development, a <u>community</u> in which people can be happy because they have <u>the ability to alternate between social contact and solitude,</u> which I deeply believe is a fundamental necessity of all human beings" (emphasis original). For solitude, people required two things: they had to be able to "enjoy their own space" separate from their families, and their families had to have their own space apart from the community. For social contact, individuals and families needed the ability to "come together within bounds of a living community with all of its diverse forms."[30] To achieve these twin objectives of isolation and togetherness, Berrurier wrote, people needed separate homes and common facilities.

Levitt would have sympathized with much of what Berrurier wanted, since he regularly said his goal was to build communities, not houses alone. Still, he was wary of the mayor's desire for "a complete interpenetration of the developer and the commune." Levitt didn't brook interference in his work. He would have readily agreed with Berrurier, however, that France was committed to a misguided idea of how to build homes for its people and that "an American spirit" could create "on the old soil of Europe" the kind of community he wanted.

Berrurier and Levitt apparently found more areas of agreement than disagreement, and a Levitt project in Le Mesnil-Saint-Denis began to take shape. After visiting Levittown, New York, the mayor quickly approved the sale of the former SAFI land to Levitt. The price was attractive: three million francs, the equivalent then of about $600,000 ($6 million today) for all 150 acres. On June 27, 1963, Levitt-France and the commune of Le Mesnil-Saint-Denis signed an agreement giving the American home-builder the go-ahead to plan a development in the town.[31] This was a good deal for Levitt, and he jumped at the chance to help save France from its housing woes by building a French Levittown.[32]

Still, the partnership with Berrurier would not be easy. In the United States, Levitt was used to steamrolling his opposition, even though he ultimately had to compromise on integrating Willingboro. Mayor Berrurier was a harder nut to crack. He inserted himself—and the town council he fully controlled—into virtually every aspect of the planning and construction of Levitt's project. From the start, Levitt agreed to abandon the wood-frame construction common to his and most other suburban American dwellings, and substitute what most French people considered more "noble" materials, brick and stone. (Although when stone proved too costly, he fought a fierce battle with the mayor to get him to compromise on cinderblocks faced with stucco.)[33] The French associated wood construction with the flimsy shacks often built on suburban lots in the 1920s and 1930s, and with the log cabins of the American frontier.[34] Berrurier also insisted, and Levitt agreed, on adopting architectural features common in the Île-de-France (the Paris region): tile or slate roofs with steep slopes; "French" windows; shutters that opened and closed rather than being merely decorative, as in Willingboro; and "noble" façades. Levitt agreed to eliminate bedroom windows on the sides of houses facing next-door dwellings, creating large blank walls that his designers hated. Berrurier maintained that these were necessary for privacy. Levitt had also agreed to sprinkle among his single-family homes a few blocks of two-story row houses and five twelve-unit apartment buildings. This was a major concession, but Berrurier wanted to make some of the dwellings accessible to people of modest means.

Substantial as these compromises were, the mayor demanded more. Levitt refused to grant any other concessions, and throughout most of 1964 and into 1965, Berrurier and company executives, including Bill Levitt himself, exchanged a series of increasingly hostile letters. Levitt demanded that Berrurier "curtail his interventions," and the mayor responded that the purpose of his interventions was to arrive at an "exemplary project."[35] Finally, an exasperated Levitt threatened to cancel the development. "I told you about a year ago," he wrote, "that we are much more qualified than you in the field of construction. . . . If we find that we can't proceed in the way that we need to, we will have no choice but to sell the land at a time most advantageous to us . . . even if the construction process has already begun."[36]

In the end, Berrurier backed off: he needed the project more than Levitt did. It seems clear that Levitt was prepared to purchase land elsewhere in the Paris suburbs if Berrurier hadn't given in. On May 19, 1965, just a week after closing the definitive deal in Le Mesnil-Saint-Denis, Andrew Lorant, the president of Levitt-France, took out an option on 450 acres of woods and farmland belonging to the mayor of Lésigny, a commune forty miles to the east.[37] The negotiations with Lorant would certainly have begun long before May 19.

With the Lésigny property in reserve, Levitt began immediately to lay the infrastructure and build his model homes in Le Mesnil-Saint-Denis. The models went on display the following October, and as with the U.S. Levittowns, the sales office was besieged with potential buyers. *Time* magazine reported that "60,000 Frenchmen poured out of Paris to gape at Levitt's recently opened American-style subdivision."[38] The three-, four-, and five-bedroom dwellings were priced from $22,000 to $32,000, about twice as much as comparable Willingboro homes, but 25 percent less than similar-sized French-built houses.[39] Altogether, there would be 595 units—360 detached single-family dwellings, 175 side-by-side duplexes and row houses, and 60 apartments.[40] The single-family lots averaged about 6,500 square feet, 500 square feet larger than those of Levittown, New York, thanks in part to Berrurier, who made Levitt create more separation between homes.[41]

By early December 1965, all 595 dwellings had been sold, although the first houses wouldn't be finished until the following July.[42] Levitt claimed to have received $100 deposits from 1,111 prospective homebuyers, and to have 450 more on a waiting list. Those who couldn't be accommodated at Le Mesnil-Saint-Denis would have priority for the Lésigny development, already in the planning stages.[43] Even allowing for Levitt hyperbole, the demand was exceptionally strong.

René Deces, who grew up in the Le Mesnil-Saint-Denis development, named Les Résidences du Château, told an interviewer that his parents put down a deposit shortly after touring the model homes and became seventy-seventh in line for a house. In November 1965, they selected their model, and they then traveled frequently to Le Mesnil-Saint-Denis to watch it going up.[44] The Deceses weren't the first family in France to install themselves in a Levitt home; that distinction went to Raymond and Rosemonde Potier, whose June 1966 move-in attracted extensive press coverage. The media-savvy Bill Levitt welcomed them in person, with cameras clicking. Levitt's marketers made the Potiers the subject of a full-page Levitt ad in *Le Monde* and other leading French papers. "Imagine their joy!" the ad proclaimed. "For the entire family, life will be transformed. Raymond will take his daily run in the forest, while Rosemond, who loves flowers, will be able to garden to her heart's content. Pascal will finally be able to ride the magnificent bicycle he received for Christmas. Chantal is thrilled. She'll be able to play her transistor radio at top volume without fear of disturbing the neighbors. The Potiers' joy can be yours."[45]

This ad, like the many others published in the spring and summer of 1966, emphasized that while the development was completely sold out, new Levitt communities were coming.[46] The ads formed part of a larger campaign that linked the Résidences du Château to the noble châteaus of the past and to the surrounding forests, where "once upon a time, the Kings of France hunted undisturbed." The Levitt homes, according to a sales brochure, were "real residences in all their nobility. Not housing blocks, but separate domains surrounded by gardens that extend into the forest close by."[47] As with Levitt's original prewar developments on Long Island's North Shore and, later, with Bowie, Maryland, the company portrayed its homebuyers as modern-day aristocrats living a gracious country life.

Like the Deceses, the Potiers chose the Arcy model, at $30,000 the second-most expensive of the Levitt homes, which easily accommodated their two children. It had four bedrooms and two baths, a large living room, a kitchen connected to a dining area, a storage room,

Photograph of Les Résidences du Château from above. (Courtesy of the city of Le Mesnil-Saint-Denis, Yvelines, France)

The Arcy, the French version of the Levitt Cape Cod. (Photograph by Edward Berenson)

The similarities between the Willingboro Cape Cod pictured here and the Le Mesnil-Saint-Denis counterpart, built at about the same time, are evident. (Willingboro Public Library, Willingboro, New Jersey, Local History Collection)

and a one-car garage. The façade featured brick-trimmed "French" windows flanked by colorful working shutters. The roof sloped sharply, but the upstairs was wide enough to accommodate two bedrooms. The other models ranged from the Dampierre, a three-bedroom side-by-side duplex, to the huge five-bedroom Barbizon. In between were the three-bedroom Chevreuse, a larger side-by-side duplex; the three-bedroom Bel Air, which could become five by converting the unfinished attic; and the four-bedroom Arcy. The Bel Air and Arcy, like the Barbizon, were detached homes on their own plots. The Dampierre had a gently sloping mansard roof covered with slate and a brick façade. The other models sported sloped, Cape Cod–style terra-cotta roofs, colorful shutters, large windows, and brick or stucco façades. Each had a one-car garage.[48]

The houses in Les Résidences du Château were built very close to the street, with much less setback than in the U.S. Levittowns. The narrow streets curve around into numerous cul-de-sacs. The plots seem cramped from the front, but they have ample backyards, many of which open onto community-maintained common lands, providing extra space.

Some of the homes have lovely "French doors" (*portes-fenêtres*) that allow light to stream in and provide easy access to the yard. In this community, like the others Levitt would build in France, homeowners were forbidden to change the footprint of their home. Remodeling was limited to converting unfinished attics, moving partitions, opening up kitchens, and turning the storage room into living space. In this, Les Résidences resembles Willingboro's stable footprints far more than the New York and Pennsylvania Levittowns, where virtually every house has been expanded, obscuring the original architecture. Since Le Mesnil-Saint-Denis and Willingboro houses had three, four, and even five bedrooms, there was less reason to expand them. What distinguishes Les Résidences from the four main U.S. Levitt developments is the existence of side-by-side duplexes, row houses, and five small apartment buildings.

In 1966, when this initial Levitt development opened, the French government still officially backed the building of *grands ensembles* rather than single-family homes. But this policy was facing growing resistance, as public opinion polls and academic studies showed that most French people still wanted their own detached homes. This was especially true in the *grands ensembles,* where 82 percent of residents said they preferred a single-family home.[49] Many French homebuilders also endorsed Levitt's experiment at Le Mesnil-Saint-Denis. "He's helping to fill a need," the builder Jacques Boulais told *Time,* "and he's giving French contractors a good lesson in the modern way to build a house."[50] Officials in the Ministry of Infrastructure followed the Le Mesnil project closely. Government inspectors, sent to report on the development in 1966, found its "urbanism perfectly well thought out," and they applauded the division of labor Levitt used to construct the dwellings. They pronounced the interior layouts "very good" and deemed the kitchen appliances and bathroom fixtures "of very high quality" and the porcelain, tilework, and hardwood flooring "first class."[51] The building trades magazine *Tuiles et briques* (Tiles and bricks) echoed this assessment, calling the development a "new genre" of housing and praising the dwellings' "varied styles" and pleasing "architectural conception." The editors also noted the "remarkable interior layouts" of the various models and their "very advanced amenities"; they especially appreciated Levitt's success in combining "traditional techniques [with] perfectly organized, rationally conceived modern methods based on formulas of 'industrial' production." They concluded that the Levitt "formula of grouping individual houses," largely unknown in France, "should be able to adapt to the French situation" and that more such developments would be "desirable." This is what Berrurier and Levitt had hoped to achieve, and they must have been pleased, despite the journal's reservations about the lack of a fully enclosed kitchen and the "somewhat thin" interior partitions.[52]

Given such positive views as well as a widespread sense, in both countries, that the United States was more modern than France and France needed to catch up, Levitt's French project garnered massive coverage in both the French and American press. In a March 1966 article devoted to Levitt and Le Mesnil-Saint-Denis, the French business magazine *Entreprise* expressed the wish that "French developers and construction companies finally be allowed to accomplish what has already been done in the United States." The editors warned that if France failed to follow the American example, Levitt's 1947 criticism of the U.S. housing industry—"If the Fords and Kaisers had had to work with the methods used in our housing construction, they would still be making the cars of 1930"—"would apply to [France] for a long time."[53]

Despite the overwhelmingly positive press coverage of Les Résidences du Château, professional architects tended to disagree. Even before a single house was built, *L'architecture d'aujourd'hui,* a glossy magazine that touted modern design, condemned Levitt's proposed houses as "symbols of bad taste, obsolescence, and the complete absence of any architectural qualities."[54] Prominent French builders rejected the architects' critique. Their role, declared the real estate promoter Franck Arthur, "should be greatly restricted in favor of engineers, who have both feet on the ground."[55]

Virtually every article about Levitt's French development made clear that the cost of a home in Le Mesnil-Saint-Denis placed it far beyond the means of most French families. Buyers of these dwellings tended to be solidly middle- and upper-middle class, and mainly in their mid-thirties to early forties. The men were engineers, middle managers, airline pilots, doctors, and successful businessmen; the women mostly didn't work outside the home.[56] Many came from prosperous families with assets and savings they could give their children. Not only were Levitt's French houses more expensive than his American equivalents, but French credit and down payment requirements made buying a house there much more difficult than in the United States. The best French terms, improved in part after pressure from Levitt, still required 30 percent down and payment of the balance over fourteen years at an interest rate of 8 to 10 percent.[57] In the United States, the thirty-year mortgage rate in 1967 was 6.4 percent, and the lower down payment and thirty-year term made monthly housing costs less than half of what they were in France. But Levitt didn't worry about his ability to sell his homes in the Paris suburbs. He reported that buyers of his Le Mesnil-Saint-Denis homes commonly gave more than the minimum down payment, thanks to financial support from relatives, and that the demand for single-family homes was such that his clientele was guaranteed. He knew as well that his mass-produced dwellings, even with the much smaller scale of building in France, were a good value and would be seen that way.[58]

French homebuyers especially appreciated that the Levitt houses came fully equipped, completely finished, and ready for them to move in.[59] With French-constructed houses, buyers had to supply kitchen appliances and hire painters and carpenters to complete the interiors; sometimes they even had to install heating units. Le Mesnil-Saint-Denis buyers also liked the efficient Levitt layouts, with minimal space lost to hallways and open plans that made the homes' public areas seem larger than they were. Levitt's built-in closets with sliding doors were also a hit, since they made bulky armoires unnecessary. The included landscaping was popular as well, since most French homebuilders didn't attend to the yards. In this initial French development, Levitt planted 350 evergreen trees, 1,300 deciduous trees, and 12,000 shrubs. He seeded every house's lawn-to-be and reserved half of the development's 160 acres as unbuilt common space.[60] Levitt's buyers saw Les Résidences du Château as the garden community he advertised, but not all liked one key feature: the lack of fences or walls surrounding each property and the prohibition against building them. To promote neighborliness and a uniform aesthetic, Levitt banned barriers from all of his developments, even though most of France's middle-class, single-family homes huddled behind them. Even so, the majority of Le Mesnil's residents voted to keep the community barrier-free.[61] Most homeowners eventually planted hedges to separate their backyards from their neighbors', but they saw the hedges as demarcating their yards rather than cutting them off, which would have violated the spirit of the development.[62]

For most inhabitants of Les Résidences du Château, the open spaces as well as the common grassy areas and fields made the community a "kingdom of children," an ideal place to raise young kids. But adolescents were often less enamored of the place. Like their counterparts in the American Levittowns, they complained of having nothing to do and no place to go. Most were too young to drive, and several complained that their fathers didn't want to take the family anywhere; after their long automobile commutes to work, "they ended up hating their cars."[63]

Although Paris wasn't terribly far, it seemed distant psychologically, partly because the landscape was so different from the city, and partly because it took a long time to get there on the traffic-clogged highways. Train service to Paris was poor, although it would improve in the 1970s and 1980s with the building of the Réseau Express Régional (RER), a commuter railroad network that connects to the Paris Métro. Some residents of Le Mesnil loved their community's tranquility, while others found it a little too calm and missed the excitement of the city. Still, for many, the community spirit in Le Mesnil compensated for the lack of stimulation. In Paris, you didn't get to know your neighbors, but in Le Mesnil, people were friendly and eager to help one another. When someone planned a shopping trip to the capital, she (it was usually a "she") asked neighboring women if they needed anything. Women took turns taking their kids to school and retrieving them at the end of the day.[64]

One uncomfortable aspect of buying into Le Mesnil involved relations with longtime residents of the old village. The new inhabitants tended to be much better off financially, and as one Levitt buyer put it, "they see us a little like colonizers," as "*les américains*" and "*les Levitts*"—foreigners who didn't belong. Another Levitt buyer commented that village women "come to the Résidences du Château to clean our houses; we don't go to the village to clean theirs."[65] Local merchants harbored particularly bitter feelings toward their new neighbors, who were said to shun them in favor of shopping in Paris. This was almost certainly untrue, but it reflected the fear that the new, wealthier inhabitants were bringing urban culture and habits into what had been a traditional rural bourg. Berrurier had wanted to bring an element of modernity to his traditional village without dis-rupting its rural character. Many locals worried he had erred too far on the side of modernity.

Levitt had no qualms about his project's modernity, and his ability to build good single-family houses at low prices made him a darling of French housing officials, who were beginning to think about how to satisfy the demand for owner-occupied separate residences. Levitt's cost-cutting methods attracted their attention, as did his "new vil-lage" under construction at Le Mesnil-Saint-Denis.[66] "Our biggest surprise," Levitt said, "was the reception given us by French govern-ment officials at all levels. They thought we had something to contrib-ute to helping solve their housing problems."[67] This statement might sound like more of Levitt's self-promotion, but the French govern-ment made its support for the American homebuilder crystal clear.

In 1966, French housing officials invited him to contribute two houses to their "Villagexpo," a seven-week (September to November) exhibit of eighty-seven single-family homes, plus another one hundred row houses and small apartment buildings, intended to display mod-ern, cost-effective building techniques.[68] A year earlier, Villagexpo's organizers had visited the United States to take a nationwide tour of single-family housing. They couldn't have failed to see one or more Levittowns, by now world-famous, and the commission's leader, Pierre Charlet, inspector general of construction at the state secretariat for housing, found himself seduced by what he called "American effi-ciency." Back in France, he wrote a highly positive report on the U.S. housing industry, and that report helped shape not only Villagexpo but the French government's plans for single-family housing for years to come. Charlet noted that builders like Levitt "assembled" houses rather than "constructing" them, and claimed that on-site assembly by specialized teams was better for single-family homebuilding than the factory prefabrication used in the *grands ensembles*.[69]

Charlet's observations were reinforced by the marketing success of Les Résidences du Château as well as the development's lavish press coverage, which emphasized its character as a "village" with headlines such as "An American Village in the Heart of the Île-de-France" and "A Real Village for Sale in the Île-de-France." Charlet also noted press descriptions of Les Résidences, which often echoed Levitt's advertise-ments, "as a group of homes in a parklike setting, comfortable but

affordable, halfway between picturesque and modern."[70] French officials used similar language to describe Villagexpo, installed in a small
town twenty miles south of Paris. The exhibit would model the government's growing desire for a new form of urbanism to complement,
and counteract, both the *grands ensembles* and the unplanned, unco-
ordinated building of isolated houses that had been typical of single-
family homebuilding in France.[71] The new urbanism would group
homes into "new villages" whose conception and layout would "guarantee all at once the privacy of family life and the ability to enjoy
common spaces designed for collective life."[72] This idea closely resembled what Berrurier had elaborated in his letter to Levitt a few years
earlier. Although the American homebuilder's prices were above the
limit for affordable housing, the French government let him display
his homes anyway. One was a wood-frame structure like those built in
the United States but rarely in France, and the other a more French-
style version of those Levitt was building at Le Mesnil-Saint-Denis.

The magazine *Les bois d'aujourd'hui,* which touted the use of wood
in construction and sent a correspondent to Villagexpo, enthused about
the Levitt models, especially the one framed with wood. The American
company's houses, the correspondent wrote, were "especially brilliant"
and "plunged us into a world of green spaces and successful architectural equilibrium."[73] The Levitt home on display was nearly identical
to the ranches being built in Willingboro and Bowie—an L-shaped
structure with a one-car garage and entryway parallel to the street and
the rest of the dwelling perpendicular to it. Villagexpo's designers
added to the model's appeal by surrounding it with lush grass accented
with flowers, bushes, and shrubs.[74] *Les bois d'aujourd'hui* called the
home "very seductive" and was one of many French publications to
have that response. According to the magazine *Réalités,* "everyone
found [the Levitt model] a hundred percent appealing."[75]

Prominent French architects complained, with justice, that they
were eclipsed at Villagexpo in favor of merchant builders like Levitt
and the French prefab housing concerns Phénix and Balency &
Schul. These companies contributed houses that ignored architectural
modernism and simply applied standardized models and mass-
production techniques to traditionalist designs.[76] The larger problem,
according to a host of architects and planners, was the massive
amount of space required to surround individual homes with separate

yards.[77] By displaying detached homes—visitors to Villagexpo largely shunned the apartments and row houses—the exposition's organizers encouraged people to take up residence miles away from Paris or other cities so they would have room for their house plus yard. Doing so, the critics said, would divide farms, forests, and open lands into small chunks of identical private spaces separate from one another and closed to the public. With no room for stores, restaurants, and bars, people would isolate themselves in their houses. "In this infinite fabric of residences utterly similar to one another," wrote the editors of *L'architecture d'aujourd'hui,* "all life dies, and even boredom, too, since monotony is nothing more than one form of death." This, the editors thought, was the dream of individual homeownership turned into a nightmare from which you never awaken. They found it horrifying that the French government seemed to be promoting this nightmare of "linear kilometers" of one damn house after the other. Does it make sense, the editors asked, "that our Ministry of Infrastructure (*Équipement*) embraces Levitt on Son [*sic*] and its pathetic European imitators, those phoenixes of the industrialized suburban box?"[78]

This dystopian view of single-family suburbia outdid Levittown's severest American critics, but as in the United States, the critics' influence was minimal. The house and yard remained by far the top choice of most French families. "Everyone was singing the praises of the single-family house," and it was "the Frenchman's dream," two French housing executives told the sociologist Christian Topalov.[79] And despite the architects' disapproval, most homebuyers, in France, as in the United States, preferred familiar, traditional designs. For many of those who aspired to a single-family home, the grouping of houses in a master plan represented an acceptable modern advance—a compromise between the isolated homestead and the dense urban neighborhood. Because Villagexpo, like Les Résidences du Château, appeared to embody this compromise, it proved wildly popular. More than 230,000 people flocked to the housing fair, some returning several times. As soon as it ended, in mid-November 1966, the dwellings went on sale, and people snapped them up.[80]

The popularity of his two Villagexpo homes, plus the hot demand in Le Mesnil-Saint-Denis, persuaded Levitt to exercise the option he had taken on the land in Lésigny, a tiny commune fifteen miles southeast of Paris. The land, which belonged to one of the many mini-châteaus of the region, was surrounded by woods and included numerous ponds and even a still-intact moat that had protected the residence, which the mayor kept for himself. The village of Lésigny contained just three hundred souls and almost nothing by way of infrastructure or services. As in his U.S. projects, Levitt had to develop it almost from scratch. In October 1967, Levitt-France's contractors began installing in Lésigny an infrastructure of sewers, water pipes, electric and telephone wires, roadways, a water purification plant, and a water tower. Because Levitt had to build a vast infrastructure, the development had to consist of no fewer than five hundred houses so as to spread the upfront costs widely enough to keep the amount per house reasonably low. The other reason, Lorant said, for building at least five hundred dwellings (Lésigny would have six hundred) was to benefit from economies of scale. If built individually, rather than as one of several hundred, a Levitt house that sold for 180,000 francs would go for 280,000.[81]

According to French government reports on the project, Levitt-France received a French government–backed loan of $4.8 million from the Crédit Foncier de France (at a low interest rate of 5 percent) and an additional $4.5 million from the Chase Manhattan Bank. The French Ministry of Infrastructure's data showed that Levitt paid just over $2 million for the land (10 million French francs) plus $3.1 million for infrastructure and preparation of the land, $11.6 million for the building of houses and facilities, and $2.67 million for advertising, taxes, interest, and administration. The total investment was $19.37 million, from which the company would ultimately register a profit of $3.58 million.[82] Although official French reports indicate that Levitt benefited from a government subsidized loan, Andrew Lorant, the chief executive of Levitt-France, denied that this was the case, telling the sociologist Topalov that the company financed its Lésigny project entirely with funds from the mother company, Levitt & Sons, and loans from U.S. banks. The Crédit Foncier de France, Lorant said, gave loans only to his homebuyers, not to his enterprise. It's unclear why Lorant made this claim, which appears to be untrue, but in any case, he needed only about half of the total investment up front. Because he built the development in successive stages and each stage sold out quickly—as in the U.S. Levittowns—the funds received from purchased homes in the first stage paid the construction costs of those in the second, the second paid the costs of the third, and so on.[83]

The first Lésigny homes went up in April 1968, and the construction crews finished between eight and fifteen a week. This pace, while much slower than in the U.S. Levittowns, was still very fast for home-building in France. French inspectors observed the process closely, partly to protect the government's investment and partly because housing officials were keenly interested in Levitt's methods. The government helped finance the Lésigny project because it considered the new effort, like the Le Mesnil-Saint-Denis development, "experimental and without any similar precedents," but highly promising. French inspectors judged the quality of construction "good," the final product "refined," and the recreation and other public facilities of "high quality, even luxurious."[84] Overall, they deemed Levitt-France a "solid" company that "provides well-constructed single-family homes with maximally comfortable facilities for a relatively well-off clientele eager to live in pleasant parts of the greater Paris region." Their report concluded: "The conceptualization of the Levitt project and their finished products enjoy the public's favor and for that reason should be encouraged."

The officials' sole reservation related to the company's "excessive profits."[85] Lorant promised to keep an eye on his profit margin, and later government reports on Lésigny maintained the positive assessment of its quality and desirability—for those who could afford it. On the whole, French officials and stalwarts of its construction industry, including Levitt's American competitor, Kaufman & Broad, were so taken by the Levitt example that it sank deep roots in France. "From the 1960s to today," writes the architectural historian Élodie Bitsindou, "essentially all of France's 'new villages' "—*lotissements concertés,* or communities built by a single developer with public facilities included and governed by strict regulations—"are the heirs of the Levitt model."[86] And by the 1980s, those new villages accounted for half of all the new single-family houses built in the suburbs of Paris.[87]

Levitt's new community, consisting entirely of single-family houses on separate plots, was designed to be more upscale than the one at Le Mesnil-Saint-Denis, with dwellings priced from $33,000 to $39,000. These prices were relatively high, but credit terms had eased, thanks to three developments: Levitt's lobbying, the French government's growing interest in promoting single-family homes, and the entry of private banks into the mortgage market.[88] The required minimum down payment on a Lésigny house was 21 percent, with the balance amortized over twenty years. Homebuyers who got their mortgages through private banks could defer principal payments for several years. For the least expensive Lésigny house, the Evry, the monthly payment with 21 percent down was 1,142 francs ($231).[89]

Besides Lésigny's more attractive financing, there were several differences between the two Levitt developments. The one in Le Mesnil-Saint-Denis was closely connected by continuous streets to the old village, as Mayor Berrurier had wanted. The new effort, Le Parc de Lésigny, was conceived as a separate enclave distinct from the tiny village nearby. With its own entrances off the main road and mostly surrounded by woodlands, the Parc de Lésigny more closely resembles an American suburb.[90] Another key difference was that in Lésigny there were no duplexes, townhouses, or apartment buildings—just six hundred homes on individual plots. The least expensive Lésigny home was thus 50 percent more costly than the entry-level ones in Le Mesnil. Still, the single-family detached homes in the two developments were roughly similar, though in Lésigny they were a bit larger and sat on bigger pieces of land.

For the new community, Levitt repeated Le Mesnil's Arcy and Barbizon models while including two new designs, the Fontainebleau and the Evry. The first, which reproduced the L-shaped ranch shown at Villagexpo, looks like a compact version of the Pennsylvania Levittown's Country Clubber. The second was a French-fried version of a Levitt ranch built in Willingboro and Bowie. As in Le Mesnil, the main structural difference was the lack of wood framing in the French models. The houses were built mainly from cinder blocks, some with solid brick façades and others faced with stucco. Erecting the masonry exterior walls required much more labor than did Levitt's U.S. homes with their precut, easily assembled wood frames. But otherwise, the French projects used a division of labor similar to the one pioneered in Levittown, New York. Interior partitions were made of plasterboard, as in the United States, and the French roofs were supported with precut wood, although topped with terra-cotta tiles.[91] As in the U.S. Levittowns and Le Mesnil, the Lésigny dwellings stood on slabs rather than basements, and the front lawns ran continuously from house to house, with no fences separating them. Inside, the homes featured parquet floors, wallpaper, bathrooms with ceramic tiles, and closets with sliding doors. This was a far cry from the rudimentary finishings in the New York and Pennsylvania Levittowns, which had spray-painted walls, asphalt floor tiles, and bamboo curtains on the closets.

Beyond the larger homes and the absence of non-detached houses, Lésigny also had a large sports and recreation complex consisting of a huge swimming pool, kiddie pool, ball fields, tennis courts, and an attractive outdoor restaurant partially covered with a redwood trellis. The sports complex gave Lésigny the feel of country club living (but without a golf course), especially in the summer. Lorant said Lésigny, unlike Le Mesnil, needed the recreation facilities to attract homebuyers. Lésigny's location east of Paris, near heavily industrial and commercial suburbs, was much less desirable than Le Mesnil-Saint-Denis's to the west of Paris, traditionally seen as prestigious and genteel. Levitt also graced Lésigny with a shopping center and an elementary school, which he deeded to the local municipality. Like Le Mesnil, Lésigny proved a commercial success, with all houses sold before they were built.[92]

Once again, the reaction in the French press was largely favorable. *L'immobilier,* a popular magazine similar to *House and Home* in the United States, found much to like, especially the homes' "luxurious" interiors, all "rationally conceived and fully equipped," and Levitt's "rational methods of construction." The magazine's editors also praised the development's "overall plan, which departs pleasantly from the habitual monotony of this kind of village." On the negative side, they pointed to the "absence of great imagination in the design of certain models" and the difficulty of getting to Paris without a car. Of the four Lésigny models, *L'immobilier* preferred the Evry, the smallest and least expensive. The editors found its interior layout especially pleasing and praised the exterior for having quoted "the style of the Île-de-France" while nodding to its "American origins." All the models, they wrote, were "classically French while discreetly inspired" by Levittown USA.[93]

The American press was especially enthusiastic about the Parc de Lésigny, taking pains to quote happy homebuyers who found Levitt homes superior to French ones. Michel Faugere, an engineer, told *House and Home*'s reporter, "The Levitt houses have much bigger rooms and better arranged kitchens than French houses. . . . We own a [French-built] house now, and . . . the differences in space and lay-out are extraordinary." Gervais Guisnel, another Lésigny homebuyer, found his four-bedroom Arcy "very pleasant" but considered the Lev-itt houses "over-equipped by French standards." He would have pre-ferred to buy his own appliances. A third buyer pronounced his new Levitt house "superb." For French people, he added, "these houses are very, very luxurious."[94] Levitt-France built on these themes in its advertising, claiming that the Lésigny development combined the quiet of the countryside with proximity to Paris via car and train. But Paris became a reasonable commute only after the nearby RER sta-tion was complete in 1970, and even then, people had to drive seven miles to the station or take a shuttle from the development.[95]

The popularity of the Parc de Lésigny, as of Les Résidences du Châ-teau and housing expositions like Villagexpo, confirmed once again the French public's overwhelming preference for single-family houses. Although only middle-class people could afford the Levitt develop-ments, the Villagexpos promoted more affordable alternatives, in which working-class people expressed an unwavering interest. This moved a team of French sociologists led by Henri Raymond and Ni-cole Haumont to try to understand the widespread desire for detached single-family homes. French social scientists had mostly dismissed this preference as an anachronism or, worse, a manifestation of petty bourgeois false consciousness that needed to be overcome. Still, how-ever seriously Raymond and Haumont took the answers they received in extensive interviews with residents of both individual dwellings and *grands ensembles,* they couldn't quite shake the idea that their respon-dents were misguided—if through no fault of their own.[96]

What the sociologists found, above all, was a widespread belief that the detached, single-family dwelling gave people more control over their space than an apartment and enabled them to stamp their homes with their own personalities. They could paint interior walls and redo their façades, move partitions, repurpose the garage, open the kitchen or enclose it, and add rooms. Occupying a rented apart-ment, or even owning one, excluded many of these efforts to "appro-priate" one's living space.[97] Owning a home also gave people a sense of security denied to nonowners, who were always vulnerable to rent increases and the whims of their landlords. For many, the sense of se-curity outweighed the burden of mortgage payments, taxes, and the costs of maintenance. The sociologists described people's attachment to the detached home as a form of "utopian thinking."

Part of what made the bungalow so desirable, even a utopian ideal, was that it offered control over one's environment. In an apartment building, and especially the dense, hastily constructed *grands ensembles,* you see and hear your neighbors, and they see and hear you. Privacy hardly exists, and intimacy is compromised.[98] This goes for members of a nuclear family as well: parents and children are crammed together in an unmodifiable space. In a detached dwelling, the parents' bedroom could be in one part of the house and the children's in another, and no bedroom is joined to a neighbor's home. The yard adds to this privacy. It not only separates one from one's neighbors but also extends privacy to family members. The husband or wife could work in the yard while the other attended to tasks inside. Children and pets could be sent outside. The yard served as an extension of the house, grafting extra play space or workspace onto the dwelling and making more room for eating and relaxing when the weather was fine.[99]

Perhaps the most important advantage of living in a single-family home was that it could be a haven from an often jarring outside world. At home, you were "at your own place" (*chez-soi*), autonomous and free in a space you controlled. At work, others were in control, and in an apartment building, you had to obey the rules and regulations of a more collective life. "When I come home," said one interviewee, "I cry with joy to be in my own place with all my things."[100]

This study was published in 1967 (and reprinted several times since), just as the French government had begun to pivot away from the *grands ensembles* and toward the single-family home—not the isolated *pavillons* of the past but the ensembles of detached dwellings pioneered by Bill Levitt. Individual homes, French officials now said, should be built as communities, as "new villages" structured around schools, stores, and recreation facilities. And builders should take advantage of economies of scale and cost-effective mass-production techniques to make homes affordably priced.

In March 1969, Albin Chalandon, France's new minister of infrastructure and housing, announced a government-sponsored competition to foster the construction of single-family houses. His objective was to "give birth to a new housing industry, one based on grouping together what until then had been separate activities—land preparation and infrastructure development, construction, and merchandizing." The final product should be ensembles of houses of which each would be "sold as a 'finished object' " and expandable "according to the needs of the families that inhabit them." This approach could have been lifted from any number of Bill Levitt's programmatic statements, especially given Chalandon's announcement that he wanted to create houses that workers and young families could afford. How would he do this? "Through forms of mass construction that will permit the rationalization of methods, the modernization and mechanization of equipment, and the industrialization of the various elements of the process."[101]

Each company entering this competition had to commit to building 7,500 single-family dwellings between 1970 and 1972, 90 percent of which would have to sell for far less than the typical price of a "pavillon"—a custom-built suburban house—and about 25 percent less than the least expensive of Levitt-France's homes. Chalandon emphasized that his goal was not a return to the ad hoc, unplanned home construction that had long been the French norm, but rather to create new communities or make connections to existing ones. Doing this wouldn't be easy. Of the 149,000 single-family dwellings built in France in 1968, only 9 percent used modern methods; the rest were solo constructions using traditional artisanal techniques and independent of any master plan.[102]

France's lack of experience with mass-production resulted in a dearth of credible entries in Chalandon's competition; the minister had to extend the deadline for submission. And although he had invited Levitt to apply, the company declined, saying it couldn't find the land on which to build 7,500 houses.[103] Chalandon's deputies advised him to cancel the competition altogether, but he persisted and eventually chose seven proposals, five of which never got started. Seeing little progress after several months, he then selected five more, most of them advanced by French companies experienced in constructing prefabricated single-family dwellings based on a few standard models. Although these companies—Phénix, Balency, Alsetex—used industrial techniques and built thousands of houses, they mostly erected them one by one rather than in "new villages" à la Levitt. Professional architects, only minimally represented on the selection committee, found these companies' "traditional," "neo-regional" designs "deplorable." But save for a few innovative alternatives, this is mostly what resulted from the competition. In the end, Chalandon and his successors succeeded in sparking the creation of single-family housing, but at price points too high for working-class families and often without masterplans for infrastructure, schools, and recreation.[104]

Still, the French government was giving its people what they wanted. The percentage of poll respondents saying they preferred a single-family home continued to grow: 78 percent in 1990; 80 percent in 1999; 82 percent in 2004; 87 percent in 2007. The main reason given for this preference was the desire for a yard, although not necessarily in a "new village," a configuration respondents thought would compromise privacy and individual freedom by placing dwellings too close to one another and imposing too many rules and regulations.[105]

People who bought into Levitt developments mostly accepted those regulations and even embraced them. Although Levitt-France bowed out of the Chalandon competition of 1969, it undertook its largest French project the following year: 1,670 homes to be constructed in Mennecy, a town about twenty-five miles south of Paris.

Having been on the lookout for buildable land after the success of Les Résidences du Château and the Parc de Lésigny, in 1970 Levitt-France found an 830-acre parcel for sale by its absentee owner, the head of a large chain of stationery stores. The property had once belonged to the dukes of Villeroy and consisted of a scenic "parc de Villeroy" that surrounded the old manor house and farmland known as the "*ferme de la Verville*." After a quick round of negotiations with the Mennecy mayor and municipal council, which had to approve any new construction project, Levitt-France bought the property for much less than the going rate and then ceded about a third of it to the commune of Mennecy. Levitt also pledged to pay for new schools, infrastructure, and recreational facilities and make them available to the entire town, not just the residents of the two linked developments he would create.[106] Always interested in connecting his homebuyers to a monied, aristocratic past, Levitt named these "new villages" the Colline (hill) de Verville and the Parc de Villeroy. The former would be a townhouse complex with medium-sized, relatively affordable units, many of which would break with a long-standing Levitt tradition by including basements. The Parc de Villeroy would be much more upscale, with large one- and two-story homes in the "California style"—

meaning they would look more American than classically French. In fact, many of the Mennecy models resemble those of Le Mesnil-Saint-Denis and Lésigny. The largest model, though, was new and featured six bedrooms, two full baths and two half baths, and a two-car garage. Most models included a working brick fireplace and fully equipped kitchens and sat on ten thousand to sixteen thousand square feet of land, much larger than the lots in Levitt-France's two earlier developments.

As it began building its Mennecy homes, Levitt-France launched a huge advertising campaign, much more extensive than the ones for its earlier projects. The headline of its first round of newspaper ads advanced a classic Levitt slogan: "For us, to build single-family homes is also to plan a new life for their inhabitants."[107] Included in the price of a house were shopping centers, swimming pools, tennis courts, gymnasiums, playing fields, schools, and daycare centers. People who visited the Mennecy projects, the ads declared, would see them as resorts, "vacation villages" whose residents "lived every evening as if on vacation." They were so desirable that residents' Parisian friends "never refused a dinner invitation." The only problem was that the Parisians had to take a long highway trip home; their hosts could stay put, as if always on a long weekend. The ads neglected to mention that the workweek commute to the capital could be brutal.[108]

Homebuyers in Mennecy resembled those in Levitt's other French developments: they were young and relatively well-to-do. In 1973, only 4 percent of Levitt's adult residents were fifty-one or older, and only 14 percent between forty-one and fifty. Eighty-two percent listed their ages as twenty-one to forty. By 1979, the adult population had grown even younger, with 90 percent between twenty-one and forty and only 10 percent forty and up. Most Mennecy families had two or three children, usually under the age of ten. A survey of the inhabitants' socioeconomic status revealed an overwhelmingly well-educated, professional group. More than three-quarters of the men worked as engineers, airline pilots (Orly Airport was close by), high-level managers, computer programmers, university professors, or high school teachers. Fourteen percent held mid-level management jobs or were technicians or schoolteachers. Only 9 percent were classified as clerical or skilled workers. As for the women, nearly 60 percent didn't work outside the home, and of those who did, most held low- or mid-level jobs. Only 5 percent of the employed women were *"cadres supérieurs"* (high-level managers), most of them high school teachers—a much higher-status profession in France than in the United States.[109]

Asked why they chose to live in Mennecy, the Levitt buyers responded as if they were reading from the Raymond/Haumont sociological study. They told researchers that they had wanted to escape the noise and bustle of the city and live in a detached house that would make them feel safe, secure, and "comfortably in my own place." They yearned for a village life surrounded by nature, a rural environment with clean air, open space, and protected places for their children to play, whether in their own yards, shared parkland, or in the development's recreational centers. They were thrilled by the community's pool and tennis courts. Many added that the Levitt homes were a great value for the money and that they could not have afforded a custom-built house of similar quality and amenities. Mennecy gave them twice the space at half the price of living in Paris. Several of Mennecy's residents were pleasantly surprised by the sociability they found in the community, especially vis-à-vis neighbors, with whom they could interact regularly while keeping the connections superficial if they wanted. Jean-Sébastien, a longtime resident of Levitt-Mennecy, dismissed as nonsense the stereotype of people living isolated lives in individual dwellings. He claimed to have close, friendly relations with his neighbors and to know a huge number of people in the community. Neighborly conversations often happened in the unenclosed front yards, while backyards, separated by hedges, lent themselves to privacy for family members and, on occasion, to closer relations with neighbors who were invited into the family space.[110]

Not everyone expressed positive views about their new community. Some complained that, as one interviewee put it, they found it impossible "to feel myself" in the house or "stamp my own personality" onto it "because they're all the same."[111] Other residents found the development monotonous, not only because of the sameness of the houses but because the Mennecyites were too similar in age, education, profession, and even dress. The writer Jean-Marc Parisis, who grew up in the Résidences du Château but whose observations applied to Mennecy as well, wrote that in winter, all the men wore cardigan sweaters with sport shirts underneath, along with pleated jeans. In the summer, they all mowed their lawns in sky-blue or salmon-colored polo shirts, Bermuda shorts, and boat shoes without socks. It was a deliberately American look. The women wore denim or corduroy pants in winter and cotton-print skirts and T-shirts in summer. While the kids were in school, they played tennis or read books and magazines on their backyard chaises longues. When they worked, it was as teachers of French and foreign languages or piano and flute.[112]

Parisis's childhood memories of the adults around him doubtless held more than a grain of truth, even if they idealized to some extent life in the community. For most of the year, it was too cold or rainy to play tennis or stretch out in the backyard with a book. During the long winter, women without jobs outside the home often found themselves isolated and bored.[113] When both wife and husband worked, the wife's workday was commonly followed by a "second shift" of meal preparation, childcare, and domestic labor.[114]

Beyond the monotony and homogeneity, the community's regulations also came in for criticism, especially the rules that forbade fences separating front yards and changing the color of shutters and façades. Several complained of the long commutes to work and the sometimes-difficult relations with residents of pre-Levitt Mennecy, many of whom saw the newcomers as "snobs," "city-people," and "foreigners."[115]

When Levitt-France began its Mennecy developments, the company's leaders believed the new project couldn't miss. It was connected to Paris by rail and highway and just six miles from the "new city" of Evry, one of six satellite towns built from scratch around Paris to absorb the burgeoning postwar population. Evry would soon grow to a half million people and was well endowed with schools, shopping centers, medical facilities, and other key services. But Mennecy itself maintained its country character, with lush woodlands and proximity to the castle and forests of Fontainebleau.[116] What Levitt didn't foresee was the economic crisis of the 1970s: the oil shocks that doubled the price of gasoline, galloping overall inflation, mounting unemployment, and rising interest rates. In this environment, demand for new single-family homes flattened. The company found itself building much more slowly than in the past and selling just two hundred to three hundred houses a year. After the oil shock of 1973, Levitt-France tried to control home prices by dropping its most expensive model, shrinking the size of plots, and using cheaper materials inside and out. It even offered the option of homes without kitchen appliances. One unintended consequence of these moves was to widen the gap of affluence between the upscale Parc de Villeroy and the mid-scale Colline de Verville, which was Levitt's second Mennecy community and the one caught in the economic vise of the 1970s. The resulting class segregation resembled that of Levittowns in Pennsylvania and Willingboro.[117] It's impossible to know whether these cost-cutting measures succeeded in juicing sales. Although Levitt-France may have slowed the rise in home prices somewhat, inflation inexorably pushed prices up. It took the entire decade to sell all of the 1,670 dwellings originally planned.[118] Still, by 1980, Levitt's two Mennecy developments stood as the company's largest European project.

While gradually building the two Mennecy developments, Levitt-France undertook a number of other projects around the country. The largest, constructed in 1970–71, was a 760-unit townhouse community named La Commanderie des Templiers, after a local monastery near Le Mesnil-Saint-Denis. Meanwhile, Levitt & Sons had been sold to International Telephone & Telegraph, which then had to divest itself of the company in an antitrust action in 1974. Levitt-France operated for three years as an independent company before being reorganized under French ownership as Levitt-France Holding in 1977. By then the enterprise was on its last legs. Between 1975 and 1981, it managed to start, but not complete, just two small developments: Le Mas de Boussard in Saint-Martin de Crau, a tiny village near Arles in southern France, and Villefontaine near Lyon. It's unclear how many homes were planned in Saint-Martin de Crau, but only one hundred were built, and the unused land was eventually sold to another company. As for Villefontaine, only eighty of the 176 dwellings begun by Levitt were finished and sold. A third community, in a beach resort near Montpellier, seems to have been conceptualized but never built. The same is true of planned developments of about one hundred houses all told (Le Clos du Moulin and Les Sables) in the communes of Cerny and Saint-Maurice Montcouronne, due south of Paris. Levitt-France submitted elaborate plans and received building permits for these projects but never moved forward.[119] The company's subsidiary, Lovim, constructed a small number of individual homes in violation of Levitt's founding premises. But late in 1980, Levitt-France, unable to withstand the challenging real estate conditions of the decade, folded its tent. It formally declared bankruptcy in 1981.[120]

Levitt-France's developments, however, live on in generally excellent shape, despite a widespread belief that the houses were "consumer goods" destined to last at most thirty years. Fanny Taillandier's 2016 novel, *Les états et empires du lotissement grand siècle. Archéologie d'une utopie* (The states and empire of the development "17th century": Archeology of a utopia), comments ironically on the supposed flimsiness of Levitt homes.[121] It is set in a distant postapocalyptic future when fixed residence no longer exists and nomads roam the Earth. The narrator is a nomad who stumbles on a long-abandoned French Levitt community. He or she—we learn virtually nothing about the narrator—notes that although people hadn't lived there for eons, the dwellings were mostly intact, standing as "identical houses, one after the other, motionless and seductive."[122]

The book begins with a short preface identifying William Jaird Levitt as the "merchant-builder [who] transplanted into Europe and France a North American model of town planning, that of the new village." This was a housing ensemble built on "virgin land all at once" using "the principles of Fordism . . . adapted to Europe's modest dimensions . . . while maintaining its physical and symbolic affinity to America's consumer society."[123] Taillandier named her fictional Levitt village "Grand Siècle" (Seventeenth Century) because of its proximity to Versailles, Louis XIV's "new village" and the first full-fledged suburb of Paris.

The development's survival, albeit with no human inhabitants, allows the narrator to conduct an archaeological investigation of its remains, whose results unfold in the rest of the text. "Rarely," the narrator declares, "have remains of the sedentary world appeared so coherent to us."[124] This Levitt-ville represents a "strange period in human history, which for a few centuries, was sedentary, pacific, and consumerist."[125] Its purpose was to grow new roots for an unrooted bourgeoisie, a class freed by cars and phones and televisions to move away from the city and skip from job to job and house to house, discarding obsolete consumer goods along the way. But the project was doomed in advance. People had to spend so much time in their cars, commuting to work and provisioning themselves at great shopping centers miles away, that their new village made them quasi-nomads for much of their lives. Rather than help people sink new roots into virgin soil, Levitt's "Seventeenth-Century Development" was the harbinger of a future in which everyone was uprooted for good.

As for Bill Levitt himself, the narrator reverts to seventeenth-century spelling and style to compare him to the great explorers and conquerors of the Grand Siècle who brought their culture and technology to the new world. But in the twentieth century, imperial conquest worked in the opposite direction, with Levitt establishing colonies in the Old World based on the Levittowns he had built in America and the suburban culture that had spread throughout the United States. Levitt "conceived of his colony as a new civilization entirely based on extremely virtuous principles: triumph of the nuclear family, predominance of leisure and calm, and the maintenance of inhabitants in a collective unit that prevented them from plunging into an individualism so costly elsewhere in the realm."[126] The new village created docile, obedient people, just as residence at Versailles under Louis XIV had turned fierce, rebellious nobles into peaceful subjects of the king.

These nobles traded their endless, bloody internecine wars for the safety and comfort of a theater seat inside the great palace of Versailles. By the late twentieth century, the inhabitants of Levitt-ville had sacrificed theater as well, preferring to stare at the TV set rather than trek into the city to see a play or opera. The bland mass culture of television, together with the rigid rules of the development, made clear that only the calm, conformist, constrained parts of the human psyche would be permitted in the development. "Seditious passions, the desire for carnage, and stormy sexuality—all the interior bombs with which all human beings in the state of nature have always been equipped" were banned from this new utopia.[127] But they couldn't be fully suppressed. Instead, they surfaced in an endless stream of distant overseas wars beamed back home in sanitized form.

Taillandier's novel speaks to Bill Levitt's deep and lingering influence in France, and like most of those who have written about this influence, she offers a negative overall assessment, albeit cleverly and creatively presented. In the common view, Levitt-villes were seductive false utopias that were able to create harmony only by attracting like-minded people with similar sociocultural attributes and then making them even more alike. This argument vastly overstates the ability of architecture and town planning to shape human life, and understates the ability of ordinary people to resist the planners' designs and impose their personalities, beliefs, values, and aspirations even on the mass-produced, cookie-cutter dwellings and "new villages" widely thought to leave little room for ingenuity and initiative.

France's Levitt communities have long served as the background for a huge amount of advertising, both in photographs and video. Most involve children, because in the Levitt-villes, "the child is king."[128] An ad for a stain-removing powder shows a young boy standing in front of a Levitt house with chocolate ice cream dripping all over his shirt. Because Levitt homes have driveways and garages, unlike many French dwellings, they are often pictured in automobile ads. One such ad shows a family-size Renault parked on a flagstone driveway next to an elaborate waterslide. Another Renault ad shows a dad washing his car in front of a Levitt home endowed with perfectly manicured grass and a forest of trees and shrubs. A Škoda ad displays another family-size car with a little boy wheeling a wagon full of huge stuffed animals and other toys toward the auto's cargo space. These ads equate like experiences—the child's fun ride and the adults' ride, the impeccable yard and the impeccable car, the child's cargo capacity and the adults'—within an American-style suburban setting (with French accents) portrayed as a haven for both.

The Levitt communities also stand as exurban havens from the ugly close-in suburbs that ring most of Paris. On the way to the Levitt-villes, you inevitably glimpse the decaying *grands ensembles* stuffed with people who lack the means to live anywhere else. These places have become notorious as the scenes of police brutality, social unrest, racial discrimination, and hostility toward France's large and increasingly alienated Muslim and non-white populations. When French commentators refer to *la banlieue* (the suburbs), this is what they mean. But the suburbs are also filled with big box stores, car dealerships, bland industrial and commercial buildings, shopping centers, and low- and medium-rise apartment buildings (many arrayed into "new towns"). From the highways that cut through this unsightly sprawl, the suburban environment looks haphazard at best.

Things begin to improve about twelve miles south of the city, when you finally clear this morass. You circumvent the charming town of Versailles and head due west to the bustling village of Le Mesnil-Saint-Denis. Les Résidences du Château is connected to the village, but it seems like a separate enclave, with curved streets, well-kept houses,

Renault advertisement showing one of France's Levitt homes. (Courtesy of the
city of Le Mesnil-Saint-Denis, Yvelines, France)

and block-long rows of townhomes. I knew there were a dozen small
apartment buildings inside the development, but it was nonetheless
surprising to see them looking so neat and prim.

In Lésigny, the two Levitt developments are separated from the old
village; entering them is not unlike entering a Levittown in the United
States. The biggest difference is that while almost all New York and
Pennsylvania Levittown houses have been altered substantially, often
obscuring the original structure, exteriors in Lésigny have remained unchanged, by local agreement. And although the Levitt style is discern-
able, its French accents are unmistakable. The brick and stucco
exteriors feature huge shutters in a rainbow of colors flanking the floor-
to-ceiling front windows.

Residents of these developments are often drawn to American culture, but one homeowner, Guillaume, has turned his house into a
shrine to the American "Populuxe" style of the 1950s and 1960s. Populuxe, writes Thomas Hine,

speaks of optimism and opulence and encompasses such tendencies as "swept-wing styling," . . . automobile company slogans that expressed . . . the speed, the motion, the fantasy available in a De Soto Fireflite or an Olds Rocket 88. It encompasses "sheer" appliances, whose flat, right-angled lines were intended to make kitchens feel as clean and efficient as scientists' laboratories or jet planes. . . . The essence of Populuxe is not merely having things. It is having things in a way that they'd never been had before, and it is an expression of outright, thoroughly vulgar joy in being able to live so well.[129]

Guillaume's kitchen mimicked a classic suburban diner, proudly displaying an authentic booth with bright red leatherette seats flanking a vintage Formica table ringed with chrome. Above the table hangs a red canopy with "Budweiser" stenciled onto all four sides. The rest of the house is draped with American paraphernalia: vintage Coke bottles and posters, a bubble gum dispenser, and framed pictures of a red 1966 Mustang parked in an early sixties service station right out of *American Graffiti*. (Guillaume has three 1960s Mustangs, the ultimate Populuxe car, in his garage and driveway.) Covering other walls are license plates from every U.S. state and posters from the fifties and sixties: "EAT HERE," "Better Sandwiches," "All you can drink COFFEE!" In the living room there's a beautiful jukebox that lights up and plays early rock and doo-wop hits from the 1950s. There are Route 66 signs, Texaco and Esso signs, a replica of a 1950s Texaco gas pump, a wood Dunlop tennis racket mounted on the wall, along with hubcaps and Coke advertisements. Prominently displayed on a living room shelf are three pairs of exquisite cowboy boots. On the back patio is, of course, a Weber charcoal grill.

Guillaume and his wife almost single-handedly, and without compensation, run the community's Centre de Loisirs, its recreational center, featuring a huge swimming pool and outdoor restaurant. The entire development, with its quiet residential streets and leisure center, reminded me of a U.S. country club community, only much more modest. Residents pay just 1,000 euros a year to use the pool and sports facilities, the costs kept low because there is no professional management.

The Levitt development at Mennecy is west of Lésigny and due south of Paris. En route the landscape shifts from densely suburban to rural. Mennecy is a charming, prosperous commune of fifteen thousand people, with lots of construction going on, mostly small to medium-sized apartment buildings. A gated community and other single-family developments have joined the Levitt development. It is mostly well kept, but some of its houses badly need a paint job and some lawns are unkempt. Streets are narrow, although somewhat wider than in Le Mesnil. The houses sit fairly close to the street, but with a greater setback than in Le Mesnil. As in the U.S. Levittowns, the community is divided into sections. There's a small shopping center in the middle of the community and a largish school built on land Levitt provided. As in all of France's Levitt communities, there is a great deal of common, unbuilt space and woods, giving the development a nice, open look. Very few fences surround the houses, although many dwellings are obscured in front by large hedges and mature vegetation. I even saw a palm tree. The houses here are worth 400,000 to 600,000 euros; when one goes on the market, it sells immediately. The local real estate agency (located in the building that was once Levitt's sales office) called the Levitt homes "prized."

One resident, Jean-Sébastien, a teacher and local historian, keeps a ton of historical artifacts from Levitt's Mennecy development. Every Levitt community, in the United States and France, has its own local historian or historians, and they help organize decennial celebrations of their towns' respective foundings. The fiftieth in Le Mesnil-Saint-Denis was especially elaborate, its theme 100 percent American. The poster advertising the event featured the stars-and-stripes and pictured a cowgirl and cowboy, a quarterback about to throw the ball, a cheerleader, a vintage Mustang, as well as burgers, hot dogs, milkshakes, and fries. The event's program included a parade of vintage American cars, a cheerleader contest, an initiation to American football, a burger party, and a square dance demonstration.[130] Celebrations like this are signs of civic pride and also of a fun-loving attachment to American popular culture that seems not in the least ironic.

The enjoyment of their homes and pride in their communities common among residents of France's Levitt developments stands apart from the critique of these places prominent in academic and journalistic writing, as well as in literature and film. Sociologists have regularly depicted Levitt villagers as suffering from petty bourgeois false consciousness, poured into molds of monotony, or isolated in identical

The All-American celebration of Les Résidences du Château's
fiftieth anniversary. (Courtesy of the city of Le Mesnil-Saint-
Denis, Yvelines, France)

homes within no-man's lands far removed from the genuine culture of
the city. Academic and avant-garde architects have generally scorned
the Levitt designs as unimaginative at best and as breeding grounds of
oppressive conformity. In a long *Le Monde* article published in 2014,
Fanny Taillandier describes Lésigny's Résidence du Parc as a "a neighborhood closed in on itself, where neither socio-economic diversity

nor cultural renewal is allowed in."[131] She softens her assessment somewhat after meeting several Résidence families, admitting that it's no "suburban nightmare housing families entirely imprisoned in their pavilions as if they were bunkers." But she can't let go of the idea that the community is fearful and suspicious of outsiders, or that some of its inhabitants are eager to turn it into a gated community. While it's true that this Levitt-ville is affluent and lily-white, there's no sign that the racial homogeneity is intentional; it's rather that the high cost of its homes places them beyond the financial reach of non-middle-class people, whatever their ethnicity or race. This is a serious problem, of course, but the same is true of most Parisian neighborhoods; stratospheric home prices exclude all but the affluent. La Résidence du Parc is a relative bargain.

Given all this writing, it's no accident that the 1997 film *Ma vie en rose* (My life in pink), which portrays the pressures of conformity and the evils of intolerance, is set in Levitt-France's Mennecy development.[132] (We know this from a realtor's "for sale" sign that reads "Levitt-Mennecy" and from many establishing shots of Levitt homes.) Much of the narrative revolves around backyard barbeques attended by the neighbors, and those neighbors are horrified when Ludovic, the son of hosts Hanna and Pierre, struts outside in a dress. Hanna and Pierre are horrified too, and things get worse when Ludovic announces the desire to marry the neighbor boy, Jerome, who appears to be gay. The problem is that Jerome's father is Pierre's boss and is furious over the budding friendship between Ludovic and Jerome, especially after another boy calls Jerome a "fairy."

The film's turning point comes during a school play, when Ludovic locks the girl who plays Sleeping Beauty in a bathroom and dons her costume to receive Jerome's kiss and awake. The audience of parents erupts in outrage, and Ludovic is kicked out of school. Shortly afterward, Jerome's father fires Pierre and effectively banishes him from the development, as he's now unable to make his mortgage payments. In the meantime, we see Ludovic mocked and bullied by the neighborhood boys, after which the child retreats into a dreamworld and marries Jerome. All the parents approve. In the real world, Pierre finds a lesser-paying job far from Mennecy. The family's new house is a dump, and their neighborhood has nothing of Levitt-Mennecy's outward charm. But in their new town, Ludovic meets Chris (born Christine), and having been liberated from Levitt-France's hatred and intolerance, finds acceptance in the new, less pretentious—but far more tolerant—town. Many current residents of Mennecy would doubtless reject the contrast as unfair, but it fits the stereotype forged from on high, a stereotype no truer to the French Levitt-villes than to their counterparts in the United States.

8 Suburbia in the Tropics

IN 1958, WHILE still building his massive Pennsylvania development and in the midst of announcing the huge, eleven-thousand-house New Jersey Levittown that would ultimately become Willingboro, Bill Levitt could be excused for being supremely confident of long-term success. But he wasn't: to hedge his bets against shrinking demand for low-cost tract housing, he began planning several smaller developments.[1] These included the Belair community near Washington, D.C., as well as clusters of a few hundred houses in northern New Jersey and on Long Island east of Levittown. He took a serious look at Florida's promising real estate market. Perhaps most notably, he also turned his attention abroad. Along with opportunities in France, which faced an extreme shortage of single-family homes, he discovered that Puerto Ricans were flocking to the island's capital, San Juan, and that much of the city's housing was subpar.[2] As Puerto Rican developers had already discovered, land was available on the outskirts of the city, and islanders, like their mainland U.S. counterparts, wanted single-family homes.

This is what Puerto Rico's then semiautonomous government, the Estado Libre Asociado (ELA), wanted as well—especially its chief executive, Luis Muñoz Marín, Puerto Rico's first popularly elected governor.[3] Muñoz Marín, who dominated the island's public life from the early 1940s to the mid-1960s, presided over Operation Bootstrap (*Operación Manos a la Obra*), a massive reform program designed to transform Puerto Rico's ailing sugarcane-based economy into a thriving industrial one. Operation Bootstrap was premised in part on a large-scale movement of people to the mainland, since the island's industrializing economy could absorb only a fraction of the tens of thousands of displaced agricultural workers.[4] In fact, the island's industrialization produced two huge migrations, one from Puerto Rico to the United States, especially New York City, and the other from the island's countryside to its cities, especially San Juan. Between 1940 and 1970, a million Puerto Ricans moved to the States, and the urban share of the island's population more than doubled, from 24 to 56 percent.[5] The majority of those who declined to leave the island flooded into San Juan, where the number of jobs could not keep up with the rapid population growth, and the housing supply fell short. A great many new and old urbanites couldn't afford the elevated rents and found themselves living in *arrabales* (shantytowns) built in swampy areas deemed unsuitable for "legitimate" construction.[6]

In the late 1950s, the Puerto Rican government resolved to rid San Juan of its festering slums and provide decent public housing for its low-income residents. But migration into the city outpaced the number of housing projects, and many shantytown residents, proud of the dwellings they had built for themselves, resisted government efforts to move them into public housing. In the projects, they would have to pay rent for the first time, obey government-imposed rules, and live cheek-by-jowl with other families. The FHA helped finance the public projects, but several of the agency's rules led to higher rents than what the Puerto Rican government had intended. Public housing remained unpopular, and elimination of shantytowns proceeded slowly at best.[7]

Accompanying the growth of the urban underclass was a fledgling middle and lower-middle class whose members benefitted from Puerto Rico's industrialization. They too needed housing, and like their mainland counterparts, they wanted to escape the increasingly crowded and run-down urban core. Developers obliged by creating *urbanizacións* (developments) built on former agricultural lands ringing the city.

Levitt would become the most prominent of these developers, but another American anticipated him by more than a decade. In 1948, just a year after the first Levittown opened on Long Island, Leonard Darlington Long began building Puerto Nuevo, a large *urbanización* of single-family houses on the outskirts of San Juan. Long was already a veteran developer, having constructed houses in Tampa and Pensacola, Florida, during and after World War I and then in Charleston, South Carolina, and Atlanta. During World War II, the U.S. Army hired him to build low-cost houses on the large military bases it was creating in Puerto Rico to protect the Panama Canal and other U.S. interests in case of German attack.[8] Through this project and others, he became familiar with the Puerto Rican housing situation and made important contacts. He got to know Muñoz Marín, then the leader of the Puerto Rican Senate, as well as Jesús Piñero, Puerto Rico's resident commissioner in Washington in the 1940s and, starting in 1946, the first native Puerto Rican appointed governor of the island. Long used those connections to gain government subsidies and regulatory relief for Puerto Nuevo, which he dubbed "the largest housing project in the world."[9] Levittown, New York, was larger, but at 4,458 dwellings, Long's was big, especially for Puerto Rico. At the time, the island had almost no suburbs except for the Eleanor Roosevelt Development, a New Deal project of 459 single-family houses for aspiring middle-class families, and a few smaller experimental efforts.[10] Those projects were dwarfed by Puerto Nuevo, where houses cost just $4,000 to $6,000, considerably less than Levitt's Long Island models.[11] Both developers—and their homebuyers—benefitted from mortgages insured by the FHA and the Veterans Administration as well as a variety of tax advantages designed to encourage single-family homeownership.[12]

When Levitt came to Puerto Rico in the early 1960s, he would learn from Long's experience. Long had figured out how to mass-produce houses using cement walls, which Levitt never did on the mainland. But in Puerto Rico, the tropical heat and aggressive termites (there was no cold season to kill them), as well as the constant danger of hurricanes, ruled out wood construction.[13] Puerto Rican builders understood that houses had to be made of cement, but cement construction was slow. Long accelerated it by devising reusable aluminum molds into which his workers would pour wet concrete. By using these molds—one for thick exterior walls and another for thin interior partitions—semiskilled laborers could make the walls for a small five-room house in less than two hours and put up the entire structure in two to five days. Long divided the construction process into forty-seven discrete steps (versus twenty-six for Levitt's wood-frame houses), and like Levitt, he devised a stationary assembly line in which worker teams moved from homesite to homesite.[14] There is no evidence that Long explicitly imitated Levitt's methods, but he couldn't have been unaware of his American counterpart.

Long's huge Puerto Nuevo project made him the pioneering builder of single-family *urbanizacións* in Puerto Rico, and not unlike Levitt in the U.S. suburbs, the pied piper of lower-middle- and middle-class flight from the city. Because San Juan was the island's only major urban center and the primary home of its budding industrial plant and infrastructure, Puerto Rican suburbanization was largely a San Juan phenomenon, although suburban developments cropped up around smaller cities as well. Puerto Nuevo was the first of a great many postwar suburbs that would turn the areas west and south of the capital into a tropical version of Long Island: a maze of single-family homes surrounded by shopping centers, fast food emporia, and traffic-choked roads and freeways. While commuters in Levittown, New York, could take the Long Island Railroad, most residents of Puerto Rican suburbs could get to their workplaces only by car.

Puerto Nuevo inspired the residential development of neighboring Bayamón, an agricultural municipality long considered too far from San Juan for residential use. But development took off after the war, and by 1963, the *San Juan Star* was calling it "an epidemic in concrete."[15] Since the war, the paper noted, 20 percent of Puerto Rico's population had "stampeded into suburbs, which recede ever farther into the surrounding cane fields." Bayamón alone had become home to sixteen suburban developments, with seventeen more under construction. Its population shot up from thirty-seven thousand in 1940 to seventy-two thousand in 1960. (By 1970, it would be 156,000.)[16] In the Sierra Bayamón development, "the bulldozers, like a swarm of relentless earth-ripping juggernauts, crawl in concerted waves over miles and miles of land, levelling hills, filling hollows, tearing the green mantle of vegetation and exposing the raw reddish earth on which the new homes will rise." Houses sprouted so fast that city services couldn't keep up. Garbage collection was spotty and flooding common, given the regular hurricanes and inadequate facilities for absorbing or redirecting the resulting overflow from the Bayamón River. Traffic had strangled the town, partly because the local government lacked the resources to modernize the town's rural roads and partly because none of the homes had any stores or services within walking distance. Ball fields, public swimming pools, and other amenities were nonexistent. Puerto Rico's early suburbs cried out for more resources and better organization.

The island's postwar suburbanization stemmed directly from Operation Bootstrap, which began with a New Deal–era land reform project designed to accelerate the decline of the island's sugar plantations and soften its extreme inequality by breaking up properties of more than five hundred acres and giving landless laborers small plots of their own. The land reform realized the unfulfilled promise of the Foraker Act of 1900, the congressional legislation that laid out the United States' relationship with its newly annexed island of Puerto Rico.[17] Foraker forbade landed domains of more than five hundred acres, but this provision went unenforced until 1936, when New Dealers in Washington and San Juan took steps both to address the misery of agricultural labors and to improve urban life.

Leading the effort was Rexford G. Tugwell, an urban economist and member of President Roosevelt's brain trust who served briefly as chancellor of the University of Puerto Rico in 1941 and from 1941 to 1946 as the appointed governor of the territory. On the mainland, Tugwell had helped create suburban "Greenbelts," the New Deal's version of garden cities, and he sought to address the country's urban problems by luring people into these new peripheral towns. He tried to do something similar in Puerto Rico by converting agricultural land into residential space. "My idea," he declared, "was to go just outside centers of population, pick up cheap land, build a whole community, and entice people to them. Then go back to the cities and tear down whole slums and make parks of them."[18] Bill Levitt might have echoed this statement, and Muñoz Marín would adopt similar views; only, as on the mainland, their ambitions would not result in neat Greenbelt towns with multifamily housing surrounded by parks and pedestrian walkways, but rather in low-rise suburban sprawl.

The effort to fix cities by surrounding them with residential areas dovetailed with Muñoz Marín's desire to improve the lives of Puerto Rico's mass of impoverished agricultural laborers—and capture their votes. The Foraker Act enabled him and other U.S. and Puerto Rican leaders to expropriate large plantations, including one belonging to the Rupert family. In 1939, the Ruperts took the matter to the U.S. Supreme Court, which ruled the expropriation constitutional in keeping with the Foraker Act.[19]

Quickly taking advantage of the ruling, in 1941 Muñoz Marín's Partido Popular Democrático (PPD), then just three years old but already Puerto Rico's dominant political organization, enacted a wide-ranging land reform (*Ley de Tierras,* or Land Law). The *Ley de Tierras* not only enshrined the expropriation provisions of the Foraker Act but also created a mechanism for slicing former plantations into plots of one to one hundred acres and distributing the smallest ones (one to three acres) to 150,000 landless agricultural workers. Earlier in his career, Muñoz Marín had advocated land redistribution as a way to foster economic equality; now he depicted the *Ley de Tierras* as providing a measure of freedom and dignity rather than a means of subsistence or of profitable agricultural production. Land would be a cultural and political asset rather than an economic one, since, as Muñoz understood, most of the plots were too small to support a family. For Muñoz Marín, the reform also symbolized Puerto Rico's independence from U.S.-based absentee landlords and from the island's neo-feudal sugarocracy; land redistribution, he said, would make formal independence unnecessary.

In taking this position, he broke with his earlier support of the island's separation from the mainland and with those who continued to argue for independence. Muñoz Marín considered his new stance a turn toward pragmatism; it would give Puerto Rico access to American capital and favorable terms of trade. But he hadn't thought through the implications of the extreme parcellation of the land. Occupying these small plots (the island's government retained formal ownership) gave Puerto Ricans a place to build a house but not a viable source of income. Land became disassociated from agricultural production and tied to one-family residences.[20]

The land reform thus gave Puerto Ricans a new sense of property as a place to build houses but no longer to grow crops. But having built their homes, former sharecroppers and agricultural laborers found that they could not stay in them, because the law that had given them land had also deprived them of an income. The breakup of plantations led to the evaporation of paid agricultural work and forced people to abandon their plots and flock to San Juan, where they parked their

Officials preparing numbered slips to be used in the drawing of lots for "*parcelas*," small plots of land on which landless farm workers could erect their homes. Near Toa Baja, Puerto Rico, July 1946. Land Authority Program. (Archivo General de Puerto Rico. Photographic Records Group: Departamento de Instrucción Pública de Puerto Rico. Photograph by Charlie Rotkin. Office of Information for Puerto Rico)

families in the expanding *arraboles* (shantytowns). The plots they abandoned were now available to developers, and even lands that were still in production became more valuable as marketable assets than as coconut or pineapple groves. Long devoted to agriculture, land became little more than real estate. When translated to the heavily populated coastal cities, especially San Juan, the new economic and cultural meaning of landed property made suburbanization conceivable and soon a reality. Muñoz Marín intended the redistributed land to give poor working families a measure of freedom and dignity; instead, his policy condemned large numbers to urban shantytowns while enriching a few megadevelopers. But the land reform also gave the island's fledgling middle class what it desired: a house and a yard, albeit in sprawling suburban tracts linked to the city only by freeways.[21]

While land reform created the preconditions of suburbanization, it also facilitated the extraordinarily rapid industrialization that took place between 1940 and 1960, as former agricultural lands became available for industrial use. By 1950, 150 new factories had been built, with more to come over the new decade. Government planners focused on petrochemicals, pharmaceuticals, and copper mining, among other concerns. To make the factories work, a new infrastructure took shape—electrical grid, water supply, modern banking system, telephone lines, and more—all subsidized and encouraged by the Puerto Rican government as part of Operation Bootstrap. The more industry developed, the less valuable and desirable agriculture became. There were exceptions: rum made from the molasses either imported or derived from the remnants of the island's sugar economy, became Puerto Rico's premier export and turned Bacardí and Company (originally Cuban) into one of the top distillers in the world. Coffee remained somewhat competitive as an export item, as did spices (Goya), juices, and a few other things. But even these agriculture-based goods had to be manufactured into marketable products, and by 1960, industry reigned supreme, although most of the investment capital came from mainland U.S. firms and banks, which then reaped the lion's share of profits. Still, Puerto Ricans also benefitted, if to a lesser degree. Average real wages for both men and women more than doubled between 1953 and 1963 and kept growing until the 1970s, when stagflation and soaring oil prices ended the boom. Ordinary people benefitted from the new electrical grid and from modernized health care and education. Average life expectancy rose from forty-six to sixty-nine years between 1940 and 1960. Even so, unemployment remained stubbornly high, at 10 percent or more, and the cities couldn't adequately house either the working or nonworking poor.[22]

Lack of jobs and housing fueled a massive migration to the mainland in the 1950s, which the PPD government encouraged by endowing San Juan with a modern airport in 1949 and creating a migration office to help place Puerto Ricans in jobs in the United States. Most settled in New York City, but some went to Philadelphia, Chicago, and other urban areas, where they faced discrimination, low-wage jobs, poor housing, and, with the economic downturn of the 1970s, high unemployment. Puerto Ricans in the United States often faced conditions little better than those they had escaped at home—and cold weather to boot. In 1975, their poverty rate was three times the U.S. average. Still, some did well on the mainland, establishing small businesses, landing government jobs, or making careers in the military.[23]

Many of those who had reached the middle class in the United States decided to return to Puerto Rico, where, by 1960, living conditions had improved markedly. Back on the island, these returnees longed for a middle-class American lifestyle and believed they had the means to maintain it. Bill Levitt understood their wishes, and in 1958, he promised to satisfy them by creating a large Levittown near San Juan.[24]

Levitt began his Puerto Rico operations with the announcement, in 1958, of two small experimental developments of a few hundred houses each in Bayamón. This announcement, covered in the United States only by Miami's Spanish-language *Diario Las Américas,* preceded a November trip to Puerto Rico in which Levitt celebrated the opening of a model home across from Bayamón's Metropolitan shopping center.[25] The three-bedroom, one-bath house would sell for $8,250 and feature amenities typical of mainland Levittowns: refrigerator, electric stove and water heater, built-in closets, and carport. No down payment or closing costs would be assessed; buyers just had to put down a deposit of $100, to be refunded at closing. At a press conference in San Juan, Levitt said that if the Bayamón project proved successful, he would build a much larger development, a new Levittown, nearby. This Levittown would resemble the mainland ones and offer affordable houses for modest middle-class families.

His plans became more specific in February 1959, when he announced his intention to build a community of ten thousand houses as soon as the Bayamón project was complete. The Levittown houses, like the Bayamón ones, would begin at $8,250 and carry a monthly payment of sixty dollars. The FHA would ensure all mortgages, and the Chase Manhattan Bank, Levitt's preferred financial institution, would finance the construction. He promised to use local builders and local labor, which didn't, however, prevent strikes against his company in Bayamón for failing to employ union workers.[26]

It took longer than expected to get the Levittown project off the ground, but by 1962, Levitt was ready to go. In January, he told a group of New York bankers that he would build three thousand houses close to Bayamón, and close to a freeway under construction that would reduce the eight-mile commute to San Juan to twenty minutes. He gave two reasons for locating his first overseas development in Puerto Rico: "One is the burgeoning economy of the Puerto Rican Commonwealth. . . . The other is the overwhelming demand for budget-priced housing which compares favorably with dwelling standards on the mainland." Levitt cited the island's strong GDP growth and the opening of 110 new industrial plants as creating a "pent up demand [that] will stand us in good stead when we enter this new market."[27]

Puerto Rico officials appeared highly favorable to the new housing project. They had become concerned over the helter-skelter mushrooming of suburban housing amid inadequate services and facilities and constant traffic bottlenecks. In July 1961, the Puerto Rico Planning Board, under the direction of the Harvard-educated Ramón García Santiago, froze all applications for building permits until it could issue new guidelines for suburban developments, which it did the following June. From then on, all sizable housing developments would have to include ball fields and other recreation facilities, along with spaces for schools, stores, bakeries, laundries, and medical centers.[28]

The new guidelines made Levitt enormously appealing because, as Santiago knew, his U.S. communities more than fulfilled them. In May 1962, Governor Muñoz Marín met personally with Levitt, who told him that he had acquired the former "Isabella" citrus and coconut plantation, about 450 acres of land in Toa Baja, a sparsely populated oceanfront town just north of Bayamón.[29] There, Levitt said, he would create a "fully planned" community of three thousand dwellings, priced between $8,000 and $16,000. In real dollars, the basic home would cost considerably less than his original Levittown, New York, Cape Cod— $4,500 in 1950 dollars versus $7,000—making the Puerto Rican development affordable to the bottom rungs of the middle class. Before building the houses, Levitt would create an infrastructure of streets, sewers, lighting, electricity, and, above all, fresh water. To store the water, the company would build a huge water tower, the first in Puerto Rico. It would loom over the low-rise community, and with "Levittown Toa Baja" painted in bold letters around its rim, it became the emblem of the development—and also a beacon for pilots descending toward Luis Muñoz Marín airport. The new Puerto Rican Levittown would include a cultural center, library, and extensive recreational facilities. There would also be police and fire stations, land for schools and churches, and full access to the beach. Levitt promised to mix together houses of different sizes and prices so the community wouldn't be segregated by class.[30]

In mid-1963, García Santiago briefly seemed to sour on Levitt's project, claiming in a memo to Muñoz Marín that the FHA might refuse to insure the mortgages on the firm's homes. García Santiago believed, mistakenly, that the FHA was concerned about Levitt's history of racial discrimination and said he'd learned that Levitt had refused to sell a home in his New Jersey project to "the ballplayer of color Willie Mays."[31] This, of course, was untrue; Mays was then playing in San Francisco, and as the highest-paid player in Major League Baseball, he could afford more than a Levitt home.[32] In any case, by 1963, Levitt had already agreed to integrate the New Jersey community. Despite his reservations, Santiago added that the lack of water elsewhere made Levitt's Toa Baja project crucial and that it should proceed. Muñoz Marín agreed, and when the homebuilder personally invited him to the ceremony marking the opening of his model homes, the governor quickly accepted.[33]

The opening took place on September 5, 1963, kicking off a "*semana de* Levittown" (Levittown week).[34] The event received wide, enthusiastic coverage from both the U.S. and insular press. "The new Levittown," declared the *Philadelphia Inquirer,* "was launched with fanfare reminiscent of the early days of the postwar housing shortage." The model homes had been "kept under armed guard" in anticipation of the formal celebration of the new development, for which Bill Levitt served as master of ceremonies along with the mayor of San Juan.[35] At the opening, Muñoz Marín called the development "a magnificent example of a community seriously dedicated to true urban progress—the kind of progress that has called the world's attention to our Commonwealth (*Estado Libre Asociado*)."[36] Muñoz Marín wanted the island he governed to stand out as a beacon of modernity and progress for the developing world, and as a shining capitalist contrast to socialist Cuba in a Cold War that was particularly intense in his Caribbean neighborhood.[37]

Levitt, speaking after Muñoz Marín, seconded his words: "The Puerto Rican Commonwealth's effort to ensure an orderly urban expansion will be carefully observed by other countries of the world and shows that other cities will benefit from the example of what's being established here." He congratulated Muñoz Marín's government for its "pioneering" spirit, its "vision" for the future, and for having "confronted the problem of urban growth so well." The Planning Board, he added, had devised excellent new guidelines because in Puerto Rico, as on the mainland, rapid metropolitan growth had resulted in "some of the world's worst examples of suburban sprawl." It was a "national disgrace" that rural beauty and tranquility had been transformed into suburban blight. Levitt claimed to be one of the few American builders to have avoided this outcome, and he again congratulated the Puerto Rican government, for "in no other part of the United States has [the chaos of suburbanization] been fought with as much vigor" as on the island.[38] Levitt's denunciation of suburban chaos would have amused his many U.S. critics, who accused him of being the key agent of ticky-tacky blight.

In congratulating Muñoz Marín, Levitt was, of course, congratulating himself for creating "perfectly planned" communities and being "the first to build an urbanización conforming to [Puerto Rico's] new planning guidelines. . . . Good planning is good business, good for the buyers and good for the builder." As Muñoz Marín and Santiago understood, "it's not enough to build houses; we try to improve people's lives." That's why his firm had made sure that all the Levittowns had spaces for churches, schools, shopping centers, parks, ball fields, community centers, and libraries and strict rules to guarantee the separation of residential and commercial areas. When developers failed to maintain this separation, as they generally did, the result was traffic-choked neighborhoods blighted by the ugliness of "hot dog stands and neon lights."[39]

The future of Levittown, Puerto Rico, would put the lie to most of Levitt's self-congratulation. But at the moment, Muñoz Marín and Santiago remained convinced that single-family homes in planned suburban developments were the best option for most Puerto Rican families, and they redesigned the property tax codes to reward people for living in them.[40]

After the dignitaries finished speaking, the Levittown celebration erupted into a fireworks display whose dazzling finale had "LEVITTOWN" spelled out in flaming letters over the Bay of San Juan. The

Ceremony marking the opening of model homes in Levittown, Toa Baja. Bill Levitt, wearing a white jacket, is sitting behind the speaker. (Colección Felisa Rincón de Gautier, Municipality of San Juan)

next day, the public was allowed in, and Puerto Ricans flocked to Toa Baja in what the *Philadelphia Inquirer* called "a solid sea of traffic" from San Juan. Police reported a mass of cars idling bumper to bumper for three miles in the searing heat. On that first weekend, Levitt claimed he sold 651 of the nine hundred homes he planned to construct in the first year.[41] Within a month, eager buyers had purchased all nine hundred, well before a single foundation had been laid.[42] "It's good to have proof that our product will export well," Levitt said.

For those who bought the first batch of houses, down payments ranged from $300 to $500, with monthly mortgage costs of sixty to ninety-six dollars. Company officials, the *Philadelphia Inquirer* reported, "stressed that the homes are designed to attract the newly emerging middle-income families of Puerto Rico."[43] The dwellings were modern versions of the vernacular Puerto Rican house, with all-cement construction, smooth horizontal and vertical lines, and flat roofs. For the footings, slabs, exterior walls, second floors, and roofs, Levitt's architects planned to use reinforced concrete—wet cement poured into wooden molds containing grids of iron bars. The interior walls would be stacks of cinder blocks. Both the exterior and interior walls would be plastered by hand in cement, which required a small army of skilled workers and made the dwellings much more expensive to build than the wood-frame houses constructed in the United States. Slatted jalousie ("Florida") windows would punctuate the exteriors to allow in light and air while keeping out the heat. Kitchens would be fully equipped with name-brand appliances, the dwelling's terrazzo floors poured into place. To avoid monotony, the houses would be painted in a variety of pastel colors. Interiors would be uniformly white.[44]

The floor plans of the five model homes were displayed in a special ten-page section of the prominent newspaper *El Mundo* devoted to Levittown. The base model (the Alhaja) was a side-by-side duplex with three bedrooms, a living room–dining room, and one bath. Next was the Broche de Oro, with three bedrooms and one bath; it was similar to the Alhaja except that it had no attached twin. For the Camafeo, Levitt added a second bath and an L-shaped living-dining room, somewhat larger than those in the Alhaja and Broche de Oro. The other two models, the one-story Diadena and two-story Esmeralda, featured four bedrooms and two baths plus ampler L-shaped living and dining rooms. The Esmeralda was the first dual-level house marketed in the San Juan suburbs. It had a terrace running more than half the length of the second floor, whose front section extended beyond the first floor to create a shaded porch facing the street. All five models had attached carports. Kitchens were tiny but well equipped, and except for the Esmeralda, which had a good-size master bedroom, the sleeping quarters were also tiny, eight by ten feet or smaller. The houses cost less than equivalent local homes, but more per square foot than those being built simultaneously in Levittown, New Jersey. The 1,079-square-foot Puerto Rican "Rancher" was priced at $13,990; its New Jersey counterpart measured 1,500 square feet and sold for just $500 more. The Puerto Rican houses were packed tightly together on plots of 2,500 to 3,300 square feet, less than half the size of even the smallest New Jersey lot.[45] When finished, the houses almost touched one another, and backyards were minuscule.

Although Levitt billed his houses as affordable, they cost more than the average Puerto Rican could pay. After the project's second year of

Levittown, Puerto Rico, homes are packed tightly together, with tiny front yards and backyards. (Photograph by Edward Berenson)

sales, the *Washington Post* reported that the new homeowners' average family income was $5,000, about 30 percent higher than the island's mean.[46] The U.S. census showed that in 1969, the median income of Levittown, Puerto Rico, families was $6,342, which means the community was the second-richest among all Puerto Rican municipalities of more than ten thousand inhabitants.[47] Even so, 25 percent of Levittowners had incomes below the official poverty line of about $4,000 per year, while 18 percent earned $10,000 or more. Residents here were also relatively well educated. The median Levittowner had 12.2 years of schooling, and 57 percent had completed four years of high school or more. As for employment, 56.4 percent were labeled "white collar," while 17.4 percent worked in industrial jobs and 29.3 percent in government. Unemployment was below average at 4.5 percent, and nearly three-quarters of men belonged to the active labor force. As in mainland Levittowns, there were huge numbers of young children: nearly half of the families had kids under age six. One especially interesting statistic was that 22 percent of Levittowners had been born outside Puerto Rico and 16.2 percent in the United States. In virtually every other municipality, more than 90 percent had been born in Puerto Rico and only 5 to 6 percent in the United States.[48]

For Levitt, the demographic here was familiar. To attract these relatively prosperous, well-educated families, he included a public relations staff in his Puerto Rico operation and accompanied the opening of Toa Baja with a major marketing and advertising campaign. The expensively produced sales brochure depicted the new community as a tropical paradise, and the cascade of newspaper ads sounded a similar note.[49] An early ad in the *San Juan Star* showed a light-skinned family in a sailboat on choppy waters. The caption reads, "The View is Levittown." No houses were in view because none had been built. Instead, the text of the ad described "palm fringed beaches" lying just "beyond a tropical seaside city," where "the architecture, the broad rolling streets, the malls, the public buildings, [are] all falling beautifully into place."[50]

Even after the first section of nine hundred homes sold much faster than expected, Levitt continued to advertise aggressively; he planned to sell thousands more. Early ads in *El Mundo* featured a smiling little girl depicted as if crayon-drawn by a child. There's a bright sun in the sky, and etched onto a large palm tree is a heart with "I like Levittown!" scrawled inside. The text proclaims, "Everyone loves Levittown because it's a modern community that offers the greatest advantages. Spectacular location. One of the most beautiful places in Puerto Rico. Very attractive houses. Low prices. There's nothing else like Levittown." It's "much closer to San Juan than many other residential areas considered close ... but it's far from the bustle," with "tranquil streets" and air always "clean and pure." Another early ad shows the same little girl, who appears to say, "Daddy and Mommy have already bought in Levittown. Have your parents already bought, too?"[51] By the time these ads ran, in November and December 1963, prices had already gone up since the opening in September; the range was now $10,750 to $15,500, nearly a 20 percent increase over the original price, doubtless buoyed by the brisk sales and perhaps also by mounting construction costs. Levitt may also have discounted the first batch of nine hundred houses to spur sales and convince future buyers of Levittown's desirability.

The first buyers moved into their homes in early 1964, and the ads that year featured the same crayon-drawn girl, only now she's playing on the beach, a bucket and shovel in her hands. Sun, surf, and palm trees grace the background. "This marvelous community," the text says, "overlooks the beautiful seascape of the Boca Vieja cove, where you can picnic under shade trees on the white and beautiful beach. . . . Imagine how good it would be to live like this." It was as if you would live right on the beach, just like the wealthy inhabitants of Malibu or Saint-Tropez, and "you would discover a different life—calm, informal, healthy, beautiful"—a land of permanent vacation with a climate "cooler and healthier" than elsewhere on the island thanks to "the constant breeze."[52] In reality, ocean breezes didn't reach many Levittown dwellings, which would be crammed tightly together not far from the beach but hardly right on it. Before long, a four-lane highway would separate the houses from the beach; it would be dangerous to cross except at traffic lights spaced far apart.

The highway wouldn't be built right away, but Levitt ads promised a short, easy drive, "just minutes from San Juan," when it was done.[53] In the meantime, the drumbeat of idyllic advertising continued. One full-page ad showed the two-story Esmeralda on what looked like a huge plot of land with no neighboring houses in sight. "Only in Levittown," beamed the headline, "can you own a two-story house with four bedrooms for $100 a month." The selling price had already gone up by $1,000 from a year earlier—from $15,500 to $16,500. But "in Levittown you get more house, more square feet of space, and more quality for your money."[54] You would also get a complete, self-contained community with every service you might need. One ad presents the same little girl, this time drawing on a blackboard to show the shopping center with its supermarkets, pharmacies, and clothing stores. In the background, she has drawn children on a playground and romping on the beach.[55]

As in the United States, Levittown, Puerto Rico, was built for families with young children, and Levitt had promised to build schools quickly. The first, which opened in September 1964, was named for President John F. Kennedy, assassinated less than a year earlier, and was the first public school in Puerto Rico built in a commercial (non-public) housing development. Its innovative architecture made it the subject of a long article in *URBE,* the island's top architectural magazine. The school boasted a modern modular design, with twenty identical prefabricated classrooms arrayed around a grassy courtyard.

Students and teachers could walk from one room to another under a canopy that shielded them from the sun and the rain. *URBE* predicted that the new school would be "a model to follow in the construction of future schools in Puerto Rico."[56] More immediately, it would serve as a model for the many other schools to be built in Levittown as the community expanded. New schools would go up at the rate of one a year.[57]

Levitt built his new Levittown, like the older ones, in sections, beginning each new subdivision when the earlier one had sold out. From 1964 to 1966, the firm finished three sections for a total of about 2,400 houses, somewhat more than originally planned. The advertisements show that in 1964 the firm dropped its semidetached base model, the Alhaja, and boosted the price of its new entry-level home to $12,990, making it about 40 percent costlier than the discontinued Alhaja. It's unclear why the company hiked its prices so much; it may be that construction costs were higher than expected, not only for the houses, but also for the schools, shopping areas, and recreation facilities Levitt had promised. Levitt may also have decided to take advantage of the brisk demand to increase profits.[58]

The Levittown homes sold so quickly and profitably that Levitt decided to buy another eight hundred acres of land just south and west of the original development. The new land was swampy and prone to flooding, so the company had to do considerable work on the site, burying miles of sewer lines beneath the watery surface and fortifying it with thousands of tons of soil. Preparing the site took such a large effort that Levitt created its own subsidiary for the project. Named Isabela after the plantation Levittown had replaced, the subsidiary bought $1.5 million of heavy equipment and hired 350 laborers for the job.[59] One of its main tasks was to create a lake and a series of twenty-foot-deep canals to sop up the area's excess rainwater and allow drainage in case of flooding. This huge undertaking resulted in the largest man-made lake in Puerto Rico, stretching over one hundred acres.[60]

Once the lake was finished, Levitt built houses around it and to the south and east. He called the new subdivision, which was just an extension of the three existing ones, Levittown Lakes. When finished, the Levittown add-on would contain more than twice as many houses as the original development, five thousand versus 2,400, and the new houses would be updated, pricier versions of the first ones. Levitt did the same thing in his mainland developments, regularly updating his models and adding new ones.[61]

On July 15, 1966, Levitt opened five new model homes to prospective buyers. On the inside, the smallest (La Florencia) resembled the original houses in Levittown, New York. It was a square box with the kitchen and living room in front and two bedrooms behind. The bathroom shared a wall with the kitchen, and there were no hallways to waste space. But the exterior was completely different from the original Cape Cods. The Puerto Rico model had cement walls and a flat cement slab for a roof. Its façade featured jalousie windows with slats made to look like redwood, giving the model some distinctiveness, at least from a distance. As he did with the Long Island original, Levitt advertised the house as "easy to expand." The next model up (La Geneve) added a bedroom but otherwise was identical to the two-bedroom version. The façade was the same, except that the living room extended beyond the dining area by three feet, creating a small porch in front, with the door facing the carport rather than the street. The Lucerne added a second bathroom and extended the house's length by about six feet. It restored the flat façade with its slatted "redwood" windows. The other two models, the one-story Jamaica and the two-story Kaluah, featured four bedrooms and two or two and a half baths. The Kaluah was almost identical to the original two-story model, except that the second-floor terrace sat on top of the carport and the floor-to-ceiling front windows also sported "redwood" slats.[62] Prices of the five models ranged from $14,990 to $19,990, with down payments of $440 to $990 and monthly mortgages of $97 to $126.[63]

To generate publicity for this new extension, Bill Levitt came to Puerto Rico to celebrate the opening of the five revamped models. Levitt executives on the scene had lined up several local dignitaries for the elaborate event, including Ramón García Santiago, the powerful president of Puerto Rico's Planning Board. In his speech, Santiago gave Levitt and Levittown effusive praise. "Unlike in other communities," he said, "the families of Levittown already have, or will soon have, the facilities and indispensable services that make for a genuine community." Levittown was a "good example of what private enterprise can accomplish in Puerto Rico" under the Planning Board's guidelines for new developments. And "in observing the growth and functioning of the neighborhoods constructed [by Levitt] we can see how to modify our ideas about the best kinds of development."[64] For Santiago, Levittown both confirmed the value of the government's housing development guidelines and provided a model for the future. Levitt's example would play a key role in shaping Puerto Rico's suburbanization in the years to come.

But Levitt wasn't about to rest on his laurels. If anything, he advertised Levittown Lakes more relentlessly than the original community. Advertisements pictured the new dwellings as perched on a lake rather than the beach. In reality, only ninety of the new houses actually faced the lake; most stood on residential streets just like those in the first part of the development.[65] No matter, Levitt's sales brochure showed two boys piloting a pair of small sailboats, with white two-story houses in the background. The ads proclaimed, "You can live on the shores of the lake," "your private lake," with "cool, crystalline" waters, where you could enjoy boating, swimming, and fishing—Levitt had amply stocked its lake. Above all, Levittown Lakes was "where the good life begins" (*Donde la Buena Vida Comienza*) and where you and your family could enjoy an "eternal vacation . . . sailing on a boat, fishing, and relaxing on your patio overlooking Levittown Lake." All this starting at $112 a month.[66]

The free publicity and advertising campaign seemed to work, as did Levittown's reputation for offering "a lot of house for the money." Some 1,500 families went to see the new model homes during the opening weekend, and three hundred put down deposits. The most popular model was the two-story Kaluah.[67] Spurred by this initial success, the aggressive marketing continued. In one ad, Levitt published an interview with one Carlos M. Dávila, vice president for finance at Burger King. Dávila "needed a place in the [San Juan] metropolitan area with easy access to my work. But at the same time, we wanted to live tranquilly . . . outside the city. We found exactly what we were looking for in Levittown Lakes. Here, we got a lot more for our money." It's no coincidence that Dávila's interview sounded just like Levitt advertising copy. He hit all the notes: the house was a great investment, perfect for the kids, and close to everything a family needs.[68]

In another "interview," Levitt's public relations people showed their understanding of Puerto Ricans' growing desire to return to the island after living on the mainland. "In 1963 we lived in New York," said Noemi Almocera de Rodriguez, president of Levittown's Newcomers'

Club, "but we wanted to move back to Puerto Rico. It was very difficult to leave everything behind—work, friends, and experiences." But
then the family took a vacation in Puerto Rico and stopped in at the
Levitt sales office. Although no houses had yet been built, they could
see that Levittown "would be an ideal place to live and raise our children." It "was a dream come true." Now, "I'm proud to say, 'I'm from
Levittown!' "[69]

Already in 1964, the *New York Times* had reported on the phenomenon of "Nuyoricans" (Puerto Rican New Yorkers) returning to the island, and in the early days of Levittown de Puerto Rico, English was
more common in the community than Spanish.[70] James Ramos Santiago, now a top official in Toa Baja, is from New York, where both of
his parents had gone as adolescents to join relatives already in the
United States. They met in their Brooklyn neighborhood and eventually moved to Long Island, where James was born. His father worked
as head waiter and then manager of a well-known Nassau County restaurant; his mother was a homemaker. His dad's job paid pretty well,
and he managed to put some money away. In 1970, friends back on
the island praised Levittown as a place friendly to returnees, and
James's parents were getting sick of the cold New York weather. They
returned to Puerto Rico when James was two, using their savings to
buy a Levittown house. As a kid, he rode his bike everywhere, just as
kids did in Levitt's mainland communities. "Levittown is a unique
place," he said. "We had a wonderful childhood because everything is
perfectly designed. We had schools, churches, commercial spaces, even
a movie theater."[71]

The family mostly spoke Spanish at home, but James took English
classes in school, and his parents had him read the *San Juan Star* and
other English-language newspapers. Not every Puerto Rican returnee
spoke good Spanish, so the municipality of Toa Baja decided to offer
Spanish courses for English-speaking Nuyoricans, and the schools offered bilingual classes.[72] When older kids learned Spanish, classmates
often mocked their accents. By 1980, two-thirds of Levittown residents belonged to families that had lived in the United States. Elsewhere on the island, Nuyoricans often had trouble adapting; but in
Levittown, many people shared the mainland background and spoke
English. The environment looked familiar, with its U.S. supermarket
chains, CVS stores, Burger Kings, and the like, and where the devel-

Entrance to the seventh section of Levittown, Puerto Rico. (Photograph by Edward Berenson)

opment's low-rise density reminded them of Long Island.[73] So did the Lions Club, the Parent-Teachers Association, and the Little League baseball teams established in the community.[74]

Returning Nuyoricans as well as middle-class islanders looking for affordable suburban homes snapped up the Levittown models as soon as they went on sale. Like the original sections of Levittown, Puerto Rico, those of Levittown Lakes sold faster than expected. Levitt opened one new section after another until seven had been built (three in the original part; four in Levittown Lakes). Eventually there would be an eighth section, known as Levittown South, making a total of eleven thousand single-family homes—about the same number as in Willingboro, New Jersey—plus several condominium projects.[75] Like Willingboro, Levittown Lakes was completed after the sale of Levitt & Sons to the International Telephone & Telegraph Corporation in 1968, and the condos mostly went up after the company was sold again to Starrett in 1976 and the former Puerto Rican subsidiary was spun off. As an independent company, Levitt Homes continued to build on the island until 2016.[76]

Despite the strong sales, the firm never let up on its advertising. To highlight the supposed peace and tranquility of Levittown Lakes, the ads always pictured the houses as if they stood on large plots with no visible neighbors. They continued to emphasize the value of the Levitt homes, the self-contained community, with its own schools, shopping centers, beach, lake, and recreation—and also the closeness to San Juan, even while stressing the development's isolation from the intensity, crimes, dirt, and traffic of the city.[77] In reality, though, Levittown was beginning to look and feel more like a city than a suburb. Residents of mainland Levittowns would have been shocked to see how dense the Puerto Rican version was, and how tiny its plots. Levittown, Puerto Rico, looked more like Los Angeles than a typical suburb, and it had a distinctly urban feel. It would feel all the more urban once the community's boulevards, intended as through streets to ease movement within the community, began to sprout shops and other services. In theory, these businesses were prohibited from residential areas and were to be located only in designated shopping centers. But when bakeries, dry cleaners, and auto parts stores began opening within residential sections, local authorities proved powerless to remove them, despite a flood of complaints.[78]

By the late 1960s, other problems had begun to plague the community. First, inflation raised prices sharply and reduced the number of potential buyers. In 1969, the least expensive Levitt house went for $16,000, the most expensive for $21,000. But labor and material costs had jumped quickly, and ads urged people to buy before home prices rose further.[79] By 1972, the cheapest house went for $20,000 and required a down payment of $2,240. The two-story home cost $27,500, with a down payment of $3,190.[80] In three years, the entry-level home had gone up in price by 25 percent, the top model by 31 percent.

At the same time, Levittown homeowners began complaining about the quality of their dwellings. Light fixtures fell from the ceiling and crashed onto dining room tables, vinyl floor tiles came loose whenever a bed, table, or other heavy piece of furniture was moved; leaks from pipes left puddles of water on the floor, and the moisture loosened or cracked the tiles. Many buyers were surprised to find that the terrazzo floors displayed on the model homes were an upgrade, and their own homes received the vinyl tiles that then caused so many problems. When residents brought their problems to Levitt officials, they were ignored. To get their attention, in 1969, members of twenty families picketed the Levitt offices in Toa Baja wielding signs accusing Levitt of failing to keep his promises, and the FHA and VA of approving defective construction. ITT-Levitt, as the company was then called, responded by bringing a $1 million lawsuit against the picketers for causing a loss of sales.[81] In the United States, Levitt was known for fixing these kinds of problems for free, but the Puerto Rican subsidiary was probably unprepared for the inflated costs.

Levittown residents also began to complain about crime. One homemaker told an *El Mundo* reporter in 1970 that she was afraid to leave her house, and that her neighbors kept their doors locked and wouldn't open them for anyone they didn't know. Another woman said she left home with her husband every morning because she was afraid to be alone in the house. Still another met her husband at his workplace every day so they could go home together. Residents added double and triple locks to their doors; some installed bars over their doors and windows. One man said he kept a baseball bat next to his bed for protection, and another admitted to having a gun, though it was illegal. A homeowner in Levittown's fifth section, where much of the crime was concentrated, told reporters that he'd sold his house because he worked nights and was not home to protect his wife and children.[82]

This intense fear of crime didn't match the reality. According to the local police, between October 1969 and February 1970, there were 108 cases of trespassing, twenty-six thefts, five robberies, seven assaults, and ten rapes in a community of about twenty-five thousand people.[83] There were no homicides, and most of the assaults didn't result in serious injury. Still, the rapes and assaults, in particular, were an obvious concern, especially since the local weekly paper, *El Tanque,* stoked the fear of crime by devoting its front pages to it. It's hard to find comparable crime statistics, but in the whole of Puerto Rico in 1972, there were 388 property crimes and 131 violent crimes per twenty-five thousand people (194 and sixty-five, respectively, for six months).[84] In San Juan in 2010 there were 201 homicides, a rate of fifty per one hundred thousand residents, or twelve for twenty-five thousand and six in half a year.[85] Except for the alarming rape statistics, Levittown was safer in the early 1970s than Puerto Rico as a whole, and, most likely, much safer than nearby San Juan. Still, Levittowners didn't feel as secure as they expected.

Levitt & Sons understandably saw the fear of crime as a threat to sales, and it readily agreed to allow the Toa Baja police department to use one of its houses as a substation. But the added police presence didn't ease the fear.[86] Homeowners continued to install bars on their windows and doors, and even on their carports. One reason for the relatively high incidence of trespassing and theft had to do with the paved alleyways Levitt had installed between some of the houses to allow kids to walk to school and recreation centers without having to cross main thoroughfares. The same alleyways gave intruders access to backyards and bedroom windows. Several older Levittowners reported having used the alleyways as shortcuts all the time, but eventually they were closed off as an anticrime measure, at the cost of making the community less friendly to teenagers.[87]

Levittowners who were frightened into selling their homes had no trouble finding buyers. Nor did Levitt & Sons want for interest in the houses it continued to build throughout the 1970s. By 1975, the community, now with seven sections, had become by far Puerto Rico's largest housing development, comprising 50 percent of Toa Baja's population. When there was no more room in Toa Baja, the eighth section, built toward the end of the decade, went up in neighboring Bayamón, although it was contiguous with the rest of the development.[88]

Levittown's popularity made the community grow too fast. Its 200 percent population increase between 1971 and 1976 overwhelmed Toa Baja's public services and public schools and led to the deterioration of the community. The mayor called Levittown's growth "huge and amazing." Just fourteen years earlier, Toa Baja had been a sparsely inhabited backwater with some coastal orchards, but much of its land was too swampy for farming or homebuilding. The tax base was minuscule, and the government in San Juan saw no reason to pump any of its meager resources into the area. Public services had remained slim, and the local government small and weak.[89]

When Levitt bought up the lion's share of the town's habitable area, along with much that was uninhabitable as well, the company had not only to build from scratch the infrastructure of streets, sewers, electricity, water purification, and sanitation. It also had to dredge a lake, drain swamps, and provide flood control for an area just a few feet above sea level, one of the lowest-lying places on the island. When Levitt finished building the community, the firm dumped the responsibility for maintaining Levittown onto the municipality of Toa Baja, which was wholly unequipped to take it on.[90] Levitt didn't, however, give up ownership of the lake it had created, and according to Toa Baja's mayor, this proved worse than if the firm had ceded it to the municipality. By 1977, Levitt & Sons had essentially ceased to exist, and its much smaller successor company lacked the resources to clean up the lake. But since Toa Baja didn't own the body of water or its surrounds, it could take only limited steps to remedy it.[91]

The results were predictable. The "crystalline waters" of Levittown Lakes advertisements became murky with filth, and the once ample fish washed up dead. The "cool, fresh breezes" wafting off the ocean now smelled of household and chemical waste, and the "palm-fringed beach" had become a garbage-strewn no-man's land where people feared to tread. Levittown's *"playa"* was now the second-most contaminated beach in Puerto Rico. Beyond the household waste dumped into the ocean, the toxic runoff from the massive Barcardí factory just east of Levittown also fouled its waters, along with those of the Bay of San Juan. In 1980, the government required the rum maker to clean up its act, which it did successfully. This didn't solve the pollution problem, but it helped.[92]

To add to these environmental misfortunes, crime continued to rise, thanks to inadequate, underfunded policing. And although highways had been built, they couldn't contain the surge of traffic; commuters simmered in their cars. Suburban sprawl doesn't lend itself to public transportation, since the population is dispersed, and although one elevated train line was constructed, it did little to ease the highway congestion.[93]

To make matters worse, the hurricanes that had always visited the island became more frequent and severe, causing massive property damage and flooding that the infrastructure, built with 1960s weather in mind, couldn't prevent or contain. Between 1900 and 1968, twenty hurricanes and tropical storms hit Puerto Rico, with one at category five, the most severe. The years from 1970 to 2000 saw the same number of major weather events in half the time. Between 2001 and 2020, Puerto was plagued with thirty-eight hurricanes and tropical storms, including nine of category five. By far the worst was Hurricane María, in 2017, which caused catastrophic damage from which the island has yet to fully recover. María hit Levittown especially hard, blowing off roofs, flooding streets and homes, and cutting off power for as long as

Toa Baja before Levittown, 1962. (Puerto Rico Department of Transportation and Public Works; Carlos A. Ramos Rosario, PR Highways and Transportation Authority, Programs Development Division Senior Manager, Pre-Construction Office)

six months.[94] The hurricane also erased much of Levittown's history, as mounds of key documents perished in flooded buildings.[95]

The storms deposited earth and debris in the pipes Levitt had installed to carry rainwater out to sea. Cleaning them required manpower and machinery that Toa Baja lacked and couldn't afford to buy. By the 1980s, channels no longer existed to drain away the rainwater that frequently deluged houses and streets. And since the government had required that Levittown's power lines be buried underground, the persistent floods knocked out electricity, cable, and telephone service.[96]

Levittown's famous amenities became unusable. Pollution made it dangerous to swim in either the ocean or the lake; crime and garbage

Toa Baja after Levittown, 1973. (Puerto Rico Department of Transportation and
Public Works; Carlos A. Ramos Rosario, PR Highways and Transportation
Authority, Programs Development Division Senior Manager, Pre-Construction Office)

kept people away from the beach; and the community's Olympic-size
swimming pool, which had once attracted international competitions,
was threatened with closing because the community lacked the means
to maintain it. For once, however, private business and local government came together, and in 1980, the facility was restored as a key
feature of the town.[97] It has remained in relatively good shape. At a
time when the public pools in the mainland Levittowns were closing
one by one, this was one way—perhaps the only way—that Puerto
Rico's Levittown surpassed its counterparts.

The pool success led a number of local officials and residents to believe Levittown would be better off as a separate municipality. The
lack of self-governance wasn't unique to Puerto Rico's version of the

development; as we have seen, the Levittowns in New York, Pennsylvania, and Maryland suffered a similar problem. In New York and Pennsylvania, the difficulty was that the community sprawled across several municipalities, each of which also included areas not part of Levittown. Non-Levittowners often didn't want to pay for services destined mainly for inhabitants of the development. Levittown, Puerto Rico, belonged to just two municipalities, with all but one section in Toa Baja, but here the issue was the lack of municipal resources to handle the massive population increase the development had wrought. As in the United States, people who lived in the town but outside Levittown didn't want to contribute to its finances.

This problem moved residents to petition the Puerto Rican legislature in 1981 to recognize Levittown as a separate city. But the mayor of Toa Baja rejected the idea on the grounds that hiving off Levittown from the larger municipality would weaken both. The huge development of the 1960s and 1970s had turned Toa Baja into the ninth-largest city in Puerto Rico, giving it clout in San Juan and qualifying it for government resources that would be denied the two midsize towns that the separation of Toa Baja and Levittown would create. An independent Levittown would have fewer rather than greater resources.[98] The mayor may have been right, and in any case, the legislature didn't agree to hive off Levittown. But Toa Baja's chief executive could be charged with special pleading. The amputation of Levittown and the demotion of his city from large to medium would have reduced his influence and turned Levittown into a rival for scarce government favors.

While some called for Levittown's independence, others took practical steps to improve the town. During the summer of 1976, the Lions Club of Levittown organized a group of volunteers to clean up the beach. The Puerto Rican government took note of the effort and gave it some help.[99] But the mounds of trash quickly returned, city officials said, because too many Levittown residents continued to drop their garbage there. Why would people carry their trash all the way to the beach, rather than simply bring it to the curb, where city trucks could pick it up?[100] Most likely because they couldn't count on the city to collect it.

By Levittown's twenty-fifth anniversary, in 1988, the portrait painted by journalists was harshly negative. Paquita Berio, a San Juan newspaper columnist who had grown up in the development, drew a stark contrast with the Levittown she had known in the 1960s. In those years, she wrote, "we ran around on the beach without fear of being assaulted. Day and night we enjoyed the pleasure of walking on the sandy beach and through the waves that caressed our feet." She and her friends walked everywhere "without fearing that a stranger would intercept us," and "neighbors visited one another, leaving our front doors open." Kids "rode their bicycles through the streets without fear." Neighbors continued to get together for birthdays and Christmas parties as the development continued to grow. But "gradually, imperceptibly at first, the ambiance began to change." Levittown faced the problems of drug addiction, alcoholism, assaults, and the fear they inspired. Residents huddled inside homes fortressed with thick iron bars. "No longer did we know who our neighbors were, and of the happy times we enjoyed in Levittown, only the memories remain."[101]

There is surely much nostalgia in this lament, a longing for innocence lost and for childhood's idyllic past. Such nostalgia comes through in the memories of people who grew up in Levittowns everywhere, whether in Pennsylvania, France, or Puerto Rico. But the regret contains an element of truth. Early in the lives of these communities, parents gave their children freer rein than kids have today, and large suburban developments like Levittown had yet to take on the problems of cities—the crime, drugs, and anomie that would plague them in later years.

Today, when you walk or drive through Levittown, Puerto Rico, you can see barred windows and doors guarding virtually every house. Some of the bars seem ornamental, but most are ugly. Their ubiquity suggests a community paralyzed by fear. It's true that iron bars aren't uncommon in other Puerto Rican suburbs, but in Levittown they're everywhere. A big part of the problem is the Puerto Rican press, which ignores Levittown most of the time but spotlights the murders and robberies when they occur. In 1993, WKAQ-TV San Juan made time to cover two Levittown murders in a pair of thirty-minute news shows. *El Mundo* regularly runs headlines like "More Robberies in Levittown," two of which involved thefts of eighteen dollars and thirty dollars.[102] Another article under the "Latest News" rubric covered "a spectacular car chase" by police of two men suspected of robbery and murder.[103] This crime took place in Levittown, but the suspects didn't come from there and could have done the deed anywhere.

Most Levittown, Puerto Rico, houses huddle behind bars. (Photograph by
Edward Berenson)

Still, there is clearly more crime in Levittown than in the 1960s, and
in general, the development hasn't aged very well. Debora Rivera, who
has lived there since 1965, said the community has become too big,
with too many stores on streets intended to be purely residential. But
the place retains some advantages. Its schools are better than those in
surrounding towns, and houses in good condition remain desirable, selling for $150,000 or more. Amneris Soto, a Levittowner since 1966,
agreed that the development has become too big. She noted less community spirit than in her childhood and lamented that the town's public
facilities have not been maintained: pools have closed, parks are neglected, the beach is unattractive, the water polluted. A recent survey of
Levittown residents found that more than half never used the amenities
that were once one of Levitt's key selling points. Respondents said they
were unsafe, inaccessible, unclean, and unappealing.[104] Soto shared
many of these concerns, especially about crime, although she added
that the press exaggerates it. James Ramos Santiago, the Toa Baja

official, said there are more robberies now than in past years, and with the increase in crime, parents no longer let their kids walk or bike around the community, as they did when he was young. And while Levittown looked fresh and new when his parents bought a house there in 1970, now it looks run down. People have stopped maintaining their lawns, and the municipality doesn't have the resources to repair streets and sidewalks, or even keep streetlights working. The lack of lighting adds to the danger of robberies and assault.[105]

These problems have led to an exodus from the community. By 2000, Levittown's population had dropped to 30,154, from a high of about forty thousand two decades earlier. And although educational attainment remained relatively high in 2000, unemployment was at 13.1 percent (compared to 10 percent for Puerto Rico as a whole), while the median household income, though still above the island's norm, was stagnant at $23,979.[106]

And then, to make matters infinitely worse, Hurricane María hit the development so hard that the extensive damage it caused remained visible six years later. The violent storm caused Levittown Lake and the canals that fed it to spill over their banks and flood much of the development, damaging more than half of the houses and trapping hundreds of people inside.[107] The electrical grid stayed down for months. Few Levittowners had insurance, and many could not afford to make repairs. Large numbers simply abandoned their unlivable dwellings, often migrating to live with their adult children or other relatives in Florida. Santiago said Levittown has lost about 15 percent of its population in the last fifteen years, and the outflow ticked up dramatically in the wake of María.

Today, some 20 percent of the houses are empty—their owners simply walked away. The U.S. Census shows a population of twenty-five thousand in 2020, a decline of 19 percent since 2010. Those who remain are older—44 percent are age sixty and up—and more female (53.4 percent) than the Puerto Rican norm, and the average income has been declining. By 2019, Levittown's poverty rate had jumped to 27.4 percent, having risen at an annual rate of nearly 5 percent. The median family income was just over $30,000, still well above the $21,000 median for Puerto Rico as a whole, but less than half that of the United States ($68,500).[108]

The Federal Emergency Management Agency (FEMA) has helped repair Levittown's infrastructure, but overall has provided only a fraction

One of the 20 percent of Levittown, Puerto Rico, houses abandoned by their owners. (Photograph by Edward Berenson)

of the resources the community needs. Hurricane recovery has been mired in Washington's indifference to the Commonwealth. There's a stark gap between FEMA's responses to natural disasters in the United States and in Puerto Rico.[109] The municipality of Toa Baja, Santiago said, has no choice but to wait for FEMA to release the funds due to the island, but meanwhile the community has deteriorated further.[110] When asked why Toa Baja doesn't simply take over the abandoned houses, Santiago gave two reasons: the town has no money to make repairs and renovations, and the houses have owners who can't be found. It's hard, though, to see why absentee owners would be a problem. Presumably the municipality could seize the properties in lieu of the taxes those owners surely aren't paying. So the fundamental problem isn't the absentee owners; it's the lack of resources to restore the damaged, abandoned homes. This is tragic, because, as Santiago notes, Puerto Rico has a dire shortage of affordable houses; there would clearly be a market for renovated Levittown homes. Santiago spoke wistfully about creating public-private partnerships to make the dwellings commercially viable, but to date this idea hasn't produced any results.[111]

Despite the problems and frustrations, many Levittown residents have positive views of the place. In a 2022 survey of 350 people, 55.5 percent of whom were current Levittown residents and 44.5 percent former ones, the current residents were asked what they liked best about Levittown, and the former residents were asked why they left. The most common responses among the current Levittowners highlighted its proximity to the city, its variety of stores and services ("Levittown is a place that has essentially everything," one respondent said), its easy accessibility from many places in the San Juan area, and its vibrant social and cultural life, with several annual festivals on the Avenida (Boulevard) Levittown. Those who had left Levittown cited crime ("It isn't safe to walk anywhere") and the deterioration of its public facilities ("The lack of streetlights is incredible"). Many also said they had left the development because the aftereffects of Hurricane María added to the feeling of insecurity ("Ever since María, I haven't felt safe here").[112]

A second Levitt *urbanización* in Puerto Rico, known as Las Delicias, has aged much better. In 1969, Levitt bought about two hundred acres of land near Ponce, Puerto Rico's second-largest city and the capital of its less frequented southern coast. Leaving the "Levittown" name behind, the firm aimed the new development squarely at the middle and upper-middle class.[113] Las Delicias proved an immediate success, as more than one thousand people flocked to the model homes on their opening weekend. Demand was so high that Levitt had to accelerate its building schedule.[114]

The houses in Las Delicias resemble those of Levittown but are larger, more comfortable, and better equipped. There are five models, including one with two stories, and just over 1,200 dwellings altogether. The average new home there cost $22,000 in 1970; to afford a place at this price level, a family needed an annual income of about $10,000, which only 9 percent of Puerto Ricans enjoyed at the time— the average income in 1970 was $6,132.[115]

Las Delicias is more colorful than Levittown, as the southern development's flat cement surfaces are painted in bright hues inspired by the colorful buildings of Ponce, known as the Pearl of the South. Unlike Levittown, Las Delicias has remained a prosperous community, with nicely maintained houses, landscaping, and many additions to the original models. People have built second stories and terraces, and converted carports and garages into extra rooms. Many houses have been remodeled on the inside. One of the loveliest is owned by a couple who bought it in 1970 after visiting the model homes.

Their one-story dwelling has four bedrooms and two baths. Some years ago, they remodeled the kitchen from top to bottom and removed the original counter that had separated it from the dining area. Now the living room, dining area, and kitchen are combined in a single open space, making the public parts of the home seem larger than they are, especially because the living room features a high vaulted ceiling. The former garage now serves as a large family room, although its shape is oddly long and narrow, in keeping with its original purpose. A closet tucked into the inside wall accommodates their washing machine, which dates from the mid-1960s and still works perfectly.

Another Las Delicias homeowner spoke perfect English; he was born and raised in New York, joined the U.S. Navy after high school, and made it his career. He and his wife bought their house in 1995, having heard through the grapevine that it was for sale. The place needed work, and they have gradually fixed it up. His wife did so much remodeling while he was stationed in Iraq that he said he barely recognized the home when he got back to Puerto Rico. Now it is large and immaculate, a substantial two-story structure. The owner said he knew his neighbors only to say hello; they never see each other socially. He's retired from the service and mostly stays home. He never goes into Ponce, even though it's only a few miles away.

As in all Levitt developments, the firm devoted space to churches, schools, community centers, tennis courts, ball fields, and other amenities. There used to be a private pool and club house that Las Delicias residents could join, but as the original owners aged and their children moved out, membership dropped, depriving the facility of money for maintenance. When the pool's filtration system failed in 2021, the remaining members decided to close it. Now it sits empty, protected by a stone wall topped with barbed wire.[116]

Still, unlike Levittown, Las Delicias has no abandoned houses, and its inhabitants seem prosperous enough to maintain and often improve their homes. It may be a key ingredient of its success that Las Delicias is only one-tenth the size of Levittown, which is by far the largest of

Puerto Rico's *urbanizaciós*. Between 1963 and 1975, in response to the apparently unquenchable demand, Levitt kept expanding the development. But the demand was not unquenchable; it lasted only as long as the relative prosperity of Operation Bootstrap. When the world economy turned sour in the mid-1970s—ending Puerto Rico's fragile economic boom—Levittown's problems began. In the wake of Hurricane María, it's unclear whether it will recover.

9 On Top of the World

AFTER FINDING UNPRECEDENTED success as a housing entrepreneur in the late 1940s and 1950s, Bill Levitt became a darling of
the media and, rare for a businessman, a household name. In 1954,
he bought out his brother, Alfred, and assumed sole ownership of
Levitt & Sons. Six years later, he took the company public and transformed a family business into a major corporation. In the process, he
kept about 80 percent of the stock for himself so as to remain firmly
in control, even while he raised a good amount of new capital.

These new resources gave him the means to begin a third Levittown in central New Jersey, but he quickly discovered that the housing market had changed dramatically since he had opened his first
two Levittowns. As we have seen, sales in the New Jersey Levittown
started strongly in 1958 but then slowed significantly. The economy
had hit a brief but sharp recession, and money was relatively tight.
Builders were also victims of their own success. Levitt and others had
done much to alleviate the postwar housing shortage, turning what
had been a strong seller's market into more of a buyer's market. It
was no longer possible to sell several thousand houses in a huge development before a single one was built. As *Business Week* put it,
looking back a decade later, "Homebuyers were rebelling against the
look-alike houses that were a Levitt trademark. . . . The old formula
of putting up sprawling, community sized 'Levittowns' was now out-
moded."[1]

In 1961, with Levittown, New Jersey, houses selling slowly, Levitt lost $1.4 million, his first unprofitable year since 1951, when he had to wait through a yearlong gap between finishing the New York Levittown and beginning to sell homes in Pennsylvania. To keep the 1961 losses from recurring, Levitt restructured his company, bringing in trained managers, engineers and architects, finance specialists, and computer technicians. As his second-in-command, he hired Richard Wasserman, who held an MBA from the University of Pennsylvania's Wharton School of Business, and surrounded him with five professionally trained senior vice presidents. These men—there were no women among the company's leaders—used market research to decide where they could build profitably and how many units each region could absorb. Once they settled on the target regions, Levitt decentralized the company, giving his ten regional managers considerable autonomy to direct Levitt projects in various parts of the country. He did the same with his newly created branches in Puerto Rico and France.[2]

The areas selected for the largest developments were the Maryland and Virginia counties surrounding Washington, D.C., the suburbs of San Juan, Puerto Rico, and the exurbs of Paris. But there were numerous small projects as well, including several in the New York City area. One of those projects was slated for Matawan Township, New Jersey, just across the Raritan Bay from Staten Island. A Levitt publication specifically positioned the Matawan development "in contrast to the first Levittown on Long Island, a mammoth community of 17,447 similar houses." In Matawan, the company would build just 1,300 houses and "offer a wide variety of different [models] priced for the middle-income market."[3] This new development would be a "Strathmore," to signal its upscale intent. Levitt no longer would, or could, sell homes for $7,000 to $10,000. Land close to major cities had become too expensive for the company to profitably build the low-cost, entry-level dwellings that had provided much-needed shelter for young, impecunious veterans and their families after World War II and the Korean War.

Matawan would be followed by another Strathmore, this one in Stony Brook, Long Island, near the state university and thirty miles northeast of Levittown. There, as in Matawan, 1,300 houses would be built using Levitt's now-standard mass-production techniques, but no two houses on the same street would look alike, at least from the outside. The Stony Brook lots were larger than those in Levittown, and so were the homes, which were priced from $17,000 to $30,000 (in constant dollars, 70 to 200 percent more than the original Levittown houses). In the new Strathmore, Levitt left intact many of the existing trees, rather than bulldozing them away, as he had done in the past.[4] As soon as the Stony Brook houses were sold out, Levitt announced a similar project, Tanglewood, to be built close by.[5]

The new approach worked. By the end of 1962, Levitt's finances were once again in the black, and his sales and profits continued to climb throughout the rest of the decade. In 1965, the company registered an increase in sales of 45 percent over the previous year, and a 22 percent increase in profits. Its $80 million in total sales that year set a record for any firm in the homebuilding industry.[6] Levitt achieved these gains at a time when the industry as a whole was languishing due to higher prices, higher mortgage rates, and shrunken demand. The size of Levitt & Sons gave it access to amounts of capital and credit beyond the reach of most other homebuilders. In 1965, Levitt secured $20 million in long-term loans from a consortium of insurance companies, at what was then the low rate of 6 percent. He also secured lines of credit worth an additional $24 million from five of New York's and Philadelphia's leading banks. These funds enabled Levitt, who served as his own mortgage broker, to offer mortgages to homebuyers at interest rates considerably lower than those of his competitors.[7]

By the end of 1966, his sales had mushroomed to $94 million, his profits to $4 million. That December, *Practical Builder* magazine honored him with its first Man of the Year award.[8] These successes stood out all the more because they starkly contrasted with the plight of the U.S. housing industry as a whole, which was mired in its worst slump since World War II. One-fifth of all U.S. homebuilders called it quits that year.[9] Levitt's sales, meanwhile, grew by at least 20 percent a year for the rest of the decade, reaching $168 million in 1968 and $200 million in 1969. By decade's end, there would be nearly one hundred thousand Levitt-built dwellings in the United States, collectively worth about $1.46 billion (about $12 billion today).[10]

By every measure, the company was on a roll. In 1963, Bill Levitt commissioned the modernist architect Edward Durell Stone to design a new company headquarters to be located in Lake Success, New

York—a choice that seemed utterly appropriate at the time, but would look ironic later on. Completed in 1968, the structure was a replica of Stone's U.S. embassy in New Delhi. It featured a two-story atrium with a fountain at the bottom and seventy-two thousand square feet of floor space. Its many windows looked out onto 4.6 elaborately landscaped acres.[11]

While this elite office building was under construction, Levitt also commissioned a faux château, dubbed La Colline (the Hill), for himself and his wife in Mill Neck, Long Island. He had evoked the Vanderbilts in his prewar housing projects, and now he sought to live like them in a mansion of his own. The house reportedly cost $3 million and had thirty rooms and sixty-eight acres of parkland, including a lighted tennis court. Another air-conditioned court was located inside the house. Levitt had become a fitness buff and played tennis every day.[12]

He turned sixty in 1967 and was in excellent shape for a man his age. He took great care of his appearance, growing a fashionable moustache and longish slicked-back hair. He dressed to the nines, although his tastes were flashy rather than elegant. His sports jackets had loud houndstooth checks and wide lapels, his winter suits were a chunky light-brown wool, and his summer suits off-white cotton or linen. Some photographs show him wearing a dark blazer with white buttons and a broad, diagonally striped shirt underneath. He also seemed to like bright-colored polo shirts with broad stripes. No one would have mistaken him for a white-shoe lawyer or Wall Street banker.[13]

Levitt loved to travel, appearing often in France and Puerto Rico to tout his projects. He kept a close eye on the developments outside Paris, but he left his Puerto Rico enterprise in the hands of its local Levitt leaders. Instead, he lounged in San Juan's best hotels, frequented its casinos, and generally tried to escape the long New York winters as much as he could.[14]

Although he paid himself an ample salary, his extremely comfortable lifestyle was rather more comfortable than he could afford. On paper he was extraordinarily wealthy, but little of that wealth was liquid because he would not give up any control over his firm, refusing to sell any of his 2.4 million shares of Levitt stock. And because he had waived dividends on virtually all of his shares, he derived little cash benefit from the company's profitability. Its estimated net value in 1966 was about $40 million ($388 million today).[15]

In 1966, frustrated with his inability to benefit personally from his company's huge profits, Levitt turned to Joel Carr, his vice president and general counsel, for advice on how to increase his liquidity. He told Carr that he now wanted to sell some of his shares in Levitt & Sons. Carr responded that a better idea, both for Bill personally and for the firm, would be to sell the company as a whole to a much larger corporation. Officially, this would be a merger, which is doubtless how Carr framed the idea to his boss, but in reality, Levitt & Sons would be sold lock, stock, and barrel.[16]

Carr quickly arranged to see Felix Rohatyn and Donald Petrie, general partners at the investment banking house Lazard Frères. They met on January 29, 1966.[17] Rohatyn and Lazard were central players in the "merger mania" of the 1960s, having brokered sixty-nine mergers between 1964 and 1968, for which the firm earned $10.6 million in fees ($100 million today).[18] Overall, there were more mergers in the 1960s than in any period since the turn of the twentieth century, before the advent of antitrust laws. Many large companies were sitting on piles of cash and highly valued stock, and rather than distribute these assets to shareholders as dividends, which would have reduced a corporation's wealth, they used it to buy up other businesses. Between 1959 and 1969, the percent of *Fortune 500* companies operating just one business dropped from 23 to 15 percent.[19]

Lazard's main client in its merger and acquisitions business was the International Telephone & Telegraph Corporation (ITT). Since 1959, under CEO Harold Geneen, the conglomerate had acquired forty-four firms in a wide variety of fields: the Avis car rental company, the book publisher Bobbs-Merrill, and Aetna in consumer finance. In 1967, ITT boasted 204,000 employees in fifty-seven countries, working in four hundred offices and plants.[20]

At their meeting, Carr told Rohatyn and Petrie that Bill Levitt "has been thinking in terms of selling some shares of his company in a secondary offering which would reduce his ownership or control from the present 80% to something below that figure." Carr wanted to discuss a merger with a "big diversified company," a transaction that would be hugely lucrative for Levitt while incurring no tax liability.[21] It's important to note that Levitt's general counsel was not a disinterested player in this game. As Rohatyn told André Meyer, another of his Lazard partners, "Mr. Petrie had been in contact for some time with Mr. Carr as part of his activities for trying to develop new business under his [Carr's] consulting arrangement with us." Carr, Rohatyn added, "is an old schoolmate of mine."[22]

So Levitt's chief lawyer, one of the builder's half-dozen top executives, had known Rohatyn for years and was apparently being paid to drum up business for Lazard. It was perfectly legal for Carr, while employed by Levitt, to moonlight as a Lazard consultant; but having Levitt seek a merger using Lazard as a go-between represented a clear conflict of interest. Carr's recommendation that Levitt sell his company, rather than some of its shares, may have been financially sound, since his boss would have had to pay stiff capital gains taxes on the proceeds of any equity sales. But there was another option: Levitt did not have to sell either the company or any stock. Levitt & Sons was doing extremely well, and its future looked bright. Unfortunately, we don't have any direct testimony from Bill Levitt and can't know if he had any reservations about selling his company. We do know that he would later regret the move.

According to Rohatyn, Bill Levitt expressed interest in Carr's idea and asked him to contact the two Lazard partners about it. Carr assured the bankers that Levitt & Sons was doing very well, but it could expand further and reap even greater profits if it had the capital to buy large amounts of land and set them aside for future development. At present, the firm had the means only to buy properties as required for each building project.[23] The ability to create a land bank would be a great hedge against inflation, which then seemed like a chronic problem. We've seen that Levitt-France had to opt out of a major project because it couldn't secure enough land.

Rohatyn was wary about Bill Levitt, calling him "a rather mercurial individual, with a highly developed sense of his own importance and requiring a somewhat highly personalized approach." But he thought the homebuilder's quirks could be managed, and that Lazard should talk with him and his general counsel. Although Rohatyn had been deeply involved with ITT, especially its acquisition of Avis—he joined the board of the new ITT subsidiary, ITT-Avis—he said he didn't immediately propose ITT as a potential acquirer. When called before the House of Representatives antitrust committee in December 1969, Rohatyn maintained, under sharp questioning, that there was no conflict of interest involved in his effort to arrange a deal for

Levitt, and that ITT had emerged as the only viable acquirer. Some
committee members found his denials questionable, since several
major companies were swallowing up merchant builders at the time.
In 1966, Westinghouse Electric had bought Florida's Coral Ridge
Properties, and Kaiser Industries had joined forces with Macco Realty
Company to develop a huge housing project near Los Angeles.[24] In his
memoir, Rohatyn wrote, "I advised him [Harold Geneen] as ITT
swooped in and, one after another, bought Canteen Grinnell, Avis,
Rayonier, Levitt and Sons, Continental Baking, Pennsylvania Glass,
and Airport Parking."[25]

It's understandable that the banker would deny any conflict of interest, but given his long relationship with Geneen and the boast in
his memoirs about advising him on the Levitt deal, among others, it
seems reasonable to suspect that Rohatyn steered Levitt toward ITT.
How hard he turned the wheel is impossible to say. He saw Levitt &
Sons as "profitable and growing" and "a saleable property," but he
also worried about "Mr. Levitt's personal ambitions and requirements
for continued unquestioned control over the operation once the company is owned by somebody else." Even so, a Levitt deal seemed to be
"a proposition worth pursuing."[26]

Lazard quickly prepared an extremely positive, twenty-seven-page
evaluation of Levitt & Sons' management, assets, profitability, efficiency, value, and potential for growth. It called Levitt "probably the
only company in the country whose name automatically connotes excellent value in single family residential construction" and added,
"Levitt creates not only new homes but new households that repre-
sent continuing purchasing power. Any firm affiliated with Levitt naturally obtains the best possible entry to this new market."[27] By March
18, 1966, just six weeks after he and Petrie met with Joel Carr, Rohatyn wrote Levitt that he had already broached the idea with Geneen, but that because of static from Washington about ITT's merger
mania, and especially its effort to acquire the American Broadcasting
Company (ABC), a deal might take a while. The banker added in a
postscript, "By the time I get back [from Paris], I will be ready to step
on a tennis court with you."[28] For Rohatyn, business and personal relationships were closely connected.

After Rohatyn's return, things moved quickly. By May, a draft document, "I.T.T.—Levitt and Sons, Inc. Merger," had been submitted to

Bill Levitt.[29] The document emphasized that a merger with the huge conglomerate would give Levitt the ability to buy lands and bank them for future development and that Levitt "would have the backing of ITT, which has extensive foreign operations and experience," at a time when the homebuilder wanted to expand its footprint in France and move into other European markets. In addition, "Levitt stockholders would receive a significant premium above the market in a merger transaction." As for ITT, it would acquire a "professionally managed company in a service business with considerable world-wide growth potential." On the draft, Bill Levitt changed his company's growth potential from "considerable" to "almost unlimited." He appeared to approve the claim that his company's ability "to help ameliorate . . . [France's and West Germany's] housing needs could redound to the benefit of ITT's entire international operation," and that ITT's backing would allow Levitt to vastly increase its business by offering luxury options such as a "two-car garage, deluxe refrigerator and . . . a full line of home furnishings. The eventual scope of such a program is large and there is no reason why Levitt could not include such services as a full line of insurance, mutual funds, mortgage services, etc., to be provided by ITT subsidiaries."[30] Much of this assessment was hyperbolic but not untypical of the era's merger/acquisitions hype.[31]

After reading the draft document, Bill Levitt addressed several questions to Rohatyn, mostly having to do with how much autonomy he would have once his firm became a wholly owned subsidiary of ITT. He also wanted to know whether his top executives would remain in place and whether he and others would be free to sell the ITT stock they received in exchange for Levitt & Sons shares. Rohatyn hedged on the question of autonomy, doubtless because he knew Geneen would want substantial control, and made clear that Levitt would be allowed to sell at most 20 percent of his ITT shares within the first two years, and never more than 50 percent.[32]

While these exchanges were taking place, the Federal Communications Commission (FCC), prodded by the U.S. Department of Justice, was raising serious questions about ITT's efforts to acquire ABC. Geneen hesitated to consummate the deal with Levitt for fear that it would sink the ABC merger, which was a far larger and, for ITT, more consequential transaction. Levitt would have to wait.[33]

The homebuilder, meanwhile, was growing concerned. Rumors of the brewing merger had substantially raised the value of Levitt & Sons' stock, while ITT's problems with the FCC had done the opposite for ITT. These developments made the deal potentially less lucrative, while limiting Levitt's alternatives. Bill told Rohatyn he was considering selling 450,000 shares of his own and the Levitt Foundation's stock (which he controlled). But as Rohatyn told his colleagues at Lazard, there were two obstacles to Levitt's stock-selling plan: the high price of Levitt & Sons' shares, and especially the fact that Bill had waived dividends until the end of 1967. He should at least wait until 1968 to make a public offering. Rohatyn added that "we should make a strong pitch that ITT is probably the best ultimate answer to Bill's problems and that during the next few months everything should be done to try to consummate that transaction on the most favorable terms possible."[34] At the time, Rohatyn and his wife together owned $122,000 ($1.1 million today) of ITT stock.[35]

On June 22, 1967, the FCC approved the ITT-ABC merger, although on a narrow four-to-three vote; the Department of Justice announced a month later that it would appeal the decision.[36] With the ITT-ABC deal officially on hold, there was no reason to delay the Levitt merger any longer, especially since it had no governmental opposition. On July 22, ITT announced the acquisition of Levitt & Sons, with Geneen's press release praising "Levitt and Sons' unique record" and calling it "the ideal vehicle for ITT to participate in the U.S. and abroad in the revolution in housing which will take place in the next decade."[37] Six months later, with the Justice Department still trying to block the ITT-ABC merger in federal court, Geneen abandoned his long-desired acquisition of the network and moved on to other prospects, including the Sheraton hotel chain, Continental Baking (Twinkie and Wonder Bread), the Rayonier Corporation (lumber and land management), and the Hartford insurance company.[38]

As for Lazard, it received $500,000 for brokering the ITT-Levitt transaction, a fee it divided with Wertheim & Company, which had been Levitt's investment banker before Rohatyn and Lazard stepped in.[39] Shortly after the deal was announced, Rohatyn joined ITT's board.[40] Was this a reward for having landed Levitt & Sons, which Geneen considered a choice acquisition, or simply confirmation of Rohatyn's longtime status as a central player for ITT? In any case, the

House committee looking into ITT's potential violations of antitrust law highlighted Rohatyn and Lazard's apparent conflicts of interest, though without accusing them of wrongdoing or of reaping untoward financial gain; Lazard's half of the brokerage fee was relatively modest. The essential question turned on Lazard's role in facilitating the anticompetitive practices of a huge conglomerate, for which the government would soon force ITT to make amends.

For the moment, both ITT and Levitt & Sons seemed excited about the merger. While it's unclear what "revolution in housing" ITT anticipated, Bill Levitt said the "merger gives us much greater flexibility, greater scope, and greater prestige. We now have the backing of a $2 billion corporation."[41] That backing would fund "a vastly accelerated expansion program" that would enable Levitt & Sons to grow worldwide. ITT's wealth and power would also permit Levitt to diversify beyond single-family homes to construct "every kind of shelter in this country and abroad—single-family homes, town houses, high-rise and garden apartments, both for sale and for rent."[42] Even more important, Levitt added, ITT's financial muscle would provide the capital for his most ambitious project yet, the creation of ten "primary employment towns" to be built from scratch in parts of the United States with open space and inexpensive land but few jobs. These towns would include homes, factories, stores, offices, schools, churches, and recreational facilities for populations of about fifty thousand. In several venues, Levitt touted this idea confidently, but naively, asserting, "We will become part of ITT, but we'll operate autonomously with the same management, same everything."[43] He doubtless thought he was an exception to ITT's rule, but nothing in Geneen's history as a CEO suggested he would give free rein to the head of a wholly owned subsidiary.

Even for Bill Levitt, putting half a million people in primary employment towns was a long-range rather than immediate goal. In the short term, the merger itself loomed above all else. When the transaction closed, on April 30, 1968, Levitt's shareholders collectively pocketed $91.25 million of stock in ITT, one of the largest and most powerful corporations in the world. Bill Levitt became ITT's largest individual shareholder, with a personal stake valued at $73 million (about $660 million today). On paper, he was now one of the richest people in the United States, shielded from tax liability as long as he didn't sell any of his shares. As part of the deal, ITT agreed to employ him for five years at a salary "commensurate with his present compensation," although at the end of his employment contract, he would be barred for five years from building any dwellings in the United States.[44] But it's no small irony that despite his new wealth, he hadn't gained any liquidity, which had been one of his objectives. And he would soon discover that as CEO of ITT's new homebuilding subsidiary, he would have none of the autonomy he had long cultivated.

The first sign of his change in status came shortly after the merger was consummated. Bill Levitt was kicked upstairs as chairman of the renamed Levitt Corporation, and his second-in-command, the highly competent but far less flamboyant Richard Wasserman, became the subsidiary's new president and chief operating officer. Geneen, always wary of the famous homebuilder, pushed him aside in favor of the forty-three-year-old, for whom the ITT chairman had "an almost fatherly affection."[45] ITT's leaders considered Wasserman's former boss too old and set in his ways to conform to the conglomerate's management structure and expectations.[46]

With no day-to-day management responsibilities and little to do, Bill Levitt had time on his hands and vast wealth stashed in ITT stock. He traveled extensively and lived extravagantly. On one of his trips, he met Simone Korchin at her Rome art gallery, an elegant space that doubled as a salon for wealthy Americans traveling or living abroad. Levitt already owned a great deal of art, most of it displayed at his château, La Colline, in Mill Neck, Long Island. He acquired a lot more on his increasingly frequent visits to Simone's gallery, during which, as Simone said many years later, he fell head over heels in love with her and vowed to divorce his wife, urging her also to get a divorce.

Bill was married to Alice Kenny, his former secretary, who had been his longtime mistress while he was married to his first wife, Rhoda. Simone was married to Barney Korchin, a Philadelphia native who had been a vice president of the Penn Fruit Company, an East Coast supermarket chain. Simone and Barney met on a boat from New York to France, where she had grown up. The history of her childhood there is murky, since her personal story has changed over time. In 1970, she told a *New York Times* reporter that her father was a French rabbi and that as a child, she had been confined to concentration camps and otherwise lived on the streets, where she collected cigarette butts to exchange for morsels of food. Four decades later, she said that her parents were Greek Jews who had taken refuge in Paris before the war and had survived the German occupation thanks to her mother's skill at poker and baccarat. She claimed to have been thrown in jail at age eleven and raped by a French policeman.[47] After the war, she lived with relatives in Brooklyn before returning to Europe and opening the gallery in Rome. She and Korchin had three daughters before the marriage petered out. Bill pursued her relentlessly, and after hasty divorces, they wed in Beverly Hills on November 19, 1969. The groom was sixty-two, the bride forty.

Simone moved into the Mill Neck mansion that Bill had built five years earlier. Not unlike Levitt's tract homes, whose designs drew inspiration from the American past—the Cape Cod, colonial, and California ranch—La Colline aped classic architecture, only the model was an eighteenth-century French manor house. It has an enclosed courtyard in front with a pair of reflecting pools. The house itself is U-shaped, with two wings flanking the main part of the residence. Impressive as it looks, it is even larger than it appears from the outside—so large that neither Simone nor Levitt's butler, who had served him for twenty years, knew how many rooms it contains. The entrance hall features a floor of black-and-white marble and an aviary with curved glass walls housing several dozen vividly colored exotic birds. In the formal drawing room, an authentic Gobelins tapestry covers one of the walls, and an eighteenth-century gilded mirror hangs over the fireplace. The seven-room master bedroom suite opens onto a private garden and includes his-and-her dressing rooms and bathrooms—each with a sunken marble tub—and an office. The bedroom itself has an all-glass ceiling and painted French paneling and is reached by a long, glass-lined hallway. There is a two-story-high library with wood-paneled walls and floor-to-ceiling bookshelves. The windows also stretch from floor to ceiling; at night, a massive crystal chandelier lights the room. The main part of the mansion contains a conservatory, swimming pool, and entertainment pavilion with a view of Long Island Sound. The kitchen wing has eight rooms facing the front of the dwelling; a separate servants' quarters looks like a typical 1960s Levitt ranch.[48]

Simone Levitt told reporters she loved the place but "would like to make the house mine." She planned to replace its reproductions of eighteenth-century furniture with genuine Louis XVI antiques and to bring in boiserie from a nearby Vanderbilt mansion. "Being French," she said, "I would like it to look like Versailles."[49] Never mind that she was off by a century—the famous French château was built in the mid- to late 1600s—the house would retain its deep French accent, and so would she.

The accent seemed to charm the many journalists who flocked to interview her following her marriage to the famous Bill Levitt. "Her openness, warmth, and enthusiasm," wrote *Newsday*'s Doris Herzig, "could win over even a jealous woman disposed to envy her good looks, her chic, her expensive clothes and her new-found wealth. It is easy to forgive her all these assets because she is so frankly overjoyed with it all."[50]

Not only was she overjoyed by La Colline; she was also thrilled by the huge pied-à-terre they had bought and extensively renovated at the Sherry-Netherland, a venerable building on Fifth Avenue.[51] Now they had a suitable place to stay in the city. She would be even more overjoyed when the couple's new yacht, three years in the making, was christened in July 1972. Bill already owned a 140-foot vessel called *Les Amis,* but wanted something really special for his new wife; she was eager to have it, especially since her husband planned to name it *La Belle Simone.* "I wanted our guests to have real luxury," she told the *New York Post*'s society and fashion columnist, Eugenia Sheppard.[52] The new boat, built in Marina di Carrara, Italy, and stuffed with Carrara marble, had a price tag of somewhere between $6 and $10 million ($46 to $76 million today).[53]

Except for the yachts belonging to the British royal family and the king of Norway, the 253-foot *La Belle Simone* was then the third-largest in the world. Among nonroyal floating palaces, only those owned by Aristotle Onassis and Charles Revson, the cosmetics entrepreneur, were bigger—and those only by twenty to thirty feet. "All my life I wanted a yacht tailored to my needs," Bill told his decorator, John Gerald.[54] "At sea you are subject to no man's laws. The captain is supreme."[55] By 1972, on the verge of resigning from the company he had sold to ITT, Levitt was captain only on his private boat. No longer was he a captain of industry.

He seemed, though, to thoroughly enjoy commanding his ship, which was more modern than those belonging to Revson or Onassis.

Simone Levitt on the grounds of her mansion, La Colline, in 1972. (Special
Collections Research Center, Temple University Libraries, Philadelphia,
Pennsylvania)

Levitt's was fully automated and could operate without much crew—
yet he employed twenty-six people from France, Italy, Spain, and
China, including four chefs, plus four English stewards who had served
on the *Queen Elizabeth*. The vessel was equipped with anticollision
radar, protected from fire by smoke alarms and a sprinkler system, and
kept cool by central air-conditioning.

In many ways, *La Belle Simone* was a floating version of La Colline.
It had a marble entryway as well as marble halls and walls. There were
parquet floors, Savonnerie rugs, Limoges china, Baccarat crystal, genuine
Louis XVI antiques, stainless steel refrigerators, and ice-cream machines.
Bill, Simone, and their many guests could enjoy the boat's kidney-shaped
pool, closed-circuit TV, and screening room. "We like to live the same
way whether we're on land or sea," Simone said.[56] The couple's master
bedroom suite, like its Long Island counterpart, had a mirrored ceiling

and his-and-hers dressing rooms and marble baths, each with gilded faucets, and a gilded bidet in hers. While their Mill Neck bedroom opened onto a private garden, the one on *La Belle Simone* opened directly onto the sea. The hull's outer walls swung open with the press of a button, allowing Bill and Simone to dive right into the water from their bedroom. If they just wanted a view, interior glass doors slid shut, creating a twelve-foot-wide picture window.

In addition to the pool, the main deck featured a huge living space that could be divided in three, into a library, drawing room, and dining room. There were two grand pianos. When used for dinner, the dining room could easily fit eighteen guests. Below deck, Bill and Simone could accommodate up to ten overnight guests in five staterooms, each with a marble bathroom. When lounging around the pool, guests were supplied with towels and terrycloth robes specially designed by Givenchy.

When the yacht was finished, the crew sailed it to New York, docking it at South Street Seaport, where Bill invited the New York press to come see it. Several showed up—one reporter called it a press conference to announce a world-class yacht. Bill and Simone had driven to the seaport in their purple Rolls-Royce with its mink-lined interior and "WL-1" vanity plates. Afterward, the boat would steam to Monte Carlo, where a spot was reserved for it right next to the one owned by Revson. Bill and Simone flew over to meet it, and after society festivities that included a visit by Princess Grace of Monaco, they took it for a spin around the Mediterranean. The bill for staffing the yacht, maintaining it, and entertaining scores of guests came to $5 million a year. "Charles Revson once told me," Levitt said, "a yacht burns money like a furnace, and I've found it's true."[57]

The *New York Post*'s Eugenia Sheppard seemed awestruck by this flaunting of wealth, and many of her counterparts were dazzled as well. But especially after the Democratic Party turned left with the nomination of Senator George McGovern for president in 1972, other commentators, including some conservatives, expressed reservations about the Levitts' ostentatious display. Harriet Van Horne, a syndicated columnist also published in the *Post*, suggested that the opulence of *La Belle Simone* "might have sickened King Farouk." "It might even be said," she wrote in her column about the boat, entitled "Let Them Eat Yachts," "that a yacht with marble halls, parquet floors,

Bill and Simone Levitt dancing on the deck of their yacht, *La Belle Simone*, docked alongside other super-yachts in Monte Carlo. The photo comes from *Paris Match*, August 1974, with the caption, "Billionaires Holiday in Monaco. The entrepreneur William Levitt waltzing with his wife Simone Levitt on one of the three decks of their yacht, 'La Belle Simone.' " (Photograph by Jack Garofalo/ *Paris Match* via Getty Images)

two grand pianos and fake leather books hiding the stereophonic sound, is going to add a certain pertinence—not to say poignance—to Sen. McGovern's charge that there's too much wealth at the top and too little at the bottom."[58]

Unfazed by such comments, though perhaps worried about McGovern's candidacy, Bill would contribute generously to Nixon's campaign.[59] Meanwhile, he and Simone joined an international social scene that extended from Monte Carlo to Venice to Palm Beach. The massively costly vessel and the glittering crowd of moguls and celebrities it attracted led journalists to think Bill was far wealthier than he was. The *Austrian Post* called him "one of the world's richest men," and a French paper labeled him "an American billionaire" with a yacht "even more luxurious than those of Onassis and Revson."[60] Even had he been paid for his company in cash and invested it wisely, he would not have been as rich as Onassis or Revson, to say nothing of Howard Hughes or J. Paul Getty. And by 1972, the value of ITT stock had begun to decline, reducing Levitt's wealth; his larger problem, though, was that he refused to sell any shares because it would have meant paying capital gains taxes. Instead, he borrowed against his ITT portfolio and used the loans to fund his and Simone's extravagant lifestyle.

Later, in her mid-eighties, Simone proudly recalled the rich and famous people who had been their guests on *La Belle Simone*. She mentioned, among others, Gregory Peck, Frank and Barbara Sinatra, Michael Caine, Harry Belafonte, Sean Connery, Julio Iglesias, Roger Moore, Hubert de Givenchy, Alan King, Anna Magnani, Adnan Khashoggi, Gina Lollobrigida, Rex Harrison, and Don Hewitt and his wife, Marilyn, who were married on the boat. "It was a fairy tale," she told the journalist Mark Seal. "Oh my God, they drank our champagne and ate our caviar. [Bill] played the piano, and I sang."[61]

Society pages were filled with accounts of the Levitts as key members of the international party set who regularly rubbed shoulders with the world's rich and famous. At a ball in Venice hosted by Count Volpi in honor of his niece, the "beautiful 18-year-old" Princess Olimpia Aldobrandini, "the international party people came from everywhere by plane, train, car, or private yacht. Both Count Theo Rossi's sailing yacht and William Levitt's 'La Belle Simone' were anchored in the Grand Canal for the weekend." The celebrities in attendance included Princess Grace, Audrey Hepburn, Marisa Berenson, and Bianca Jagger.[62] That same weekend, "some 80 guests were ferried back and forth to La Belle Simone for a buffet luncheon." Pictures accompanying Eugenia Sheppard's article about the gathering showed Simone Levitt posing with the fashion designer Hubert de Givenchy, and São Schlumberger, wife of the oilman, industrialist, and art collector Pierre Schlumberger. Another photo was captioned "Elsa Martinelli [the actress and fashion model] aboard *La Belle Simone*."[63]

The following year, the *Daily Mail* credited Levitt with having recently made 120 million pounds, more than twice what he had actually gained in the ITT deal, and noted that he had "moored his opulent motor yacht La Belle Simone at Tower Bridge and on Monday invited a mere 50 guests for lunch."[64] Other columns pictured the Levitts at Capri, Palm Beach, and again at Monaco, where "the two biggest and most famous American yachts," Levitt's and Revson's, "anchored . . . right next to each other, [so] naturally the group went all-out for a round of parties." The Levitts "entertained around 60 at a dinner dance on their yacht." Simone appeared in "Givenchy's white evening slacks and jacket, open over a jeweled bra." The other guests included Rosemarie Kanzler "in white and rubies . . . Princess Liechtenstein . . . Countess Cigogna, Sir George Weidenfeld; Mrs Gregory Peck," and others.[65]

Beginning in 1972, the Levitts combined partying with philanthropy, especially for Jewish charities. Increasingly, they wanted to be known not only as ultrarich members of the yachting set but as people who devoted their money and energy to good causes. Of course, jet-setting and philanthropy are closely related, and press coverage of the Levitts began to combine the two. Bill chaired the United Jewish Appeal in the New York area, and in 1972 hosted a party in Palm Beach honoring people who had given $100,000 or more to the charity. The following evening, he and Simone attended the Red Cross Ball and afterward took the most elite guests, including "the Henry Fords," on a cruise aboard *La Belle Simone*. At yet another Palm Beach event, the society columnist Charles van Rensselaer chronicled a dinner at Nando's ("serving pasta to the rich and famous") in honor of Bill Levitt, "the philanthropist-builder." Afterward, during three days aboard *La Belle Simone*, Van Rensselaer discovered that "Simone and Bill, despite their vast wealth, are basic, simple, wonderful people. I feel it a great honor and pleasure to know them."[66] Shortly before this cruise, Simone had expressed cynicism about all the people who rushed to kiss up to her and Bill after they launched their yacht. "I never knew I had so many friends," she told a *New York Times* reporter, as if that wasn't the point of building a $10 million mega-yacht.[67]

The most visible of the Levitts' philanthropic efforts was the three-day-long celebration of the State of Israel's twenty-fifth anniversary, in August 1973. No one suspected that just two months later, Israel would be fighting for its life in the Yom Kippur War. Bill had been giving significant sums to Israel for decades, and when Prime Minister Golda Meir visited the United States in March 1973, he helped raise huge amounts for the United Jewish Appeal, scoring an invitation to the state dinner in Meir's honor hosted by President Nixon.[68] Four months later, Bill cochaired Israel's silver anniversary, a splashy event for which he underwrote most of the costs. He also paid for the restoration of a mid-nineteenth-century structure originally financed by the British banker Sir Moses Montefiore. The first Jewish habitation erected outside the walls of Jerusalem's Old City, it later became an almshouse for impoverished Jews. The building was threatened during the 1948 Arab-Israeli War but brought under full Israeli control during the Six-Day War of 1967. Unveiled during the twenty-fifth anniversary festivities, the restored building was converted into a guesthouse for important cultural figures visiting Israel. The renovation cost Levitt $1.5 million, and he also contributed to a pair of newer structures, a theater and a convention center, flanking the older one. Together with Jerusalem's mayor, Teddy Kollek, Levitt called it Mishkenot Sha'ananim, or "peaceful dwelling place."[69] Levitt's bill for the three-day celebration came to another $1.5 million.

The guests at the celebration included 450 members of the international glitterati, who watched Rudolf Nureyev dance in the Caesarea, the ancient Roman amphitheater discovered and restored just five years earlier. The event was in large part a tribute to Golda Meir, Israel's seventy-four-year-old prime minister, and at the Caesarea, Nureyev sang a rendition of "Hello, Dolly" in which he substituted "Golda" for "Dolly." Bill and Simone sat with the prime minister, who enjoyed a warm relationship with the couple.[70] The following evening began with a reception hosted by Teddy Kollek, who called Bill Levitt his friend and was repeatedly photographed with him. A show followed, featuring Yves Montand, Peggy Lee, Alan King, Harry Belafonte, Pablo Casals, Isaac Stern, and Josephine Baker, the African American performer turned French cultural icon.[71] A *Times* reporter called the program "a disorganized hodgepodge of opera, pop, Druze folk dances, and borscht-belt humor." Fortunately, he added, the evening was saved when "the spectacular Josephine Baker . . . swept down the stone steps of David's Tower in a black dress shot with silver and a full cape of white feathers." She captivated the audience with her version of "Bill," a song from *Showboat* about a mixed-race woman abandoned by her white husband, and especially, "La Vie en Rose."[72]

Before leaving the stage, Baker departed from her script and talked about befriending the Palestinian porter who cleaned her room in the Jerusalem Intercontinental Hotel. He invited her to visit him and his family in their humble home in the West Bank village of Bethany, and she spent two hours there over coffee. After returning to Jerusalem, Baker bought the family a refrigerator, an amenity extremely rare in their world.[73]

The *New York Times* reporter sent to cover the celebration couldn't help but notice the strangeness that an event marking the survival of a tiny nation surrounded by mortal enemies should be fashioned as a bash for the rich and famous. Such a luxe, celebrity-studded weekend, he wrote, was odd in "socialist, egalitarian Israel, where society seldom rises above the kibbutz level." Yet it had hosted the excesses of a typical celebrity gala. The Levitts and a few others arrived in their yachts and held fancy dinners with attendees dressed by the world's top designers. "The fashion highlight of the weekend," the journalist wrote, "was provided, predictably, by Simone Levitt and Robin Duke, both permanent fixtures on various best-dressed lists." Duke wore a "fitted Pucci," Levitt "a free-flowing Valentino." Simone was equally well dressed when she and Bill hosted a farewell lunch on their yacht. "It's a way to say goodbye," Bill concluded.[74]

While generously supporting Israel and the United Jewish Appeal, the Levitts also made handsome contributions to hospitals and other medical facilities, especially the North Shore University Hospital on Long Island. In February 1972, Simone chaired a black-tie benefit for the facility that drew one thousand donors and included Governor William Cahill of New Jersey, Ambassador George H. W. Bush, astronaut Alan Shepard, journalist Walter Cronkite, and the actresses Arlene Dahl and Joan Bennett.[75]

For these efforts, especially those on behalf of Israel, Bill received the Man of Conscience Award in December 1973. The honor came from the interfaith Appeal of Conscience Foundation, which seeks to recognize "visionary business executives with a sense of social responsibility who use their resources and vast reach across borders to better serve the global community."[76] The award was given during a black-tie event at New York's Hotel Pierre, with the usual assortment of well-dressed guests in attendance. This was exactly the kind of legitimation Levitt had worked to achieve. Six months later, Simone received an award of her own, the Woman of the Year from the women's division of the Anti-Defamation League. Bill presented the award, as his wife "accept[ed] it with a brief but meaningful little speech."[77]

While enjoying these honors and spending freely on philanthropy, politics, and entertaining on their yacht, the Levitts were also lavish with each other, often in highly public, even narcissistic, ways. In early 1973, the couple commissioned Aaron Shikler, who had painted

President and Jackie Kennedy in the White House, to do portraits of each of them. When the pictures were ready, Bill and Simone hung them on either side of their drawing-room doors at La Colline and invited forty dinner guests to see them. "They are real people and I painted them that way," said Shikler, the Levitts' guest of honor. "Bill Levitt's canvas especially comes to life," wrote Eugenia Sheppard, while Simone's seemed to stand out a bit less. Although she wore a red satin dress for the sittings, "Shikler changed the color to beige."[78]

For the couple's fifth wedding anniversary in 1974, Simone took six months of singing lessons and recorded an album of fifteen songs, with her face sketched on the cover. She presented the album to her husband at a dinner dance she hosted in a posh Manhattan restaurant. The title song was "Just My Bill" (also known as "Bill"), the same tune Josephine Baker had sung in Israel.[79] It's an ode to a far from perfect man, whom the singer loves dearly despite everything.

Although Bill doubtless appreciated the gift of song, he wanted to be the main gift-giver in the family. "He celebrated my anniversary every month for ten years," Simone recalled late in life, her memory of the diamonds and rubies he had showered on her still vivid decades later. We don't know the total value of these baubles, but we can extrapolate from the diamond ring that, according to Simone, Sotheby's appraised at $800,000 in 1995.[80] Even allowing for inflated memories, the jewelry Bill gave her over the years must have cost millions.

Throughout the 1970s, society columnists regularly commented on her jewelry. "It was a great night for jewels," wrote the *Post*'s Sheppard of a fashion show for the rich and famous held in the Palace of Versailles. In a competition for the best piece of jewelry, Simone Levitt's diamond necklace came in third, just behind those of Mrs. Antenor Patiño and Marie-Hélène de Rothschild. For Simone, "Gérard" had "designed her new diamond necklace just to reach her cleavage."[81] On another occasion, a celebrity dinner in Washington, D.C., a society columnist for the *Star-News* commented ironically on a woman who criticized Simone's makeup but "who would have given an eyetooth for Simone's fabulous diamond and blood red ruby necklace."[82]

The Levitts loved to show off Simone's jewels, and on a May 1975 trip to Las Vegas she brought along five diamond and sapphire pieces. During their stay at Caesars Palace, the jewelry was stolen, or so they claimed in a $5 million lawsuit against the hotel. After a three-day trial in U.S. district court, the jury ruled in the Levitts' favor, calling the hotel guilty of "gross negligence" for its lack of security and ordering it to pay the couple the estimated value of the jewelry, about $550,000. Although the verdict was overturned on appeal, the case provides evidence of the jewelry's worth—more than $100,000 for each piece.[83]

After 1975, Bill and Simone Levitt appeared less often in the *Post*'s society columns. The novelty of their extravagant yacht had doubtless worn off. But Sheppard and others still commented regularly on their yachting sojourns, elaborate dinners, and appearances at high-profile events, including political fundraisers. After Watergate, Bill switched to supporting moderate Democrats, and in September 1976, he paid $5,000 to attend an exclusive Manhattan cocktail party for Jimmy Carter, saying the former Georgia governor "is going to be the greatest president since Abraham Lincoln." The then-thirty-year-old Donald Trump also appeared at the gathering, where he declared, less hyperbolically but ironically in view of later developments, "I think it's important we get some Democrats in office."[84]

At the time of Carter's election, the press still portrayed Bill Levitt as a fabulously wealthy "real estate magnate," but it would soon become clear that he was struggling to keep up appearances. Simone would come to suspect that it was Bill who took the jewelry from their Las Vegas hotel room, presumably to sell it, and then played double or nothing with his lawsuit against Caesars Palace.[85] The hotel's successful appeal of the verdict boded ill for the future of Bill and Simone.

10 The Fall

AFTER HE SOLD his company to ITT in February 1968 and agreed to turn over its day-to-day operations to his deputy and surrogate son, Richard M. Wasserman, Levitt expected the conglomerate to fund "a vastly accelerated expansion program" by its new subsidiary. No longer would "ITT-Levitt," its name soon restored to Levitt & Sons, limit itself to single-family housing.[1]

This optimism seemed well founded at first. The ITT deal had given Levitt a huge fortune, and for his ceremonial role as the home-builder's chairman, he continued to receive a handsome salary of no less than $175,000 a year for at least five years.[2] ITT also poured money into Levitt & Sons. In 1969, it financed the construction of a 140,000-square-foot factory to build modular homes on assembly lines designed to churn out fully finished parts that could be assembled at a homesite in forty-eight hours. Even Levitt's mass-produced Cape Cods couldn't be built that fast, and although the new modular homes were more expensive than the original Levittown houses, the factory-produced houses were still affordable, priced from $20,000 to $25,000 ($162,000 to $202,000 today). Some of these houses would contribute to a Department of Housing and Urban Development effort, known as Operation Breakthrough, to create subsidized affordable housing in American cities. Wasserman planned seven of these modular housing factories with the goal of stamping out four thousand dwellings a year.[3]

ITT also bankrolled Levitt's building of multiple-family dwellings, especially garden apartments, and the construction of "cluster housing" in which single-family dwellings would be packed close together on small lots but would share common lands and recreational facilities.[4] Levitt had tried this approach on a small scale in France with considerable success. It was designed to economize on land without depriving inhabitants of open spaces. ITT also served as Levitt's banker, offering mortgages at below-market interest rates on six hundred Levitt homes on Long Island that were selling slowly. Perhaps most important, the conglomerate enabled Levitt to buy large amounts of land, including one hundred thousand acres of prime Florida real estate north of Daytona Beach, through a newly created subsidiary called the ITT Levitt Development Corporation. Levitt advertised this land as providing homesites on which buyers could have the company build one of its home models "for vacationing or retirement" or "as a hedge against inflation."[5] With this huge bank of land, the subsidiary could also sell parcels to other homebuilders or create parks for mobile homes, which the company also began constructing.[6] In 1971, the ITT Levitt Development Corporation reported it was selling this Florida land at double the rate it had projected.[7] One final ITT contribution to Levitt was its purchase of United Homes in Portland, Oregon, enabling Levitt to realize its long-deferred goal of building on the West Coast.[8]

ITT-Levitt was riding high. In 1971, the company's sales reached their highest dollar amount ever, while its profit exceeded $6 million, breaking all prior records.[9] Levitt remained the largest homebuilder in the country. But building costs and mortgage rates were increasing rapidly. Wasserman was keen to keep housing costs down, as Bill Levitt had been, because inflation had driven home prices so high in the late 1960s that three-quarters of Americans couldn't afford the typical newly built home. With the prices of land, labor, and capital all rising rapidly after 1970, Levitt's success in building affordable housing would be difficult to maintain. Wasserman claimed to be comfortable heading up an ITT subsidiary, despite the conglomerate's track record of heavy-handed micromanagement of its components. But Geneen's "fatherly affection" for Wasserman enabled the younger man to keep his boss at bay.[10] "They have been smart enough," Wasserman said, "to let us maintain our vitality and our freedom."[11]

This freedom didn't last. In early 1971, less than three years after becoming president of ITT-Levitt, Wasserman quit in disgust. So did eight of the other twelve Levitt executives. Two years later, a former Levitt executive told *Business Week* that Geneen was over-managing the company, imposing a bureaucratic straitjacket that prevented Wasserman from responding nimbly to changes and opportunities in the market. The result, as Bill Levitt put it, was that "we began to lose people. We began to get raided" by other large homebuilders like Kaufman & Broad. "ITT had a gold mine," Levitt said, "and didn't know what to do with it."[12] The ITT approach also prevented Levitt supervisors from responding to events on the ground. "ITT didn't give its field managers any latitude," explained Ken Adelberg, Levitt's chief engineer in Bowie, Maryland. "Any time a decision had to be made . . . they had to go to the top [ITT] executives, who were out playing golf."[13] Bill Levitt noted the same problem: Geneen's "management system didn't lend itself to this kind of business. . . . In this business you've got to be able to turn on a dime."[14] Never once, Bill added, did Geneen consult him, even though he officially remained on the ITT payroll and was one of the company's largest shareholders.[15]

What Levitt said, while largely true, was far from the full explanation for Levitt & Sons' troubles under ITT's ownership. At least as important were ITT-Levitt's unsuccessful efforts to expand its range of activity, and the financial losses that resulted. Its factory-built modular homes proved a spectacular bust. It cost far more to produce home parts on an assembly line than it did using Levitt's long-standing, once-revolutionary method: transporting all the components of a dwelling to each site and then having specialized crews go from house to house, each crew performing one step of the operation. ITT had gone to great expense to build a modular home factory in Battle Creek, Michigan, but had to shut it down after only two years. In addition, changes in tax laws stripped apartment construction of its profitability, especially given the inflated costs and interest rates of the early 1970s. And ITT-Levitt's homebuilding efforts in the Pacific Northwest foundered after Boeing, one of the region's main employers, laid off thousands of workers.[16]

These developments proved costly, especially in the wake of the Nixon administration's antitrust actions against ITT. Since the mid-1960s, politicians, writers, and press commentators had taken aim against the conglomerate for having grown too large, too powerful, and overly focused on making profits rather than producing useful things. In 1970, the *Washington Post* columnist Nicholas von Hoffman wrote that ITT "contributes nothing to productivity, efficiency, or creativity. The companies they own were doing well before they were purchased." ITT operated purely in "the domain of fiscal manipulation and profit-hyping accomplishments of dubious social utility."[17] Three years later, the British writer Anthony Sampson devoted an entire book to excoriating ITT, lambasting Geneen and other top executives for greed and corruption and especially for the company's ability to bully other businesses and even sovereign nations.[18] The book appeared after ITT faced accusations of making large contributions to the Republican Party in exchange for leniency in the antitrust case, and for efforts to persuade Nixon officials to intervene against Chilean president Salvador Allende, who had nationalized the Chilean Telephone Company, 70 percent of which belonged to ITT.[19] The Nixon administration did intervene to topple Allende, though not because of ITT's prompting, and Geneen succeeded in softening, but not squelching, the Justice Department's antitrust case.[20]

Richard McLaren, Nixon's assistant attorney general in charge of the Antitrust Division, took steps to overturn ITT's 1969 acquisition of the Hartford Fire Insurance Company and to block its purchase of the Grinnell Corporation, the nation's largest maker of fire protection equipment, which the Justice Department saw as overly entwined with Hartford. ITT fought hard against McLaren, intensely lobbying other key members of the administration, some of whom would later be investigated for perjury and obstruction of justice in connection with ITT's efforts to influence them.[21] The conglomerate also unleashed a public relations barrage, after which it won some key cases in court. McLaren planned to appeal those decisions to the Supreme Court but finally decided to negotiate a settlement with ITT's lawyers, which is what ITT wanted. In June 1971, the two parties announced a consent decree in which ITT would be allowed to retain Hartford, which it wanted badly, in exchange for divesting itself of companies whose total revenue equaled that of Hartford. The list included the Canteen Corporation, which made vending machines; Avis; parts of Grinnell; two life insurance companies; and Levitt & Sons. The deadlines for divestiture were September 1973 for Canteen and Grinnell, and September 1974 for Avis and Levitt.[22] Although ITT made quick gains from

selling 50 percent of Avis and found buyers for most of the other companies, the effort to unload Levitt ran into serious trouble.[23]

At first it looked like ITT would benefit from the sale of Levitt. The
homebuilding subsidiary registered record sales and profits in 1971,
and under Wasserman's experienced management, seemed in good
shape. But the next year, ITT had to book large losses from the failed
modular housing project, as well as from weak demand for its apartment buildings and the inability to sell many homes in Seattle. To
make matters worse, mortgage rates of 9 percent and rising, plus inflated construction costs, dramatically reduced the demand for new
homes nationwide. Levitt's balance sheet turned upside down: its
1971 profit of $6 million morphed into a loss of nearly $6 million the
following year. In 1973, it took a $14 million loss.[24]

The more Levitt's balance sheet suffered, the harder it became for ITT
to find a buyer. It didn't help that the conglomerate also had trouble dis-
posing of its unsold half of Avis. Given the company's cloudy future,
Levitt continued to hemorrhage top executives; replacing them was
hard. After Wasserman left, in mid-1971, ITT took six months to find a
new chief executive.[25] And the new president, Gerhard R. Andlinger,
could not stop the losses: $64.8 million in 1974 and $28.5 million in
1975. Thanks to credits from ITT, the official 1975 loss understates the
actual amount.[26] All told, ITT sank at least $250 million into the flailing
homebuilder between 1969 and 1975, and the antitrust decree required
it to continue pouring in money. Geneen called the acquisition of Levitt
& Sons one of the worst decisions ITT had ever made. It continued to
hurt the company financially for nearly a decade.[27]

These losses, along with a general stock market slump after the oil
shock of 1973, made it impossible for ITT either to mount a public offering for Levitt (as it did for the unsold parts of Avis) or to find a private buyer. Even Bill Levitt didn't want his old company back.[28] After
ITT missed the government's September 1974 deadline for unloading
Levitt & Sons, the case was then turned over to a Connecticut judge,
who appointed a trustee, Victor Palmieri and Company, to assume
control of the troubled subsidiary. Palmieri's charge was to transform
the enterprise into a "viable home-building company" and sell it as a
profitable concern.[29]

In the early 1970s, Palmieri and Company had become well known
in the Northeast as the real estate firm brought in to manage key as-

sets of the Penn Central Transportation Company. The huge railroad concern had declared bankruptcy in 1970, just two years after its creation through the merger of three ailing, venerable companies, the Pennsylvania Railroad, the New York Central System, and the New York, New Haven, and Hartford Railroad.[30] On the surface, it seemed surprising that Palmieri and Company, originally a West Coast firm, was selected to oversee the remaining profitable parts—largely real estate—of the elephantine conglomerate. Palmieri and Company was a relatively small outfit, with just $2 million is assets against $1.9 million in liabilities as of June 1977.[31] But Victor Palmieri was an extraordinarily energetic entrepreneur who, according to his critics, had had become prominent "due to his influence with the important people he knows."[32] In 1967, President Lyndon Johnson named him deputy executive director of the National Advisory Commission on Civil Disorders (known as the Kerner Commission), charged with examining and proposing solutions to the massive urban unrest of the time. Palmieri came to know the commission's deputy director, John Lindsay, the mayor of New York City from 1966 to 1973. After serving on the Kerner Commission, Palmieri worked on California congressman John Tunney's Senate campaign, during which he is said to have made connections to the Kennedy clan—Tunney had been Ted Kennedy's roommate while both were students at the University of Virginia School of Law. Palmieri's aide on the commission was the Yale-educated attorney John Koskinen, who would later work for Lindsay and Connecticut senator Abraham Ribicoff. In 1973, Koskinen joined Palmieri as a principal of his company.[33]

In September 1973, the trustees overseeing the Penn Central bankruptcy hired Palmieri "to develop, sell or lease" the conglomerate's properties, worth $1 billion all told.[34] Among those properties were the rail yards on Manhattan's West Side between Thirtieth and Thirty-Ninth streets and Fifty-Ninth and Seventy-Second streets, as well as what was then the Commodore Hotel, situated next to Grand Central Terminal. The train station itself had belonged to the New York Central Railroad and to Penn Central after the merger of 1968.

In 1974, a young real estate developer named Donald Trump proposed to buy these properties. Handling the negotiations for Penn Central was Palmieri's vice president, Edward P. (Ned) Eichler, a California real estate man whose father had founded a Levitt-like housing firm called Eichler Homes. Palmieri would make a fortune in fees—pegged at $21 million by the *Wall Street Journal*—for his firm's management and disposition of Penn Central holdings, and he was present at the creation of Trump's Manhattan real estate empire; Donald's father, Fred Trump, had owned properties in the outer boroughs but never broke into "the city."[35]

Although two other buyers offered considerably more for the rail yards, Trump's tight political connections with New York City mayor Abe Beame and New York governor-elect Hugh Carey—Trump had contributed to their electoral campaigns—convinced Eichler that the young developer "seemed best positioned in the New York market to get rezoning and government financing" because zoning was a "highly political activity in the City of New York." Many of Penn Central's major shareholders and creditors were unhappy with Trump, but Eichler pushed the sale through. He conceded that the offer made by one of the other bidders, the Starrett Company, "would generate more money than the Trump deal," but that "the rezoning will only be the result of an especially powerful political effort, which Trump is much more likely to pull off." This notion seemed dubious, since Starrett had been a major New York City developer since the 1920s, having erected the Empire State Building.[36] In any case, Eichler's job became easier after Trump got Starrett to withdraw its offer, apparently by reminding Starrett's owner, Henry Benach, that they were partners in the Brooklyn housing project known as Starrett City, the largest federally subsidized project in the United States, and that Trump owned a much larger share.[37] In 2007, Trump called Starrett City "probably the greatest tax shelter ever made."[38] Eichler offered Starrett "other parcels," one of which would be a streamlined Levitt & Sons.[39]

On taking over Levitt as its trustee, Palmieri labeled the company "a bleeding elephant" and set out to reduce its costs. He cut its workforce from 750 to 150, shed unprofitable operations—apartment buildings, mobile homes, and commercial manufacturing—and sold its subsidiaries in France and Spain plus its homebuilding operations in several U.S. metropolitan areas. He then sold $57.5 million of Levitt-owned land, much of it unbuildable, back to ITT. Palmieri's most dramatic move, and possibly its greatest cost-saver, was the sale of Levitt's palatial, multimillion dollar headquarters in Lake Success, New York.[40] The firm moved into an undistinguished office building in Greenwich, Connecticut. Nothing more poignantly symbolized the downfall of the once-mighty Levitt & Sons. Bill himself refused to move to the new office, deciding at the end of 1975 to leave the firm once and for all, despite an employment contract good until 1977.[41]

These drastic cuts appeared to work, and in 1976 the Levitt company showed its first profit in five years, with net income of $2.2 million. The next year it made $4.4 million. Total sales were modest, but not bad considering that Levitt, now called the Levitt Corporation, was operating only in the D.C. and Chicago areas plus Puerto Rico.[42] The stripped-down company could now be sold, and Palmieri quickly found a buyer: none other than the Starrett Housing Company, which paid $30 million, about one-third the price, not allowing for inflation, that ITT had paid Bill Levitt nine years earlier. Donald Trump brokered Starrett's acquisition of the Levitt Corporation, which named as its new president Edward Eichler, Trump's confederate in the Penn Central transactions.[43] When asked by a *Newsday* reporter to comment on the Starrett purchase, Bill Levitt blamed ITT for having "made a shambles of his former company," which it had "completely mismanaged." It was now "far from the highly profitable and respected firm I had sold."[44] The whole antitrust business made him "very frustrated, very disheartened, very depressed," but he was convinced that "someday, I'll have it all back again."[45]

During all the years that Levitt & Sons languished in antitrust limbo, Bill Levitt was far from inactive. Although he spent a great deal of time on his yacht and was a fixture in high society, he repeatedly told reporters he had no plans to retire. "Sure I play hard," he said at age sixty-nine, "but I also want to keep working hard."[46] He remained healthy and vigorous, played tennis several times a week, and, being contractually barred by ITT from building housing in the United States, invested in a variety of other ventures. Since he left no financial records, it's impossible to know how he paid for his extravagant lifestyle as well as his philanthropy and widespread investments. He clearly intended for the media and members of high society to believe he possessed a large fortune, but there is reason to doubt he did.

Bill Levitt's wealth was lodged almost entirely in ITT stock, and its value declined precipitously—along with the stock market in general—throughout the 1970s. During the recession of 1973–74, which followed OPEC's steep increases in oil prices and the end of the postwar

Bretton Woods system, which had pegged the dollar to gold and most other currencies to the dollar, the Dow Jones Industrial Average dropped 45 percent. It sank another 20 percent over the rest of the decade.[47] *Newsday* investigative reporter Kimberly Greer said that Bill Levitt owned seven hundred thousand shares of ITT, and that the value of each share had dropped from $104 in 1968 to $12 in 1974, a decline of 90 percent.[48] She cites no source for these numbers, and although the 1968 number is correct, the 1974 one isn't. Records of the New York Stock Exchange show a decline to a low of about $30 a share in 1973, an uptick to a high of $58 in 1974, and a low of $27.50 in 1975.[49] These are nominal values. Given the inflationary spikes of the 1970s—over 10 percent in 1975 and over 9 percent in 1979—the stock's real value was considerably lower.[50]

Even though Levitt's ITT stock didn't fall as much as Greer thought, it dropped to less than a third of its 1968 value by 1975—before accounting for inflation. Bill was much poorer in 1975 than he had been seven years earlier, but he wasn't exactly poverty-stricken. He continued to earn ample dividends on his ITT stock—ninety-five cents a share in November 1968, $1.05 a year later, $1.24 in 1972, $1.40 in 1974, and $1.60 in 1975.[51] These rising dividends partly offset the decline in share values and gave him cash for his lifestyle and investments. In 1969, his dividend amounted to $735,000 ($6.3 million today); by 1975, it was $1.12 million ($6.5 million today).

By any measure, Bill Levitt was wealthy. But he led an extraordinarily lavish life, and the worse his financial situation became, the more ostentatiously he lived and the more generously he gave. He seemed to need to convince himself and others that he remained as flush in 1975 as he had been when he sold his company. His cash dividends weren't enough to sustain this pretense. He borrowed heavily against his ITT shares, and as their value fell, his debt burden grew.[52]

Needing new sources of cash, he began to invest in a wide variety of ventures. In late 1971, he made two successive purchases of stock in Parkway Distributors, a company that operated a chain of drugstores and a mail order pharmaceuticals and cosmetics business. Two others joined him in the second purchase, which gave Levitt and his associates a controlling interest in the company. Levitt announced he would join the company's board and become an active participant. He paid $5.4 million for the first tranche of four hundred thousand

Parkway shares, and with his two colleagues, another $5.64 million for the second tranche.[53] He held on to Parkway for several years, but it did lackluster business, and he sold his interest in 1977 for $8.9 million, less than his original investment, even without counting inflation. He and a partner also created a film production and distribution company. The first film they distributed was Federico Fellini's *The Clowns* (1970), a prestige production that made little money in the United States.[54] Levitt quickly liquidated the firm but, in the meantime, invested millions in TownHouse Records, which also went south and by 1980 had lost him $13.8 million.[55]

In other investments, Levitt found himself a victim of international politics. Shortly before the Yom Kippur War of 1973, he led an effort to prospect for oil in the Sinai Peninsula, which Israel had seized during the Six Day War of 1967. Levitt assumed 12 percent of the venture's cost in exchange for 12 percent of the future profits. Several U.S. oil companies took on another 25 percent, with the Israeli government accounting for the rest. These investments were gravely threatened by the Camp David Accords of 1978, under which Israel pledged to return the Sinai to Egypt in exchange for normal diplomatic relations between the two countries and an end to the state of war that had existed since 1948. Levitt and his fellow investors, fearing that Israel would forfeit the rights to any oil discovered in the Sinai, met with Israeli prime minister Menachem Begin in an effort to convince him to maintain Israeli control. Begin refused to alter the agreement, making Levitt's large investment evaporate into thin air.[56]

Persisting with investments in troubled parts of the world, Levitt announced, in June 1977, a plan to build fourteen thousand condominium garden apartments in Tehran. The development, to be called Levittshahr, would include clusters of two-, three-, and four-story buildings, the first of which would be finished by the end of 1977. Construction and land purchases would amount to $500 million. Units would cost between $30,000 and $40,000, making them affordable only to the comfortable middle class. "We hope to bring to Iran," Levitt said, "a little bit of the innovations we've brought to the United States," including central air-conditioning, modern bathrooms, and large closets.[57] He had considered building in South America and Nigeria, but according to Edward Cortese, his vice president for marketing, he chose Iran because it "looked more stable."[58] Meanwhile, the Starrett Corporation, which had bought Levitt from ITT, made a larger investment in Tehran homebuilding and actually finished some units.[59] Both Levitt and Starrett downplayed the unrest that had broken out in Iran in the fall of 1977. As Cortese observed in November 1978, "We were about to break ground just before the recent turmoil began, but now we're waiting for things to settle down." Cortese told journalists that the Iranian radicals' anti-Americanism wouldn't extend to Levitt and his projects. "Ours is a more popular concept," he said.[60] This was, of course, wishful thinking: in December 1979, less than a year after the Iranian Revolution, Levitt announced the cancellation of the Tehran project, taking a loss of $5 to 10 million. He lost another $8 million on an Iranian drip irrigation project confiscated by the Khomeini regime. Starrett did even worse; its losses reached $38 million.[61]

Apparently undaunted by the Iran fiasco, Levitt looked south to Venezuela, where in 1981 he claimed to have signed "the largest and most detailed housing contract in the history of the industry in the United States as well as any other part of the world." The contract promised the construction, near Valencia, of at least 25,500 low-cost housing units plus the installation of infrastructure designed to accommodate another thirty thousand units. The total construction costs would come to $700 million. The first dwellings to be built would be two-family, semidetached houses; once these were completed, the next phase would include several apartment buildings. The project would include "elaborate plans for transportation, including buses, monorails, etc." The Venezuelan government pledged to subsidize the mortgage interest, which was usually high, and to buy $75 million of any dwellings that were unsold six months after being completed. The project would be exempt from state and local taxes.[62] The announced terms of this deal sounded too good to be true, and they were. Venezuela was a major oil exporter, and when oil prices began a steep decline in 1980, dropping from a high of $153 a barrel in April 1980 to $95 less than two years later and continuing to fall from there (prices adjusted for inflation), the government could no longer afford the expensive Levitt project and canceled the deal.[63] Once again, Bill not only lost millions in upfront investment but also the chance to make many millions, at a time when he desperately needed an infusion of cash.

A big reason for Levitt's business woes was a set of Florida projects that seemed highly promising at first. To sell homes in the Sunshine

State, Bill banked on his stellar reputation among people who had bought his homes in the Northeast and now planned to retire in Florida. He had been "depressed," his associates said, while banned from building housing in the United States; in 1978, as soon as the ban was lifted, he created a privately owned homebuilding firm called the International Community Corporation (ICC), bought more than three thousand acres in central Florida near Orlando, and announced he would create a new Levittown there.

Bill's former company, now known as the Levitt Corporation after its sale to Starrett, objected to Bill's use of the term "Levittown" and sued in federal court to force him to drop the name. During his employment by ITT (1968–77), he was contractually obligated not to build, sell, or lease any residential property in the United States. After 1977, he could reenter the business but could not use the names "Levitt," "Levittown," or "Strathmore" in any of his building projects, or do anything that would suggest to potential homebuyers that any enterprise of his was a new incarnation of the Levitt company. In selling out to ITT, Starrett argued, Bill Levitt had relinquished not only his company as an economic entity but also the rights to his name and reputation.[64]

Starrett's lawsuit, filed in July 1978 and appealed by Levitt three months later, bore the strange abbreviated title of "*Levitt Corp v. Levitt*."[65] To the casual observer it sounded as if Levitt was suing itself. In reality, the new Starrett subsidiary was taking legal action against a private citizen named William J. Levitt, whose transgressions included a press release that asked, "Who is the real Levitt?" suggesting it wasn't the Starrett subsidiary, which employed no one named Levitt. Bill had also announced plans to build "a new Levittown in the United States" and that prospective buyers should address themselves to "Levitt Industries, Inc." He placed ads in the *Washington Post, New York Times,* and other papers touting his new "Levittown Florida" and suggesting that his company was still "Levitt & Sons," the company that had "constructed more than 130,000 homes in scores of communities worldwide."[66]

U.S. district court judge George C. Pratt agreed with Starrett that Bill Levitt had unlawfully infringed on trademarks that belonged to the Levitt Corporation, causing confusion between Bill's projects in Florida and those of the Starrett subsidiary. The judge ruled that Bill must remove all references to "Levittown," "Levitt," "Levittown &

Sons," and the like from his venture's publicity, and that for a period of two years, he must refrain from using his own name in connection with any projects undertaken by his new company, the ICC. Bill had feared that potential customers wouldn't realize that ICC houses were Levitt houses, and that they would think the ones being built by the Levitt Corporation were his. Even if this were true, the court ruled, it didn't change the fact that Levitt had given up the right to use his name, goodwill, and reputation as trademarks. "When a business purchases trademarks and goodwill," the judge wrote, "the essence of what it pays for is the right to inform the public that it is in possession of the special experience and skill symbolized by the name of the original concern, and of the sole authority to market its products. . . . To protect the property interest of the purchaser, then, the courts will be especially alert to foreclose attempts by the seller to 'keep for himself the essential thing he sold.' "[67]

Evidence that Bill tried to do just that can be seen in scores of communications from potential ICC homebuyers that indicated the belief, the judge wrote, "that they would be dealing with the company responsible for the Levittowns of the Northeast." And in fact, "many inquiries came from residents of Levitt-built projects in the Northeast who desired to move to warmer climes," including "significant numbers of letters . . . addressed to Mr. Levitt personally [that] waxed nostalgic" about their Levitt homes. The appeals court affirmed the district court's ruling, concluding, "it is precisely this goodwill for which Levitt Corporation paid Mr. Levitt."[68]

The legal reasoning was sound, but from a layperson's point of view it defied common sense. Why shouldn't homebuyers associate Bill Levitt's name with the communities he built, and why should Starrett's Levitt Corporation, a stripped-down version of the original with few accomplishments of its own, get credit for what Bill Levitt had achieved? This was especially true in Bowie, Maryland, where Starrett's Levitt Corporation finished the construction begun by Levitt & Sons. The Starrett subsidiary did such shoddy work that Prince George's County officials found more than 2,500 building code violations in just 122 homes and cancelled the Levitt Corporation's license to build there. "Rain pours in the ceiling," said one homeowner, and "there's a two-inch rise in the upstairs floor." Added another, "We don't have the right insulation; the flashing is bad . . . a wall is warped, and the shutters have fallen off."[69] A Levitt Corporation project in Fairfax County, Virginia, was even worse. "The floor in the recreation room is buckling and the plumbing is leaking in several places," reported one new homeowner there. Several of the development's townhouses had been cited for "leaking basements, improperly supported walls, and floor trusses that were laid upside down." Edward Eichler, Levitt Corporation's president, had to replace his entire senior field management staff in Virginia and bring in "higher paid and higher skilled" carpenters from other projects. One subcontractor called the Fairfax development "the worst site I've ever worked on in Virginia."[70]

These problems, important as they were to homeowners, did nothing to dent Eichler's case against Bill Levitt. And a slew of letters Bill received about his new Florida community proved Eichler's point that Bill was illegally using his reputation to sell new homes. One letter writer couldn't have been clearer: "I recently made a reservation deposit on your new Levittown, Florida home priority #432 strictly on the 'Levitt' reputation sight unseen."[71] Another writer referred to a *Washington Star* article "about your proposed Levittown-Orlando."[72] Others asked Bill for a brochure "on the project to be built under Levitt and Sons in Orlando" and for "information about 'Levittown' " located east of Disney World. Many identified themselves as current or former residents of the Levitt & Sons developments in Willingboro and Bowie.[73]

Bill Levitt's counterargument, which the appeals court rejected, was that the injunction preventing him from using his name and reputation "deeply imperiled" the $70 million of mortgage commitments made by two lenders for his Florida project. The lenders had given him their money, Levitt said, "out of a firm belief that members of the public familiar with me personally would have sufficient confidence in the . . . project to risk the purchase of a home." The court order also prevented Levitt from making clear that the Levitt Corporation's negligence in its Bowie and Fairfax developments had nothing to do with him. Bowie residents, however, seemed to know the difference. "The hearts and minds of Bowie," wrote a *Washington Post* reporter, "are still with William J. Levitt," and he quoted one longtime resident as saying, "A lot of people from Bowie are already trying to sign up" for Levitt's Orlando homes.[74] In any case, Bill shrugged off the injunction with an ad in the *New York Post* for his Orlando development that proclaimed the "Return of a Legend, William J. Levitt . . . the nation's No. 1 home builder and developer of the famed Levittowns."[75]

Despite Bill Levitt's professed concerns, he got the mortgage loans, though far less than the $70 million he claimed, and began building what he planned as an "adult" community, by which he meant a development for older couples who wanted, sooner or later, to retire in Florida. Since he couldn't call the place Levittown, he named it Williamsburg, after his first name. The Williamsburg models were small by 1980s standards, with just two or three bedrooms, and designed in a "tropical" style like those in Levittown, Puerto Rico, with cinder block walls and stucco exteriors. In addition to Puerto Rico, Levitt had experience with this kind of structure in France, where wood-frame houses were considered flimsy. Like virtually all Levitt homes, the Williamsburg models sat on concrete slabs, and like most early Levittown models, they were one-story ranches. Within a few months of announcing the project, Levitt had received six thousand deposits to reserve a home, and by the end of 1980, he had completed one thousand, with plans for another eight thousand, including townhouses and garden apartments. The smallest of the single-family dwellings was the 1,070-square-foot Ardsley 1A, with two bedrooms and two baths. The largest was the Crofton, with 1,873 square feet of living space, three bedrooms, two baths, a garage, and a portico in front. Plots were small—just one-quarter acre.

Prices ranged from $34,000 to $56,000, making even the costliest model less expensive than the mean U.S. home price in 1980 of $75,000. But the mortgage rate in January 1981 weighed in at 14.75 percent, which doubtless explains why nearly 40 percent of Levitt's Florida homebuyers paid cash. Many had sold their homes in Levittown, New York, for a nice profit—half of Williamsburg buyers came from the New York area—and used the proceeds to buy into the Florida community. Aaron Frankel, a retired schoolteacher, sold his Levittown, Long Island, home in 1979 and purchased a Williamsburg house. "His [Levitt's] reputation was top-notch," Frankel explained. "We practically bought it sight unseen."[76] In 1981, Bernice Rosen sold her Levittown, Pennsylvania, house for $50,000, five times her purchase price in 1953. She then bought a dwelling in Williamsburg for $49,900. "Levitt gives us an excellent value for the money," she said, echoing generations of Levitt buyers.[77] Virtually all of those who purchased homes in Williamsburg, and also in Levitt's next Florida development, Williamsburg-Tampa, did so because of the Levitt name.[78]

The new development, however, had problems. This was the first time Levitt had used tile roofs rather than asphalt shingles in a U.S. development—he'd used tile in France, Spain, and Puerto Rico, where subcontractors had experience with the material—and many Florida roofs leaked. Levitt fixed the problem and guaranteed the work for five years, but several new residents complained that Bill didn't attend to the work personally, as he had in his Levittowns.[79] Such memories were tinged with rose-colored nostalgia, but in the 1940s and 1950s, Bill wasn't spending months on his yacht entertaining the rich and famous. Those who bought his modest Levittown homes could identify with him, look up to him, and although many of his Orlando homebuyers still thought highly of him, he seemed much more distant now. Levitt appeared unworried by this change in perception. "It is nice to be visible," he told a journalist, "I enjoyed it in the old days, it was fun. But . . . when you are running a ship you can't also be a seaman."[80] It was not a metaphor he would have used in the old days, when he didn't own a yacht with a twenty-six-person crew. Still, the retirees attracted to Levitt's Florida development couldn't help noting that at age seventy-four he remained extremely active, as they too wanted to be in their new adult community, with its warm weather and ample recreational facilities.[81]

Most of Levitt's Florida homebuyers wanted to love their new homes and also to give him the benefit of the doubt. But many became impatient waiting for their roofs to be fixed, and then other problems began to plague them: bad insulation, drainage issues, and poor paving in the streets. Levitt was slow to address these defects, and Williamsburg residents now complained en masse to the county commissioner, who responded by placing a moratorium on new building permits in Williamsburg. Levitt blamed new environmental regulations imposed after the project was underway for the delays in fixing the construction snafus. He had had to spend large sums on a sewage disposal system, which the county then deemed environmentally unsound. That ruling forced him to slow construction and therefore sales. With less money coming in, he didn't have the funds to repair the streets or redo faulty insulation. Homeowners and prospective buyers encountered similar problems in Williamsburg, Tampa, where homebuilding slowed to a snail's pace. People who had placed deposits on houses that were supposed to be completed in a few months found themselves waiting a year or more.[82]

They would continue to wait, usually in vain. Unbeknownst to anyone outside Bill Levitt's tiny circle of top executives, most of whom had been with him since the glory days of Levittown, the Florida projects were inadequately financed from the beginning. Long gone were the days when Bill could receive large amounts in construction money from the FHA and count on rapid sales to keep cash coming in. In 1978, when he began his Orlando Williamsburg, he borrowed $11.1 million from several lenders and put up virtually no money of his own. Normally, banks required the builder to contribute 20 percent up front, but Levitt's reputation was such that the banks waived the payment. Bill "was able to incur as much credit as he could," an attorney for Barclays Bank told *Newsday* in 1986, "because of his history."[83] But when Levitt borrowed this money, he was already some $14 million in debt from his failed investments and overseas housing busts.[84]

To stabilize his finances, he desperately needed the Williamsburg project to succeed. He appeared to have plenty of interested homebuyers, but instead of sinking the entire new construction loan into the Williamsburg development, he quickly spent more than half of it on other things. According to a Price Waterhouse audit examined by *Newsday,* he took $1.85 million for personal expenses and $190,000 for new overseas investments. He then transferred another $30,000 to Channel Enterprises, Ltd., the company he had set up to manage his yacht, and gave $4.5 million to another company, W.J. Levitt Inc., of which he was the sole owner. He used this large sum to pay himself a salary of $750,000 along with generous salaries for his top executives. By the end of 1980, two years after the Williamsburg project began, he had stripped $10 million out of the $11 million construction loan given to the ICC, the Levitt company in charge of the development. Of that $10 million, he took $5.29 million for himself, including $402,840 to keep his massively expensive yacht afloat, and an unknown amount spent on jewelry for Simone and various business dealings abroad. In using the money this way, Levitt violated his agreements with his lenders, which had restricted it to the development of Williamsburg. Since the $11 million loan wasn't secured by any real property, auditors for Price Waterhouse feared that it would never be repaid.[85]

In interviews and court depositions, Levitt argued that he had done nothing wrong in removing money from one of his companies to fund others, and that his extensive wealth served as his collateral. "Everything I've got I use as collateral for bank loans," he said in a court deposition. "The loans are to me, and I, in turn, lend them to my company."[86] This was patently false, since the $11 million in loans to the ICC were exclusively for the purpose of building his Williamsburg community.

This wasn't the first time Levitt had improperly diverted large sums of money. In 1981, the New York state attorney general charged that between 1974 and 1980, he illegally withdrew $8 million from his charitable foundation and deposited it in his personal bank accounts.[87] It seems highly likely that this money paid for his extravagant lifestyle, especially the upkeep of his yacht and Mill Neck mansion, along with the elaborate entertaining he and Simone did in both venues. It seems likely as well that the foundation money helped the Levitts buy millions' worth of jewelry, art, and haute couture, as well as their twelve-room Manhattan penthouse apartment. These expenditures made everyone think that Bill and Simone were fabulously wealthy, the equals of the richest people in the world. In 1982, *Forbes* magazine said Levitt possessed $100 million in assets and ranked among the four hundred wealthiest people in the country. In reality, he was massively in debt.[88] Still, the awestruck journalistic accounts of his apparent wealth convinced bankers that Bill represented no credit risk.

In December 1980, two banks, Centerre Bank in St. Louis and the National Bank of North America, showered him with $20.4 million in loans. He used about half of that money to repay the $10 million he had taken from the loans made to the ICC and another $4 million to restore funds he had snatched from his charitable foundation. The rest, about $5 million, went to American Express, which had financed his doomed venture in Iran. Levitt secured the new $20.4 million loan with Simone's jewelry collection, their yacht, the Mill Neck mansion, and ICC stock. There is no record of him selling his ITT stock, which had dropped to $28 a share by the beginning of 1979 (the equivalent of $13.42 in 1968, when ITT shares were worth over $100 each), so he must have still owned it.[89] Perhaps the reason he didn't use it as collateral as well is that its value had dropped to an inflation-corrected

12 percent of its original value. In any case, with his ICC stock as collateral, Bill was forbidden to take any more money out of the ICC for purposes other than building homes and infrastructure for Williamsburg. Yet he continued to siphon off ICC funds for his personal expenses, including his permanent lunch table at the Plaza Hotel.[90]

In hindsight, it is clear that Levitt had been living a life of illusory wealth since at least the mid-1970s. His income from salary and ITT dividends could not begin to cover his purchases of art, clothing, and jewelry, to say nothing of the maintenance of his yacht and seventy-acre estate. Nor could they cover his multimillion-dollar losses in Iran, Israel, and Venezuela, or the costly failure of his investment in TownHouse Records. At first, he borrowed against his ITT stock, but as the value of his portfolio plummeted, he had to take out a series of loans at increasingly elevated interest rates—loans issued to the ICC, his construction company, loans to repay earlier loans, and "loans" from his charitable foundation, which had accumulated dividends from the one-hundred-thousand-plus shares of ITT stock it owned and perhaps from tax-sheltered sales of the shares themselves.

By 1978, when Levitt began his Florida building project, his finances were a shambles. Although "no one knew it then," as a former Levitt executive later told the *Washington Post*, his lavish lifestyle floated on a sea of debt.[91] His Florida projects might have restored his balance sheet, since the state was about to hit a growth spurt, but his mounting debts prevented him from giving Williamsburg the resources required to build a viable community there. The result was shoddy infrastructure, poorly built houses, and an inability to keep up with the initially strong demand for his Florida homes. Thanks to this demand, he continued to receive thousands of deposits on homes he promised to build, but with no resources to pay contractors, either for work already done or for new work, the homes remained an unfulfilled promise. And now, in addition to defrauding banks, he began to defraud his customers, many of them Levittown homeowners who had long regarded Bill Levitt as a hero.

"I lived in a Levitt house on Long Island for thirty years," Bernice Kamen told the *Newsday* investigative reporter Kimberly Greer. "Just his name was like magic to us." But when Kamen and her husband moved in 1983 to what Levitt had advertised as a thriving retirement community near Tampa, they found that only 3 percent of the promised houses had been built and that their home was surrounded by vacant lots and half-built dwellings, left unfinished because the properties had been foreclosed. Her new surroundings, she said, were a "ghost town. . . . Levitt has been a tremendous disappointment to us."[92] Hundreds of other customers, many of them also veterans of earlier Levitt communities, expressed similar disappointment, often tinged with anger. Many had put down deposits on homes promised them in a few months' time, yet two years later, no house was in sight. Several had sold their homes up north, quit their jobs, and moved to Florida, where they ended up squatting in motels, apartments, and other temporary quarters. When they asked the ICC to return their deposits, usually between $5,000 and $15,000, they were ignored or given the runaround. One retirement-age couple, who had put up more than $13,000, said they had had "blind faith in the Levitt name," and he stiffed them without remorse. Another Florida buyer, whose promised house was fifteen months overdue, had tried to cancel the deal. But "they won't return the $14,000 deposit. They won't pay interest on it. They won't produce a house."[93]

When asked to explain the situation, Bill Levitt responded that he couldn't repay the deposits because he didn't have the money. But withholding the deposits violated Florida law, and knowing this, he prioritized refund requests submitted by lawyers who threatened legal action. He ignored the rest, and when his own executives told him this was unacceptable, he shrugged them off. "It happens," he said. "It is not pleasant, but it happens."[94]

Beyond his once-loyal customers, Levitt also shortchanged his loyal contractors, many of whom had worked for him in the glory days. A Long Island contractor who had moved to Florida with Levitt had to sue him for $75,000 in unpaid bills. Another Long Islander, who considered "Bill a personal friend," filed liens against him for nearly $400,000 of unpaid work. An Orlando contractor went out of business because Levitt failed to pay him, and yet another had to raid his children's college savings accounts to keep his business afloat. The president of a roadside billboard advertising company let Levitt's unpaid bills ride for more than two years because of the builder's reputation. He believed "Levitt's past successes" meant the company was "solid and sound and would stand by its obligations." He eventually had to sue. By December 1984, unpaid contractors' bills totaled more than $3 million. The owner of a concrete company told *Newsday*, "There are people who would shoot Bill Levitt if he came down here."[95]

By 1983, even some of Levitt's top executives, people who counted Bill as a close friend, were suing him for unpaid salary, benefits, and bonuses. Levitt's attorneys, having warned him that it was illegal to use homebuyers' deposits for purposes other than building their homes, now sued him for unpaid legal bills. They also made clear that he didn't have the right to use money intended for the maintenance of recreation facilities for his personal use. "They would raid clubhouse funds," former Levitt employees charged, "and pay the bills . . . for his maid, the housekeeper, the chauffeur." One executive told *Newsday* that these transgressions "have virtually destroyed our reputation and credibility with our buyers, homeowners, employees, contractors, suppliers, and governmental agencies and their representatives."[96] When Levitt did agree to pay, said one ICC official, "we knowingly write bad checks." Rather than make amends, Bill accused his executives and attorneys of mismanagement, incompetence, and insubordination. His woes were everyone's fault but his own.[97]

Levitt's longtime collaborator Nelson Kamuf explained his friend's failures in Florida as the result of his having "lost contact with the [homebuilding] industry." Levitt, he added, "has lived in the past for the last five, ten years. . . . He thought that the magic name would work magic any place he decided to drop the anchor."[98] This explanation, though doubtless partially true, didn't go far enough. By the early 1980s, Bill Levitt seemed increasingly to live in a reality of his own making. He claimed his projects were well-funded, and any cash flow problems were temporary. Complaints were to be expected, but they were easily resolved and not to be taken seriously. Worse, he apparently continued to believe his next big score was just around the corner. Amid the bitter complaints and lawsuits over his Williamsburg-Orlando development, he announced a second Williamsburg near Tampa. In Orlando, he had at least built about two thousand homes, however defective. In Tampa, his cash flow problems, unpaid bills, and homeowner complaints, among a cascade of other problems, limited him to just 125 finished dwellings.[99] By 1984, when all construction in the two Williamsburgs ceased, local officials had cancelled Levitt's building permits, unpaid contractors were refusing to work for him, and foreclosures required him to give up land on which he had planned to build.

Despite these devastating setbacks, or perhaps because of them, Levitt traveled to New York City in December 1984, accompanied by Simone and her three daughters, to hold a press conference announcing yet another Florida development, Poinciana. He made the announcement in a packed room at the Helmsley Palace, an elegant hotel in Midtown Manhattan, laying out what he said would be his largest project ever, a $2 billion, twenty-six-thousand-unit development on seven thousand acres near Orlando. A subsequent advertisement promised that Poinciana would feature "master planning, painstakingly done, overlook[ing] nothing to make this beautiful setting into a true residential park. . . . It is ideal that a family should live here and be able to do so at a price it can comfortably afford."[100] Levitt billed the new venture as a "primary employment town" that would have its own industry and service sector and provide some sixteen thousand jobs. The *New York Times* and several other outlets covered the press conference uncritically, and it generated massive publicity followed by one thousand deposits, much to the amazement of Floridians all too familiar with the reality on the ground.[101]

In Florida, local leaders, builders, and real estate agents considered Levitt's newest proposal pie in the sky; they doubted his ability to attract industry and create thousands of jobs. Villa Poinciana, they said, would be at best a bedroom community or a mecca for retirees, but they also expressed deep skepticism over Levitt's ability to build so many housing units, especially since his Williamsburgs in Orlando and Tampa were still largely unfinished. "Here he was making all these grandiose announcements," said one of Levitt's unpaid contractors, "when everyone in Central Florida was trying to nail him for payment."[102] The doubters would soon learn that their worries were vastly understated: things were far worse than even the worst pessimists believed.

Levitt, of course, condemned the naysayers.[103] And undaunted, he found a bank, Old Court Savings & Loan, that was willing to partner with him on the Poinciana development and promise him a loan of $17.5 million, with an immediate advance of $9 million. It quickly became apparent, however, that Old Court was anything but a viable business partner. In 1985, its president was indicted for misappropriating deposits from another savings and loan it owned. The state of Delaware, where Old Court was chartered, placed the bank in receivership and dissolved the alliance with Levitt on grounds that the ICC had "completely lost credibility with various county agencies and the public because of his failure to perform as required in Williamsburg-Orlando and Williamsburg-Tampa." No other bank stepped in to save Poinciana, preventing Levitt from proceeding with the project. Even so, he continued to place full-page ads for the development in major Northeastern newspapers. "Poinciana Park," the ads asserted, "is perhaps the most desirable residential area in the U.S. today."[104] Amazingly, deposits again poured in, totaling three thousand by mid-1985. Few of them were returned. "I was terribly impressed by Levitt," said one hopeful Poinciana homebuyer. "That is what kills me. The whole basis of trust was in his name." It goes without saying that no Poinciana houses were ever built.[105]

Bill Levitt's response to *Newsday*'s series of articles about his Florida disasters shows, again, just how much his reality departed from the one understood by virtually everyone who knew the situation. In a letter to *Newsday,* Levitt claimed he was about to receive new financing for his Williamsburg and Poinciana projects, but that the lenders backed off after reading the paper's pieces. There is no record, however, that any new financing was in the works. Levitt attributed the series' "erroneous and libelous information" to a former ICC official "discharged for his incompetence." Once again, the homebuilder's problems were entirely due to the misdeeds of others. And he said of Williamsburg homeowners, against a mountain of evidence, that "the overwhelming majority are happy." He also maintained that he still possessed "very substantial assets," although they were "not liquid." Among those assets was La Colline, which was real, but Williamsburg and the unbuilt Poinciana could hardly be considered assets, even illiquid ones, given the millions of dollars in lawsuits against him for these projects. He also listed as an "asset" the U.S. government's proceedings against Iran for property it had confiscated from American citizens. He would eventually receive $3.8 million in compensation, far less than the $25.6 million he had claimed. This entire Iranian sum would be applied to his debts.[106] Finally, Levitt asserted, as he had many times before, that he was a graduate of NYU, even though he had dropped out.[107] In addition to Levitt's response, *Newsday* published a letter to the editor from a Long Island contractor who admitted to being unaware of the homebuilder's

Florida troubles but found it impossible to believe that "a good human being like Levitt [can] become the thief and perpetrator of frauds you paint him."[108]

While the lawsuits over unreturned deposits, unpaid salaries, and stiffed contractors simmered in Florida courts, investigators for the New York state attorney general delved into Levitt's personal use of funds from his charitable foundation, which enjoyed tax advantages unavailable to individuals or commercial enterprises. In June 1983, a New York court imposed a fine of $1.03 million on him for illegally removing $8 million from his foundation. Shortly afterward, New York state attorney general Robert Abrams filed another suit against Levitt alleging that he misused another $5 million from the Levitt Foundation in a complex scheme involving the Bar-Ilan University in Tel Aviv, a Tel Aviv bank, and a shell company based in Zurich. After several years of depositions, investigations, and testimony, Levitt finally agreed to repay $11 million to his family foundation. To make that payment, he was forced to sell his Mill Neck mansion, for which he received $9.2 million.[109] He then dragged his feet for nearly five years before fully reimbursing the foundation.[110] He had already had to sell *La Belle Simone,* most of his wife's jewelry, his art collection, and his Manhattan apartment to pay off a variety of creditors. And even after liquidating his mansion and most of its contents, he still wasn't even. To pay off loans from the defunct Old Court Savings & Loan, he forfeited seven thousand acres of Florida real estate that had been bought for the Poinciana development, as well as land in his two Williamsburg developments.[111] When he failed to comply with a court order to repay nearly $1 million in deposits he collected for homes never built, the New York State Supreme Court barred him from advertising any homebuilding projects in the state and from collecting deposits on any dwellings planned for the future. The New York state attorney general also asked the court to forbid Levitt to build any new housing in the state—the state where he had established his reputation as the genius builder of low-cost homes.[112] Despite these legal actions, which state officials considered harsh but fully justified, Levitt doled out the required reimbursements slowly, hoping in vain to erase these debts and all his other ones with the $25.6 million he had claimed in compensation for his Iranian real estate debacle. But once again, he was living in his own reality. The $3.8 million he finally received from the Iran-United States Claims Tribunal proved little more than a drop in the bucket.[113]

Still another example of his massive self-deception was his effort to impress Joe Biden by spearheading a large contribution to his 1988 reelection campaign for the Senate, widely seen as a prelude to Biden's running for president in the Democratic primaries. To raise a sizable donation, Levitt had eight of his employees and eight of their relatives write checks to Citizens for Biden for $1,000 each, then the maximum permitted individual contribution. Levitt immediately reimbursed the $16,000 with funds from his charitable foundation, which was doubly illegal. Federal campaign finance laws forbade the solicitation-reimbursement scheme, and New York law forbade the transfer of tax-exempt foundation money to individuals for their personal use. When the Biden campaign got wind of Levitt's scheme, it returned the money.[114]

In the face of these financial and personal debacles, Levitt clung to his own deluded reality. In early 1989 he announced to the *New York Times* "some plans for something in the Orlando area . . . it could be very big." By then, even the *Times,* which had long supported him, and his most diehard supporters no longer took him seriously.[115] It didn't help that he had been evicted from his office in Greenvale, New York, for failing to pay his rent. He had no choice but to move his business activity, such as it was, to his Mill Neck estate, which the new owner had temporarily leased back to him. Life there with Simone must have been extraordinarily sad. Their two grand pianos had been sold, their art collection no longer graced the walls, the property itself bleak and unkempt. He'd had to let most of his staff go.[116]

In September 1990, having been forced to leave La Colline for good, Levitt was in court again for failing to repay the millions he had illegally siphoned from the family foundation. His lawyer told the judge that William J. Levitt, the master builder of the postwar era, was "truly destitute" and couldn't pay a cent. David Samuels, the New York state assistant attorney general prosecuting the case, didn't buy the claim. If Bill was destitute, how could he afford his $3,500-a-month condo and pair of brand-new cars? Levitt claimed friends were helping him, to which Samuels answered that he was "not entitled to live in splendor."[117] But by then, splendor was little more than a memory for Levitt. Once again, he blamed others for his misfortune, this time his attorney, whom he sued, unsuccessfully, for malpractice.[118] Not until 1992 did Samuels and Levitt come to an agreement, as the assistant attorney general seized what he believed were the home-builder's last remaining assets. Levitt was now "truly destitute" and in poor health, the end very near.

But, as always, Bill dreamed of a spectacular comeback, a new effort that at long last would strike gold. "I have a regular organization ready to punch in full time," he told Hofstra University professor Stuart Bird in an interview filmed in December 1993. Confined to a hospital bed, gravely ill with kidney disease and a ruptured intestine, the eighty-six-year-old Levitt assured Bird that his new enterprise would be brilliantly run by two of his young relatives, an architect and a banker. In the interview, Levitt's voice is raspy, barely above a whisper, but he's fully coherent. He tells Bird that he doesn't want to be remembered, because he doesn't want to die. He eagerly defines his legacy as "a guy that gave value for low-cost housing, not somebody who gave value for half a million dollar houses. Anybody could do that."[119] In this and other interviews given late in life, Levitt preferred to reminisce about his good times rather than answer questions about what had gone wrong. "In an interview last year," wrote *Newsday*'s Kimberly Greer, "the founder of Levittown claimed that his original accomplishment will always far overshadow his recent problems. 'We are in the history books,' he said."[120]

Levitt was certainly in Donald Trump's historical memory. In a July 2017 speech before the Boy Scouts of America's National Jamboree, the new president began with a prepared message meant to inspire the forty thousand scouts gathered there. But he quickly veered off script and landed on a strange riff about Bill Levitt, who had been dead for twenty-five years and was unknown to virtually everyone in the audience. Levitt in his prime, Trump said, was "an unbelievable success," had made a vast fortune, and took great pride in his work. "At night," the president reported, Levitt would "go to these major [housing] sites with teams of people and he'd scout the sites for nails and sawdust and small pieces of wood. And they cleaned the sites so when the workers came in the next morning, the sites would be spotless and clean. And he did it properly."

Levitt did take pride in his work, but there's no record of his spending the wee hours scouring his developments for stray nails. He and his father, Abraham, however, did glide through his completed Levittowns behind the wheel of a Cadillac checking to see that lawns had been properly mowed and the properties remained free of fences and clotheslines. In any case, Trump didn't intend to leave his audience with a positive view of the man he claimed to have idolized in his youth. The president was speaking extemporaneously and segued to a story, perhaps invented as well, about a fancy party given by Steven J. Ross, the creator of Time Warner, for New York City's rich and famous. "I see a hundred people," the president said, "some of whom I recognize, and they are big in the entertainment business." As he worked the room, Trump said, he saw "sitting in the corner . . . a little old man who was all by himself. Nobody was talking to him. I immediately recognized that that man was the once-great William Levitt of Levittown."[121]

The point of this story seems to be that Trump was young and vital and on his way up, while the "once-great" Levitt was an elderly has-been, a tragic figure who had ceded his place at the summit of New York real estate to Donald Trump. While Levitt shrank into a corner completely alone, Trump was en route to becoming president of the United States.

The riff, which had nothing to do with the Boy Scouts, then turned inappropriate as Trump alluded to Levitt's womanizing and hedonism to this audience of teenage boys. But the president's rumination on Levitt suggests that the homebuilder had made a big impression on the young real estate developer, just as he had on the media during his heyday and on the inhabitants of his Levittowns to this day.

A great many Levittowners saw him as a towering figure. "To the original residents," said Lynne Matarrese, who wrote about the community, "he was a hero. No matter what happened to him [later], he was their savior. He was just wonderful. He could do no wrong." Toward the end of his life, Bill returned the compliments, telling reporters, "You know, the 60,000 people of Levittown are much more my friends than the people of Park Avenue. Oh, God, yes more than most of those I entertained on my yacht."[122]

On January 28, 1994, five weeks after Levitt's interview with Stuart Bird, the homebuilder died at North Shore University Hospital, the facility to which, in better days, he had contributed huge sums. He died there as a charity patient. Newspapers everywhere published obituaries and some added editorials as well. The *Bucks County Courier Times,* the paper that served Levittown, Pennsylvania, called him "a legend [and] one of the forward thinkers who helped revolutionize American life. He is a true American success story—a man who got rich by seeing a need and meeting it on a grand scale. But it was not greed that drove him. It was an overriding concern to provide for millions of Americans in need—good people with young families and strong values who could only afford modest homes." Nowadays, the editors lamented, there were far too few builders willing to create affordable housing. "There is more money . . . in luxury developments." This statement is even more true today than it was in 1994. The editorial ended on an almost worshipful note: "William Levitt will forever be a hero—not just to Levittowners, but to America."[123]

The *Philadelphia Inquirer* began its obit on the front page and extensively quoted Levitt's son James, who called him "a very dynamic person, very well-liked." He "played a great piano" and was "a great party-giver, a good family man. He was everything. . . . He had charisma." In a recent interview with me, James offered a more nuanced view, saying, "I loved him; I idolized him, but I didn't really know him." Bill "was not a great father," James said. "He was great to everybody except his children." He recounted one incident that, if true, explains his ambivalence. After James dented the Corvette his father had given him for an eighteenth-birthday present, Bill sold the car without telling his son. "He loved to give and take away. . . . In a simple nutshell, he liked to have his power over us." The sale of the car soured their relationship for a long time. After college, James moved to Los Angeles, where he became a film producer, making two movies with modest success. "Somebody should have made a book or a movie about *my* life. I was really interesting when I was young." The statement reveals just how much the son wanted to be famous like his father. When I asked James why his father went downhill after so much success, he answered that Bill had been "bowled over by Harold Geneen and wasn't thinking rationally about what the sale of his company would mean." James saw firsthand the disaster of his father's attempted comeback in Florida: "I did work for him for four miserable years [1979–83] in Florida. That was a failure. . . . I just blanked that whole portion of my life."[124]

Many of the obituaries quoted David Halberstam and the urban historian Kenneth Jackson comparing Levitt to Henry Ford and calling him one of the most significant businessmen of the twentieth century. Virtually all of the obits emphasized Levitt's outsized role in the suburbanization of postwar America, either directly as a builder or indirectly as a model for other builders. Assessing his impact on the New York region, Joshua Ruff, a curator at the Long Island Museum, compared Levitt with Robert Moses, calling the homebuilder "just as important as Moses as far as what Long Island became."[125] The *New York Times* quoted the historian Jon C. Teaford, who claimed that "throughout the country, every metropolitan area had its own version" of the Levitt family "building scores of houses along the suburban fringes." Levitt's boast that he succeeded "in meeting a demand with a product no one else can meet" was a typical exaggeration.[126] He didn't invent mass-produced, low-cost housing, and other builders also met the postwar demand for this kind of dwelling, but Levitt was arguably the most important and influential of them all.

Most obits didn't neglect the negative aspects of the Levitt phenomenon. They took note, often prominently, of Levitt's policy of excluding African Americans from his developments, although they rarely mentioned the lasting effects of this exclusion. Most of the obits described his dramatic decline, but mainly as a sad coda to the real story of his life. Perhaps that's all it was. Tens of thousands of homebuyers never ceased to consider him a hero. Returning to Levittown, Long Island, for the community's fortieth anniversary in 1987, the eighty-year-old William J. Levitt, bankrupt and shorn of his home and his office, found himself embraced by a huge, enthusiastic crowd. "It might have been General Douglas MacArthur returning [from] the Philippines," wrote a *Newsday* reporter. And Levitt, who badly needed a dose of love amid all his troubles, spoke proudly of his place in history, of "wind[ing] up in the *Encyclopedia Britannica*." For those who attended the celebration, said Tom Carroll, chair of the anniversary committee, "regardless of what's happened, he's still the founder of Levittown and we love him." "Levittown," added the Nassau County executive Thomas S. Gulotta, "is what America is all about."[127]

Epilogue
Levitt's Legacy

BILL LEVITT'S LEGACY is anything but straightforward. It can't be reduced to a negative story of racial exclusion, a positive story of heroic homebuilding for returning veterans, the sad architecture of "little boxes," or any other singular narrative. Each of those stories is true, but none paints the whole picture. Nor can the contradictions among them be satisfactorily resolved. It's true that Levitt created unprecedented opportunities for young families to become homeowners and build a measure of family wealth, but he simultaneously excluded African Americans from those same possibilities. White opportunities were premised on Black exclusion. Their exclusion left a terrible legacy but also a moral ambiguity. Most of the white families that took advantage of the Levittowns did so because they could afford nothing else, and because it cost less to buy there than to rent in nearby New York City, Philadelphia, or Washington, D.C. (and later, in Paris and San Juan). Most of Levitt's white buyers weren't consciously trying to avoid having Black neighbors, although some clearly were. Still, the white people who bought into Levittown must have been aware that Blacks were barred, and if they had qualms about choosing a segregated community, most pushed them aside because the price was right. The "pure" thing to do would have been to reject Levitt's racism and refuse to buy homes there, and some did just that. But most Levittowners didn't see themselves as beneficiaries of an undeserved privilege, the happenstance of being white. Many would come to understand this uncomfortable fact only later in life, and some would work for the integration of African Americans into their communities.

Although the FHA tacitly, and sometimes explicitly, endorsed Levitt's racist policies and the courts ratified them for more than a decade, Levitt's exclusions were controversial and ultimately overturned, at least as a matter of law. Thanks to a series of court rulings, Levittown, New Jersey, became an integrated community, although most whites eventually fled. Bowie, Maryland, however, became more racially integrated than most U.S. suburbs and has stayed that way. But the two original Levittowns, in New York and Pennsylvania, remain almost entirely white, making the Levitt legacy there enduringly unfair. The main way Americans have built family wealth has been through owning a home and having it appreciate in value. Since 1963, home prices have gone up more than two and half times faster than the consumer price index, the standard measure of inflation.[1] The whiteness of Levittown denies this benefit to African Americans.

Levitt's genius was to reduce the cost of homes at a crucial point in U.S. history by quickly and dramatically increasing the supply. He thus made home-buying affordable to people with modest incomes, at least in the mainland United States—in France and Puerto Rico, he catered to the upper 10 percent. In the United States, a Levitt house was a key ingredient of what could be called the "long New Deal," a vision of relative social equality perhaps unprecedented in American history.[2] From the late 1940s to the early 1970s, key features of the New Deal—social security, labor protections, government-guaranteed mortgages, progressive taxation, Keynesian economic policy—were maintained, even enhanced, by both Republican and Democratic administrations, eager to show Cold War rivals that capitalism worked. These benefits improved the lives of working- and lower-middle-class Americans, as did the G.I. Bill and the prosperity grounded in U.S. economic dominance. White Americans gained by far the most from these developments, but Black Americans also saw their fortunes increase, although not until the 1960s, when the civil rights movement helped propel some African Americans into the middle class, and in Willingboro and Bowie, into a Levitt house.[3]

One price of affordability was critical disdain. As the premier architect of postwar suburbia, Levitt dotted his landscapes with houses that critics deemed ticky-tacky, architecturally banal, and oppressively uniform. His Cape Cods and ranches, it was claimed, turned their inhabitants into lemmings of conformity. But the overwhelming majority of those who bought his houses thought they were just fine and considered the ability to own them a small miracle. Later, they would transform their homes in myriad distinctive ways; as Herbert Gans showed long ago, the charge of conformism was vastly overblown. Levittown didn't make the individuals who lived there substantially different from who they would have been elsewhere.

Non-Americans would repeat the criticisms of U.S. critics, for although Levittown has long been known as quintessentially American, Levitt built successful, desirable suburban developments abroad, making his mark in France and especially Puerto Rico. These projects contributed to the Americanization of the West; had Levitt retained his company rather than selling it to ITT, he might have continued to build in France, created the German developments he had planned, and made a substantial impact in Spain rather than a minor one. Because Europeans, like Americans, often prefer single-family houses, other homebuilders have imitated Levitt's methods in the Old World and enjoyed considerable success.

The sale to ITT was a mistake, and it raises questions about his acumen as a businessman and his understanding of business trends, especially the merger-mania of the late 1960s. Levitt apparently believed, against all evidence, that Harold Geneen, ITT's CEO, would allow him to run Levitt & Sons as he had before the buyout. But Geneen quickly pushed the famous homebuilder aside and left him with nothing to do. This must have been galling to Levitt, perhaps even more than he perceived; self-knowledge wasn't his forte. He not only thrived on running his own company and the attention it earned him; he also wanted to be more than just a successful businessman earning piles of money. He wanted to build communities, not just houses, and shape how people lived. His houses were designed for nuclear families, with open-plan interiors to foster togetherness and compact kitchens with space only for Mom. But he also wanted families to leave their separate dwellings and come together with other families in public facilities—swimming pools, ball fields, and shopping centers. He valued neighborliness but, unlike Robert Frost, thought it was the absence of fences that made good neighbors. So he banned them from Levittown yards. To foster community belonging, he divided his massive developments into sections or "parks," each one small enough for residents to know one another. Levittowns were not to be engines of anonymity but collections of small towns anchored by the schools, churches, and synagogues for which he set aside ample land. Although not observant himself, he wanted Levittowners to attend religious services. In the early years, many did.

Levitt seemed satisfied with what his massive developments had accomplished, but he sought to do even more to shape people's lives. In the late 1960s, he unveiled a visionary, if unrealistic, plan to build "primary employment towns" of fifty thousand people, modern-day utopian communities providing jobs and housing in parts of the country lacking both.[4] Whether he knew it or not, Levitt's pipe-dream communities were distantly related to those of the nineteenth-century socialists Robert Owen, Henri de Saint-Simon, and Charles Fourier, who also envisaged self-sustaining towns and villages with habitats and workplaces close together. Levitt would have disliked the socialists' communal eating and living arrangements, although in his Levittowns, sociability was important. Perhaps the nearest ancestors to Levitt's "primary employment towns" were Ebenezer Howard's garden cities and their postwar successors, places intended not as suburbs but as complete, self-sufficient municipalities.

Levitt's imagined communities wouldn't have been more successful than Saint-Simon's, Fourier's, or Howard's and, in retrospect, it's clear that his visionary, innovative talents had limits. They worked well in the two decades following World War II but faltered in the late 1960s. Immediately after the war, he perceived better than most other homebuilders the unique opportunities of the time, snapping up large expanses of farmland close to New York City and Philadelphia at prices low enough to market houses for as little as $7,000. Between 1947 and 1967, he sold far more dwellings than most of his competitors put together, thanks mainly to the mass-production techniques he pioneered and to economies of scale. He also took advantage of a seller's market in which homebuyers were willing to live in houses similar to thousands of others in exchange for affordable prices and what were then novel creature comforts for the working and lower-middle class—well-equipped kitchens and bathrooms, air-conditioning, built-in cabinets and closets, and private, semi-landscaped yards. But when the sellers' market subsided in the mid-1960s, and buyers became choosier, Levitt set up shop overseas. He did well in France and Puerto Rico, but U.S. sales slowed in Willingboro, and he never completed his ambitious plans for Bowie. It's impossible, of course, to know how Levitt & Sons would have fared had he rejected Felix Rohatyn's advice to sell it, but it seems likely that the company would have struggled amid the stagflation and high interest rates of the 1970s and 1980s.

Although selling out to ITT made Levitt a wealthy man, most of that wealth existed only on paper, in the stock certificates whose value held no guarantees. Since the terms of the sale to ITT barred him from U.S. homebuilding for a decade, he turned to other enterprises, making a series of disastrous investments: a drugstore chain, a record company, oil prospecting. He even lost money in real estate. The millions he sank into housing projects in Iran and Venezuela evaporated in the face of unstable regimes and shaky local economies. He seemed to have forgotten that his earlier achievements were built on unprecedented support from the U.S. government. His original, mass-produced Cape Cod aped the "minimum house" devised by the FHA, and he could sell thousands of them (and subsequent models) thanks to government-backed mortgages with payments stretched over thirty years. These government guarantees minimized the risk to banks, which in turn reduced interest rates and therefore monthly payments, allowing thousands to become homeowners for sixty dollars a month. In inflation-adjusted dollars, this would amount to $790 today, just 35 percent of the average monthly mortgage payment ($2,200) in 2024.[5]

Levitt had always sought status, and with his Levittowns, he achieved it through real accomplishments. After being sidelined by Geneen and finding himself with no company to manage and nothing to do, he turned to philanthropy and jet-setting, replacing the reality of success with its trappings—the Long Island mansion, Fifth Avenue penthouse, expensive art, jewelry for his trophy wife, high-profile donations, and especially his yacht. By the late 1970s, all of this floated precariously on a cascade of debt.

In 1978, after being contractually barred from homebuilding in the United States for a decade, he came back to the business with plans for developments in Florida. But the real estate market had changed. From the late 1940s to the early 1960s, his buyers could borrow money at 4 to 5 percent with little or no down payment. By 1978, mortgage interest hovered around 10 percent and was rising sharply; it would peak at 16.6 percent in 1981.[6] Still, he could have adapted to the new situation. His reputation enabled him to take out sizable bank loans for his Florida projects; had he sunk them into home-building rather than his expensive lifestyle, the new developments might have succeeded, despite the high interest rates. Many of his potential Florida buyers, eager to retire to a Levitt house, had paid off Levittown mortgages and, after selling their houses, had the cash to buy in Florida without taking on debt. New Levitt homes in Tampa and Orlando could sell for relatively modest amounts because land in those regions was still relatively cheap. As interest rates gradually moderated after 1985, Levitt could have benefitted from Florida's position at the leading edge of a Sunbelt boom that enticed millions of people to the state. Between 1980 and 2000, Florida's population grew by 63 percent, from 9.8 million to over sixteen million.[7]

Still, Levitt faced far more regulations and stringent building codes in Florida than he had two decades earlier in New York, Pennsylvania, New Jersey, or Maryland, where local authorities were weak. In Florida, Levitt had to cut corners to keep prices down, and it showed in the quality of his houses. Even if he hadn't misappropriated his construction loans for his personal use, he still might not have had the wherewithal to make his Florida developments succeed. He had sold his first Levittown homes at age forty. By the time he resumed home-building after the ITT debacle, he was over seventy, no longer the energetic, business-hungry young man who created affordable housing for the masses. He increasingly lived in a reality of his own making, stubbornly refusing to admit to fraud and failure, and fleecing his loyal customers. Year after year, even on the hospital bed where he lay dying as a charity patient, he insisted that his next business coup was on the horizon.

Beyond the reasonable prices, perhaps the greatest selling point of a Levittown house was the ample yard surrounding it. People took pride in their lawns and the other greenery Levitt installed. But by allotting six thousand to twelve thousand square feet of land to each house, Levitt, like his counterparts elsewhere in the country, limited the number of houses that could be built on a given parcel of land. These limits were then set in stone by the zoning laws enshrined in every Levitt development and the thousands of others like them.

Today, as the country faces a shortage of at least four million homes, the inability to build additional dwellings on Levitt-style lots keeps the housing supply artificially low, and housing prices and rents artificially high.[8] France faces a similar situation thanks in part to its Levitt developments and the suburban preference for low-density housing they helped to inspire. The mayor of Le Mesnil-Saint-Denis actually wanted Levitt to make lot sizes even larger than he had intended.[9]

In the United States, soaring real estate values have been a boon for homeowners in Levittowns and other suburbs nationwide, but for the low-wage workers who service the middle and upper-middle class as nannies, gardeners, and handymen, or who work as hospital orderlies, retail clerks, busboys, and unskilled laborers, homeownership has become impossible. Even rents in communities close to their jobs are often beyond their means.[10] A growing suburban underclass now lives in pockets of poverty, some on the edges of Levittown itself, and in other, similar areas of the United States. Its members dwell in increasingly dilapidated structures, built for single families but now sheltering two or more families in garages, attics, partitioned living rooms, additions, and even backyard sheds. Some homeowners who struggle to make mortgage and property tax payments can afford to stay in their homes only by sharing them with renters. In other cases, especially in the poorest suburban areas, slumlords have bought run-down or abandoned houses and illegally turned them into multifamily dwellings or even rooming houses for single adults. Such "informal housing" serves a need for affordable living space, but because it's illegal and thus unregulated, it often creates hazardous, even life-threatening conditions. Local authorities tend to ignore these arrangements until a fire or a burst septic tank creates visible harm. Only then do they enforce building codes and root out informal housing in the neighborhood. These actions add to the dearth of affordable shelter and often turn poorly housed people into homeless ones.[11]

This situation has forced some public authorities, usually governors, to concede that the single-family, house-and-yard ideal, so successfully encouraged and exploited by builders like Levitt, can't be sustained. Officials have learned a lesson from the informal (generally illegal) conversion of single-family properties into multifamily ones and have begun to allow or even encourage the building of "accessory dwelling units" (ADUs)— converted garages, additions, even freestanding structures—so that a second family can live safely and legally on a property zoned for just one. ADUs, however, have been controversial and are often opposed by home-owners who fear "overcrowding" and "changes in the character of the community," which can mean anything from overtaxing local services to attracting poorer, non-white people. Suburban officials are fully aware of these fears, and although many understand the need for more affordable housing, they are reluctant to tamper with the single-family norm.[12]

On Long Island, for example, where there is some support for ADUs, many localities have followed the lead of Hempstead, New York, in opposing them. In 1975, it passed a law designed to reinforce "the intention of Levitt & Sons, Inc." to maintain "certain land in the Town of Hempstead as a planned suburban community of one-family dwellings." The ordinance limited the use of garages and other struc-tures to a professional office for the homeowner.[13] A second residence on the property was prohibited, and it remains illegal in Hempstead and most American suburbs.

In 2022, when New York's governor, Kathy Hochul, proposed to require the building of a few hundred new ADUs statewide, she was met with a chorus of opposition. Don Clavin, the Hempstead town supervisor, called the proposal "an attack on the suburban way of liv-ing." Another Nassau official, John Hrvatin, executive director of the Freeport Housing Authority, denounced the governor's efforts to override local control as "just too radical."[14] Long Island leaders, Re-publicans and Democrats alike, often claim that ADUs will worsen the area's traffic nightmare, make scarce parking even scarcer, add to school overcrowding, and overburden social services.[15]

These worries are not unfounded, thanks to Levitt's devotion to de-tached single-family dwellings, which has made Nassau County look a lot like Los Angeles. Both have sprawling, low-rise built environ-ments that are at once too dispersed for mass transit to be practical and too dense to allow for smoothly flowing traffic and ample park-ing. In both Los Angeles and Nassau County, almost nothing is within walking distance, and stores are grouped into strip malls and shopping centers along major thoroughfares. You can't get anywhere without a car. Levittowns, like most postwar suburbs, were premised on the private automobile, making traffic jams a fact of life, not only on the infamous Long Island Expressway, where even the lane for high occupancy vehicles routinely slows to a crawl, but also on the various "turnpikes" that cut through the suburban sprawl. The same is true, of course, of Los Angeles's freeways and countless other highways that span U.S. suburbia and the parts of cities that resemble it.

In California, which has an especially acute shortage of affordable housing, and where the average new home costs over $1 million, the state legislature has passed a series of bills designed to promote the construction of ADUs on single-family lots. Successive bills were necessary because municipalities and other local jurisdictions were using every legal means available, including zoning rules, environmental laws, and homeowners' associations, to block ADUs. The state has overcome many of these obstacles, and the number of permitted ADUs has jumped from one thousand built in 2016 to twenty-four thousand in 2022. Some of these units had already existed illegally, so the overall number of new secondary dwellings built since 2016 may be only fifty thousand to sixty thousand in a state of thirty-nine million people.[16]

Beyond the hostility of local governments, a key obstacle to ADUs is the expense of building them. On average, it costs $167,000 to create an ADU in California—$148,000 in Los Angeles and $237,000 in the Bay Area, where an ADU can cost $800 per square foot, or $400,000 for a tiny dwelling of just twenty by twenty-five feet. Most homeowners need financing to build them, but banks are reluctant to offer it. Since a main motivation for creating an ADU is to give a homeowner extra income, many are deterred by the high construction bills, together with a host of bureaucratic barriers.[17] ADUs are better than nothing, but they do little to dent Levitt's single-family legacy.

Beyond ADUs, one potential remedy for the U.S. housing shortage is to erect apartment buildings close to train and subway stations. But this too has evoked ferocious opposition. In early 2023, Hochul proposed legislation that would require cities and their close-in suburbs to rezone areas within a half-mile of subway and train stations to allow for fifty units per acre—Levitt's smallest properties made room for, at most, seven per acre. The farther from the city, the lower the number of required new units, but suburbs fifty miles out would still have to construct fifteen units per acre on land within ten minutes' walking distance from a train station.[18] In Nassau County, which has 478,000 housing units, mostly single-family dwellings, Hochul's proposal would have added just 14,340 new units over three years, less than five thousand a year.[19]

Despite these modest goals and a heavy publicity campaign, the bill was buried under an avalanche of opposition from homeowners and legislators representing both political parties. "Her plan would flood YOUR neighborhood with THOUSANDS of new apartments" asserted one mailing. Others warned that Long Island would become New York City's "sixth borough."[20] During the 2020 presidential campaign, Donald Trump had promised "all of the people living their Suburban Lifestyle Dream [sic] that you will no longer be bothered or financially hurt by having low-income housing built in your neighborhood."[21] In 2024, after once again failing to get legislative support, Hochul gave up, stripping higher-density housing from the state budget.

The power of New York's suburban homeowners and the officials they elect has made the state a laggard even compared to the rest of the United States, which hasn't exactly been eager to build denser housing. Between 2010 and 2018, New York issued fewer building permits per capita than virtually every other highly suburbanized state in the country.[22] It's no wonder that the average home price in Nassau County hovers around $700,000, and that rents commonly sop up 35 to 50 percent of family income. An acute example of how difficult it is to create multifamily housing is the Matinecock Court project in East Northport, a Long Island town of twenty thousand. The 146-unit affordable housing development was first proposed in 1978, but a series of lawsuits by local homeowners, plus one by the NAACP, stalled the project for forty-five years. Ground was finally broken in 2023.[23]

Homebuilding on Long Island has been especially difficult, but denser housing is an uphill battle almost everywhere. Homeowners and local officials nationwide have blocked efforts by state governments to foster homebuilding through rezoning and through softening environmental and other regulations used to prevent development. California, though modestly successful with ADUs, has been unable to promote high-density housing near transit stops or to bypass environmental rules never meant to stymie homebuilding but routinely used to thwart it, especially by wealthy communities eager to remain exclusive.

In Colorado, Governor Jared Polis failed in 2023 to get state lawmakers to allow him to override local control over development and require municipalities to build multifamily housing near transit stations. The following year, he managed to enact a housing bill over the fierce opposition of local leaders. This relatively strong measure permits ADUs and rezones for higher density housing in populous localities, but it depends on developers' willingness to build and softens earlier language imposing penalties on efforts to skirt the law.[24]

Other states, too, have seen glimmers of success. Oregon and Washington have recently passed laws authorizing multiunit buildings in areas zoned for single families, but because of inflation and high interest rates, few units have been built. In 2023, Florida, a state with soaring housing costs and one of the highest proportions of low-wage workers in the country, enacted a bill that promises to boost the number of affordable housing units by changing zoning rules, providing state grants and subsidies, and offering tax breaks. It also prohibits rent control, which helps existing renters but often discourages the building of new housing. A few other states, red as well as blue, have enacted legislation allowing for ADUs in single-family precincts.[25] Most of these bills are modest, but they reflect the growing recognition that suburban towns will not promote more abundant housing on their own; state governments must require them to build. Suburban homeowners benefit from scarce housing, since it keeps their home values high, and they often want to maintain the exclusions that high prices and low density create. Also, few localities want to be the first in their areas to build new housing, for fear of having to bear the burdens of increased traffic, crime, crowded schools, and stressed services, while lightening the load of neighboring communities. What's needed is the ability to distribute new housing throughout a variety of municipalities, so that the effects are spread as evenly as possible. Only a state government can do this successfully, but given the enduring appeal of the Levitt-style house and yard and the often fierce opposition to seeding apartment buildings into suburban landscapes, governors struggle to require suburbs and cities to permit denser housing.

Many governors have come to understand that all new housing helps, whether rented or sold at market rates or below. Advocates for boosting the supply of market-rate dwellings argue convincingly that as new housing goes up, even expensive housing, older housing will become available to lower-income people as prosperous ones move into the new dwellings. If the supply of new units rises enough, the cost of older residences will fall.[26] Most places that have enacted zoning changes and other incentives to build new housing haven't yet seen prices come down significantly—again, inflation and high interest rates discourage construction—but Houston stands out as an exception and, perhaps, a promise for the future.

Rather than permitting ADUs, officials there have reduced minimum lot sizes to as low as 1,400 square feet—the typical minimum nationwide is about ten thousand square feet. Suburban areas have commonly kept minimum lot sizes high, requiring builders to buy as much as an acre for a single house, typically a large, expensive one to justify the high cost of the land. Houston's reform encourages townhouse construction and allows owners to turn single-family properties into multifamily ones. A detailed study of Houston's housing reforms concludes that by reducing minimum lot sizes, the city has "facilitated infill construction"—seeded existing land with more housing—"to a level unprecedented in US history since the adoption of zoning in the twentieth century."[27]

Even in Houston, however, costs haven't fallen enough to make dwellings affordable to families with low incomes. Boosting the supply of market-rate housing can help, but it's also essential to build public housing, offer housing subsidies, or both.[28] It's well known, though, that public housing is expensive to construct, unpopular politically, and thus in extremely short supply, especially in suburbs where nearly half of Americans live. This too is a legacy of Levitt.[29] Early in his career, he told Senator Joseph McCarthy's housing committee that public housing is socialistic and inefficient and that homes should be built by private entrepreneurs like him. This was a message McCarthy wanted to hear, and although the Truman and Eisenhower administrations kept many of the New Deal's reforms in place, the provision of public housing wasn't one of them.[30] Still, even in the absence of additional subsidized housing, if cities and suburbs could more easily turn single-family properties into multifamily ones and cut regulatory red tape, our housing situation would improve significantly.[31] But Levitt's lasting influence makes such reforms difficult at best. Once a solution to a dire housing shortage, the Levitt legacy has boxed us into a new shortage that will be harder to fix.

Notes

PROLOGUE

1. Val Duncan, "Home-Rush Mobs Levitt; 375 Houses Sold," *Newsday*, May 12, 1949.

2. Kenneth T. Jackson, *Crabgrass Frontier: The Suburbanization of the United States* (New York: Oxford University Press, 1985), 232.

3. Quoted in Ron Rosenbaum, "The House That Levitt Built," *Esquire*, December 1983, 382. See also P.M. Hauser and A.J. Jaffe, "The Extent of the Housing Shortage," *Law and Contemporary Problems* 12, no. 1 (Winter 1947): 3–15.

4. For an excellent summary of the literature on housing discrimination against African Americans in the first half of the twentieth century, see David R. Roediger, *Working toward Whiteness: How America's Immigrants Became White* (New York: Basic, 2005), ch. 6. See also Paige Glotzer, *How the Suburbs Were Segregated: Developers and the Business of Exclusionary Housing, 1890–1960* (New York: Columbia University Press, 2020); Richard Rothstein, *The Color of the Law: A Forgotten History of How Our Government Segregated America* (New York: W.W. Norton, 2017); Arnold R. Hirsch, "Less Than *Plessy*: The Inner City, Suburbs, and State-Sanctioned Residential Segregation in the Age of Brown," in *The New Suburban History,* ed. Kevin M. Kruse and Thomas J. Sugrue (Chicago: University of Chicago Press, 2006), 33–56; Sheryll Cashin, *The Failures of Integration: How Race and Class Are Undermining the American Dream* (New York: Public Affairs, 2004).

5. "The Industry Capitalism Forgot," *Fortune*, August 1947, 61–67, 167–70.

6. Michael Grunwald, "Character Emerges in a Uniform Town. Everytown, USA Marks 50th Year with Spirit of Individuality," *Boston Globe,* October 13, 1997.

7. Levittown Historical Society and Museum, Facebook, https://www.facebook.com/Levittown-Historical-Society-And-Museum-1364661420227399.

8. W.D. Wetherell, "The Man Who Loved Levittown," in *The Man Who Loved Levittown* (Pittsburgh: University of Pittsburgh Press, 1985), 5–7. See also Steve Bergsman, *Growing Up Levittown: In a Time of Conformity, Controversy*

and Cultural Crisis (Mesa, AZ: SMB COMM, 2011); Pam Conrad, *Our House: The Stories of Levittown* (New York: Scholastic, 1995).

9. "4,000 Houses per Year," *Architectural Forum*, April 1949, 84; "Long Island: Our Story," special issue, *Newsday*, August 2019.

10. "4,000 Houses," 84.

11. "4,000 Houses"; *Time*, January 31, 1949, 60.

12. "1,500 Mob Levitt, Buy 650 Homes in 4 Hrs.," *Newsday*, August 16, 1949.

13. John D. Allison, "An Analysis of Levittown, New York; with Particular Reference to Demand Satisfaction from Mass-Produced Low-Cost Housing" (PhD diss., New York University School of Business Administration, 1956), 99.

14. Geoffrey Mohan, "Suburban Pioneers," *Newsday*, September 28, 1997, part of the *Newsday* series "Levittown at Fifty." Abrams's story and those chronicled below were collected for Mohan's retrospective. This material would reappear verbatim in the *Newsday* series "Long Island: Our Story" in August 2019.

15. Quoted in Rosalyn Baxandall and Elizabeth Ewen, *Picture Windows: How the Suburbs Happened* (New York: Basic, 2000), 167.

16. Ibid.

17. Quoted in ibid., 135.

18. "Lessons of Leadership: Revolutionizing an Industry, William J. Levitt, the Country's Biggest Homebuilder," *Nation's Business*, February 1967, 55.

19. "Up from the Potato Fields," *Time*, July 3, 1950, 67–72; Richard Lacayo, "William Levitt, Suburban Legend," *Time*, December 7, 1998, 148–52.

20. Ed Brown, "Giants of the 20th Century: The Sultans of Sprawl," *Fortune*, June 21, 1999, 129–30.

21. The last two quotes in the paragraph are from Chad M. Kimmel, "Levittown, Pennsylvania: A Sociological History" (PhD diss., Western Michigan University, 2004), 54.

22. "Levitt's Progress," *Fortune*, October 1952, 156.

23. "Up from the Potato Fields"; Eric Larrabee, "The Six Thousand Houses That Levitt Built," *Harper's*, September 1948, 80.

24. "Levitt's Progress," 155.

25. "4,000 Houses," 84.

26. Baxandall and Ewen, *Picture Windows*, ch. 6.

27. "Levitt's Progress," 155.

28. Ned P. Eichler, *The Merchant Builders* (Cambridge, MA: MIT Press, 1982), 68; "Up from the Potato Fields."

29. "4,000 Houses."

30. Christopher C. Sellers, *Crabgrass Crucible: Suburban Nature and the Rise of Environmentalism in Twentieth-Century America* (Chapel Hill: University of North Carolina Press, 2012), 64.

31. Keeanga-Yamahtta Taylor, *Race for Profit: How Banks and the Real Estate Industry Undermined Black Homeownership* (Chapel Hill, NC: University of North Carolina Press, 2019), 77.

32. Sellers, *Crabgrass Crucible*, 64–65.

33. Quoted in ibid., 64.

34. Quoted in "Rental Policy to Remain Unchanged at Levittown," *Newsday*, June 1, 1949.

35. Quoted in Rachelle Blidner, "Legacy of Exclusion Is Tough to Shed," *Newsday*, November 17, 2019; Bruce Lambert, "At 50, Levittown Contends with Its Legacy of Bias," *New York Times*, December 28, 1997.

36. Julia C. Mead, "Memories of Segregation in Levittown," *New York Times*, May 11, 2003. See the ad for Ronek Park reproduced in Christopher C. Verga, *Civil Rights in Long Island* (Charleston, SC: Arcadia, 2016), 78.

37. Tim Keogh, *In Levittown's Shadow: Poverty in America's Wealthiest Postwar Suburbs* (Chicago: University of Chicago Press, 2023), esp. ch. 3. See also Andrew Wiese, *Places of Their Own: African American Suburbanization in the Twentieth Century* (Chicago: University of Chicago Press, 2004).

38. Quoted in Lambert, "At 50, Levittown Contends with Its Legacy of Bias."

39. Mead, "Memories of Segregation."

40. For these efforts, see Thomas J. Sugrue, *Sweet Land of Liberty: The Forgotten Struggle for Civil Rights in the North* (New York: Random House, 2008).

1 PRELUDE TO LEVITTOWN

1. Biographical information on the Levitts is limited. The best source, from which I drew most of the information below, is Charlie Zehren, "The Dream Builder," *Newsday*, September 28, 1997, part of the *Newsday* series "Levittown at Fifty."

2. "Up from the Potato Fields," 67–71.

3. "An Early Levitt & Sons Tudor," *The Founders of Levitt and Sons Blog*, Thefoundersoflevittandsons.wordpress.com.

4. Zehren, "Dream Builder."

5. Jennifer Fauci, "A Little Bit of Heaven," *Manhasset Press*, May 2, 2019; Levittown Beyond, "Strathmore at Manhasset," Levittownbeyond.com; Strathmore, "About Strathmore," https://strathmore.us/about-strathmore.

6. Fauci, "Little Bit of Heaven"; Boyden Sparkes, "They'll Build Neighborhoods, Not Houses," *Saturday Evening Post*, October 28, 1944, 42–47.

7. Strathmore, "About Strathmore."

8. Quoted in Richard Longstreth, "The Levitts, Mass-Produced Houses, and Community Planning in the Mid-Twentieth Century," in *Second Suburb: Levittown, Pennsylvania*, ed. Dianne Harris (Pittsburgh: University of Pittsburgh Press, 2010), 130. This article provides an excellent overview of the Levitt phenomenon.

9. Longstreth, "The Levitts," 131; Henry Blodget, "For a Reminder of What Inflation Does to Your Money, Check Out the Cost of Living in 1938," *Business Insider*, October 3, 2014.

10. "Promoter Wraps House in Cellophane," *Life*, May 10, 1937, 50.

11. "They Dress Them Up," *Architectural Forum*, November 1934, 383.

12. Baxandall and Ewen, *Picture Windows*, 74–75; Longstreth, "The Levitts," 133.

13. "Industry Capitalism Forgot."

14. A.C. Shire, "The Industrial Organization of Housing: Its Methods and Costs," *Annals of the American Academy of Political and Social Science* 190

(March 1937): 37–49, quoted in Greg Hise, *Magnetic Los Angeles: Planning the Twentieth-Century Metropolis* (Baltimore: Johns Hopkins University Press, 1999), 72–73.

15. "Industry Capitalism Forgot."

16. Hise, *Magnetic Los Angeles,* masterfully documents and examines these prewar discussions and experiments and shows how they bore fruit in California during the war and after 1945.

17. FHA report from 1936, quoted in ibid., 69.

18. Ibid., 83.

19. Jackson, *Crabgrass Frontier,* 193–96.

20. Ibid., 196; Baxandall and Ewen, *Picture Windows,* 56.

21. Eichler, *Merchant Builders,* xvi.

22. Jackson, *Crabgrass Frontier,* 197–98.

23. Ibid., 198.

24. On the role of realtors in tying race to property values, see Glotzer, *How the Suburbs Were Segregated.*

25. Jackson, *Crabgrass Frontier,* 200.

26. Ibid.

27. Ibid., 202.

28. Larrabee, "Six Thousand Houses," 85.

29. Ibid.

30. Rosenbaum, "House That Levitt Built," 385.

31. United States Census Bureau, "Historical Census of Housing Tables: Homeownership," https://www2.census.gov/programs-surveys/decennial/tables/time-series/coh-owner/owner-tab.txt; Federal Reserve Bank of St. Louis, "Homeownership Rate in the United States," https://fred.stlouisfed.org/series/RSAHORUSQ156S.

32. Jackson, *Crabgrass Frontier,* 206.

33. Ibid., 207.

34. Ibid., 202.

35. Hise, *Magnetic Los Angeles,* chs. 4–6.

36. Jackson, *Crabgrass Frontier,* 208.

37. Ibid., 209.

38. Mead, "Memories of Segregation."

39. Wiese, *Places of Their Own,* ch. 8.

40. Rosenbaum, "House That Levitt Built," 382.

41. William Levitt, interview with Stuart Bird, 1993, Mercer Museum.

42. Longstreth, "The Levitts," 136. See also Hise, *Magnetic Los Angeles,* chs. 2, 4, 5, 6; Joe Applegate, "Westchester: Suburb Where LAX Is King," *Los Angeles Times,* July 2, 1989.

43. Longstreth, "The Levitts," 138.

44. "Lessons of Leadership."

45. Ibid.

46. Zehren, "Dream Builder."

47. Barbara M. Kelly, *Expanding the American Dream: Building and Rebuilding Levittown* (Albany, NY: SUNY Press, 1993), 155.

48. Lynne Matarrese, *The History of Levittown, New York* (Levittown, NY: Levittown Historical Society, 1997), 31–33. Matarrese exaggerates the importance of the golden nematode in the origins of Levittown. For a more nuanced view, see, Kelly, *Expanding the American Dream,* 154–55; and Robert F. Keeler, *Newsday: A Candid History of the Respectable Tabloid* (New York: Arbor House William Morrow, 1990), 134–35.

49. Longstreth, "The Levitts," 140; Paul Manton, "The Lost Year of 1946," *The Patch,* March 28, 2012; Paul Manton, interview with author, July 8, 2022. Manton is the president of the Levittown Historical Society.

50. Longstreth, "The Levitts," 140–43.

2 LEVITTOWN, NEW YORK

1. David Behrens, "The New Frontier," in "Long Island: Our Story." Throughout this book, the inflation conversions should be seen as approximate, based as they are on aggregate measures of "how the buying power of the dollar has changed over the years by using the latest Bureau of Labor Statistics (BLS) inflation information provided in the Consumer Price Index (CPI)." See U.S. Inflation Calculator, https://www.usinflationcalculator.com. "Today" means 2024.

2. "4,000 Houses," 88.

3. Allison, "Analysis of Levittown," 24–25.

4. Steve Fraser and Gary Gerstle, eds., *The Rise and Fall of the New Deal Order, 1930–1980* (Princeton: Princeton University Press, 1989); Gary Gerstle, *The Rise and Fall of the Neoliberal Order: America and the World in the Free Market Era* (New York: Oxford University Press, 2022), ch. 1.

5. U.S. Senate, Joint Committee Study and Investigation of Housing, Hearings, 80th Cong., 1st sess., 1947–48. On the McCarthy hearings, see Baxandall and Ewen, *Picture Windows,* ch. 8. See also Richard O. Davies, *Housing Reform during the Truman Administration* (Columbia: University of Missouri Press, 1966).

6. Mary Lou Williamson, ed., *Greenbelt: History of a New Town, 1937–1987* (Norfolk, VA: Donning, 1987).

7. Baxandall and Ewen, *Picture Windows,* 87.

8. "Rush Maps for Levitt Rentals as 6,000 Ask $60 Homes," *Newsday,* May 29, 1947.

9. This discussion of Levitt's vertical integration of the once-dispersed home-building process is drawn from "4,000 Houses."

10. John Thomas Liell, "Levittown: A Study in Community Planning and Development" (PhD diss., Yale University, 1952), 104.

11. Larrabee, "Six Thousand Houses."

12. Frederick Winslow Taylor, *The Principles of Scientific Management* (New York: Harper, 1911); Anson Rabinbach, *The Human Motor: Energy, Fatigue, and the Origins of Modernity* (Berkeley: University of California Press, 1992).

13. Quoted in Keeler, *Newsday,* 133.

14. Quoted in Kimmel, "Levittown, Pennsylvania," 60. Behind the scenes, Bill Levitt was working on local Republican leaders, promising to send his considerable insurance business to agents of their choosing. See Keeler, *Newsday,* 134.

15. On *Newsday*'s effort to support Levitt in changing the building code, see Keeler, *Newsday,* 132–34.

16. Arnold Abrams, "Product of the Times," *Newsday,* October 4, 1987. One veterans' group sent a telegram dated May 26, 1947, to Hempstead officials, exclaiming: "Working people wish to register proxy for Island Trees approval." Levittown Public Library, Local History Collection.

17. Joshua Ruff, "Levittown: The Archetype for Suburban Development," *American History Magazine,* December 2007, https://www.historynet.com/levittown-the-archetype-for-suburban-development/; Tony Insolia, "How Levitt Fought Bid to Kill Levittown: The Levittown Decade," *Newsday,* October 1, 1957.

18. "DA Calls Levitt on DeKoning Tie," *Newsday,* October 10, 1953; Insolia, "How Levitt Fought Bid"; Keogh, *In Levittown's Shadow,* 60–61.

19. "Up from the Potato Fields."

20. Liell, "Levittown: A Study," 108.

21. Levitt & Sons, *The Story of Total Construction* (Lake Success, NY, n.d.).

22. Liell, "Levittown: A Study," 107.

23. "4,000 Houses," 91.

24. Tom Bernard, "New Homes for $60 a Month," *American Magazine,* April 1948, 47; "4,000 Houses," 90.

25. "4,000 Houses," 88.

26. Levitt built eight hundred houses in 1947; 5,200 in 1948; 4,192 in 1949; 4,755 in 1950; and 2,500 in 1951. Figures from the Levittown Historical Society.

27. "4,000 Houses," 90.

28. E. Rachlis and J. E. Marqusee, "The Levitts and Their Towns," in *The Landlords* (New York: Random House, 1963), 237.

29. Quoted in Zehren, "Dream Builder."

30. Quoted in Longstreth, "The Levitts," 142.

31. "Up from the Potato Fields"; *Income of Families and Persons in the United States: 1950,* U.S. Department of Commerce (Washington, DC, March 25, 1952).

32. Liell, "Levittown: A Study," 115.

33. Michele Ingrassia, "The House That Levitt Built," *Newsday,* September 28, 1997; Tim Seeberger, "Frank's Place: Lloyd Wright's Solo Long Island Project Remains at Ease with Itself," *Long Island Press,* September 20, 2017, https://www.longislandpress.com/2017/09/20/franks-place-lloyd-wrights-solo-long-island-project-remains-at-ease-with-itself/; RightPath Windows and Restoration, "Project: 9A Myrtle Avenue (Rebhuhn House)," https://www.rpwindowsandrestoration.com/blog/2018/5/10/project-9a-myrtle-ave.

34. "4,000 Houses," 90.

35. John Normile and Robert M. Jones, "$50,000 Worth of Ideas in a Low-Cost Home," *Better Homes and Gardens,* August 1949. See the diagram on p. 39.

36. Ingrassia, "House That Levitt Built."

37. Ibid.

38. Ibid.

39. Ibid. Like the ad, magazine and newspaper articles commonly assumed the reader was male. "Maybe your wife will develop a phobia about always walking on hard tile," asserted an early article in the *New York Times Magazine.* See

Ralph G. Martin, "Life in the New Suburbia," *New York Times Magazine,* January 15, 1950.

40. "4,000 Houses," 88.

41. Kelly, *Expanding the American Dream,* 103–4; Normile and Jones, "$50,000 Worth of Ideas."

42. Rachlis and Marqusee, "Levitts and Their Towns," 235.

43. "4,000 Houses," 84.

44. Tom Maguire, "Buyers Storm Levitt for 2,500 New Homes," *Newsday,* January 19, 1949.

45. For the social characteristics of early Levittown, see Liell, "Levittown: A Study."

46. Ibid., 112.

47. Allison, "Analysis of Levittown," 13–16.

48. Ibid., 28.

49. Ibid., 28–29.

50. Liell, "Levittown: A Study," 101.

51. Ibid., 29, 81.

52. On garden cities, see Ebenezer Howard, *Garden Cities of To-Morrow* (1898; repr., London: Dodo, 2009); Robert Beevers, *The Garden City Utopia: A Critical Biography of Ebenezer Howard* (London: Palgrave Macmillan, 1988). After World War II, Britain's Labour government addressed its housing shortage in part by building thirty-two "new towns" based on the garden city idea. This was the United Kingdom's public-sector alternative to the U.S. Levittowns. See Guy Ortolano, *Thatcher's Progress: From Social Democracy to Market Liberalism through an English New Town* (Cambridge: Cambridge University Press, 2019).

53. Liell, "Levittown: A Study," ch. 5.

54. Tony Insolia, "Levittown: First 10 Years of a Dream: The Levittown Decade," pt. 1, *Newsday,* September 30, 1957; Allison, "Analysis of Levittown," 108.

55. Allison, "Analysis of Levittown," 152ff.

56. Quoted in ibid., 172.

57. Ibid., 231.

58. Ibid., 216.

59. *Income of Families and Persons in the United States: 1950.* The statistics on Levittown's inhabitants around 1950 come from a large sample collected and analyzed by Liell, "Levittown: A Study."

60. Allison, "Analysis of Levittown," 123.

61. Baxandall and Ewen, *Picture Windows,* 151.

62. Liell, "Levittown: A Study," 217. The age structure would remain roughly the same through the mid-1950s. See Allison, "Analysis of Levittown," 102–4.

63. "4,000 Houses," 85.

64. Lewis Mumford, *The City in History* (New York: Harcourt, Brace, and World, 1961), 486.

65. William Levitt, "What! Live in Levittown?" *Good Housekeeping,* July 1958, 176.

66. John Keats, *The Crack in the Picture Window* (Boston: Houghton Mifflin, 1956), 10.

67. John Keats, "The Crack in the Picture Window," *Esquire*, January 1, 1957, 70–72.

68. "After Hours," *Harper's*, February 1958, 80.

69. "How Individuality Got a Second Chance," *House Beautiful*, February 1956, 96–101, 146–51, 169.

70. *Thousand Lanes: Levittown's Own Magazine*, inaugural issue, November, 1951, 3. There's a collection of issues from the 1950s and 1960s in the Hofstra University Library, Special Collections.

71. Kelly, *Expanding the American Dream*.

72. Suzanne Gleaves, "Levittown Revisited," *New York Herald Tribune*, August 16, 1964.

73. Herbert Gans, *The Levittowners: Ways of Life and Politics in a New Suburban Community* (New York: Pantheon, 1967), showed that most urban neighborhoods were composed of people who belonged to the same racial, ethnic, and religious groups. See also Mollie Keller, "Levittown and the Transformation of the Metropolis" (PhD diss., New York University, 1991), 226.

74. On Levittown's ethnic diversity, see Ruff, "Levittown: The Archetype."

75. Neva R. Deardorff, "The Religio-Cultural Background of New York City's Population," *Milbank Memorial Fund Quarterly* 33, no. 5 (April 1955): 155–56; Liell, "Levittown: A Study," 234–36; Statista, "What Is Your Religious Preference: Protestant, Roman Catholic, Jewish, Another Religion, or No Religion?," https://www.statista.com/statistics/245478/self-described-religious-identification-of-americans/.

76. William M. Dobriner, *Class in Suburbia* (Englewood Cliffs, NJ: Prentice-Hall, 1963), 93–103.

77. For the U.S. African American population, see *We the Americans: Blacks*, U.S. Department of Commerce, Economics and Statistics Administration Bureau of the Census (Washington, DC, September 1993), 4.

78. Gleaves, "Levittown Revisited."

79. "Say Negroes Got Levitt 'No,' " *Newsday*, June 7, 1949.

80. Ibid.

81. Quoted in Mohan, "Levittown through the Years."

82. "NAACP Anti-Bias Plea Rejected by FHA Head," *Atlanta Daily World*, November 10, 1948.

83. "No Grounds for Levitt Probe: DA," *Newsday*, March 8, 1949.

84. "In View of His Good Work," unsigned editorial, *Newsday*, March 12, 1949.

85. Quoted in Daniel Immerwahr, "Shallow Consensus: Political Culture in Levittown, Long Island, 1947–1963" (unpublished manuscript, Columbia University, 2002), Levittown Public Library, Local History Collection, 132.

86. "Charge Rally to Rap Levitt Leases Run by 'Outsiders,' " *Newsday*, April 12, 1949.

87. Quoted in David Kushner, *Levittown: Two Families, One Tycoon, and the Fight for Civil Rights in America's Legendary Suburb* (New York: Walker, 2009), 44.

88. Quoted in Kelly, *Expanding the American Dream*, 164.

89. Kushner, *Levittown*, 45.

90. Mohan, "Levittown through the Years."

91. Liell, "Levittown: A Study," 186.

92. Arnold Abrams, "Goodbye Levittown. The Early Years," *Newsday*, October 4, 1987; Verga, *Civil Rights in Long Island*, 74.

93. "Liberals Quiz Levitt on Racial Bias in Levittown," *Newsday*, February 16, 1952.

94. Martha Biondi, *To Stand and Fight* (Cambridge, MA: Harvard University Press, 2003), 231.

95. Citizens Committee for a Better Levittown, "A Preliminary Report of Your Self Survey," February 1956, Levittown Public Library, Local History Collection.

96. John C. McCullough and Roland T. Moriarty, "Junto's $30,000,000 Deal for Levitt," *Philadelphia Sunday Bulletin*, February 26, 1950.

97. Ibid.; "The Whole Town's Talking: The Junto," *Time*, October 20, 1941, 5.

98. *The Autobiography of Benjamin Franklin* (Cambridge, MA: Harvard Classics, 1909), Kindle Book, location 903; Benjamin Franklin Historical Society, "Junto Club," http://www.benjamin-franklin-history.org/junto-club/.

99. Stan Benjamin, "Junto Has Come a Long Way since Franklin," *Harrisburg Evening News*, March 18, 1954.

100. "Junto's $30,000,000 Deal."

101. "Absentee Landlord Venture Makes $100,000 for Junto," *Philadelphia Evening Bulletin*, October 16, 1951.

102. Junto Corporation, Temple University, Urban Archives (hereafter TUUA).

103. "Junto's $30,000,000 Deal."

104. As reported in "Absentee Landlord Venture," "Not a penny was taken from the Junto treasury."

105. "People," *Architectural Forum*, April 1950, 20; "All Levittown Rental Houses Sold to a School in $26,500,000 Deal," *New York Herald Tribune*, February 26, 1950; "Absentee Landlord Venture." See also Daumant Kusma [member of the Junto board] to Dr. Albert Owens [president of the Junto Corporation], June 20, 1950, Junto Schools, Inc. Minutes, Acc #433, box 2, folder 10, TUUA.

106. Kusma to Owens, June 20, 1950.

107. "Junto, Inc. Minutes of Meeting of Junto, Inc, January 4, 1951," "Junto Schools, Inc. Minutes, Junto Administration Minutes Jan–Feb. 1951," acc 433, box 2, folder 12; George F. Kearney to Phillip Klein, October 25, 1955, Junto, Administration, Correspondence and Minutes, 1950–1956, acc 433, box 2, folder 11, TUUA.

108. "Junto Probed by Government," *Philadelphia Evening Bulletin*, July 16, 1954; " 'Windfall' Gain Denied by Levitt," *Philadelphia Inquirer*, July 16, 1954; "Probe of Junto by US Revealed," *Philadelphia Inquirer*, August 9, 1954; Bernie Bookbinder, "$5,000,000 No 'Windfall': Levitt," *Newsday*, July 16, 1954.

109. Jenni Buhr, "Levittown as a Utopian Community," in *Long Island: The Suburban Experience*, ed. Barbara M. Kelly (Interlaken, NY: Heart of the Lakes, 1990), 72.

110. Kelly, *Expanding the American Dream*, 68–69.

111. Ibid., 69–73.

112. Lizbeth Cohen, *A Consumers' Republic: The Politics of Mass Consumption in Postwar America* (New York: Knopf, 2003), 217–19. For the long history of racial exclusion in housing, see Rothstein, *Color of the Law*.

3 THE LOSS OF INNOCENCE

1. Obituary of Harry A. Kalish, *Philadelphia Inquirer,* May 5, 1999. See also Dilworth Paxson LLP, dilworthlaw.com. See, in addition, Kenneth Warren, *Big Steel, the First Century of the United States Steel Corporation, 1901–2002* (Pittsburgh: University of Pittsburgh Press, 2001); Henry Goldman, "Suburbia—30 Years Later, Levitt's Still Developing," *Philadelphia Inquirer,* November 14, 1982. "32 years ago . . . he [Levitt] received a call from Philadelphia lawyer Harry Kalish, who told him that U.S. Steel was planning to build a $400 million plant in Lower Bucks County."

2. Warren, *Big Steel,* 208–10.

3. Alfred S. Levitt, "A Community Builder Looks at Community Planning," *Journal of the American Institute of Planners* 17, no. 2 (1951): 80–88; Longstreth, "The Levitts," 147–49.

4. Levitt, "Community Builder," 82.

5. Longstreth, "The Levitts," 149.

6. "Sky's the Limit," *American Builder,* March 1952, 125.

7. "New Towns," *Architectural Forum,* November 1951, 95.

8. Quoted in Longstreth, "The Levitts," 161.

9. Kalish obituary.

10. Kimmel, "Levittown, Pennsylvania," 18.

11. Ibid.

12. Interview with Levitt in the film *A City Is Born: Levittown, PA* (Columbia Broadcasting Network, 1954).

13. "Levitt's Progress," 156.

14. Arthur J. Fox, Jr., "Levittown, Pa . . . a City from Scratch," *Engineering News Record,* December 4, 1952, 35.

15. "Levitt's Progress," 156.

16. David R. Vásquez, "Levittown: How It Grew," *Advance of Bucks County,* November 17, 1983; Christopher Sellers, "Suburban Nature, Class, and Environmentalism in Levittown," in Harris, *Second Suburb,* 291; Barry Norman Checkoway, "Suburbanization and Community: Growth and Planning in Postwar Lower Bucks County, Pennsylvania" (PhD diss., University of Pennsylvania, 1977), 167ff.

17. "Labor Violence Hits Levitt in Pa," *Newsday,* May 17, 1952.

18. "New Towns," 138.

19. Kimmel, "Levittown, Pennsylvania," 154.

20. Quoted in Curtis Miner, "Picture Window Paradise," *Pennsylvania Heritage* 28, no. 2 (Spring 2002): 18.

21. See Hasia R. Diner, *Roads Taken: The Great Jewish Migrations to the New World and the Peddlers Who Forged the Way* (New Haven: Yale University Press, 2015).

22. David Diamond, "The Wonder Years," *Delaware Valley,* May 1991, 44.

23. "New Towns," 137.

24. Kimmel, "Levittown, Pennsylvania," 138.

25. For the history of shopping malls and their sociocultural significance, see Cohen, *Consumers' Republic,* pt. 3.

26. Diamond, "Wonder Years," 59.

27. State Museum of Pennsylvania, "Levittown: Building the Suburban Dream," 2002, http://statemuseumpa.org.

28. "New Towns," 142.

29. Quoted in Craig Thompson, "Growing Pains of a Brand New City," *Saturday Evening Post*, August 7, 1954, 72.

30. Charles R. Allen, Jr., "Levittown in Bucks County," *The Nation*, May 31, 1952, 525.

31. Allen Ward, "Levittown, PA: Negroes Not Wanted," *Bucks County Traveler*, June 1954, 11–12.

32. "New Levitt Houses Break All Records," *House and Home*, February 1952, 99.

33. Kimmel, "Levittown, Pennsylvania," 82–83.

34. Diamond, "Wonder Years," 44; "Levitt's Progress," 161.

35. "New Levitt Houses Break All Records," 98.

36. Vásquez, "Levittown: How It Grew"; Thompson, "Growing Pains," 26; "Birth of a City," *Reader's Digest*, December 1952, 74; Diane Harris, " 'The House I Live In': Architecture, Modernism, and Identity in Levittown," in Harris, *Second Suburb*, 210.

37. Chad M. Kimmel, "Revisiting Levittown, Pennsylvania: Changes within a Postwar Planned Community," *Proteus: A Journal of Ideas* 18, no. 2 (Fall 2001): 89.

38. Kimmel, "Levittown, Pennsylvania," 106.

39. Ibid., 88.

40. "Sky's the Limit," 122; Dave Rosenbluth, "And Now Levitt Repeats His LI Housing Miracle," *Newsday*, June 6, 1952.

41. Penn Kimball, " 'Dream Town'—Large Economy Size," *New York Times Magazine*, December 14, 1952, 38.

42. Quoted in Miner, "Picture Window Paradise," 15.

43. Kimball, "Dream Town," 12, 36.

44. Longstreth, "The Levitts," 154–55.

45. "The Big Move," *Ladies' Home Journal*, March 1953, 151.

46. "Biggest New City in the US," *House and Home*, December 1952, 87; Curtis Miner, "The Evolution of 1950s Kitchen Design in Levittown," in Harris, *Second Suburb*, 254ff.

47. Harris, " 'House I Live In,' " 211.

48. Ibid. See for example, Barbara Ehrenreich, *Fear of Falling: The Inner Life of the Middle Class* (New York: Pantheon, 1989).

49. Quoted in Miner, "Evolution of 1950s Kitchen," 256.

50. Ibid., 266–67.

51. "The Fastest Selling Houses in the USA," *House and Home*, August 1953, 128.

52. Quoted in Harris, " 'House I Live In,' " 231.

53. Teddy Pulerwitz, interview with author, December 4, 2023.

54. Sellers, "Suburban Nature," 287–88.

55. Ibid., 295.

56. Ibid., 290.

57. "Levitt Keeps Experimenting with the Expansion Attic," *House and Home*, February 1954, 123.

58. "After 25 Years of Experimenting, Bill Levitt Bets on Two Bargains in Quality for 1955," *House and Home*, November 1954, 136–43; "Sky's the Limit," 124.

59. Miner, "Picture Window Paradise," 19; Harris, " 'House I Live In,' " 204. The population figures are for 1960.

60. David Popenoe, *The Suburban Environment: Sweden and the United States* (Chicago: University of Chicago Press, 1977), 124.

61. Kimmel, "Revisiting Levittown," 90.

62. Miner, "Evolution of the 1950s Kitchen."

63. Harris, " 'House I Live In,' " 237.

64. Checkoway, "Suburbanization and Community," 150.

65. Peter Charapko, interview with author, January 30, 2022. Charapko grew up in Fairless Hills, Pennsylvania.

66. Quoted in Kimmel, "Levittown, Pennsylvania," 28.

67. "Giant Steel Mills Displace Farmers," *New York Times*, January 31, 1951.

68. Marvin Bressler and Charles Westoff, "Leadership and Social Change: The Reactions of a Special Group to Industrialization and Population Influx," *Social Forces* 22 (March 1954): 237; Kimmel, "Levittown, Pennsylvania," 28.

69. Quoted in David Halberstam, *The Fifties* (New York: Open Road, 1993), 132.

70. Bressler and Westoff, "Leadership," 239.

71. "Steel Boom on the Delaware," *U.S. News and World Report*, February 29, 1952, 26.

72. Checkoway, "Suburbanization and Community," 158.

73. Ibid., 158–59.

74. Ibid., 159ff.

75. Historic Fallsington, http://www.historicfallsington.org.

76. Checkoway, "Suburbanization and Community," 177–78; Marie Jahoda, *Community Influences on Psychological Health—An Exploratory Study* (unpublished study, New York University Research Center for Human Relations and U.S. Public Health Service, 1955).

77. Jack Rosen, "Five Years Later: Report on Levittown," *Bucks County Traveler,* June 1957.

78. Ellen Karask, "Levittown: After 20 Years Has the 'Dream Community' Test Succeeded?," *Philadelphia Inquirer*, July 2, 1972.

79. Herbert Gans, introduction to *Levittowners*.

80. Karask, "After 20 Years."

81. "The Levittowners Outlast Their Critics," *Philadelphia Inquirer,* June 26, 1977.

82. Popenoe, *Suburban Environment*, ch. 6.

83. Ibid., 155.

84. Ibid., 152–55.

85. Ibid., 158–63.

86. "Children of Levittown," *Philadelphia Inquirer*, December 12, 1982.

87. Ibid.; Roediger, *Working toward Whiteness*, 163–66; Thomas Lee Philpott, *The Slum and the Ghetto: Immigrants, Blacks, and Reformers in Chicago, 1880–1930* (New York: Wadsworth, 1991); John Logan, *The Ethnic Neighborhood, 1920–1970* (working paper, Russel Sage Foundation, 1995).

88. From a Facebook page, I gathered the names of people who had grown up in the 1950s and 1960s, Levittown's heyday.

89. Peter Fritzsche, "Epilogue: The Suburbs of Desire," in Harris, *Second Suburb*, 362.

90. George Strachan, interview with author, January 28, 2021.

91. Gary J. Gray, *A Levittown Legacy: 1960 Little League Baseball World Champions* (Lemont, PA: Mount Nittany, 2019).

92. Andrea Eisenberg, interview with author, February 23, 2022.

93. Dennis Bauer, interview with author, July 16, 2020.

94. Quoted in Dale Russakoff, "The American Dream: Fired Up and Melted Down," *Washington Post*, April 12, 1992. U.S. Steel recorded parts of Fairless's speech in its company-produced film, "Levittown's New Neighbor" (1953).

95. Ibid.

96. Warren, *Big Steel*, 245–52.

97. Ibid., 255.

98. Ibid., 326.

99. Quoted in Russakoff, "American Dream." See also Warren, *Big Steel*, 327; "Steelmaking's Decline," *Washington Post*, April 12, 1992.

100. "US Steel Shuts Down Majority of Fairless Works," *Philadelphia Business Journal*, August 14, 2001.

101. Tom Sofield, "Large U.S. Steel Site in Falls Twp. Sold for $160 Million," Levittown Now, December 2020, https://levittownnow.com/2020/12/29/large-u-s-steel-site-in-falls-twp-sold-for-160-million.

102. Quoted in Russakoff, "American Dream."

103. Ibid.

104. David M. Anderson, "Levittown Is Burning! The 1979 Levittown, Pennsylvania, Gas Line Riot and the Decline of the Blue-Collar American Dream," *Labor: Studies in Working-Class History of the Americas* 2, no. 3 (2005): 46–65.

105. "Rioting Follows Protests by Truckers in Levittown, Pa," *New York Times*, June 26, 1979. The *Bucks County Courier Times*, June 24–26, 1979, covered these events extensively.

106. Quoted in Anderson, "Levittown Is Burning!," 48.

107. Ibid., 49.

108. Ibid., 59–62.

109. Bucks County, "Bucks County's Top 50 Employers," https://www.bcedc.com/about-bucks-county/bucks-county-facts/largest-employers.

110. Anita Getz, interview with author, August 18, 2020.

4 THE RACIAL EXPLOSION

1. After being forgotten, ignored, or quickly glossed over for decades, the racial strife accompanying the Myerses' move to Levittown in 1957 has been rediscovered in a series of excellent works. See Kushner, *Levittown: Two Families;* Thomas J. Sugrue, "Jim Crow's Last Stand: The Struggle to Integrate Levittown," in Harris, *Second Suburb*, 175–99; James Wolfinger, " 'The American Dream— For All Americans': Race, Politics, and the Campaign to Desegregate Levittown," *Journal of Urban History* 38, no. 3 (2012): 430–51.

2. Sugrue, "Jim Crow," 176. See also William O'Neill, *American High: The Years of Confidence, 1945–1960* (New York: Free Press, 1986), 12–13; Gwendolyn Wright, *Building the Dream: A Social History of Housing in America* (New York: Pantheon, 1981), 242–43; Anthony Jackson, *A Place Called Home: A History of Low-Cost Housing in Manhattan* (Cambridge, MA: MIT Press, 1976), 244; Wiese, *Places of Their Own*.

3. Wolfinger, "American Dream," 432–33.

4. Ibid., 433.

5. For ample evidence of the NAACP's efforts on housing, see NAACP Papers, General Office File, Housing, Madison Jones, 1955, II-A-313.

6. Sugrue, "Jim Crow," 177.

7. "Memorandum from the National Association for the Advancement of Colored People to the Fund for the Republic's Commission on Race and Housing," September 1, 1955, NAACP Papers, General Office File, Housing, Madison Jones, 1955, II-A-313.

8. Wolfinger, "American Dream," 436.

9. Undated memo, clearly from 1955, NAACP Papers, General Office File, Housing, Madison Jones, 1955, II-A-313. See also "NAACP Sues to Force Sales to Negroes in Levittown," *Philadelphia Bulletin*, December 13, 1955.

10. "Federal Court Dismisses Levitt Discrimination Case," *Defender*, March 16, 1955.

11. "Levittown Case Is Dismissed," *Philadelphia Bulletin*, March 16, 1955.

12. Sugrue, "Jim Crow," uncovered the largely unknown and unheralded Quaker effort.

13. Jane Reinheimer to George Loveless, May 27, 1955, TUUA, NAACP file.

14. Daisy D. Myers, *Sticks 'n Stones: The Myers Family in Levittown* (York, PA: York County Heritage Trust, 2005), 11. This memoir by Daisy Myers, mostly written a few years after their move to Levittown but not published until much later, is an invaluable source of information about her and what she and her husband endured.

15. Ibid., 12–14.

16. Ibid., 15–22.

17. Ibid., 23.

18. Ibid., 24.

19. Lewis Wechsler, *The First Stone: A Memoir of the Racial Integration of Levittown Pennsylvania* (Chicago: Grounds for Growth Press, 2004), 17.

20. Ibid., 12.

21. The next three paragraphs summarize material in ibid., 13–19.

22. Barbara Moffett to Lucy Carner, Paul Blanshard, and Frank Loescher, "Negro Family Moving into Levittown," July 24, 1957, "Phila. Y.M. Race Relations Comm. Projects: The Levittown Crisis, 1957," Friends Historical Library, Swarthmore College. See also Sugrue, "Jim Crow," 183–84.

23. Moffett, "Negro Family Moving into Levittown"; Sugrue, "Jim Crow," 183–84.

24. "First Negro Family Moves into Levittown," *Bristol Daily Courier and Levittown Times*, August 13, 1957.

25. Wechsler, *First Stone*, 4.

26. "5 of 200 Seized at Levittown Home of Negro," *Philadelphia Bulletin,* August 14, 1957.

27. Ibid.

28. "Police Quell 2nd Levittown Crowd," *Philadelphia Inquirer,* August 15, 1957.

29. Sugrue, "Jim Crow," 192, reveals that the AFSC intervened to prevent the neighbors of Levittown's second Black couple, Kenneth and Julia Mosby, from selling their house to a third Black family. The Quakers feared that another sale to African Americans "might touch off panic selling and even start the development of a 'Negro' section."

30. Myers, *Sticks 'n Stones,* 43–44.

31. The following narrative relies on reports in the local paper, the *Bristol Daily Courier,* August 15–22, as well as the *Philadelphia Bulletin* and *Philadelphia Inquirer* for the same dates.

32. Telegram from Bucks County sheriff C. Leroy Murray to Governor George Leader, August 15, 1957, 2:45 p.m., George M. Leader Papers, Pennsylvania State Archives, Subject File 9–0188 box 31, Levittown State Police Action, M-Z, 1957 (folder 2). There is a copy of the telegram at the Mercer Museum, Doylestown, Pennsylvania.

33. Quoted in Myers, *Sticks 'n Stones,* 35.

34. Quoted in ibid.

35. "Jewish Labor Unit Fights for Civil Rights, Liberties," TUUA.

36. Stephen J. Remsen to Emanuel Muravchik, national director, Jewish Labor Committee, August 19, 1957, "Jewish Labor Committee," box 32 (hereafter JLC), TUUA.

37. "Legal Means Sought to Force Negroes to Leave Levittown," *Bristol Daily Courier,* August 16, 1957.

38. Remsen to Muravchik, August 19, 1957, JLC, TUUA.

39. Confidential memorandum from Albert Vorspan to Jules Cohen, national coordinator, National Community Relations Advisory Council [a Jewish Umbrella organization now called the Jewish Council for Public Affairs], JLC, TUUA.

40. Stephen J. Remsen, "All Quiet in Levittown???," September 9, 1957, JLC, TUUA.

41. "Levittown's Shame," *Trenton Evening Times,* August 16, 1957.

42. "Both Factions Urge Peace in Solution," *Bristol Daily Courier and Levittown Times,* August 17, 1957.

43. Myers, *Sticks 'n Stones,* 76.

44. Ibid.

45. Ibid., 46.

46. Quoted in "Integration Troubles Beset Northern Town," *Life,* September 2, 1957, 43.

47. MSC 803, Levittown Collection Publications, Race Relations, box 4, folder 11, Mercer Museum.

48. Quoted in Wolfinger, " 'American Dream,' " 441.

49. Myers, *Sticks 'n Stones,* 95.

50. Wechsler, *First Stone,* 22.

51. Ibid., 60.

52. Ibid., 41.

53. "First Negro Family in Levittown," *Philadelphia Bulletin,* August 19, 1957.

54. "More Meetings Planned on L'town Issue," *Bristol Daily Courier,* August 19, 1957; "Crowd Menaces Levittown Home Despite Troopers," *Philadelphia Inquirer,* August 18, 1957.

55. "More Meetings Planned."

56. Remsen, "All Quiet."

57. *Bristol Daily Courier,* August 20, 1957.

58. "State Troopers Break Up Crowd. Man Held for Disorderly Conduct," *Bristol Daily Courier,* August 20, 1957.

59. Ibid.

60. Ibid.

61. "State Troopers Ban Crowds. Township Policeman Felled," *Bristol Daily Courier,* August 21, 1957.

62. "An Appeal," *Bristol Daily Courier,* August 28, 1957.

63. *Crisis in Levittown,* directed by Dan Dodson (Dynamic Films, 1958).

64. Ibid.

65. Dan Dodson, Myrtle Irene Brown, David H.K. Flagg, and June Sokolov, "Discussion Guide for Dan Dodson's 'Crisis in Levittown' " (self-published, 1958). The guide says, "William Myers is neither a professional nor non-professional block buster. He moved to Levittown because he needed a large home for his family. There is no evidence to support the rumor that the Myers were sponsored by any outside group whatsoever."

66. Albert Vorspan to Jules Cohen, confidential memorandum, August 26, 1957, JLC, TUUA.

67. Ibid.

68. Robert King, interview with author, July 24, 2020.

69. "State Troopers Ban Crowds."

70. Ibid.; "Rock Injures Policeman in Levittown Row," *Philadelphia Bulletin,* August 21, 1957.

71. "State Troopers Ban Crowd."

72. "Quiet Night Prevails in Levittown," *Bristol Daily Courier,* August 22, 1957.

73. Claire Berenson, interview with author, June 27, 2020.

74. "Synagogue Cited for Fight on Bias," *New York Times,* November 21, 1957.

75. "Quiet Night Prevails."

76. "Levittown Purchase Tale Branded False by NAACP," press release, NAACP, August 22, 1957, NAACP Papers, Housing—Pa. Levittown.

77. Dorothy Anderson, "Politicians Leading Campaign to Chase Myers Out of Levittown," *Philadelphia Tribune,* September 7, 1957. "Our informant said Bill Levitt arranged to put up the $15,000 to be offered to Myers to make him move."

78. "Betterment Group Sets Radio Meeting," *Bristol Daily Courier,* August 23, 1957. "Mr. Myers disclosed that Paul R. Beckert, Levittown attorney and assistant district attorney, was the person who had offered him $15,000 for his new home."

79. Myers, *Sticks 'n Stones*, 52.

80. "Betterment Group Sets Radio Meeting."

81. For a catalogue of the various forms of harassment against the Myers family, see *Commonwealth of Pennsylvania v. Eldred Williams, James E. Newell, Howard H. Bentcliffe, Mrs. Agnes Bentcliffe, John R. Bentley, David L. Heller, John Thomas Piechowski, Mrs. John Barbazon*, In the Court of Common Pleas of Bucks County, no. 8, September Term, 1957, Friends Historical Library, Swarthmore College, RG2_800 box 9 PYM Levittown; Wechsler, *First Stone*, 61–68, 88. See also Marvin Bressler, "The Myers' Case: An Instance of Successful Racial Invasion," *Social Problems* 8, no. 2 (Fall 1960): 136; "Racial Ordeal in Levittown," *Look*, August 19, 1958, 86.

82. Myers, *Sticks 'n Stones*, 71.

83. *Pennsylvania v. Williams*; Wechsler, *First Stone*, 61–68, 88.

84. Sugrue, "Jim Crow," 191.

85. Berenson, interview with author.

86. Sugrue, "Jim Crow," 189; Myers, *Sticks 'n Stones*, 60–61.

87. Wechsler, *First Stone*, 84.

88. *Pennsylvania v. Williams*.

89. "Levittown Man Held in Jail on Charges of Printing 'KKK,'" *Bristol Daily Courier*, October 18, 1957; "Court Grants Injunction in Myers," *Bristol Daily Courier*, October 24, 1957; "8 in Levittown Barred from Racial Violence by Court Injunction," *Philadelphia Inquirer*, October 22, 1957; Wechsler, *First Stone*, 108–9.

90. "Bias Defendant Suffers Attack," *Doylestown Daily Intelligencer*, February 1, 1958; "Defendant Collapses in Myers Case," *Bristol Daily Courier*, February 1, 1958; "Mistrial Caused by Heart Attack in Bucks Court," *Philadelphia Inquirer*, February 1, 1958.

91. "Levittown Man Fined in Bias," *Philadelphia Inquirer*, February 27, 1958.

92. "Permanent Ban on Bias Handed to 7 in Levittown," *Philadelphia Inquirer*, August 16, 1958.

93. RGA4/112 box 9, Fair Housing Council. Ser.2, Case Files, Ford-Myers 43 Deepgreen Lane, Levittown (closed 6/16/61), Friends Historical Library, Swarthmore College.

94. "Bucks Jaycees Honor Negro," *Philadelphia Daily News*, January 19, 1965.

95. World Population Review, "Levittown, Pennsylvania, Population 2022," https://worldpopulationreview.com/us-cities/levittown-pa-population.

96. The Little Rock school integration crisis began on September 4, 1957, three weeks after the Myers family took possession of their Levittown house and while the anti-Myers harassment remained intense. When nine African American students were prevented from entering the Little Rock Central High School, the media spotlight shifted from Levittown to Little Rock, and in the wake of other civil rights struggles in the South, the Levittown incident was forgotten. This chapter owes a large debt to Daisy Myers and Lewis Weschler for their gripping personal narratives of this event and also to the three historians, Kushner, Sugrue, and Wolfinger, acknowledged in note 1, who rescued this crucial story from oblivion.

97. Unidentified newspaper clipping in Case Files, Ford-Myers, Friends Historical Library.

98. Myers, *Sticks 'n Stones,* 93.

99. Ibid., 93–94.

100. Ibid., 102.

5 INTEGRATION AND ITS DISCONTENTS

1. John W. Flamer, field secretary, NAACP, to Gloster B. Current, director of branches, January 24, 1955, NAACP Papers, housing discrimination to 1955. Thurgood Marshall, the NAACP chief counsel, and Roy Wilkins, its executive secretary, were copied on this letter. "Levitts Get Tract for Jersey Housing," *New York Times,* January 28, 1955.

2. Quoted in Mark S. Guralnick, "The Experiment," *Philadelphia Magazine,* February 1982, 200.

3. Interview with Sidney W. Bookbinder, March 2, 1981, Willingboro Historical Society Oral History Project (hereafter WHSOHP), conserved in the Willingboro Public Library, Local History Collection (hereafter WPLLHC).

4. Madison S. Jones, NAACP field secretary, to Ulysses S. Wiggins, New Jersey State Conference of Branches, January 28, 1955, NAACP Papers, housing discrimination to 1955; Madison S. Jones to John W. Flamer, February 9, 1955, NAACP Papers, housing discrimination to 1955; "Levitts Get Tract for Jersey Housing."

5. "A Piece of History," *Burlington County Times,* August 14, 2012.

6. The story of the New Jersey Levittown's origins and development follows Gans, *Levittowners,* ch. 1.

7. Interview with J. Cresswell Stuart, March 31, 1983, WHSOHP.

8. "Talk with Cresswell Stuart, December 10, 1958," Herbert J. Gans Papers, Columbia University (hereafter HJGP), box 11, folder 1, series I.1.

9. Gans, *Levittowners,* 5–6.

10. Quoted in ibid., 9.

11. William J. Levitt, letter to the editor, *Business Week,* August 30, 1958, 5.

12. "Celebrating a Rich, Diverse History," *Philadelphia Inquirer,* September 21, 2008.

13. Longstreth, "The Levitts," 171–72.

14. On Neutra, see Thomas Hines, *Richard Neutra and the Search for Modern Architecture* (New York: Oxford University Press, 1982).

15. Longstreth, "The Levitts," 171–72.

16. "Jersey Levittown Split on Restoring Willingboro Name," *New York Times,* October 20, 1963; Bookbinder interview.

17. "Calkins Media Continues Its Expansion," *Burlington County Times,* June 24, 2007. The *Levittown Times* was renamed the *Burlington County Times* in 1961. Calkins also owned the *Doylestown* (PA) *Intelligencer,* which covered news from Levittown, Pennsylvania.

18. Gans, *Levittowners,* 13–14.

19. "Look How Bill Levitt Is Meeting the Changing Market: More House, More Money, More Value," *House and Home,* September 1959, 140.

20. "6 Best Homes for the Money," *American Home,* February 1961, 38.

21. "Bill Levitt's Third Big Town: More Value for Less Money," *House and Home,* August 1958, 80.

22. "Look What Bill Levitt Is Doing Now with His Story-and-a-Half Model," *House and Home,* November 1960, 110–11.

23. Quoted in ibid.

24. "The Planning of Levittown: Talk with William Levitt, June 8, 1959," HJGP, box 11, folder 1.

25. "Talk with Bill Levitt, Jr., and Alex Polett, March 23, 1959," HJGP, box 11, folder 2; Gans, *Levittowners.* For an excellent summary of the book's major findings, see Herbert J. Gans, "An Anatomy of Suburbia," *New Society* 261 (September 28, 1967): 432–31.

26. "Russians Inspect Homes at Levittown, NJ," *Philadelphia Inquirer,* February 24, 1960.

27. "Levitt's Relationship to the Community: Talk with Ira Goldman, August 25, 1959," *Philadelphia Inquirer,* February 24, 1960.

28. "The Planning of Levittown" and "Planning in Levittown: The Public Hearing for the Master Plan, April 7, 1959," *Philadelphia Inquirer,* February 24, 1960.

29. "Third Levittown Gets Underway," *New York Times,* June 6, 1958.

30. Ibid. See also NAACP report, "Levittown, New Jersey," June 24, 1958, JLC-SUB, Levittown, N.J.: Discrimination Case, 1958, folder 15, TUUA.

31. Gans, *Levittowners,* 373.

32. L.1957 c.56: An Act to Amend the "Law Against Discrimination," approved April 16, 1945 (P. L. 1945, c. 169).

33. Interview with Reverend Willie James, April 7, 2005, WHSOHP; Richard J. Vinnacombe, "Integration in the Planned Suburban Community: A Comparison of Levittown, Pennsylvania and Willingboro, New Jersey" (MA thesis, Glassboro State College, 1973), 110–11.

34. State of New Jersey, Department of Education, Division Against Discrimination, June 10, 1958, Harold A. Lett Papers, Charles F. Cummings New Jersey Information Center, Newark Public Library (hereafter Lett Papers).

35. See Todd's credit report in Lett Papers. The report specified that he was a "Negro."

36. Roy Wilkins to Samuel Williams, president, New Jersey State Conference of Branches, NAACP, June 19, 1958, Lett Papers.

37. Press release from Sam Brown, director, New Jersey region, American Jewish Congress, February 5, 1959, TUUA; "Bias Charge Threatens U.S. Aid to Housing in Jersey," *New York Times,* June 21, 1958.

38. Vinnacombe interviewed Lett in 1973. See Vinnacombe, "Integration," 15.

39. Ibid., 114; ACLU New Jersey, "On the Front Lines of Freedom," https://www.aclu-nj.org/en/news/front-lines-freedom-aclu-njs-50th-anniversary; New Jersey Committee Against Discrimination in Housing, minutes of executive board meeting, December 19, 1958, TUUA; James A. Pawley, New Jersey Committee Against Discrimination in Housing, to Steven Remsen, Jewish Labor Committee, October 6, 1958, JLC, TUUA; memo from Steven Remsen, Jewish Labor Committee, June 26, 1958, JLC, TUUA.

40. Press release, National Community Relations Advisory Council, June 6, 1958, NAACP Papers, NAACP Administration, 1956–65. Housing—New Jersey Levittown, 1956–60.

41. Harold Lett, "How Newtown Removed Racial Restrictions: A Factual Case History," Lett Papers, 3. Newtown was the fictional name Lett substituted for Willingboro.

42. 56 N.J. Super. 542 (App. Div. 1959) 153 A.2d 700.

43. "Visit to Levittown, NJ, June 28," HJGP, box 1, folder 11.

44. Gans, introduction to *Levittowners.*

45. "We pick our lot in Levittown, June 30," HJGP, box 1, folder 11.

46. Ibid.

47. Ibid.

48. "The first 3 days in Levittown NJ, Oct 20," HJGP.

49. Ibid.

50. Ibid.

51. Gans lived in Willingboro from 1958 to 1960 and published his book about the community in 1967. The publication process was long in part because his participant observation had been so thorough—too thorough for the sociologist colleagues Gans had asked to read the 1,200-plus-page manuscript, and especially for prospective editors, who made clear that the typescript would have to be dramatically cut. See HJGP, box 8, folder 6. Gans also sent the manuscript to Bill Levitt's son, William, Jr., and to another top Levitt executive, Alexander Polett, both of whom provided detailed comments. See HJGP, box 6, folder 1. As soon as the book was published, Gans faced a defamation suit by Herbert H. Smith, the Willingboro planner involved in the development of the community. Smith alleged that the sociologist had grievously damaged his professional reputation by claiming, falsely, that he was under Levitt's thumb. Gans's publisher, Random House, was also named in the suit, which was eventually dismissed in a summary judgment by a New Jersey court. See HJGP, box 64, folder 1. Four years before beginning the study of Levittown, New Jersey, Gans had proposed to examine life in Levittown, Pennsylvania, and nearby Fairless Hills. The proposal wasn't funded, and the young sociologist dropped the idea. Gans also had trouble securing funding for the Levittown, New Jersey, project, having been turned down for major government grants. He got some support from the University of Pennsylvania. See "A Research Proposal for Studies in the Bucks County New Towns," HJGP, box 5, folders 2 and 3.

52. Gans, *Levittowners,* 372.

53. Ibid., 373.

54. "Talk with Bill Levitt, Jr. and Alex Polett, March 23, 1959," HJGP, box 11, folder 2.

55. Gans, *Levittowners,* 374.

56. "Talk with Mayor Kennedy on Zoning and on Politics, March 25, 1959," HJGP, box 11, folder 2.

57. "Talk with Charles and Loretta Vansciver, January 5, 1959," HJGP, box 11, folder 1.

58. *Levitt Sons v. Div. Against Discrimination,* 56 N.J. Super. 542, 153 A.2d 700 (App. Div. 1959), July 22, 1959.

59. "Committee for Open Occupancy in Levittown, December 10," HJGP, box 1, folder 11.

60. *Levitt & Sons, Inc. v. Division Against Discrimination in State Department of Education,* 31 N.J. 514, 158 A.2d 177 (N.J. 1960), February 9, 1960.

61. "Levitt Appeals Housing Bias Decision," *Philadelphia Inquirer,* February 17, 1960; "Supreme Court Refuses Levitt Plea in Bias Suit," *Philadelphia Inquirer,* June 14, 1960; Gans, *Levittowners,* 374.

62. Lett, "Racial Restrictions," 4.

63. Ibid., 4.

64. Gans, *Levittowners,* 375.

65. Ibid.

66. Ibid., 376; Vinnacombe, "Integration," 123.

67. Gans, *Levittowners,* 376.

68. Ibid., 377; Vinnacombe, "Integration," 130.

69. Ibid.

70. Gans, *Levittowners,* 379.

71. Ibid.

72. J.D. Mullane, "As Willingboro Turns 60, a Look Back at Tumultuous Times," *Burlington County Times,* October 18, 2018.

73. Roy B. Paige, "The Impact of Afro-Americans on Willingboro Once Racial Barriers Were Lifted in 1960," typescript in WPLLHC.

74. Gans, *Levittowners,* 383–84.

75. "Living Together," *Wall Street Journal,* December 28, 1970.

76. Interview with Reverend Willie James, April 7, 2005, WHSOHP.

77. "Living Together."

78. "The Small, Economy Levittown," *Business Week,* June 9, 1962, 62.

79. Quoted in the *Burlington County Times*'s *Accent!,* December 14, 1975, 4.

80. Wikipedia, s.v., "List of Recessions in the United States," https://en.wikipedia.org/wiki/List_of_recessions_in_the_United_States.

81. PMI Properties, "100 Years of Mortgage Interest Rates," https://pmicreativespaces.com/2013/06/24/100-years-of-mortgage-interest-rates/.

82. Gans, *Levittowners,* 22–23; *Income of Families and Persons in the United States: 1960,* U.S. Department of Commerce, Bureau of the Census (Washington, DC, 1962). The inflation calculator is somewhat misleading with respect to housing, since home prices have risen much faster than the overall rate of inflation.

83. Gans, *Levittowners,* 23.

84. See the sales brochures in WPLLHC.

85. *Census of Population, 1970: Per Capital Income, Median Family Money Income, and Low Income Status in 1969 for States, Standard Metropolitan Statistical Areas and Counties: 1970,* U.S. Department of Commerce (Washington, DC, June 1974). For the Willingboro figures, see "W'boro Has 3% on Welfare, Median Income of $13,125," *Burlington County Times,* August 31, 1972.

86. "Living Together."

87. "Celebrating a Rich, Diverse History."

88. Mullane, "As Willingboro Turns 60."

89. "Middle-Class Willingboro Makes Gains in Race Harmony," *Philadelphia Inquirer,* November 10, 1974.

90. Guralnick, "Experiment," 201.

91. Township of Willingboro, "Human Relations Commission Report," September 18, 1972, WPLLHC.

92. Ibid.

93. "Middle-Class Willingboro Makes Gains."

94. "Blacks Find Willingboro Popular with Realty Firms," *Philadelphia Inquirer,* November 10, 1974.

95. John McLaughlin, "Is Willingboro a Camelot?," *Philadelphia Daily News,* November 15, 1976.

96. *Linmark Associates, Inc., et al. v. Township of Willingboro et al. Supreme Court of the United States.* 431 U.S. 85; 97 S. Ct. 1614; 52 L. Ed. 2d 155; 1977 U.S. LEXIS 81, May 2, 1977: 3.

97. Ibid.

98. McLaughlin, "Camelot."

99. "Middle-Class Willingboro Makes Gains."

100. Guralnick, "Experiment," 202.

101. For African American income growth, see National Center for Education Statistics, "Median Family Income," https://nces.ed.gov/pubs98/yi/yi16.pdf. See also "Living Together."

102. *Linmark v. Willingboro.*

103. "Blacks Gain Sway in Two Suburbs," *Philadelphia Inquirer,* November 22, 1993.

104. See Wiese, *Places of Their Own,* 212.

105. "Blacks Gain Sway."

106. Ibid.

107. For statistics on the racial composition of the student body, see "Equality, Not Diversity: Can Largely Segregated Districts Like Willingboro Teach Their Students Well?," *Philadelphia Inquirer,* May 18, 2004. For population figures, see *Census of Population and Housing, New Jersey: 2000,* U.S. Department of Commerce Economics and Statistics Administration U.S. Census Bureau (Washington, DC, May 2003).

108. "Equality, Not Diversity."

109. Ibid.

110. State of New Jersey, "New Jersey High School Proficiency Assessment," https://www.nj.gov/education/assessment/results/njask/njask05/hspa/longitudinal_graphs.pdf.

111. "Equality, Not Diversity."

112. NCHEMS Information Center, "College-Going Rates of High School Graduates," http://www.higheredinfo.org/dbrowser/?year=2004&level=nation&mode=data&state=&submeasure=63.

113. "Equality, Not Diversity."

114. Ibid.

115. Ibid.

116. The next two paragraphs are based on near-daily reports in the *Burlington County Times.* See, for example, Josh Bernstein, "State: Ethics Lapses by W'boro Board," *Burlington County Times,* July 29, 2005.

117. United States Census Bureau, "Median Household Income: 2004," https://www.census.gov/content/dam/Census/library/visualizations/2006/demo/2004-state-county-maps/med-hh-inc2004.pdf; "Equality, Not Diversity."

118. David Rusk, "The 'Segregation Tax': The Cost of Racial Segregation to Black Homeowners" (Brookings Institution, Survey Series, October 2001).

119. Ibid., 8.

120. Ibid., 10. *Census of Population and Housing, New Jersey: 2010,* U.S. Department of Commerce Economics and Statistics Administration U.S. Census Bureau (Washington, DC, 2012).

121. "Small, Economy Levittown."

122. In its annual reports to shareholders—Levitt & Sons had gone public in 1960—the company announced a rapidly rising net income after taxes from $1.389 million in 1963 to $3.983 million four years later. Net income per share rose during this period from $0.46 to $1.28, an increase of nearly 150 percent. The company's sales rose from $39 million in 1963 to $93.6 million in 1967.

6 LEVITTOWN GOES UPSCALE

1. "The Shooting of the Century," *Life,* November 14, 1955.

2. Allison McNearney, "Truman Capote, a Cyanide Pill, and a Shocking High Society Murder," Daily Beast, March 20, 2022, https://www.thedailybeast.com/truman-capote-a-cyanide-pill-and-a-shocking-high-society-murder.

3. Jim O. Neill, Bob Greene, and Stan Brooks, "Grand Jury to Probe Woodward Case," Tony Insolia, "Ann and Father—Strangers since '23," "A Mystery of Contradictions," and "Nab Prowler in Woodward Case," all *Newsday,* November 1, 1955; Milton Bracker, "Wife Kills Woodward, Owner of Nashua," *New York Times,* October 31, 1955. The coverage continued in these and many other papers for several days. See also Truman Capote's short story, "La Côte Basque, 1965," *Esquire,* November 1975. The story was an excerpt from his never-finished book, posthumously published as *Answered Prayers, The Unfinished Novel* (New York: Random House, 1987). Also see Dominick Dunne, *The Two Mrs. Grenvilles* (New York: Crown, 1985). Dunne's book was made into a miniseries for Showtime in 1987 and a Showtime documentary in 2005.

4. "Long Island: Our Story."

5. "Zeckendorf or Levitt," *Business Week,* April 20, 1957, 50–52.

6. Ibid. See also the appellate court briefs in the case: Court of Appeals of Maryland, September Terms, 1957. No. 46. *Webb & Knapp, Inc. v. The Hanover Bank and John W. Ludewig.*

7. See the anonymous "Levitt and Sons," a forty-two-page history of the Belair acquisition and the Levitt development in the Belair Mansion Archives (hereafter BMA).

8. Text of Levitt announcement in BMA.

9. "Zeckendorf or Levitt," 52; "Levitt Project Here Will Cost 100 Million" and "Developer of Belair Is Dynamic Builder," *Washington Sunday Star,* December 6, 1957; "Levitt Moves In and Pastureland Becomes a Town," *Washington Post,* January 28, 1962.

10. "Levitt's Biggest Opening," *Washington Post,* October 15, 1960.

11. "Levitt Sales at Belair Top $20.4 million," *Evening Star,* June 17, 1961.

12. All quotes from James A. Jacobs, "Beyond Levittown: The Design and Marketing of Belair at Bowie, Maryland," in *Housing Washington: Two Centuries of Residential Development and Planning in the National Capital Area,* ed. Richard Longstreth (Chicago: Center for American Places, 2020), 91.

13. Julie Ernstein, "Landscape Archaeology and the Recent Past: A View from Bowie, Maryland," in *Preserving the Past,* vol. 2, ed. Deborah Slaton and William G. Foulks (Washington, DC: National Park Service, 2000), 97–103.

14. Interview with Rize quoted in ibid., 100.

15. Ibid., 101; "Eric Felter and the Obscure Art of Street Naming," *Levitt Life,* January–February 1970, 7, 19.

16. Jacobs, "Beyond Levittown," 88–89.

17. *Evening Star,* September 17, and November 26, 1960.

18. *Evening Star,* January 24, 1961; *Harper's,* February 1960, 42.

19. *Evening Star,* August 11, 1962.

20. *Evening Star,* January 14, 1961; March 16, 1962; November 15, 1963; March 31, 1962; January 21, 1963.

21. *Evening Star,* June 1 and November 22, 1963; September 10, 1961.

22. "Levitt's Biggest Opening"; "John B. Willmann, "Home Builders Can Still Smile Despite National Downturn," *Washington Post,* October 22, 1960; "Value Is Stressed by Levitt," *Philadelphia Inquirer,* October 18, 1960. See also Kruse and Sugrue, *New Suburban History,* 1.

23. "Belair at Bowie" sales brochure, downloaded from the Belair at Bowie Facebook group.

24. Jacobs, "Beyond Levittown," 95.

25. "Levitt Gives Mansion to Bowie for Town Hall," *Washington Post,* July 11, 1964.

26. "6 Best Homes for the Money," *American Home,* February 1962, 17; "Levitt's Maryland House Wins Award," *Philadelphia Inquirer,* July 2, 1961.

27. Unpublished papers written for Professor Richard Longstreth's graduate course, "Historic Preservation: Principles and Methods" (spring 2000), BMA.

28. Quoted in Jacobs, "Beyond Levittown," 98.

29. Zillow, "Bowie, MD, Housing Market," https://www.zillow.com/bowie-md/home-values/.

30. Quoted in Jacobs, "Beyond Levittown," 98.

31. Ibid., 87.

32. "Belair Now Has 5500 Families," *Washington Post,* September 17, 1966. According to the *Washington Post*'s real estate editor, John B. Willmann, buyers had to wait about five months for their home to be built. "Builder Levitt Is Looking for New Worlds in This Area," *Washington Post,* April 11, 1964.

33. Jackson Diehl, "Rise and Fall of Levitt Era," *Washington Post,* October 14, 1978.

34. *Washington Post,* October 22, 1966.

35. *Washington Post,* May 28, 1966, and June 24, 1967.

36. Jacobs, "Beyond Levittown," 98–99.

37. Ibid., 99–100.

38. *Evening Star,* July 27, 1963.

39. Jacobs, "Beyond Levittown," 101–4.

40. Ibid., 105.

41. *Evening Star,* November 22, 1962.

42. Jacobs, "Beyond Levittown," 104–6.

43. Ibid., 108. *American Home,* February 1962. The Belair Country Clubber appears as the magazine's cover photograph.

44. "Levitt and Sons," BMA, 14–15; display ad, *Washington Post,* November 24, 1961.

45. "Bowie Belair, the Old and the New," *Washington Star,* June 14, 1964.

46. Jacobs, "Beyond Levittown," 108–9; Peter Osnos, "It's Smart and Wealthy in Bowie," *Washington Post,* April 24, 1969; "Levitt and Sons," BMA, 19–20; "Trade Board Survey," *Bowie Blade and Post Times,* April 24, 1969.

47. "Levitt and Sons," BMA, 22–23.

48. Jacobs, "Beyond Levittown," 108–9; Osnos, "Smart and Wealthy"; "Levitt and Sons," BMA, 19–20; "Trade Board Survey," *Bowie Blade and Post Times,* April 24, 1969.

49. "Purchase of Belair Tract Spurs View," *Belair News,* July 12, 1962.

50. Levittown Beyond, "Maryland," LevittownBeyond.com; John B. Willmann, "Levitt Projects 4,500 Homes for New Year," *Washington Post,* October 22, 1966.

51. "Townhouses Sold Out," *Washington Post,* July 12, 1969.

52. Helen Dewar, "Levitt Plans Development near Dulles," *Washington Post,* January 23, 1969.

53. "Levitt Project Here"; "Belair Rejects Sale to Negro," *Sunday Star,* June 9, 1963; "Levitts Refuse Home to Negro in Md.," *Newsday,* June 11, 1963. For Levitt's full statement on his whites-only policy, see the *Suburban Times,* June 13, 1963.

54. "Negro Charges Levitts Violate Housing Order," *Evening Star,* December 17, 1962.

55. "Levitts Refuse Home."

56. "Belair to Continue Negro Housing Ban," *Evening Star,* August 14, 1963.

57. *Suburban Times,* June 20 and 27, 1963; "Belair Picks Armstrong Race Issue 'Moderate,' " *Evening Star,* June 21, 1963.

58. "Bowie-Belair, the Old and the New," *Evening Star,* June 14, 1964.

59. Quoted in ibid.

60. *Evening Star,* August 4, 1963.

61. Quoted in Longstreth, "Historic Preservation."

62. Washington Area Spark, "Counter-Demonstrators Say 'Keep 'em White,' " Flickr, https://www.flickr.com/photos/washington_area_spark/15465915151/in/photostream/.

63. "Levitt Office Picketed by Episcopal Ministers," *Evening Star,* August 16, 1963.

64. "Bowie-Belair, the Old and the New."

65. "CORE Balks at Ending Picketing in Belair," *Evening Star,* August 20, 1963; "Injunction Bars Belair Pickets," *Washington Post,* August 18; "8 Pickets Are Jailed at Belair," *Washington Post,* September 15, 1963.

66. "Levitt May Lift Racial Bar Here," *Washington Post*, June 30, 1962. "Levitt Discusses Belair Integration," *Evening Star*, June 30, 1962.

67. Donald L. Hymes, "17 CORE Demonstrators Convicted in 30 Minutes for Sit-Ins at Belair," *Washington Post*, February 14, 1964.

68. Michael Drosnin, "Levitt Vows to Aid Displaced Negroes," *Washington Post*, June 8, 1967.

69. Thomas Grubisich, "Bowie-Belair. Typical Only on the Surface. A Trip Down Knowledge Lane Shows Suburban Sprawl," *Washington Post*, January 1, 1970.

70. Douglas Feaver, "Bowie Church's Problem: Meshing Tradition, Instant Suburbia," *Washington Post*, December 27, 1969.

71. On the African American population of Prince George's County, see Wiese, *Places of Their Own*, 269–84.

72. Aaron Latham, "Proposal to Annex Bowie Village Heavily Favored by Bowie Voters," *Washington Post*, July 14, 1968. On the annexation and the controversy surrounding it, see "Annexation Petition Given to City Council," *Belair News Express*, April 24, 1968; *Prince George's County News*, February 29, May 28, and June 20, 1968; *Bowie Blade*, February 22, 23, and 29, and May 23, 1968.

73. See the full-page Levitt ad in the *Washington Post*, May 4, 1968.

74. *Washington Post*, June 1, 1968, and March 8, 1969. See the various external renderings and floor plans collected in BMA. In the end, only the townhouses were built, as Levitt scaled back its plans in Belair Village following the company's sale to ITT in 1968.

75. *Washington Post*, May 16, 1969.

76. See, for example, *Washington Post*, June 1, 1968, July 28, 1968, and October 18, 1969.

77. This film, *Suburbia USA*, produced and directed by André Carbe (Bavarian Television, 1965), is excerpted in a documentary by Jeff Krulik, *Tales of Belair at Bowie*, which first aired on Maryland PBS on February 20, 2021, https:// video.mpt.tv/video/tales-of-bel-air-at-bowie-yysowm.

78. Jackson Diehl, "Levitt's Firm Surrenders Its County Building License. Cited for 2,500 Building Violations," *Washington Post*, December 15, 1978.

79. Kim Chappell, "Bowie: City Boasts 10th Highest Medium Income in Nation," *Washington Post*, April 1, 1984.

80. Tom Vesey, "The Graying of Bowie," *Washington Post*, January 28, 1982.

81. Bowie State University, "Bowie State University History," https://www. bowiestate.edu/about/history/.

82. Wiese, *Places of Their Own*, 269–72.

83. On the busing battle, see "Busing Foes Jam Meeting at Bowie," *Saint George's Sentinel*, August 19, 1971.

84. On the country's desegregation plan, see Douglas Watson, "Massive Busing of Pupils Mulled," *Washington Post*, July 29, 1971.

85. Thomas Grubisich, "Can Poor Find Life in Bowie?," *Washington Post*, May 18, 1972.

86. Chappell, "Bowie."

87. Demographia, "Change in Median House Value: 1990–2000 Census," http://www.demographia.com/db-statehouse$2000.htm; DQYDJ, "Historical US

Home Prices: Monthly Median from 1953–2024," https://dqydj.com/historical-home-prices/.

88. Jonathan Kaufman, "Where Blacks Have More Than Whites, Racial Tension Erupts," *Wall Street Journal,* February 8, 2001; Tracy A. Reeves, "Anger at Pr. George's Deepens Racial Schism," *Washington Post,* November 6, 2000.

89. Quoted in Wiese, *Places of Their Own,* 276.

90. Reeves, "Anger."

91. Kaufman, "Where Blacks."

92. Wiese, *Places of Their Own,* 272.

93. Census figures cited in Lonnea O'Neal Parker, "For Whites in Prince George's County, a Mirror on Race," *Washington Post,* July 27, 2006.

94. Kaufman, "Where Blacks"; Reeves, "Anger."

95. Kaufman, "Where Blacks."

96. Reeves, "Anger."

97. Ibid.

98. Kaufman, "Where Blacks."

99. Wiese, *Places of Their Own,* 279–81.

100. Reeves, "Anger."

101. Eugene L. Meyer, "The Big Boom in Bowie: Bowie's Roads of Discovery," *Washington Post,* April 21, 1999.

102. Ibid.

103. "Bowie Voters Keep Mayor, Elect First Blacks to Council," *Washington Post,* April 3, 2002.

104. City of Bowie, Maryland, "Community Profile," Department of Planning and Economic Development, August 2013, https://www.cityofbowie.org. See also Statistical Atlas, "Race and Ethnicity in Bowie, Maryland," https://statisticalatlas.com/place/Maryland/Bowie/Race-and-Ethnicity.

105. City of Bowie, "Community Profile." See also United States Census, "Quick Facts: Bowie, Maryland," https://www.census.gov/quickfacts/bowiecity-maryland; Karyn Lacy, *Blue-Chip Black: Race, Class, and Status in the New Black Middle Class* (Berkeley: University of California Press, 2007), 59.

106. City of Bowie, Maryland, "Tim Adams, Mayor, City of Bowie," https://www.cityofbowie.org/2520/Tim-Adams-Mayor.

107. Mike Bargeron, interview with author, August 22, 2023.

108. Two unpublished papers from Longstreth course, "Historic Preservation."

109. Bargeron, interview with author.

7 BILL LEVITT IN PARIS

1. "The Levittown Look Takes on a French Style," *Business Week,* October 23, 1965, 65. See also "Pourquoi Levitt vient-il construire en France," *Entreprise,* March 3, 1966.

2. Benoît Pouvreau, "Des 'maisons nouvelles' pour en finir avec les 'pavillons de banlieue,' " in *Désirs de toit: Le logement entre désir et contrainte depuis la fin du XIXe siècle,* ed. Danièle Voldman (Paris: Éditions Créaphis, 2010), 98.

3. A United Nations study in 1961 showed that France lagged far behind other developed countries in the construction of single-family homes. The United

Kingdom led the way, with single-family homes constituting 78 percent of its dwellings built that year. The United States was a close second at 76 percent, while Belgium registered 70 percent, the Netherlands 56, and West Germany 49. The corresponding percentage for France was just 32. See Norma Evenson, *Paris: A Century of Change, 1878–1978* (New Haven: Yale University Press, 1979), 252.

4. For the original postwar survey in which 72 percent of respondents said they preferred a single-family home, see Catherine Bonvalet et al., *Désirs des français en matière d'habitation urbaine: Une enquête par sondage de 1945* (Paris: INED Éditions/Institut national d'études démographiques, 1947). See also Susanna Magri, "Le pavillon stigmatisé. Grands Ensembles et maisons individuelles dans la sociologie des années 1950 à 1970," *L'année sociologique* 58, no. 8 (2008): 180, 192–93; Nicole Haumont, *Les pavillonnaires: Étude psychosociologique d'un mode d'habitat* (Paris: L'Harmatton, 2001); Kenny Cupers, *The Social Housing Project: Housing Postwar France* (Minneapolis: University of Minnesota Press, 2014), 3.

5. On the influence of Le Corbusier, see Magri, "Pavillon stigmatisé," 180–81. For a perspective that downplays Le Corbusier's influence, see Cupers, *Social Housing,* 41–45. On Le Corbusier, see Jean-Louis Cohen and Tim Benton, *Le Corbusier: Le Grand* (New York: Phaidon, 2008); Cohen, *Le Corbusier* (New York: Taschen, 2015); Antony Flint, *Modern Man: The Life of Le Corbusier, Architect of Tomorrow* (New York: New Harvest, 2014).

6. Magri, "Pavillon stigmatisé," esp. 171–77.

7. The best recent discussion of the French approach to postwar housing is Cupers, *Social Housing.* See also Magri, "Pavillon stigmatisé"; Annie Fourcaut, "Qu'elle était belle la banlieue," *L'histoire* 315 (January–February 2006): 75–83.

8. Herrick Chapman, *France's Long Reconstruction: In Search of the Modern Republic* (Cambridge, MA: Harvard University Press, 2018); Cupers, *Social Housing,* 8.

9. Catherine Bonvalet, preface to the 2018 reprint of *Désirs des français,* 19.

10. Fourcaut, "La banlieue," 77–78; Evenson, *Paris,* 235–36.

11. Bonvalet, preface to *Désirs des français,* 6–7.

12. Fourcaut, "La banlieue," 78; Cupers, *Social Housing,* 102; Evenson, *Paris,* 238.

13. Cupers, *Social Housing,* 20–40.

14. Ibid., 38.

15. Ibid.

16. Fourcaut, "La banlieue," 78–79.

17. Evenson, *Paris,* 241.

18. Quotations in this paragraph in Evenson, *Paris,* 246.

19. Jean Duquesne, quoted in ibid., 247.

20. Christiane Rochefort, *Les petits enfants du siècle* (Children of heaven) (Paris: Grasset, 1961), 101.

21. Ibid., 158.

22. Magri, "Pavillon stagmatisé," 184, 191–97.

23. Municipal archives, Le Mesnil-Saint-Denis (hereafter MA LMSD). These local archives don't have any particular organization, except to make clear that this quotation was reproduced in a series of documents prepared for the fiftieth

anniversary of the town's Levitt-built community, Les Résidences du Château. I'm grateful to town leaders for making these materials available to me.

24. Commune du Mesnil-Saint-Denis, "Avis du maire sur le projet de construction dit 'Les Résidences du Parc' au Mesnil Saint Denis," July 29, 1964, MA LMSD.

25. "Une firme américaine sur le marché français du logement," *Le Monde,* February 15, 1962; "Small Economy," *Business Week,* June 9, 1962, 62–63; *Paris-press-l'intransigeant,* April 18, 1962, clipping in Archives nationales, 19800092/58.

26. "Small Economy," 63.

27. Ibid.

28. "Historique," MA LMSD, elaborately documents the complex proceedings that unfolded between the mid-1950s and early 1960s.

29. Raymond Berrurier to William Levitt, December 22, 1962, MA LMSD.

30. Ibid.

31. Agreement between SAFI and Gretima, June 7, 1963, MA LMSD.

32. There is very little published writing on Levitt's operations in France and his influence on the housing market there. The excellent exception to this silence is Isabelle's Gournay's three articles: "Romance, Prejudice and Levitt's Americanization of the Middle Class House in France," in *National Stereotypes in Perspective: Americans in France, Frenchmen in America,* ed. William L. Chew III (Amsterdam: Éditions Rodopi, 2001), 401–28; "Levitt France et la banlieue à l'américaine: Premier bilan," *Société française d'histoire urbaine* 5 (2002): 167–88; "Levitt en région parisienne," in *Construire dans la diversité: Architecture, contextes et identités,* ed. Daniel Le Couédic and Jean-François Simon (Rennes: Presses universitaires de Rennes, 2005), 99–109.

33. Commune du Mesnil-Saint-Denis, "Avis du maire."

34. Gournay, "Romance, Prejudice," 404.

35. See Raymond Berrurier to Levitt-France, April 24, 1964; Levitt-France to Berrurier, December 17, 1964; and F.M. Javitte and A.H. Neyzi to Berrurier, June 19, 1964, MA LMSD.

36. William Levitt to Raymond Berrurier, March 2, 1965, MA LMSD.

37. Cabinet et services rattachés aux ministres chargés de la Construction puis de l'Équipement: Société Levitt-France, 1966–1974, Archives nationales, 19950343/14.

38. "A Lesson from Levitt," *Time,* December 10, 1965, 108.

39. "Levitt France: U.S. Floor Plans in Gallic Garb," *House and Home,* September 1965, 9.

40. Jean Michel Michenaud, email to author, August 25, 2022. Michenaud worked for Levitt in France for many years and is one of Le Mesnil-Saint-Denis's best local historians.

41. For the number of units, see M. Denechau, Credit foncier de France to Bureau des enquêtes, October 26, 1967, Archives nationales, 19800092/58.

42. On the rapid sales, see Andrew L. Lorant, letter to the editor, *New York Times,* February 10, 1994. Lorant was president of Levitt-France from 1964 to 1975.

43. "U.S. Homes Woo World, Levitt Says," *Philadelphia Inquirer,* January 30, 1966.

44. René Deces, "Témoinages," MA LMSD.

45. The Potiers' move-in made it into the *Washington Post:* "First Levitt-Built Home in France Is Occupied," June 11, 1966. For the ad, see *Le Monde,* June 9, 1966.

46. See, for example, *Le Monde,* May 14 and September 30, 1966.

47. "Commercialisation," MA LMSD.

48. For the features and floorplans of Les Résidences homes, see "Commercialisation," MA LMSD.

49. For the definitive study that both showed the preference for single-family homes and explained it, see Henri Raymond, Nicole Haumont, Marie-Geneviève Dezès, and Antoine Haumont, *L'Habitat Pavillonnaire* (Paris: Institut de sociologie urbaine, Centre de recherche d'urbanisme, 1966). The 82 percent figure is page 1 of the 2001 edition (Paris: L'Harmattan).

50. Ibid.

51. Unnamed *directeur* in the Ministry of Infrastructure to M. Le Neveu, UCIP, November 17, 1966; M. Valette, survey of Les Résidences du Château, September 26, 1967. Both documents in Archives nationales, 19800092/58.

52. "Un ensemble de constructions unifamiliales," *Tuiles et briques* 69 (first trimester 1967): 27–30.

53. "Pourquoi Levitt vient-il construire en France," *Entreprise,* March 3, 1966.

54. "Pavillons de banlieue français. Made in USA," *L'architecture d'aujourd'hui,* March 1965, 21.

55. Franck Arthur, interview with Christian Topalov, 1970, CNRS archives du site Pouchet (CNRS Pouchet). I'm grateful to Christian Topalov for giving me access to this unpublished material. No specific date is indicated on the interview transcripts, but it's clear they were conducted in 1970.

56. Jean-Marc Parisis, *A côté, jamais avec* (Paris: Lattes, 2016), 31. Parisis is a well-known French novelist who grew up in Les Résidences du Château.

57. For details on the financing of home purchases in the 1960s, see Christian Topalov, *Le logement en France: Histoire d'un merchandise impossible* (Paris: Presses de la Fondation nationale des sciences politiques, 1987), ch. 9. See also John L. Hess, "French Home Buyers Pleased by a 'Levittown' Outside Paris," *New York Times,* January 29, 1967; "Levittown Look Takes on a French Style," 69; "Levitt France: Gallic Garb," 9.

58. Hess, "French Home Buyers Pleased."

59. Ibid.; Philippe and Denise, "Témoignage," and Decez, "Témoignage," MA LMSD.

60. "1962–1968. La période Levitt," MA LMSD.

61. For sentiment about fences, see Jean-Charles Depaule, "Les nouveaux villageois," *Constellation,* October 1966, 110.

62. Dorine Viltrouvé and Sophie Rodriguez Vieira, current residents of Le Mesnil-Saint-Denis, interview with author, June 4, 2022.

63. Depaule, "Nouveaux villageois," 111.

64. Ibid.

65. Ibid., 112–13.

66. Gournay, "Levitt France et la banlieue," 171.

67. "Levittown Look Takes on a French Style," 70.

68. "Préfabrication mais diversité," *La maison française,* May 1967, 200.

69. Anne Bossé and Marie Laure Guennoc, *Villagexpo. Un collectif horizontal* (Paris: Creaphis, 2013), 24. This wasn't the first trip to the United States by French housing officials and architects interested in modernizing their home construction industry. Those visits began during the New Deal, when the U.S. government intervened heavily, as we have seen, in the housing market, and continued after the war in connection with the Marshall Plan.

70. Bossé and Guennoc, *Villagexpo,* 20–25.

71. There were exceptions to this rule. During the first decade after World War II, the French government undertook several experimental efforts to build relatively comfortable, and affordable, single-family homes. Perhaps the most successful was a development at Noisy-le-Sec on the outskirts of Paris. But only a few dozen homes were built there, and the effort wasn't repeated elsewhere. French housing officials were fully aware of Levittown, New York, having visited the development in 1951 and underlining its success in creating affordable housing. One private company, Maisons Phénix, drew inspiration from Levitt, but it relied on factory prefabrication and couldn't match the American homebuilder's cost-effectiveness and scale of building. Maisons Phénix did, however, construct a substantial number of single-family homes, though mostly as individual projects rather than Levitt-style communities. The company would remain one of the largest homebuilding firms in France. See Nicole C. Rudolph, *At Home in Postwar France: Modern Mass Housing and the Right to Comfort* (New York: Berghahn, 2015); Monique Eleb and Lionel Engrand, *La maison des français: Discours, imaginaires, Modèles (1918–1970)* (Brussels: Éditions Mardaga, 2020), 185.

72. "Visite au village du meilleur et du pire," *Les bois d'aujourd'hui,* December 1966, 26.

73. Ibid., 25.

74. See the photograph in ibid., 27.

75. Quoted in Gournay, "Romance, Prejudice," 415.

76. Voldman, *Désirs de toit,* 112–13.

77. Rudolph, *At Home,* 193.

78. Pierre Parat and Ch. H. Arguiliere, "L'individuel, rêve, tendances, cauchmar," *L'architecture d'aujourd'hui,* February–March, 1968, 8, 10.

79. Interview with Christian Topalov, CNRS Pouchet.

80. Voldman, *Désirs de toit,* 115.

81. Andrew Lorant, interview with Christian Topalov, CNRS Pouchet.

82. Cabinet et services rattachés aux ministres chargés de la Construction puis de l'Équipement: Société Levitt-France, 1966–1974, Archives nationales, 19950343/14.

83. Lorant, interview with Topalov.

84. MM. Duthion and Laffon to the Chef de la délégation du trésor, ministère de l'économie et des finances, Mission de contrôle des prêts à la construction, June 2, 1969, Archives nationales, 19950343/14.

85. Ibid.

86. Élodie Bitsindou, "Les périurbains d'Auvergne-Rhône-Alpes au prisme des nouveaux villages pavillonnaires. Méthodologie pour une analyse des lotissements concertés," *Les carnets de l'inventaire. Études sur le patrimoine culturel*

en Auvergne-Rhône-Alpes, July 5, 2021, https://inventaire-rra.hypotheses. org/6782. See also Gournay, "Levitt en région Parisienne," 101.

87. Jean-Yves Chailleux, preface to *Impact économique et financier pour les communes d'accueil des operations de logements individuels* (Paris: Direction régionale de l'équipement, 1981).

88. Topalov, *Logement en France,* ch. 9; Sabine Effosse, *L'invention du logement aidé en France: L'immobilier au temps des Trente Glorieuses* (Histoire économique et financière de la France) (Paris: Institut de la gestion publique et du développement économique, 2013), ch. 7, pt. 2.

89. C. Perdriau to Monsieur Vaello, ministère de l'économie et des finances, September 21, 1971, Archives nationales, 19950343/14: Société Levitt-France.

90. Le Parc de Lésigny, "L'opération Levitt à Lésigny," https://www.parcdele signy.com/operation-levitt-lesigny.

91. For a thorough description of the Parc de Lésigny community and its construction, see "Un grand chantier de maisons," *Tuiles et briques* 77 (first trimester 1969): 64–67.

92. Duthion and Laffon to the Chef de la délégation du trésor, June 2, 1969.

93. "Teste visite Nouveau Village: Le Parc de Lésigny," *L'immobilier* 83 (January 1969): 19–21.

94. "18,000 Frenchmen Can't Be Wrong: 'Levitt—C'est Magnifique,' " *House and Home,* December 1967, 5.

95. See, for example, the ads in *Le Monde,* February 28, 1970, and April 3, 1971.

96. Magri, "Pavillon stigmatisé"; Raymond et al., *Habitat Pavillonnaire,* 48–52, conclusion.

97. "Appropriation" was the term used by the Marxist philosopher Henri Lefebvre, who wrote the preface for *L'Habitat Pavillonnaire.* See the English translation of the preface in Henri Lefebvre, *Key Writings* (London: Bloomsbury Academic, 2017), 147–49.

98. Raymond et al., *Habitat Pavillonnaire,* 80–83.

99. Ibid., 75–77.

100. Raymond et al., *Habitat Pavillonnaire,* 86.

101. Albin Chalandon, Présentation du concours pour la promotion de maisons individuelles, March 31, 1969; Concours de la maison individuelle, résultats, Archives nationales, 19840342/329–330.

102. Voldman, *Désirs de toit,* 117.

103. Ibid.

104. Ibid., 118–22.

105. Bonvalet, preface to *Désirs des français,* 13–14.

106. For the history of the Levitt developments at Mennecy, see Monique Roussel, "Les marges de l'urbanisation: Forms et processus de périurbanisation" (doctoral diss., Université de Paris 1 Panthéon Sorbonne, 1987); Roussel, "Mennecy-Levitt ou 'un certain bonheur de vivre,' " *Mennecy et son histoire* 76 (June 2002): 11–34.

107. *Le Monde,* November 7, 1970.

108. *Le Monde,* February 12, June 3, and April 15, 1972.

109. Roussel, "Mennecy-Levitt," 24.

110. Jean-Louis Siran, *Les nouveaux villages: Étude comparative des modes de vie et de sociabilité dans les nouveaux villages et du mode de vie de travailleurs urbains ayant choisi un logement en milieu rural* (Paris: Centre scientifique et technique du bâtiment service sciences humaines, 1978), 36–38, 74, 114. Jean-Sébastien Detrait, interview with author, June 4, 2022.

111. Siran, *Nouveaux villages,* 112.

112. Parisis, *A côté, jamais avec,* 31–33.

113. Siran, *Nouveaux villages,* 75.

114. Arlie Hochschild, *The Second Shift: Working Families and the Revolution at Home* (1989; repr., New York: Viking Penguin, 2021).

115. For the last two paragraphs, see Roussel, "Mennecy-Levitt," 24–32.

116. Ibid., 13–14.

117. Siran, *Nouveaux villages,* 9–12.

118. Roussel, "Mennecy-Levitt," 18.

119. Roger Jacquelin of Levitt-France to the Direction départementale de l'équipement, département of the Essonne, August 3, 1978, Archives départementales de l'Essonne, 1553W 3612; Levitt-France to mayor, Saint-Maurice Montcourrone, November 28, 1979, Archives départementales de l'Essonne.

120. See Société Levitt-France, various "Enquêtes bureaux" from 1975 to 1978, Archives nationales, 19950343:14. See also Pierres & Terres, pierres-et-terres.org, for the Levitt community near Lyon.

121. Fanny Taillandier, *Les états et empires du lotissement grand siècle. Archéologie d'une utopie* (Paris: Presses universitaires de France, 2016), Kindle Book.

122. Ibid., loc. 48.

123. Ibid., loc. 12.

124. Ibid., loc. 74.

125. Ibid., loc. 127.

126. Ibid., loc. 485.

127. Ibid., loc. 849.

128. The homeowners' associations in Lésigny and Mennecy make money by giving advertising agencies, film companies, and video music producers permission to shoot in their developments. In Lésigny alone, twenty-six films and clips have been shot since 2005. See Le Parc de Lésigny, "Quand le parc plaît aux médias," https://www.parcdelesigny.com/medias-parc-lesigny.

129. Thomas Hine, *Populuxe* (New York: Knopf, 1987), 4.

130. "Les résidences du château à 50 ans," MA LMSD.

131. Fanny Taillandier, "Lésigny, c'est l'Amérique!," *Le Monde,* October 17, 2014.

132. *Ma vie en rose* (My life in pink), directed by Alain Berliner (Sony Pictures Classics, 1997).

8 SUBURBIA IN THE TROPICS

1. "How They Sell: Mass Builder Levitt Becomes a Marketer as Buyers Get Choosy," *Wall Street Journal,* December 4, 1964.

2. Guillermo A. Baralt, *Una de Cal y Otra de Arena: Panorama Histórico de la Construcción en Puerto Rico: 1493–2004* (San Juan: La Asociación de

Contratistas Generales de América, 2008), 242ff; Mónica Leonor Cruz Declet, "Del Individualismo al Colectivismo: Reformuler La Vivienda Suburbana Para Revitalizer le Lago de Levittown" (MA thesis, School of Architecture, University of Puerto Rico, 2023), 20. According to Declet, in 1950, 35 percent of Puerto Rican dwellings were substandard.

3. On Muñoz Marín, see Fernando Picó, *Luis Muñoz Marín, Perfiles de su Gobernación, 1948–1964* (San Juan: Fundación Luis Muñoz Marín, 2003). For the governor's preference for single-family housing, see Anibal Sepúlveda Rivera, "Viejos Cañaverales, Cases Nuevas: Muñoz versus le Syndrome Long," in Picó, *Luis Muñoz Marín,* 202. See also "Big Renewal Plan Ordered," *San Juan Star,* October 24, 1963. According to the *Star,* Carlos Alvarado, director of the Urban Renewal and Housing Corp, said, "The Governor stressed that whatever plans are designed to deal with the [housing] problem should follow the long-standing public policy of preparing construction of individual housing units whenever feasible."

4. On Operation Bootstrap and its effects, see César J. Ayala and Rafael Bernabe, *Puerto Rico in the American Century: A History since 1898* (Chapel Hill: University of North Carolina Press, 2007), esp. ch. 9.

5. Aníbel Sepúlveda Rivera, *Puerto Rico Urbano: Atlas Histórico de la Ciudad Puertorriqueña* (San Juan: Carimar, 2004), 4:62.

6. For population and employment figures for San Juan, see Ramón García Santiago, president, Junta de Planificación, to Luis Muñoz Marín, July 6, 1961, archives of the Fundación Luis Muñoz Marín (hereafter FLMM), A 010 3. See also Baralt, *Una de Cal,* 241; Rivera, *Puerto Rico Urbano,* 62.

7. Jorge Duany, "From the *Bohío* to the *Caserío:* Urban Housing Conditions in Puerto Rico," in *Self-Help Housing, the Poor, and the State in the Caribbean,* ed. Robert B. Potter and Dennis Conway (Knoxville: University of Tennessee Press, 1997), 188–216. On the FHA and rents, see the memo from Heriberto Alonso, executive assistant of the governor, n.d., but probably March 1960, FLMM, Oficina del Governador, 011.321 Minutas: Viviendas S.F. 1966, 64, 62, 1960–59. On the shantytown problem, see Carlos Alvarado to the governor's staff, November 6, 1959, ibid. See also Marygrace Tyrrell, "Colonizing Citizens: Housing Puerto Ricans, 1917–1952" (PhD diss., Northwestern University, 2009), 290; El Caño Martín Peña, San Juan, Puerto Rico, https://equitableresilience.mit. edu: "Communities fought to keep their land and stay in their communities, despite government attempts to displace the dense '*arrabales.*' "

8. Rivera, *Puerto Rico Urbano,* 72.

9. Quoted in Rivera, "Viejos Cañaverales," 170. The information on Long comes from this excellent article.

10. Long doubtless drew some inspiration from the Roosevelt Development built in Hato Rey, a former suburb now part of San Juan. See Tyrrell, "Colonizing Citizens," 188–90.

11. Ibid., 172–81, 307.

12. Rivera, *Puerto Rico Urbano,* 70.

13. Puerto Rico was plagued with an especially aggressive termite species. See Tyrrell, "Colonizing Citizens," 276.

14. Ibid., 179.

15. Eddie Lopez, "Bayamón—an Epidemic in Concrete," *Sunday San Juan Star Magazine*, September 29, 1963, 16. All quotes in the paragraph are from this article.

16. Rivera, *Puerto Rico Urbano*, 64–65.

17. On the Foraker Act, see Sam Erman, *Almost Citizens: Puerto Rico, the U.S. Constitution, and Empire* (New York: Cambridge University Press, 2019), esp. chs. 1–3.

18. Quoted in Rivera, *Puerto Rico Urbano*, 55.

19. Rubén Nazario Velasco, "Pan, Casa, Libertad. De la Reforma Agraria a la Especulación Inmobiliaria," in Picó, *Luis Muñoz Marín*, 145–66.

20. Ibid., 152; Rivera, *Puerto Rico Urbano*, 56–57.

21. This discussion follows Velasco, "Pan, Casa, Libertad," 144–64.

22. Ayala and Bernabe, *Puerto Rico*, ch. 9.

23. Ibid. On Puerto Rican migration to New York, see Audrey Celestine, *La fabrique des identités—l'encadrement politique des minorités caribéennes à Paris et New York* (Paris: Karthala, 2018).

24. Alana Cassanova-Burgess, "La Brega in Levittown," NPR podcast, April 20, 2021.

25. "Viviendas a bajo costo," *Diario Las Américas*, November 26, 1958.

26. "Policía protege piquetes que se realizan en Campo Alegre," *Diario Las Américas*, June 26, 1959.

27. Both quotes are from "Levitt to Build 3,000 Houses in Puerto Rico," *Philadelphia Inquirer*, January 28, 1962.

28. "Reunion sobre Programa de Vivienda," September 18, 1962, FLMM, A 011 321; Lopez, "Bayamón."

29. "Levitt in Puerto Rico: Nine Years of Growing," *Levitt Life*, January–March 1972, 8; "Levitt & Sons hace valiosa aportación al progreso de P.R.," *El Mundo*, March 22, 1975, which provides a page-long history of Levitt & Sons in Puerto Rico.

30. Memo by Heriberto Alonso, executive assistant to the governor, May 18, 1962, FLMM, A 011 321.

31. Ramón García Santiago, July 23, 1963, FLMM, A 0103.

32. Mary Kay Linge, *Willie Mays: A Biography* (New York: Greenwood, 2005), 151.

33. Luis Muñoz Marín to William J. Levitt, July 3, 1963, FLMM, Reading File—Gobernador, July and August 1963.

34. "Inauguran Levittown," *URBE* (September 1963): 14, 90–92.

35. "Inauguran Levittown," 14.

36. Oscar B. Teller, "Levittown, P.R., Off to Flying Start," *Philadelphia Inquirer*, September 15, 1963.

37. Already in the 1940s, Muñoz Marín had abandoned the socialist flirtations of his youth to embrace what he hoped would be a reformed capitalism. On Muñoz Marín's politics, see Francisco A. Catalá Oliveras, "Guerra, Dorfman y la Realidad práctica de Muñoz," in Picó, *Luis Muñoz Marín*, 208–27. See also the comments by Jorge Lizardi-Pollock about Puerto Rico and the Cold War in Cassanova-Burgess, "La Brega in Levittown."

38. "Inauguran Levittown," 90, 92; "Dice nuevas Guías planificación servirán de ejemplo a otros países," *El Mundo,* September 14, 1963.

39. "Inauguran Levittown," 92; "A Guide to the Guidelines," *San Juan Sunday Star Magazine,* September 29, 1963.

40. Rivera, *Puerto Rico Urbano,* 70.

41. Teller, "Levittown, P.R."

42. "Levitt Sells 858 Homes in Puerto Rico," *Washington Post,* November 9, 1963. The *Philadelphia Inquirer* reported that Levitt planned to build nine hundred houses in the first year, while the *Washington Post* said the total was 858.

43. Teller, "Levittown, P.R."

44. For the construction methods, see "Levitt Life Interview: Carl Palmisicano," *Levitt Life,* January–March 1972, 7. See also Baralt, *Una de Cal,* 312. I'm grateful to the architectural historian Jorge Lizardi-Pollock, who explained to me how the houses were built.

45. "Levittown de Puerto Rico," *El Mundo,* September 14, 1963.

46. "Levitt Progresses in Puerto Rico," *Washington Post,* August 21, 1965.

47. *Census of Population: 1970,* Puerto Rico, "General Social and Economic Characteristics," Chapter D.

48. Ibid.

49. "Levittown de Puerto Rico."

50. *San Juan Sunday Star Magazine,* September 29, 1963.

51. *El Mundo,* December 14, 1963.

52. *El Mundo,* May 2, 1964, April 24, 1965, and March 26, 1966.

53. *El Mundo,* May 29, 1965.

54. *El Mundo,* November 28, 1964.

55. *El Mundo,* October 31, 1964.

56. "Escuela Elemental John F. Kennedy—Levittown, Puerto Rico," *URBE* 23 (June, July, August 1967): 44–47.

57. Ibid, 47.

58. *El Mundo,* June 26, 1965.

59. "People Make the Difference in Puerto Rico," *Levitt Life,* January–March 1972, 10.

60. "Crean lago artificial en la urb de Levittown," *El Mundo,* May 6, 1966.

61. "Levittown Lakes inaugurado," *La Voz de Levittown,* July 1966.

62. For the floorplans and external renderings, see Levittown Beyond, "Levittown Lakes," http://levittownbeyond.com/LevittownLakes.html.

63. Levittown Lakes advertisement, *El Mundo,* October 8, 1966; "Levitt Opens Puerto Rico Town-within-Town," *Washington Post,* July 16, 1966; "Levittown Lakes inaugurado."

64. "Levittown Lakes inaugurado."

65. The lakefront homes are clearly visible on the Puerto Rican government's taxation map of the area. See Portal Casastro Digital y Productos Cartográficos, https://catastro.crimpr.net/cdprpc/.

66. *El Mundo,* September 24, 1966, September 28, 1968, and March 28, 1970. Prices had gone up in the second year of the development.

67. "Desde Levittown Lakes" and "Modelo tipo Kuluah es favorito de compradores," *La Voz de Levittown,* August 1966; "Levittown Lakes inicia oficialmente ventas," *La Voz de Levittown,* December 1966.

68. *El Mundo,* February 1, 1969.

69. *El Mundo,* March 29, 1969.

70. Merrill Folsom, "Puerto Rico's Two Faces," *New York Times,* January 19, 1964.

71. James Ramos Santiago, director, Office of Economic Development, Tourism, and Culture, Municipality of Toa Baja, interview with author, June 5, 2023.

72. "Help Fight Monolinguality [*sic*]: Free Spanish Classes at Cultural Center," *La Voz de Levittown,* May 1966. In the June issue of *La Voz,* the Lutheran Church announced that because so many Levittown residents were "from the United States," it would hold services in English.

73. Folsom, "Puerto Rico's Two Faces"; Margot Hornblower, "A Political, Cultural Identity Crisis: Puerto Rico and the U.S.," *Washington Post,* June 23, 1981; "Life in Levittown," 1979, Archives of the Bucks County Historical Society.

74. *La Vox de Levittown,* May and June 1968.

75. On the rapid sales, see "La oportunidad llama dos veces," August 5, 1967, and "Vamos para la tercera," January 20, 1968, *El Mundo.* For overall sales, see "Levitt in Puerto Rico," 9.

76. "Levitt Homes se acoge a la ley federal de quiebras," *El Nuevo Día,* May 8, 2015.

77. *El Mundo,* September 7, 1968. "Mucho más que una casa!"

78. Carlos Raú Saavedra, "Funciones del comite de ciudadanos de Levittown," *La Voz de Levittown,* April 1966.

79. "Vecinos exponen," *El Mundo,* February 25, 1969.

80. Levittown Beyond, "Levittown Lakes."

81. "Residentes de 2 urbanizaciones protestan mala condición casas," *El Mundo,* July 7, 1969; "Levitt Sues 20 Families on Picketing," *Washington Post,* July 26, 1969.

82. "Vecinos exponen problema insecuridad en Levittown," *El Mundo,* February 14, 1970.

83. Ibid.

84. John A. Arthur, "Social Change and Crime Rates in Puerto Rico," *International Journal of Offender Therapy and Comparative Criminology* 36, no. 2 (Summer 1992): 108.

85. "San Juan se coloca como la segunda capital con más asesinatos en Latinoamérica," *Primera Hora,* March 8, 2020.

86. Tony Santiago, "Más robos en Levittown," *El Mundo,* September 30, 1970.

87. Santiago, interview with author; Debora Rivera, Levittown real estate agent, interview with author, June 15, 2023.

88. Rivera, interview with author. See also, "Levitt in Puerto Rico"; Paquita Berio, " 'Picolino' se confiesa," *El Reportero,* June 13, 1981; "Con su mirada puesta hacia el futuro de Toja Baja," *El Reportero,* September 14, 1984.

89. "Levittown: Crecimiento desmedido le causa infinidad de problemas," *El Mundo,* June 14, 1977.

90. For the list of the developments built by Levitt & Sons and its successors, the Levitt Corporation and Levitt Homes, see Levittown Beyond, "Levitt & Sons Communities Worldwide," http://levittownbeyond.com/LevittCommunities.html. For the Madrid development, see "Levitt construye urbanización en España," *El Mundo,* April 12, 1975, and the Spanish subsidiary's website, www.levitt.es.

91. "Levittown: Crecimiento desmedido."

92. "La secunda playa más contaminada," *El Reportero*, June 13, 1981.

93. Ibid.

94. Wikipedia, s.v., "List of Puerto Rico Hurricanes," https://en.wikipedia.org/wiki/List_of_Puerto_Rico_hurricanes; Michael Deibert, *When the Sky Fell: Hurricane Maria and the United States in Puerto Rico* (New York: Apollo, 2019).

95. Santiago, interview with author.

96. Ibid. Rubén Pomales Rodriguez, city planner, Office of Planning and Territorial Order, Toa Baja, interview with author, June 5, 2023.

97. Jesús Rodrígues, "Club de natación de Levittown. Esfuerzo de toda una comunidad," *El Mundo*, July 12, 1981.

98. "Es Levittown un Pulpo Para Toa Baja?," *El Reportero*, June 13, 1981; Luis A. Caban, "Rechazan municipalidad para Levittown," *El Mundo*, May 19, 1988.

99. "Coordinan conservación y limpieza de playas locales," *El Mundo*, August 20, 1976.

100. "Campaña de ornato 'verde y amarillo,' " *El Reportero*, November 16, 1985.

101. Paquita Berio, "Toa Baja da la bienvenida al 'boom' del progreso," *El Vocero*, March 7, 1988.

102. "Más robos en Levittown," *El Mundo*, December 30, 1970.

103. Carlos Rubén Rosario, "Lo matan en el mismo local que quería comprar," *El Mundo*, April 22, 1989.

104. Declet, "Del Individualismo," 43.

105. James Ramos Santiago, Debora Rivera, and Amneris Soto, interviews with author, June 15, 2023.

106. United States Census for 1980, 1990, 2000, 2010, and 2020; Macrotrends, "Puerto Rican Unemployment Rate 1960–2024," https://www.macrotrends.net/countries/PRI/puerto-rico/unemployment-rate.

107. Declet, "Del Individualismo," 42.

108. Santiago, interview with author. The podcast Cassanova-Burgess, "La Brega in Levittown," also said 20 percent of Levittown houses have been abandoned by their owners. For various statistics, see the U.S. Census for 2020 and Declet, "Del Individualismo," 37–38, 113–15. In 2020 the U.S. poverty level for a family of four was $26,200. ASPE: Office of the Assistant Secretary for Planning and Evaluation, "2020 Poverty Guidelines," https://aspe.hhs.gov/topics/poverty-economic-mobility/poverty-guidelines/prior-hhs-poverty-guidelines-federal-register-references/2020-poverty-guidelines.

109. Santiago, interview with author.

110. On the slow response by the U.S. federal government, see Declet, "Del Individualismo," 42.

111. Santiago, interview with author.

112. Declet, "Del Individualismo," 41.

113. "Levitt & Sons inicia construcción comunidad 'Las Delicias' en Ponce," *La Voz de Levittown*, May 1969.

114. "Millares de personas asisten a inauguración de 'Las Delicias,' " *La Voz de Levittown*, September–October 1969.

115. "Levitt Life Interview," 7.

116. These observations are based on my trip to Ponce and Las Delicias on June 14, 2023. I spoke with several residents and had a long discussion with a retired high school teacher who was well informed about the history of the community.

9 ON TOP OF THE WORLD

1. "Levitt's Secret Is Change," *Business Week,* July 29, 1967, 47.

2. Ibid., 48–50; "The Small, Economy Levittown," 62–63; "After the Levittowns," *Time,* May 19, 1967, 118.

3. "Levitt Returns to Building Activity in New York Area," *The Levittimes,* June 1961, 1. This is a Levitt & Sons in-house publication conserved in the Bucks County Historical Society's Mercer Museum.

4. Francis Wood, "New Levitt Community Has Settled Look," *Newsday,* October 12, 1964.

5. "Levitt Opens Second LI Project," *Newsday,* June 1, 1966.

6. "Levitt Sets Sales Record," *Newsday,* June 12, 1965.

7. Leroy Adams, "Levitt & Sons: A General Motors in Brick and Nails," *Washington Post,* November 13, 1966.

8. "Levitt Lauded," *Washington Post,* December 24, 1966. The *Post*'s story reported the *Practical Builder* Award.

9. "Appetite for More," *Time,* August 4, 1967, 74–75.

10. "After the Levittowns," 118; Dennis Duggan, "Biting into a $70 Apple," *Newsday,* November 25, 1969.

11. "Medical Center to Buy Levitt's Headquarters," *Newsday,* December 30, 1976.

12. Zehren, "Dream Builder."

13. Beginning in the late 1960s, photographs of Levitt appeared regularly in the society pages of the *New York Post* and other newspapers.

14. Ibid.

15. See the analysis of Levitt & Sons prepared by Lazard Frères, the investment bank representing Levitt in its efforts to find a buyer for the firm, in "Investigation of Conglomerate Corporations," hearings before the antitrust subcommittee of the Committee on the Judiciary, House of Representatives, 91st Congress, on International Telephone & Telegraph Corporation, November 20, 21, 26, and December 3, 1969, Serial No. 91–23, Part 3 (hereafter ITTAH), 800. These hearings provide an extraordinarily rich and detailed account of ITT's acquisition of Levitt & Sons, a deal brokered by Felix Rohatyn, a key partner at Lazard. Rohatyn would soon become famous, and reviled, for restructuring New York City's finances in the face of a potential bankruptcy. See Felix G. Rohatyn, *Dealings: A Political and Financial Life* (New York: Simon and Schuster, 2010); Felix Rohatyn and Hélène Demazure, *Un banquier dans le siècle: L'homme qui a sauvé New York de la faillite* (Paris: Saint Simon, 2011).

16. Felix Rohatyn to André Meyer, February 1, 1966, ITTAH, 774.

17. On Rohatyn and New York's fiscal crisis, see Kim Phillips-Fein, *Fear City: New York's Fiscal Crisis and the Rise of Austerity Politics* (New York: Metropolitan, 2017).

18. ITTAH, 237.

19. Andrei Shleifer and Robert W. Vishny, "Takeovers in the '60s and the '80s: Evidence and Implications," *Strategic Management Journal* 12 (Winter 1991): 51.

20. "Appetite for More," 74–75.

21. Rohatyn to Meyer, February 1, 1966, 774.

22. Ibid.

23. Ibid.

24. "Appetite for More," 74–75.

25. See Rohatyn's testimony in ITTAH, 207ff; Rohatyn, *Dealings*, 37.

26. Rohatyn to Meyer, February 1, 1966, ITTAH, 801.

27. "Levitt and Sons, Incorporated," Lazard's analysis of the company, March 9, 1966, 25–27, ITTAH, 803–4.

28. Felix Rohatyn to William Levitt, March 18, 1966, ITTAH, 805.

29. "I.T.T.—Levitt and Sons, Inc. Merger," May 10, 1966, ITTAH, 808ff.

30. Ibid., 813–15.

31. Robert Sobel, *The Rise and Fall of the Conglomerate Kings* (New York: Basic, 1999); Brett Cole, *M&A Titans: The Pioneers Who Shaped Wall Street's Mergers and Acquisitions Industry* (New York: Wiley, 2008).

32. ITTAH, 839–42.

33. Donald A. Petrie to Felix C. Rohatyn, January 10, 1967, ITTAH, 858–59.

34. Felix Rohatyn to André Meyer, February 28, 1967, ITTAH, 860–62.

35. Felix Rohatyn to Hon. Emanuel Celler, chairman, Committee on the Judiciary, House of Representatives, January 14, 1970, ITTAH, 877.

36. "ITT to Acquire Levitt; Its ABC Merger Is Stalled," *Wall Street Journal,* July 24, 1967.

37. Ibid. See also "ITT and Levitt and Sons, Inc. Agree on Acquisition Terms," ITTAH, 873.

38. This was actually the second FCC vote, the first of which had approved the transaction six months earlier. The Justice Department, however, forced the FCC to reopen the case, hence the second vote. On the ITT-ABC merger, see David Wayne Piehl, "The ABC-ITT Merger Case: An Analysis of the Arguments Presented by the Participants" (PhD diss., Northwestern University, 1977), 343; James Ridgeway, "The Voice of ITT," *New Republic,* July 8, 1967, https://newrepublic.com/article/90833/the-voice-itt.

39. Joel Carr to Lazard Frères and Co., February 12, 1968; Lazard to Wertheim & Co., February 14, 1968, ITTAH, 875–76.

40. Ibid., 879.

41. Quoted in "Levitt's Secret Is Change," *Business Week,* July 29, 1967, 47.

42. Quoted in "Changes Set by Levitt," *Washington Post,* March 2, 1968.

43. Ibid.

44. Internal Revenue Service to Levitt and Sons, Inc., January 19, 1968, ITTAH, 1363.

45. Quoted in "How Levitt Lives with a Conglomerate," *Business Week,* December 26, 1970, 52.

46. Zehren, "Dream Builder."

47. For Simone's changing story, see Robert Mc.G Thomas, Jr., "To Simone Levitt, Posh Home Isn't Everything," *New York Times,* December 6, 1970; Rich

Cohen, "La Belle Simone," *New York,* November 8, 2013, https://nymag.com/news/features/simone-levitt-2013-11/. When Thomas interviewed her, she was living in Levitt's huge Mill Neck mini-Versailles. When Cohen began meeting with her, she was eighty-four and living in a rented one-bedroom in Manhattan.

48. On the Levitt mansion, see Thomas, "To Simone Levitt"; Doris Herzig, "When Levitt Builds for Himself," *Newsday,* June 1, 1970; Linda Saslow, "Former Levitt Estate Is a Showcase," *New York Times,* May 29, 1988.

49. Quoted in Herzig, "When Levitt Builds."

50. Ibid.

51. Eugenia Sheppard, *New York Post,* June 8, 1972.

52. Eugenia Sheppard, *New York Post,* April 2, 1971.

53. Among the many press stories on the new Levitt yacht, see Rita Reif, "A Little Levittown Rivaling the Taj Mahal—and She Floats," *New York Times,* July 19, 1972; Eugenia Sheppard, "On Land or Sea," *New York Post,* July 14, 1972; Rhoda Amon, "The Yacht That Levittown Built," *Newsday,* July 15, 1972.

54. Quoted in Reif, "Little Levittown."

55. Quoted in Amon, "Yacht That Levittown Built."

56. Quoted in Sheppard, "On Land or Sea."

57. Ibid.

58. Harriet Van Horne, "Let Them Eat Yachts," *New York Post,* July 17, 1972.

59. During the 1972 presidential campaign, Levitt made a significant enough contribution to the Nixon reelection effort as to warrant a "Dear Bill" thank-you note from the president. See Richard Nixon to William J. Levitt, November 30, 1972, in the Hofstra University Library's Special Collections Department, Levitt, William J., 1907–1994, and Levitt, Simone Korchin, 1935–. Scrapbook, 1970–1973.

60. *Australian Post,* October 19, 1972. The French clip is undated but clearly from the fall of 1972. Levitt and Korchin Scrapbook.

61. Quoted in Mark Seal, "The Good Life Aquatic," *Vanity Fair,* May 2004, https://archive.vanityfair.com/article/2005/5/the-good-life-aquatic.

62. Eugenia Sheppard, *New York Post,* September 8, 1972.

63. Hofstra Scrapbook.

64. "Lady Bird Johnson Looks in on London," *Daily Mail,* July 11, 1973.

65. Eugenia Sheppard, "It Happened in Monaco," *New York Post,* August 23, 1973.

66. Charles van Rensselare, "Why Didn't He Paint Me with My Dog?," *Palm Beach Post-Times,* February 25, 1973. "Serving pasta to the rich and famous," quote from "After 55 Years, Nando's Will Call It Quits," *South Florida Business Journal,* January 5, 1998.

67. "To Club Members' Relief, Luncheons Have Nothing to Do with Charity," *New York Times,* October 8, 1972.

68. Dorothy McCardle, "Golda Meir: 'We Are Not Alone,' " *Washington Post,* March 2, 1973.

69. Eugenia Sheppard's column, *New York Post,* August 16, 1973. Sheppard's piece featured a large photograph of Simone and Bill Levitt.

70. "The three are old friends": Eugenia Sheppard, *New York Post,* August 15, 1973. See also Prime Minister Golda Meir to William J. Levitt, December 14,

1970, in Hofstra Scrapbook. The letter was addressed, "Dear Bill" and signed, "Love to Simone and to you, Golda."

71. For coverage of this event, see Terrance Smith, "Celebrities Enliven a Three-Day Party, 'Salute to Israel,' " *New York Times,* August 14, 1973; Sheppard, *New York Post,* August 15–16, 1973.

72. Smith, "Celebrities Enliven."

73. Ibid.

74. Ibid.

75. Louis George, "The Oriental Slant," *Palm Beach Life,* February 1972.

76. PR Newswire, "Appeal of Conscience Honors . . ." https://www.prnews wire.com/news-releases/appeal-of-conscience-foundation-honors-italian-prime-minister-mario-draghi-with-2022-world-statesman-award-and-robert-kraft-founder-chairman-and-ceo-of-the-kraft-group-and-jean-paul-agon-chairman-of-the-loreal-group-with-appe-301627683.html. The 2022 awardees were Robert Kraft, the billionaire owner of the New England Patriots, and Jean-Paul Agon, chairman of the L'Oréal Group. On Levitt's award, see Eugenia Sheppard, *New York Post,* December 13, 1973.

77. Eugenia Shepard, *New York Post,* May 10, 1974.

78. Eugenia Sheppard, *New York Post,* May 11, 1973.

79. Eugenia Sheppard, *New York Post,* November 21, 1974.

80. Cohen, "Belle Simone."

81. Eugenia Sheppard, *New York Post,* November 30, 1973.

82. "The Liveliest White House," *Washington Star-News,* October 21, 1973.

83. Michael Alexander, "Gem Verdict for Levitts," *Newsday,* November 25, 1977; Tom Demoretcky, "Levitt Loses Theft Award," *Newsday,* July 10, 1979.

84. Jane Perles, "Those Weren't Peanuts at Democrats' Party," *New York Post,* September 1, 1976.

85. Cohen, "Belle Simone."

10 THE FALL

1. Quoted in "Changes Set by Levitt," *Washington Post,* March 2, 1968.

2. The salary figure is listed in the opinion in the case *Levitt Corporation v. William J. Levitt by Chief Judge Irving R. Kaufman of the United States Court of Appeals for the Second Circuit,* February 22, 1979.

3. "Housing Enters the Era of the Superbuilder," *Business Week,* December 26, 1970, 51.

4. "Levitt Is Moving into Apartments," *Washington Post,* September 6, 1969.

5. See the full-page ads in the *Washington Post,* October 15, 1970, March 23, 1971, and June 29, 1971.

6. "Levitt Firm to Produce Mobile Homes," *Washington Post,* December 12, 1970. On the one hundred thousand acres, see Robert Reno, "ITT Settlement: What Was Not Said," *Newsday,* April 6, 1972.

7. "Sales High at Palm Coast," *Washington Post,* June 5, 1971.

8. "Housing Enters," 52.

9. Scott R. Schmedel, "ITT Finds It Difficult to Earn Top Dollar in Divestiture Program," *Wall Street Journal,* January 8, 1974.

10. "Housing Enters," 52.

11. "How Would You Like the Business Back?," *Business Week*, November 3, 1973, 58.

12. Quoted in Howard Schneider, "An Ageing Levitt Is Hardly Retiring," *Newsday*, December 20, 1975.

13. Quoted in Jackson Diehl, "The Rise and Fall of Levitt Era," *Washington Post*, October 14, 1978.

14. Ibid.

15. Schneider, "Ageing Levitt."

16. Schmedel, "ITT Finds It Difficult." For Levitt's modular homes enterprise, see Levittown Beyond, "Levitt Building Systems," http://levittownbeyond.com/LevittBldgSys.html.

17. Nicholas von Hoffman, "ITT and Its Power," *Washington Post*, July 20, 1970.

18. Anthony Sampson, *The Sovereign State of ITT* (London: Hodder and Stoughton, 1973). See also Robert Sobel, *ITT: The Management of Opportunity* (New York: Times, 1982), 255ff.

19. "Papers Show I.T.T. Urged U.S. to Help Oust Allende," *New York Times*, July 3, 1972.

20. Sobel, *ITT*, ch. 16.

21. Priscilla S. Meyer, "ITT Saga (cont.), Agnew, Connally, Stans Linked to ITT Effort in the Hartford Case," *Wall Street Journal*, March 19, 1973.

22. For a blow-by-blow account of the antitrust developments, see Sobel, *ITT*, chs. 13–16.

23. Schmedel, "ITT Finds It Difficult."

24. Ibid.

25. Ibid.

26. "Levitt & Sons Reduced Its Debt Owed to ITT $14 Million in Quarter," *Wall Street Journal*, February 11, 1976.

27. "Selling What's Left of Levitt," *Business Week*, November 24, 1975, 46–47.

28. "How Would You Like," 58. Levitt told *Business Week* that he was "thinking about" Geneen's offer to sell the company back to him, but was willing to purchase only a small piece of what, under ITT, had become a bloated enterprise. Levitt said that this partial purchase was acceptable to ITT, but when he and ITT representatives went to the Justice Department, which was managing the conglomerate's divestitures, they were told, "We'd like to see the whole thing sold in accordance with the divestiture order." Quoted in Jerry Morgan, "Even Levitt Shuns Levitt & Sons," *Newsday*, October 26, 1974. For ITT's difficulties in selling Levitt and Avis, see "Victor Palmieri Named by Judge to Manage Levitt Unit of ITT," *Wall Street Journal*, January 15, 1975.

29. Eisler, *Merchant Builders*. Eisler, discussed later in this chapter, became Levitt's chief executive in 1975.

30. Joseph R. Daughen and Peter Binzen, *The Wreck of the Penn Central* (Boston: Beard Books Little, Brown, 1999).

31. John D. Williams, "Victor Palmieri Finds a Nugget of Gold in the Ashes of the Penn Central Railroad," *Wall Street Journal*, January 27, 1978.

32. Quoted in ibid.

33. Wayne Barrett, "Behind the Seventies-Era Deals That Made Donald Trump," *Village Voice,* January 22, 1979. This piece is the second in a two-part series of top-notch investigative journalism that places the young Trump in the context of New York City politics, high finance, and the unwinding of several prominent bankruptcies.

34. See the profile of Victor Palmieri in "Palmieri: Real Estate Doctor," *Business Week,* February 3, 1975, 32–34.

35. Ibid.; Williams, "Palmieri Finds."

36. For Starrett's history, see Funding Universe, "Starrett Corporation History," http://www.fundinguniverse.com/company-histories/starrett-corporation-history/.

37. All quotes and information in this paragraph are from Barrett, "Seventies-Era Deals."

38. Charles V. Bagli, "Sale of Brooklyn Housing Complex Would Benefit Trump," *New York Times,* September 6, 2017.

39. Barrett, "Seventies-Era Deals."

40. "Purchase by Hospital," *New York Times,* March 13, 1977.

41. Howard Schneider, "When Levitt Moves, Levitt Will Stay," *Newsday,* December 6, 1975.

42. "Starrett Housing Signs Contract to Buy Levitt," *Wall Street Journal,* February 14, 1978.

43. Barrett, "Seventies-Era Deals." Barrett wrote that Trump refused to disclose his fee for making this deal.

44. Quoted in "William Levitt Says Firm Being Bought Isn't His," *Wall Street Journal,* February 16, 1978.

45. Quoted in Schneider, "Ageing Levitt."

46. Ibid.

47. Macrotrends, "Dow Jones—DIJA—100 Year Historical Chart," https://www.macrotrends.net/1319/dow-jones-100-year-historical-chart.

48. Kimberly Greer, "William J. Levitt: The Empire Crumbles," *Newsday,* February 16, 1986. This piece was one of several in a series on Levitt published in *Newsday* that month. These articles are gems of investigative reporting, and in 1987 they earned Greer the Gerald Loeb award for Distinguished Business and Financial Journalism. See Wikipedia, s.v., "Gerald Loeb Award Winners for Large Newspapers," https://www.wikiwand.com/en/Gerald_Loeb_Award_winners_for_Large_Newspapers; "Levitt's Secret Is Change," *Business Week,* July 29, 1967, 55, also reported that Bill Levitt received seven hundred thousand shares of ITT common stock. The total deal transferred nine hundred thousand shares of ITT common to Levitt & Sons' shareholders. See Glen Padnick, "ITT to Acquire Levitt & Sons Inc.," *Newsday,* July 24, 1967.

49. For stock quotations, see relevant issues of the *New York Times,* 1968–75.

50. Federal Reserve Bank of St. Louis, "Economic Data," Stlouisfed.org/fred2.

51. *Wall Street Journal,* November 14, 1968, November 13, 1969, November 11, 1971, November 9, 1972, December 31, 1974, November 13, 1975.

52. Zehren, "Dream Builder."

53. "Levitt Signs to Acquire Parkway Distributors; Plans Role in Managing," *Wall Street Journal*, December 15, 1971.

54. "Levitt to Form Film Concern," *Wall Street Journal*, May 19, 1971.

55. Kimberly Greer, "He's a Man with Big Ideas," *Newsday*, February 16, 1986.

56. Abraham Rabinovich, "Levitt Has Share in Sinai Oil Hunt," *Newsday*, May 11, 1976; *New York Times*, November 6, 1978; *Newsday*, August 27, 1980.

57. Leonard Sloane, "Levitt Co-Founder, in New Company, to Build Community in Iran," *New York Times*, June 16, 1977; Daniel Kahn, "Levitt to Sell Discount Drug Stores," *Newsday*, April 7, 1978.

58. Jerry Morgan, "Levitt Firm Sees No Threat to Plan," *Newsday*, December 11, 1978.

59. James Carberry, "Starrett Housing Corp. Achievements Upstaged by Insider-Trading Charges," *Wall Street Journal*, April 13, 1978; Encylopedia.com, s.v., "Starrett Corporation," https://www.encyclopedia.com/books/politics-and-business-magazines/starrett-corporation.

60. "Shah's Keen on Levittown," *New York Post*, November 28, 1978.

61. "Levitt Cancels Tehran Project," *New York Post*, December 7, 1979; Greer, "Big Ideas."

62. "Levitt Plans Venezuelan Housing," *New York Times*, November 25, 1981.

63. Macrotrends, "Crude Oil Prices—70 Year Historical Chart," https://www.macrotrends.net/1369/crude-oil-price-history-chart. The price would fall all the way to $30 a barrel in March 1986 and would stay relatively low until 2004.

64. Stanley Reed, "William Levitt, 73, in Business, but Not as 'Levitt,' " *New York Times*, January 25, 1981. See also the narrative history in *Levitt Corporation v. William J. Levitt*, Court of Appeals for the Second Circuit, Appellate Case File 78–7520–78–7606. This huge, nearly three-hundred-page file is housed in the National Archives in Kansas City.

65. *Levitt Corporation v. William J. Levitt*.

66. *Levitt Corporation v. William J. Levitt*, 5, and the original opinion by Judge Pratt, 12.

67. *Levitt Corporation v. William J. Levitt*, 9. The part within single quotes refers to a key precedent.

68. Ibid., 11.

69. Jackson Diehl, "Levitt's Firm Surrenders Its County Building License," *Washington Post*, October 9, 1978; Diehl, "12 P.G. Families Sue Levitt Homes," *Washington Post*, September 7, 1979.

70. Jackson Diehl, "Levitt Project Snarled in Disputes," *Washington Post*, December 15, 1978.

71. Sidney J. Appel to William Levitt, July 22, 1978, in Appellate Case File.

72. Straty Zervados to William Levitt, July 7, 1978, in Appellate Case File.

73. Ibid.

74. Diehl, "Rise and Fall."

75. *New York Post*, October 20, 1978; Appellate Case File.

76. Quoted in Kimberly Greer, "Florida Suburbs, Levittown-Style," *Newsday*, January 12, 1985. See also John B. Willmann, "You Can Call Him Levitt,"

Washington Post, October 27, 1979; Steven A. Morgenstern, "Bill Levitt: Still Building at 73," *New York Times,* February 1, 1981.

77. Quoted in Greer, "Florida Suburbs."

78. Ibid.

79. Ibid. See also Reed, "William Levitt, 73."

80. Quoted in Greer, "Florida Suburbs."

81. "Levitt Pioneers New Concept in Building Towns," *Philadelphia Inquirer,* March 22, 1981.

82. "Levitt Pioneers New Town Concept," *Newsday,* January 12, 1985.

83. Quoted in Kimberly Greer, "The Empire Crumbles: When Levitt's Magic Stopped," *Newsday,* February 17, 1986. Jack Snyder, "Levitt's Fortune Dwindles," *Washington Post,* May 16, 1987, gave the same assessment of Levitt's demise, although in much less detail.

84. Greer, "Empire Crumbles."

85. Ibid.

86. Quoted in ibid.

87. Ibid.

88. Ibid. "The Forbes Four Hundred," *Forbes,* September 13, 1982, 148. Levitt was ranked in the same category, "over $100 million," as several members of the Rockefeller family; William Clay Ford, the grandson of Henry Ford; Katharine Graham, owner of the *Washington Post;* and Joseph A. Albertson, owner of a huge supermarket chain.

89. For ITT's stock price, see *New York Times,* January 8, 1979.

90. Greer, "Empire Crumbles."

91. Snyder, "Levitt's Fortune."

92. Kimberly Greer, "They Banked, and Lost, on Levitt's Good Name," *Newsday,* February 18, 1986.

93. Ibid.

94. Quoted in ibid.

95. Ibid.

96. Greer, "Empire Crumbles."

97. Greer, "They Banked, and Lost."

98. Quoted in ibid.

99. Greer, "Empire Crumbles."

100. Advertisement found in the Mercer Museum, Doylestown, Pennsylvania.

101. Lee A. Daniels, "Levitt Starts $2 Billion Project," *New York Times,* December 12, 1984.

102. Greer, "They Banked, and Lost."

103. Robert Guenther, "Florida Project Tests Whether Levitt Still Has Magic Touch," *Wall Street Journal,* May 8, 1985.

104. Ibid. On the Old Court situation, see also Emily Sachar, "Levitt's Fla. Project Hit by S & L Woes," *Newsday,* May 20, 1985.

105. Sacher, "Levitt's Fla. Project"; Kimberly Greer, "Levitt Loses 7,000 Acres to Debt: Forfeits Land for 26,000-Unit Florida Development," *Newsday,* April 21, 1987.

106. Kimberly Greer, "Levitt Awarded $3.8 Million for Lost Iran Housing Project," *Newsday,* April 29, 1987.

107. For Levitt's response to *Newsday,* see "Levitt Responds to *Newsday* Series" and "Reply from *Newsday* Editor," *Newsday,* March 23, 1986.

108. Armand J. Regateiro, Jr., "Levitt's LI Legacy," *Newsday,* February 25, 1986.

109. Kimberly Greer, "Levitt to Repay Family Charity $11M," *Newsday,* January 23, 1987; Greer, "Levitt Sells Estate: $9.2 M for LI Property Will Go to Repay Debts," *Newsday,* November 20, 1987.

110. Alvin E. Bessent, "Levitt's Legal Tangles Settled," *Newsday,* April 1, 1992.

111. Greer, "Levitt Loses 7,000 Acres," *Newsday,* April 21, 1987.

112. Kimberly Greer, "Court Freezes Levitt Home Sales," *Newsday,* January 21, 1987.

113. Greer, "Levitt Awarded $3.8 Million."

114. Kimberly Greer, "Levitt Campaign Donations Probed," *Newsday,* September 20, 1987.

115. Michael T. Kaufman, "Tough Times for Mr. Levittown," *New York Times,* September 24, 1989.

116. Snyder, "Levitt's Fortune."

117. Shirley E. Pearlman, " 'Truly Destitute': Lawyer: Levitt Lives on Friends' Largesse," *Newsday,* September 19, 1990.

118. Alvin E. Bessent, "No Closings Yet in Levitt Lawsuits," *Newsday,* October 25, 1990.

119. William Levitt, interview with Stuart Bird, 1993.

120. Kimberly Greer, "Levitt at a Loss," *Newsday,* October 4, 1987.

121. "Trump Hails and Slights Developer, and Family Fumes," *New York Times,* July 29, 2017.

122. Sidney C. Shaer and Bob Keeler, "Dream Builder: With His Levitt Houses, He Transformed the Suburbs," *Newsday,* January 30, 1994.

123. "William Levitt: Vision and Courage: The Legacy of a Giant," *Bucks County Courier Times,* February 1, 1994.

124. James Levitt, interview with author, August 12, 2021.

125. David Everitt, "Pivotal Development: The Route to Subdivisions Full of Cookie-Cutter McMansions Began in Levittown," *New York Times,* February 25, 2007.

126. Eric Pace, "William J. Levitt, 86, Pioneer of Suburbs, Dies," *New York Times,* January 29, 1994, for the last two quotes in the paragraph.

127. Joan Kelly, "Town Turns 40: Homecoming for Levitt," *Newsday,* October 11, 1987.

EPILOGUE

1. Joseph Nguyen, "Is There a Correlation between Inflation and Home Prices?," Investopedia, November 22, 2023, https://www.investopedia.com/ask/answers/correlation-inflation-houses.asp.

2. Frazer and Gerstle, *Rise and Fall of the New Deal Order;* Gerstle, *Rise and Fall of the Neoliberal Order.*

3. Black Demographics, "African American Income from Truman to Trump," October 13, 2022, https://blackdemographics.com/data-chart-african-american-income-from-truman-to-trump-1948-2021.

4. Buhr, "Levittown as a Utopian Community." As her title suggests, Burh argues that Levittown was itself a utopian effort.

5. Andrew Dehan, "Average Monthly Mortgage Payment," Bankrate, https://www.bankrate.com/mortgages/average-monthly-mortgage-payment.

6. Peter Miller, "Mortgage Rates Chart," The Mortgage Reports, June 21, 2024, https://themortgagereports.com/61853/30-year-mortgage-rates-chart.

7. Macrotrends, "Florida Population, 1900–2023," https://www.macrotrends.net/global-metrics/states/florida/population.

8. Jared Brey, "How States Are Addressing the High Cost of Housing," *Governing*, Spring 2024, https://www.governing.com/urban/how-states-are-addressing-the-high-cost-of-housing; Daniel McCue and Sophie Huang, "Estimating the National Housing Shortfall," Joint Center for Housing Studies of Harvard University, https://www.jchs.harvard.edu/blog/estimating-national-housing-shortfall.

9. Commune du Mesnil-Saint-Denis, "Avis du maire"; "Logement: Une crise prévisible," *Le Monde,* September 7, 2023.

10. For an excellent study of poverty in Long Island and what has become a sizable suburban underclass, see Keogh, *In Levittown's Shadow.*

11. Ibid.

12. When the village of Tarrytown, New York, where I live, proposed to allow up to two dozen new ADUs a year, residents erupted against the idea, with anti-ADU yard signs sprouting up everywhere. In a public meeting, someone said, "You don't know what kind of people will occupy these units."

13. Town of Hempstead, Building Zone Ordinance, article XV LPRD, Levittown Planned Residence District (LPRD), December 29, 1975.

14. "Town, County Officials: No to ADUs," *Long Island Herald,* February 10, 2022.

15. Town of Hempstead, February 18, 2022.

16. Owen Minott, "Accessory Dwelling Units in California," Bipartisan Policy Center, https://bipartisanpolicy.org/blog/accessory-dwelling-units-adus-in-california/.

17. Terner Center for Housing Innovation, UC Berkeley, "Reaching California's ADU Potential: Progress to Date and the Need to ADU Finance," August 2020, https://ternercenter.berkeley.edu/wp-content/uploads/pdfs/Reaching_Californias_ADU_Potential_2020.pdf.

18. WSHU Public Radio, Long Island News, "Hochul Wants to Build Hundreds of Thousands of Homes near Train Stations," February 6, 2023, https://www.wshu.org/long-island-news/2023-02-06/hochul-wants-to-build-hundreds-of-thousands-of-homes-near-train-stations.

19. Timothy Bolger, "Will Hochul's Affordable Housing Plan Turn Long Island into the Sixth Borough?," *Long Island Press,* January 19, 2023.

20. Michael Hill, "Uproar on Long Island as NY Looks to Spur Housing Development," *Long Island Press,* April 7, 2023; Ross Barkan, "The Many Enemies of Affordable Housing," *New York,* April 24, 2023, https://nymag.com/intelligencer/2023/04/kathy-hochuls-plan-for-affordable-housing-was-doomed.html.

21. Donald J. Trump (@realDonaldTrump), Twitter, July 29, 2020, https://x.com/realDonaldTrump/status/1288509568578777088.

22. Bolger, "Hochul's Affordable Housing Plan."

23. Hill, "Uproar on Long Island"; David Winzelberg, "Site Work to Start on Long-Awaited Affordable Housing Project," *Long Island Business News,* January 7, 2023.

24. Marianne Goodland, "Colorado Gov. Jared Polis Signs Major Housing Bill, Pushing High-Density Development," Colorado Politics, May 29, 2024, https://www.coloradopolitics.com/news/housing-bills-colorado/article_8baf2a88-1200-11ef-b298-0f22d5e30e56.html.

25. Jared Brey, "Florida's Republican-Led, Nearly Unanimous Housing Reforms," *Governing,* April 5, 2023, https://www.governing.com/community/floridas-republican-led-nearly-unanimous-housing-reforms; Brey, "How States Are Addressing."

26. Vicki Been, Ingrid Gould Ellen, and Katherine O'Regan, "Supply Skepticism: Housing Supply and Affordability," NYU Furman Center, August 2018, https://furmancenter.org/research/publication/supply-skepticismnbsp-housing-supply-and-affordability.

27. Emily Hamilton, "The Effects of Minimum-Lot-Size-Reform on Houston Land Values" (Mercatus working paper, George Mason University, 2023).

28. Been et al., "Supply Skepticism," 7, 13.

29. Elizabeth Kneebone and Alan Berube, "Post-Pandemic Poverty Is Rising in America's Suburbs," Brookings, October 11, 2023, https://www.brookings.edu/articles/post-pandemic-poverty-is-rising-in-americas-suburbs/.

30. U.S. Senate, Joint Committee Study and Investigation of Housing, Hearings, 80th Cong., 1st sess., 1947–48. On the McCarthy hearings, see Baxandall and Ewen, *Picture Windows,* ch. 8. See also Davies, *Housing Reform during the Truman Administration.* For the afterlife of the New Deal, see Fraser and Gerstle, *Rise and Fall of the New Deal Order;* Gerstle, *Rise and Fall of the Neoliberal Order,* ch. 1.

31. There is a huge debate both in the media and among academic and public policy specialists over the causes of our crisis of affordable housing and how to solve it. It would take another book to do justice to this debate. Here are some of those who favor a larger supply of market-rate housing: Ezra Klein, "Why Housing Is So Expensive—Particularly in Blue States," *New York Times,* July 19, 2022; Jenny Schuetz, *Fixer-Upper: How to Repair America's Broken Housing Systems* (Washington, DC: Brookings Institution Press, 2022); Kevin Erdmann, *Shut Out* (New York: Rowman and Littlefield, 2019); Kevin Erdmann's substack, "Erdmann Housing Tracker," https://kevinerdmann.substack.com; Been et al., "Supply Skepticism"; Hamilton, "Minimum-Lot-Size-Reform"; David Dayen, "A Liberalism That Builds Power," *American Prospect,* May 25, 2023, https://prospect.org/economy/2023-05-25-liberalism-that-builds-power; Darrell Owens substack, on "Yes in My Backyard" housing reform, https://substack.com/@darrellowens; Matthew Yglesias's substack, "Slow Boring," https://www.slowboring.com.

Index

Illustrations are indicated by page numbers in *italics*.